EDENS ZERO

13

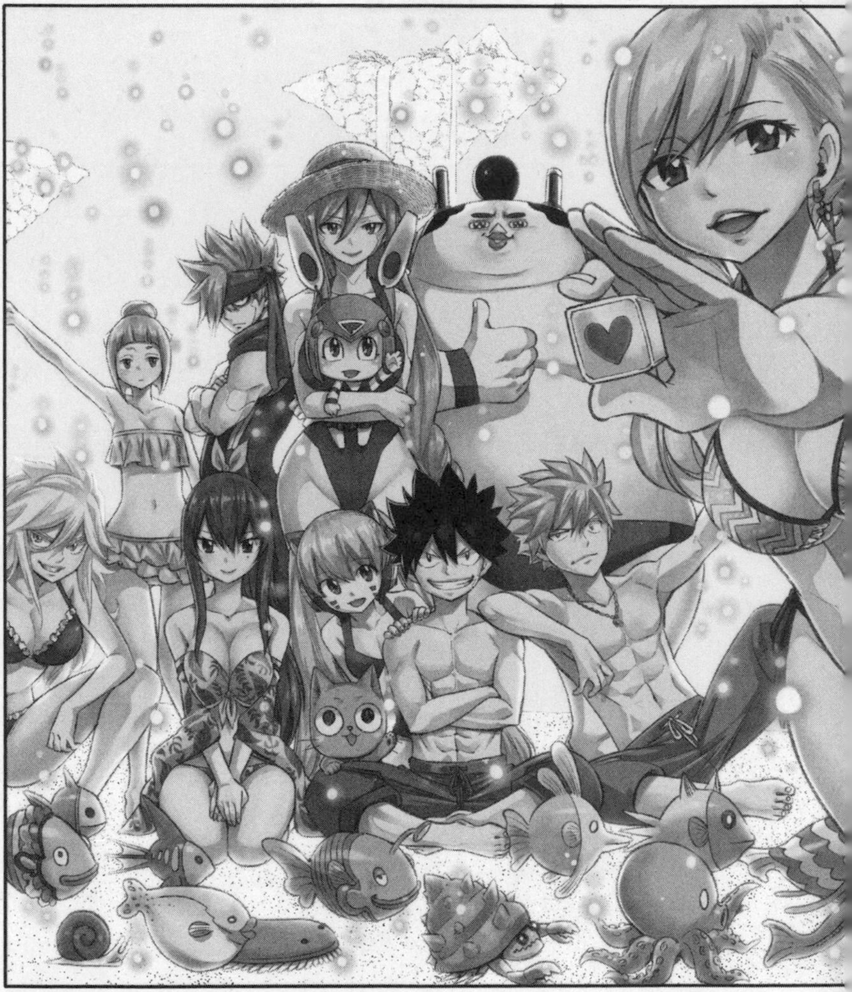

HIRO MASHIMA

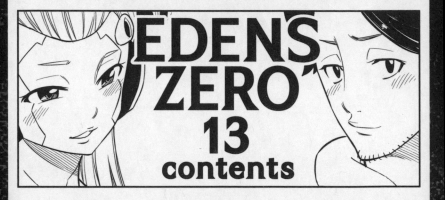

EDENS ZERO 13 contents

EDENS ZERO

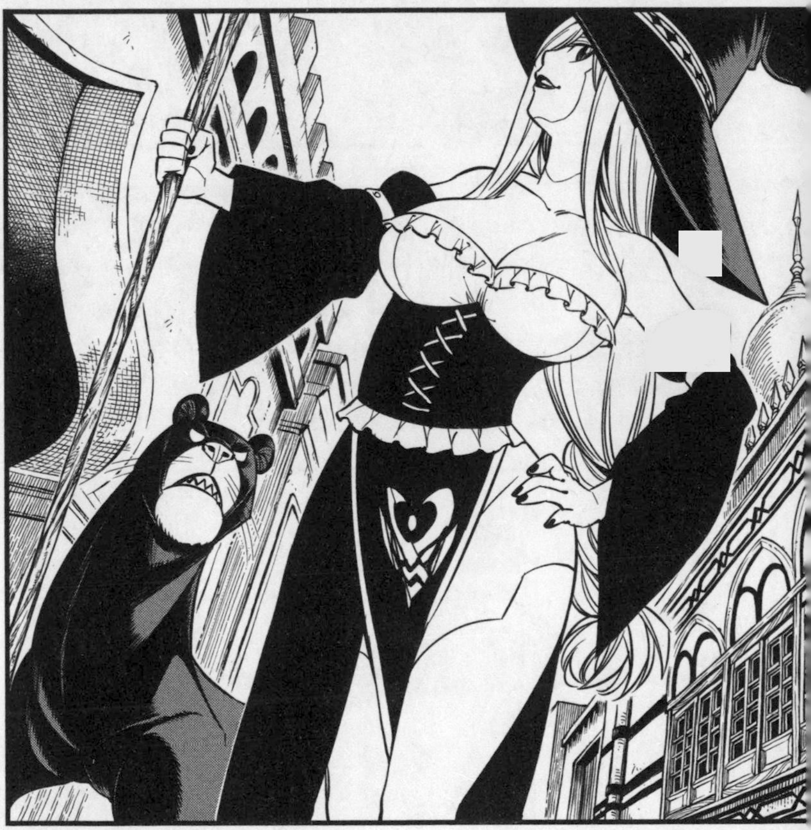

CHAPTER 105: DRAGONFALL

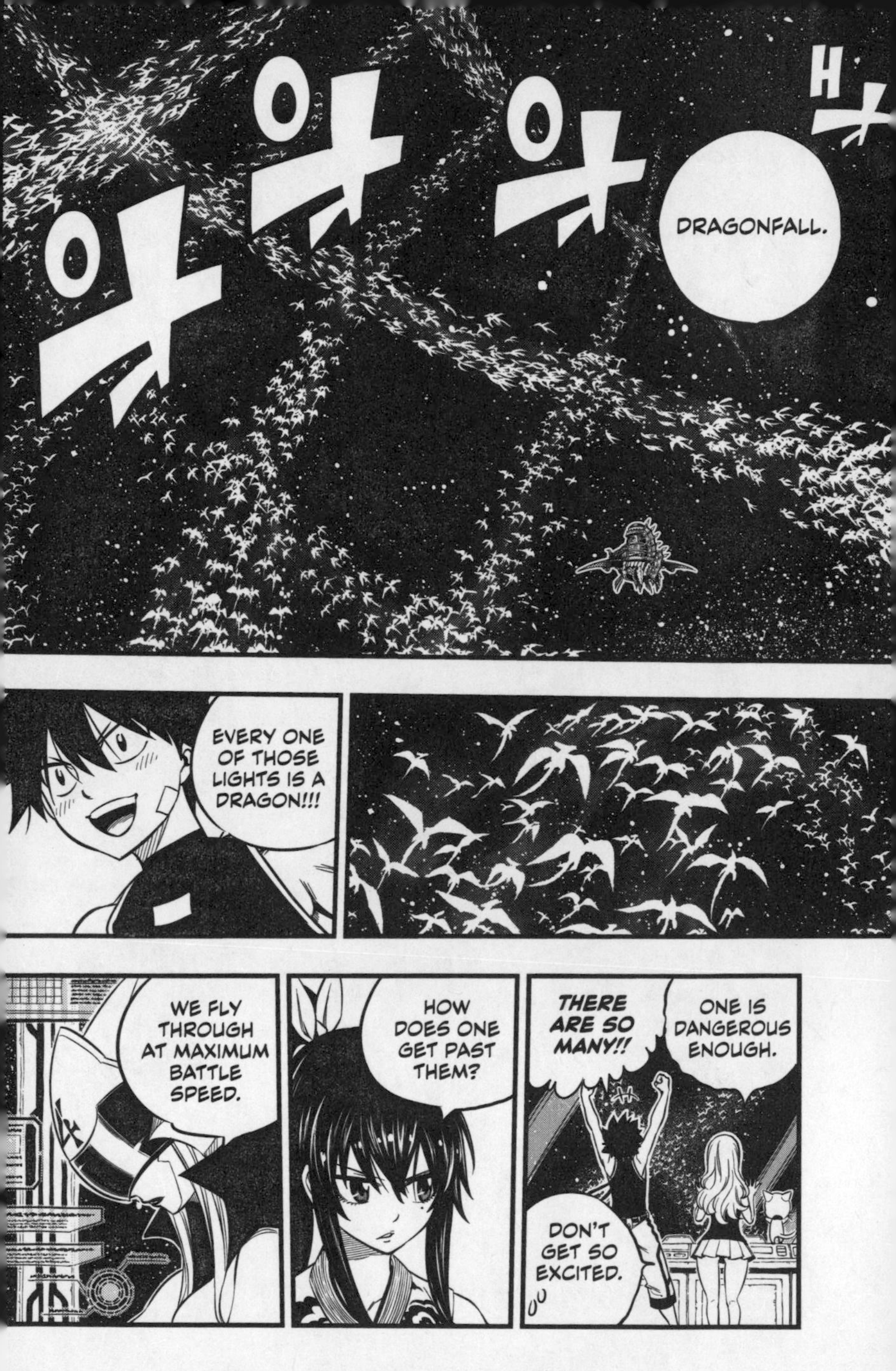
DRAGONFALL.
EVERY ONE OF THOSE LIGHTS IS A DRAGON!!!
ONE IS DANGEROUS ENOUGH.
THERE ARE SO MANY!!
DON'T GET SO EXCITED.
HOW DOES ONE GET PAST THEM?
WE FLY THROUGH AT MAXIMUM BATTLE SPEED.

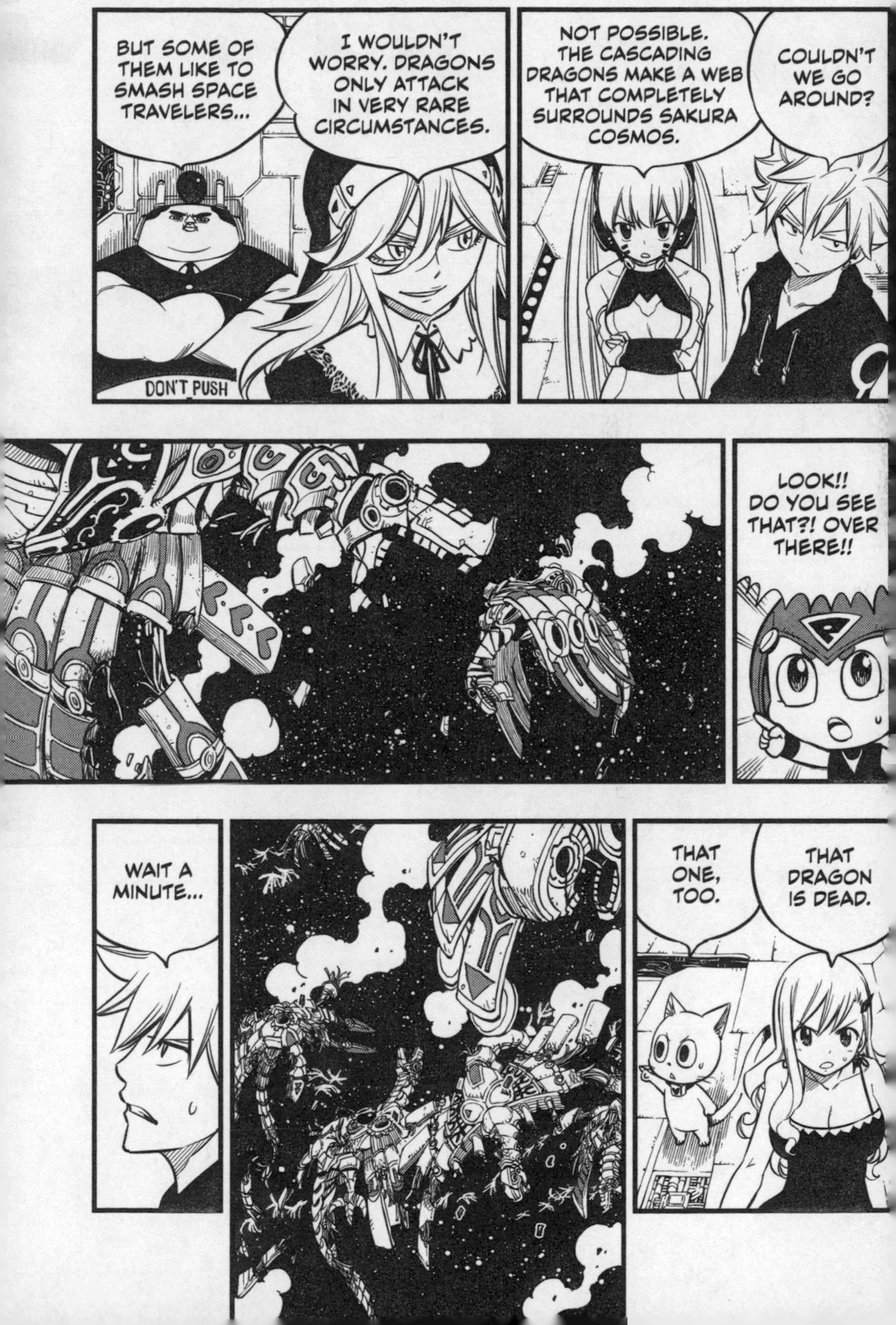
COULDN'T WE GO AROUND?
NOT POSSIBLE. THE CASCADING DRAGONS MAKE A WEB THAT COMPLETELY SURROUNDS SAKURA COSMOS.
I WOULDN'T WORRY. DRAGONS ONLY ATTACK IN VERY RARE CIRCUMSTANCES.
BUT SOME OF THEM LIKE TO SMASH SPACE TRAVELERS...
DON'T PUSH
LOOK!! DO YOU SEE THAT?! OVER THERE!!
THAT DRAGON IS DEAD.
THAT ONE, TOO.
WAIT A MINUTE...

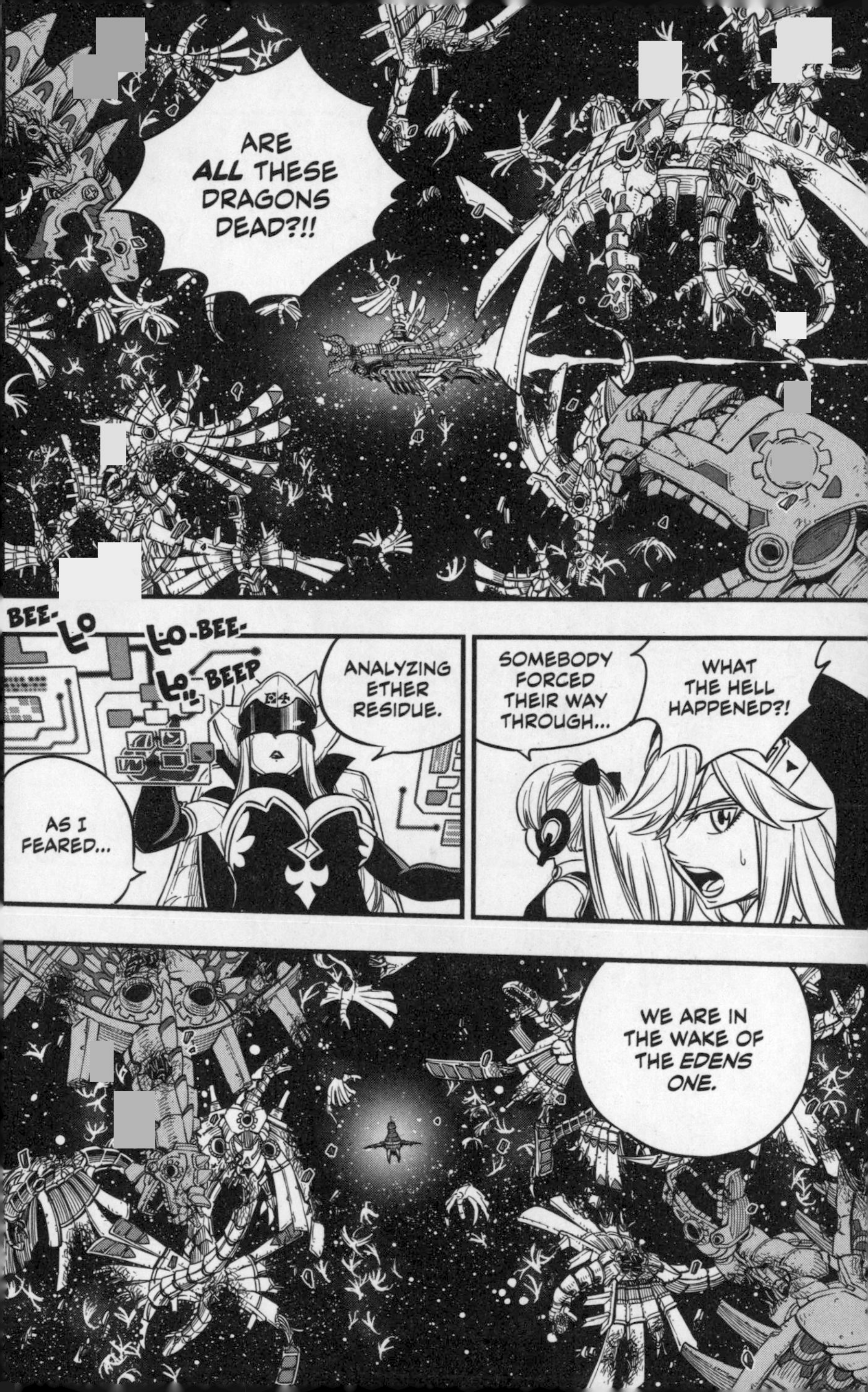
ARE *ALL* THESE DRAGONS DEAD?!!
WHAT THE HELL HAPPENED?!
SOMEBODY FORCED THEIR WAY THROUGH...
ANALYZING ETHER RESIDUE.
BEE-
BEE-
BEEP
AS I FEARED...
WE ARE IN THE WAKE OF THE *EDENS ONE.*

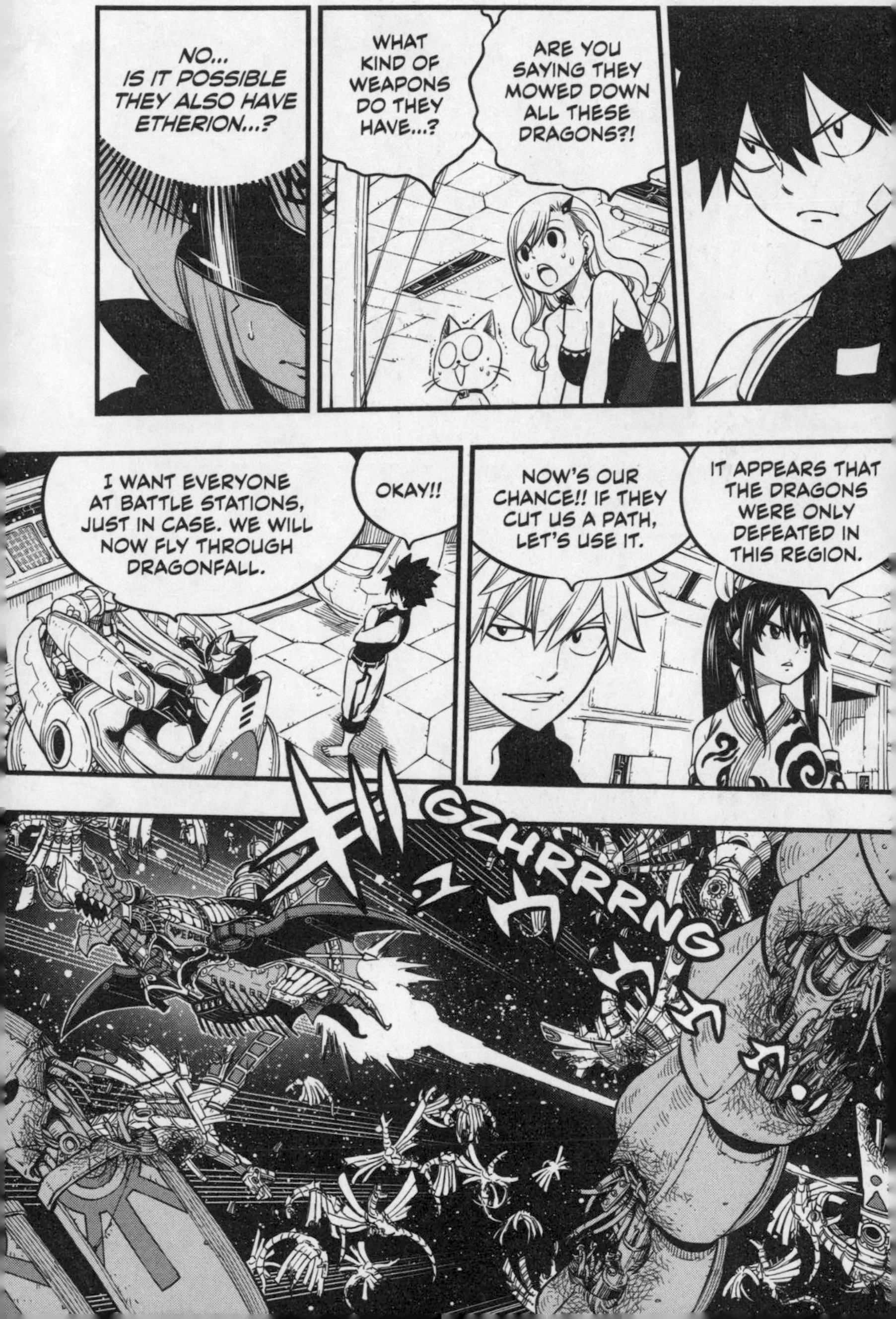
ARE YOU SAYING THEY MOWED DOWN ALL THESE DRAGONS?!
WHAT KIND OF WEAPONS DO THEY HAVE...?
NO... IS IT POSSIBLE THEY ALSO HAVE ETHERION...?
IT APPEARS THAT THE DRAGONS WERE ONLY DEFEATED IN THIS REGION.
NOW'S OUR CHANCE!! IF THEY CUT US A PATH, LET'S USE IT.
I WANT EVERYONE AT BATTLE STATIONS, JUST IN CASE. WE WILL NOW FLY THROUGH DRAGONFALL.
OKAY!!
GZHRRRNG

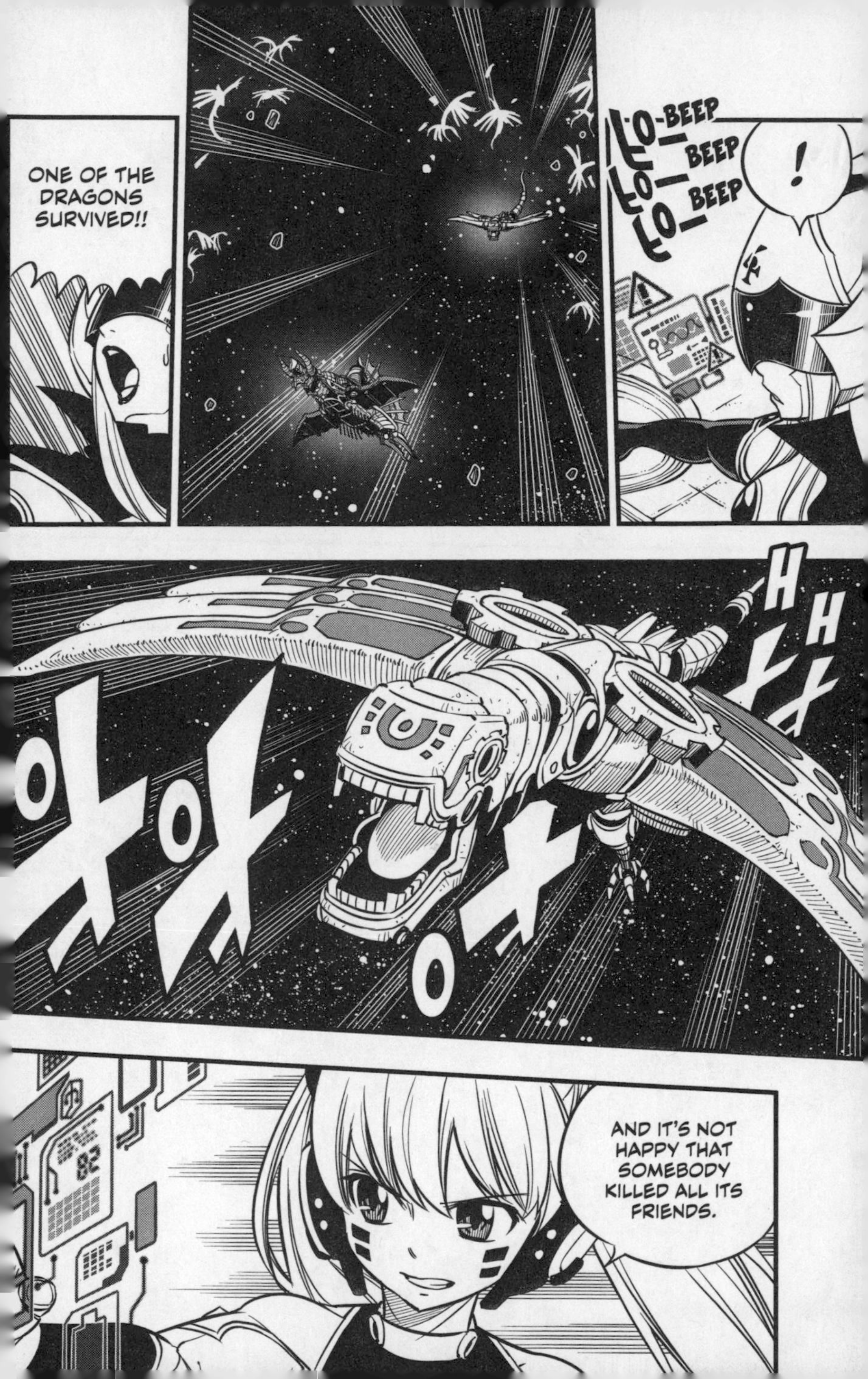
BEEP
BEEP
BEEP
!
ONE OF THE DRAGONS SURVIVED!!
AND IT'S NOT HAPPY THAT SOMEBODY KILLED ALL ITS FRIENDS.

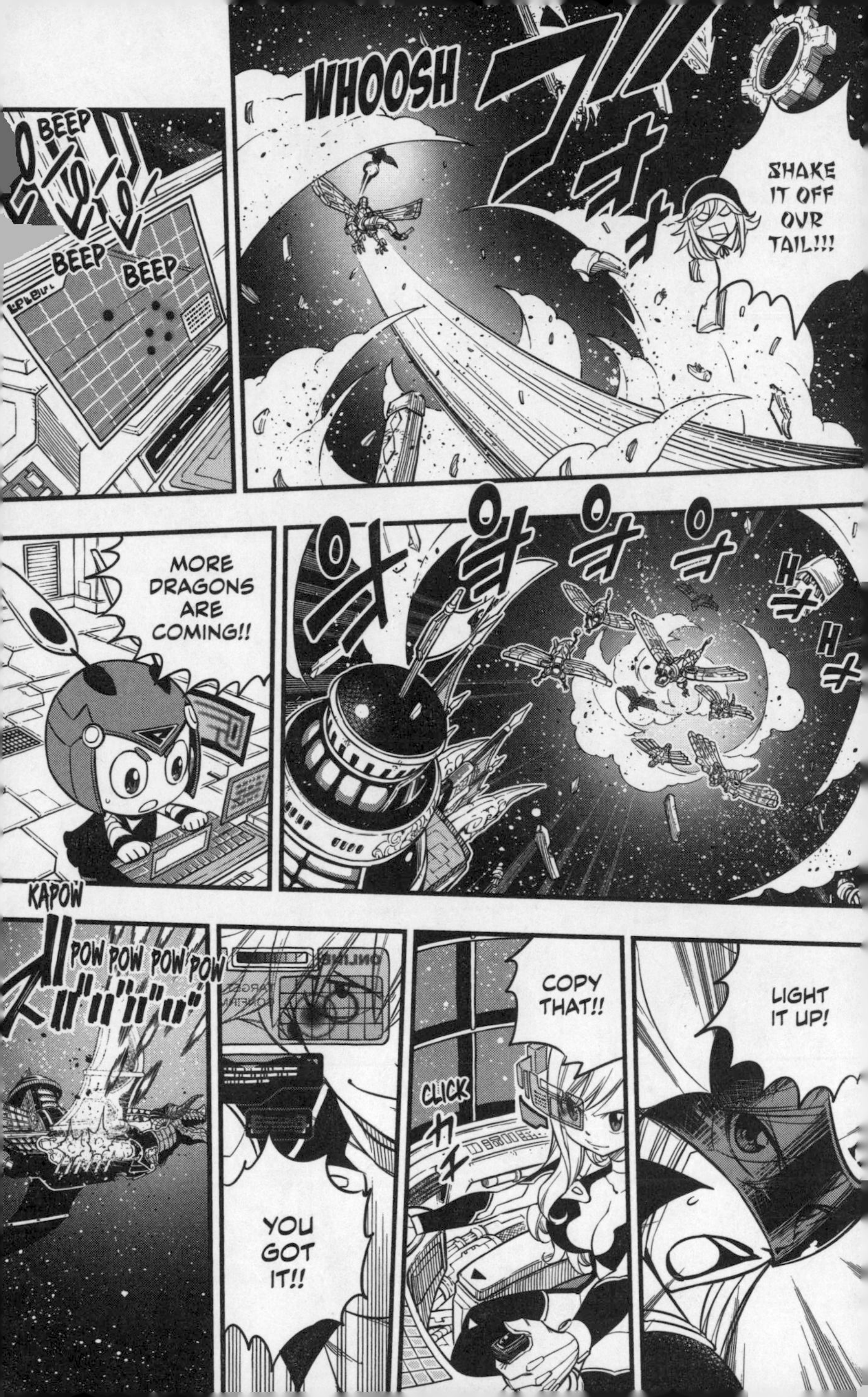
WHOOSH
SHAKE IT OFF OUR TAIL!!!
BEEP
BEEP
BEEP
H
H
MORE DRAGONS ARE COMING!!
LIGHT IT UP!
COPY THAT!!
CLICK
YOU GOT IT!!
KAPOW
POW POW POW POW

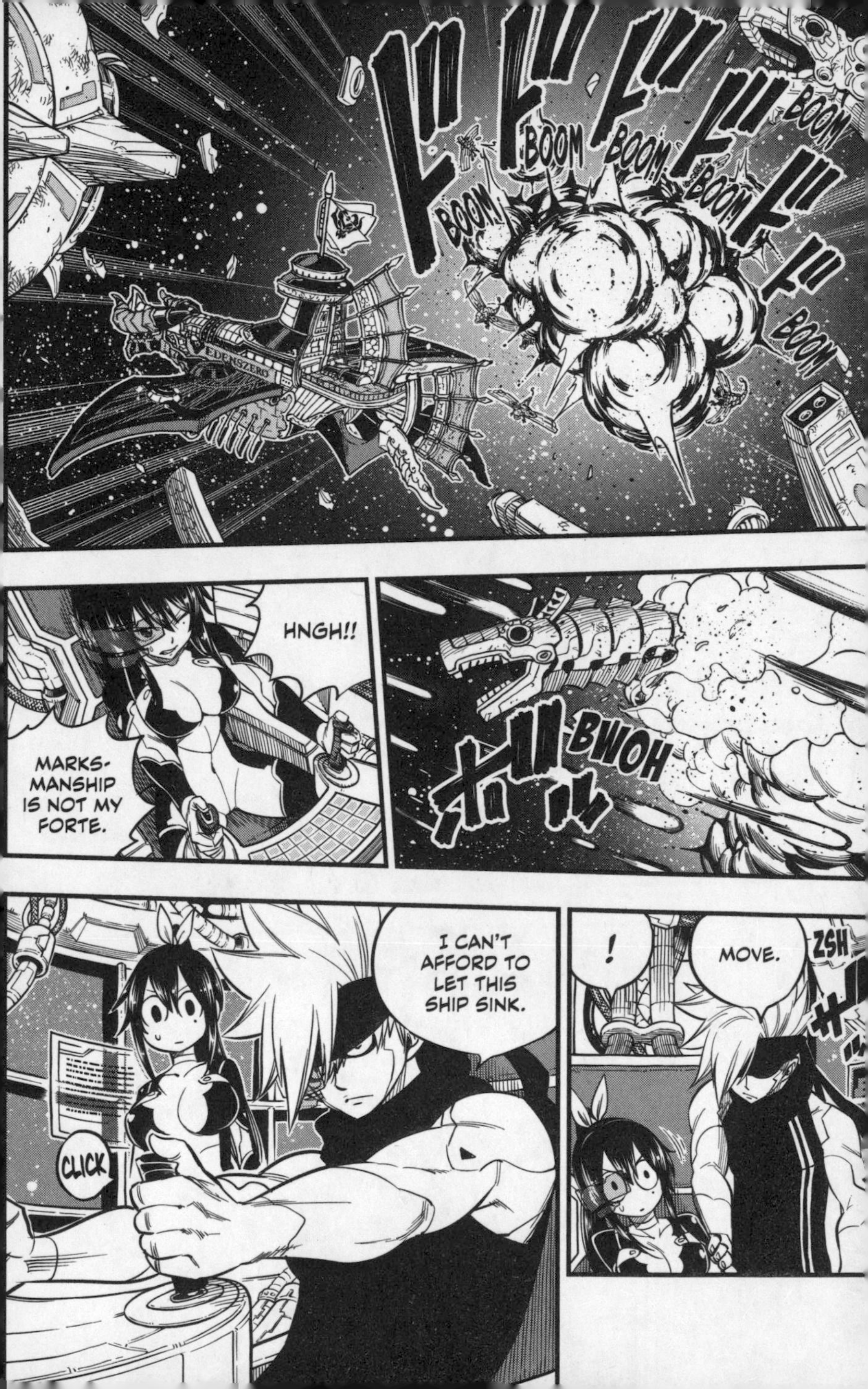
BOOM
BOOM
BOOM
BOOM
BOOM
BOOM
BWOH
HNGH!!
MARKS-MANSHIP IS NOT MY FORTE.
ZSH
MOVE.
!
I CAN'T AFFORD TO LET THIS SHIP SINK.
CLICK

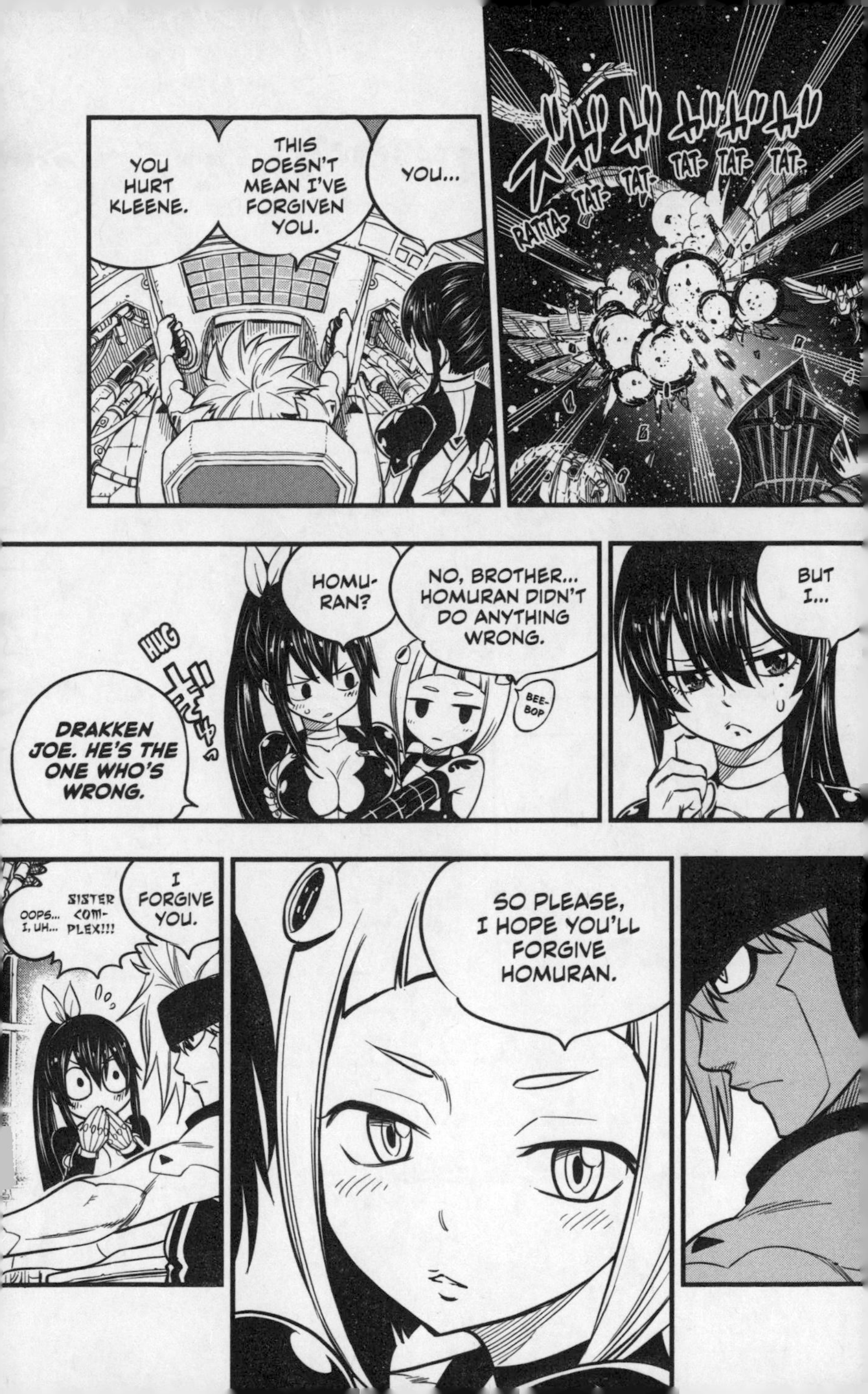
RATTA-TAT-TAT-TAT-TAT-TAT-TAT
YOU...
THIS DOESN'T MEAN I'VE FORGIVEN YOU.
YOU HURT KLEENE.
BUT I...
NO, BROTHER... HOMURAN DIDN'T DO ANYTHING WRONG.
HOMU-RAN?
BEE-BOP
HUG
DRAKKEN JOE. HE'S THE ONE WHO'S WRONG.
SO PLEASE, I HOPE YOU'LL FORGIVE HOMURAN.
I FORGIVE YOU.
SISTER COM-PLEX!!!
OOPS... I, UH...

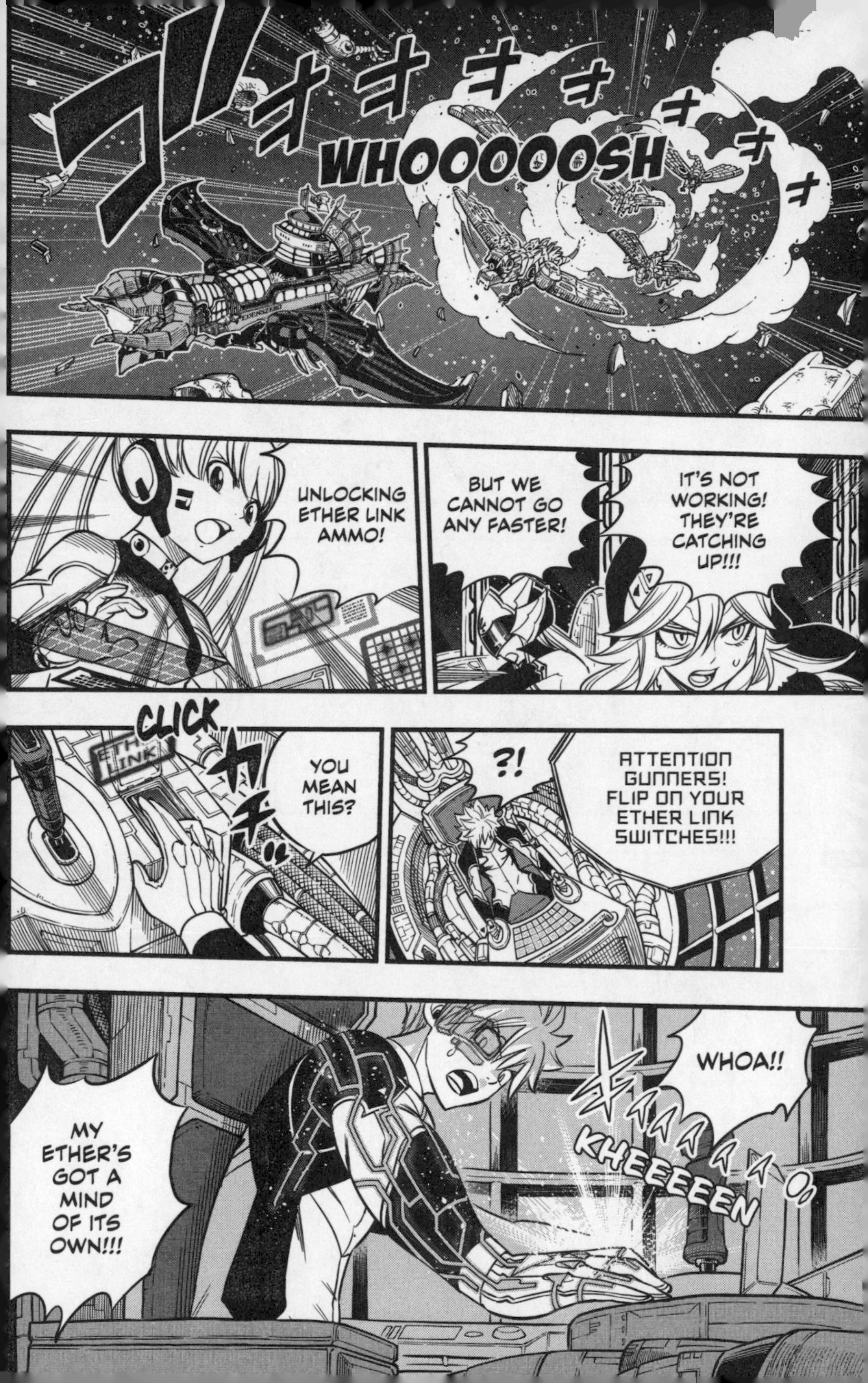
WHOOOOOSH
IT'S NOT WORKING! THEY'RE CATCHING UP!!!
BUT WE CANNOT GO ANY FASTER!
UNLOCKING ETHER LINK AMMO!
ATTENTION GUNNERS! FLIP ON YOUR ETHER LINK SWITCHES!!!
?!
YOU MEAN THIS?
CLICK
WHOA!!
KHEEEEEEN
MY ETHER'S GOT A MIND OF ITS OWN!!!

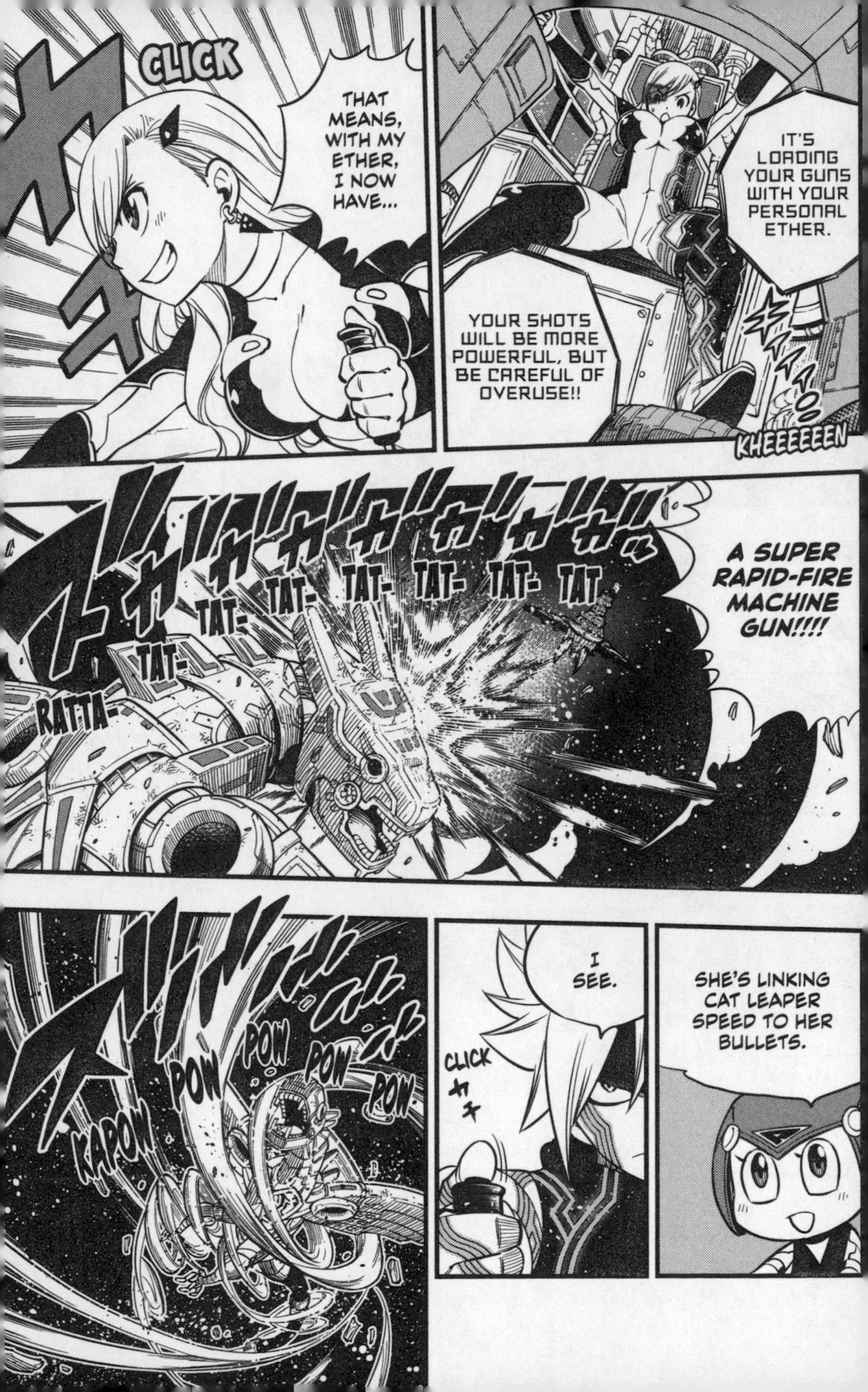
IT'S LOADING YOUR GUNS WITH YOUR PERSONAL ETHER.
YOUR SHOTS WILL BE MORE POWERFUL, BUT BE CAREFUL OF OVERUSE!!
KHEEEEEEEN
CLICK
THAT MEANS, WITH MY ETHER, I NOW HAVE...
A SUPER RAPID-FIRE MACHINE GUN!!!!
RATTA-TAT-TAT-TAT-TAT-TAT-TAT-TAT
SHE'S LINKING CAT LEAPER SPEED TO HER BULLETS.
I SEE.
CLICK
KAPOW POW POW POW POW

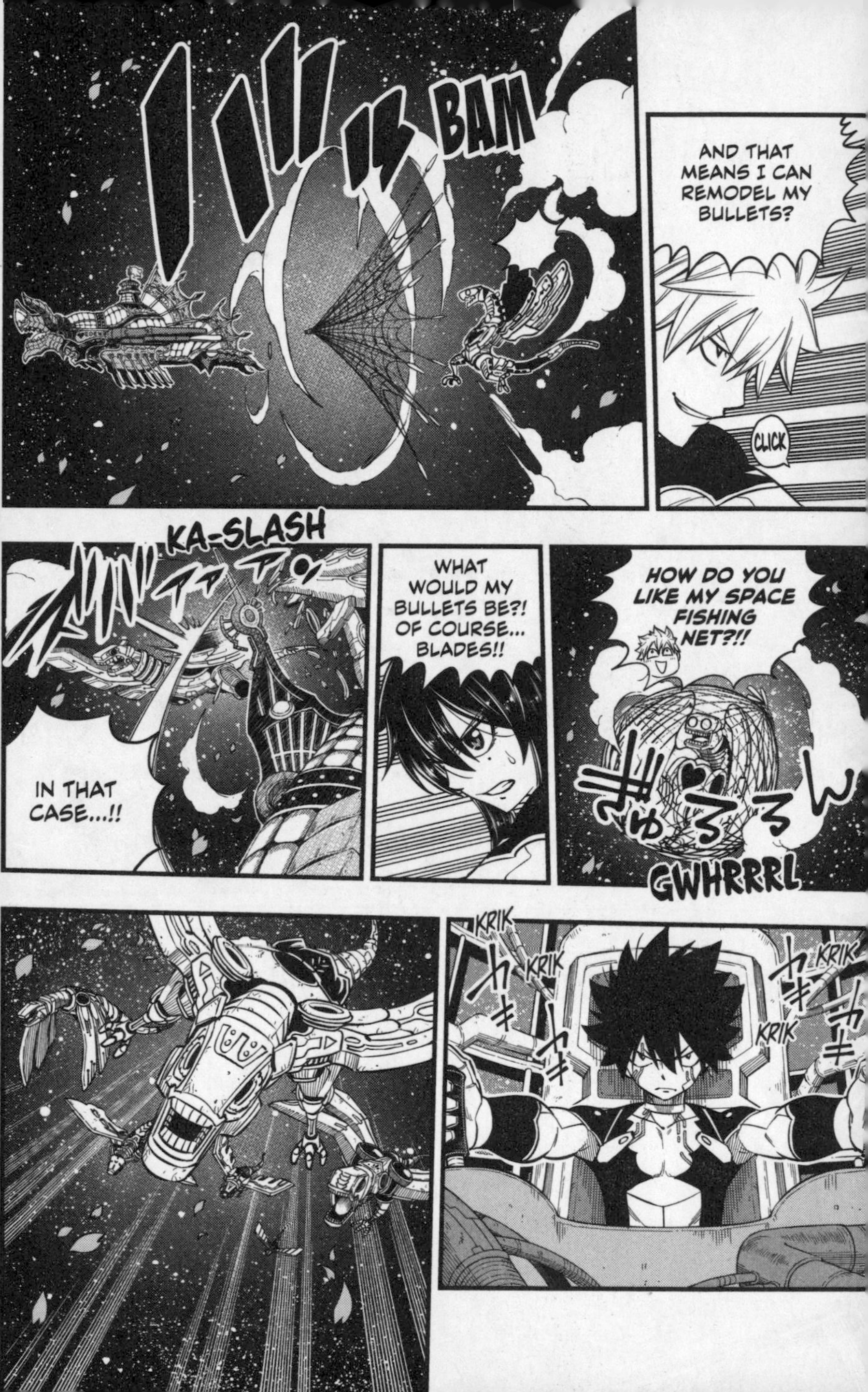
AND THAT MEANS I CAN REMODEL MY BULLETS?
CLICK
BAM
HOW DO YOU LIKE MY SPACE FISHING NET?!!
GWHRRRL
WHAT WOULD MY BULLETS BE?! OF COURSE... BLADES!!
KA-SLASH
IN THAT CASE...!!
KRIK
KRIK
KRIK
KRIK

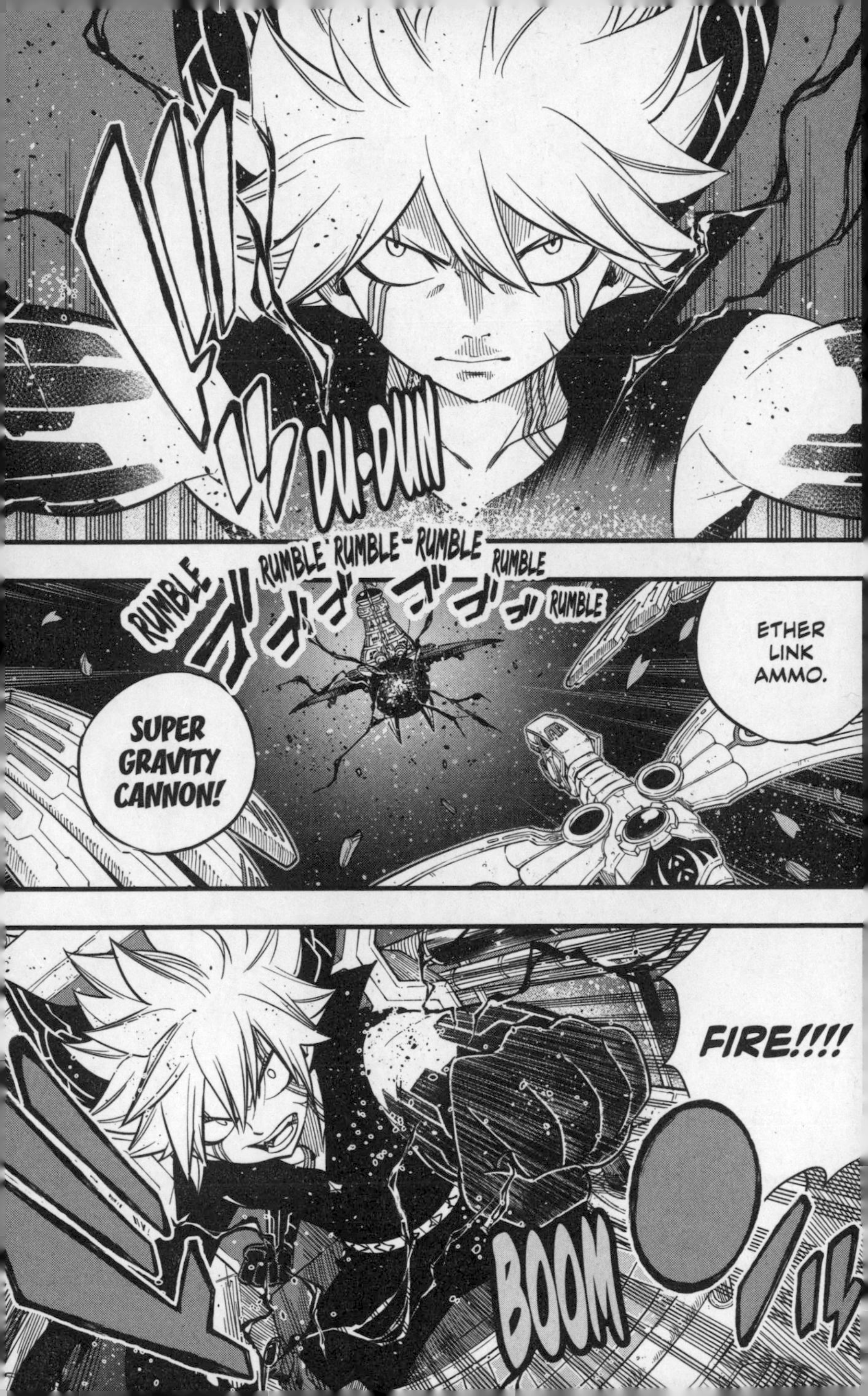
DU-DUN
ETHER LINK AMMO.
RUMBLE RUMBLE RUMBLE-RUMBLE RUMBLE RUMBLE
SUPER GRAVITY CANNON!
FIRE!!!!
BOOM

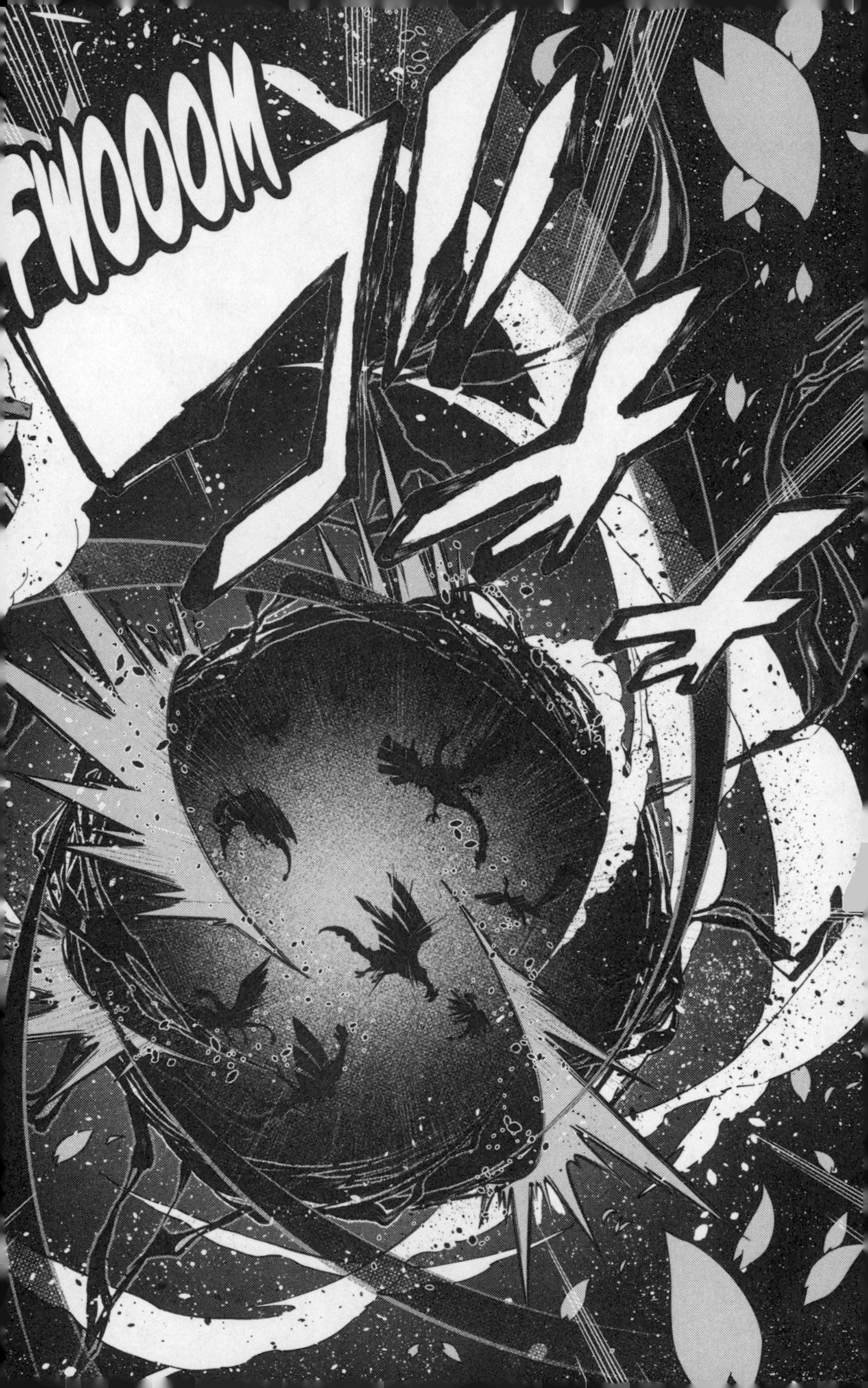
FWOOOM

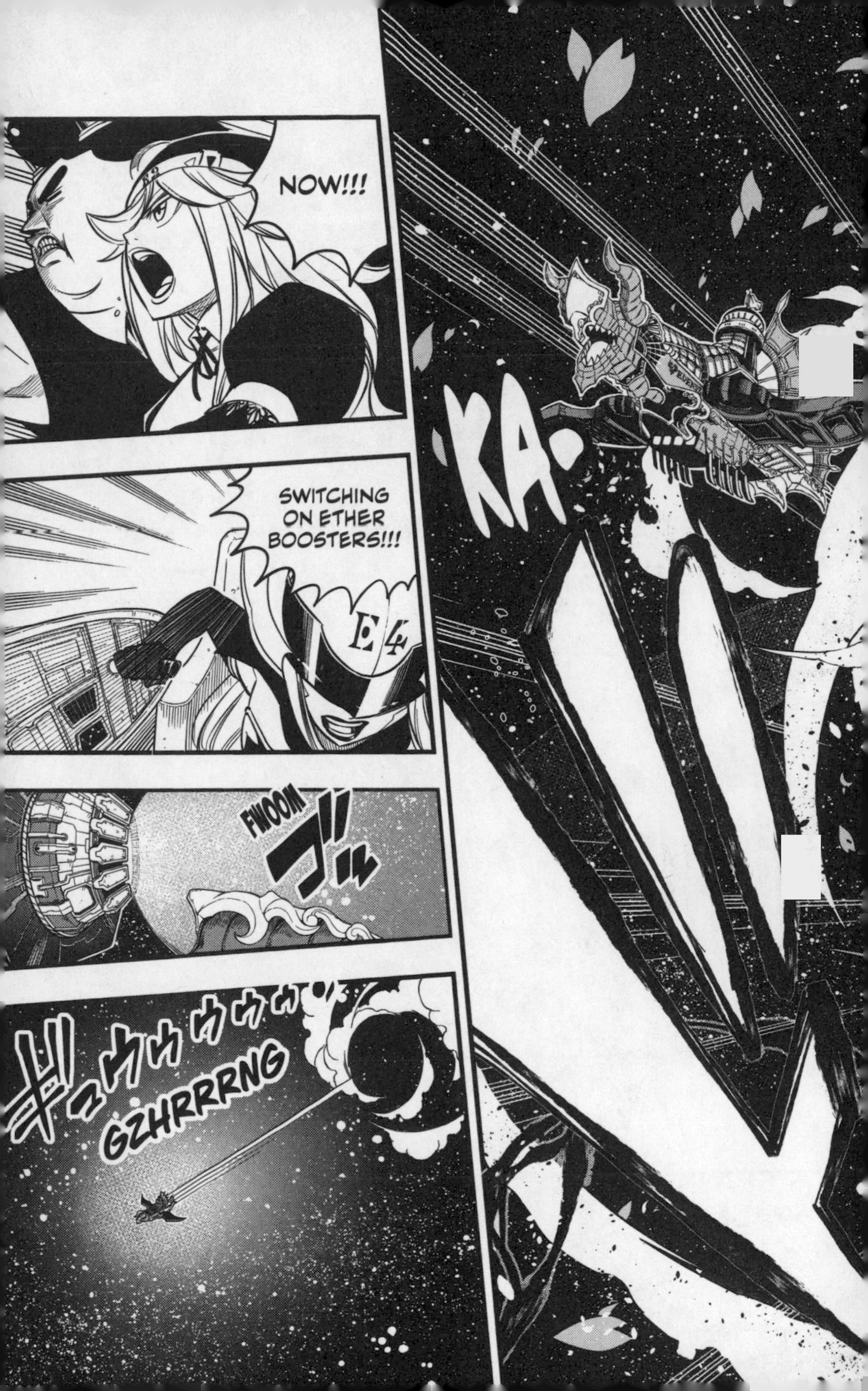
KA-
NOW!!!
SWITCHING ON ETHER BOOSTERS!!!
FWOOM
GZHRRRNG

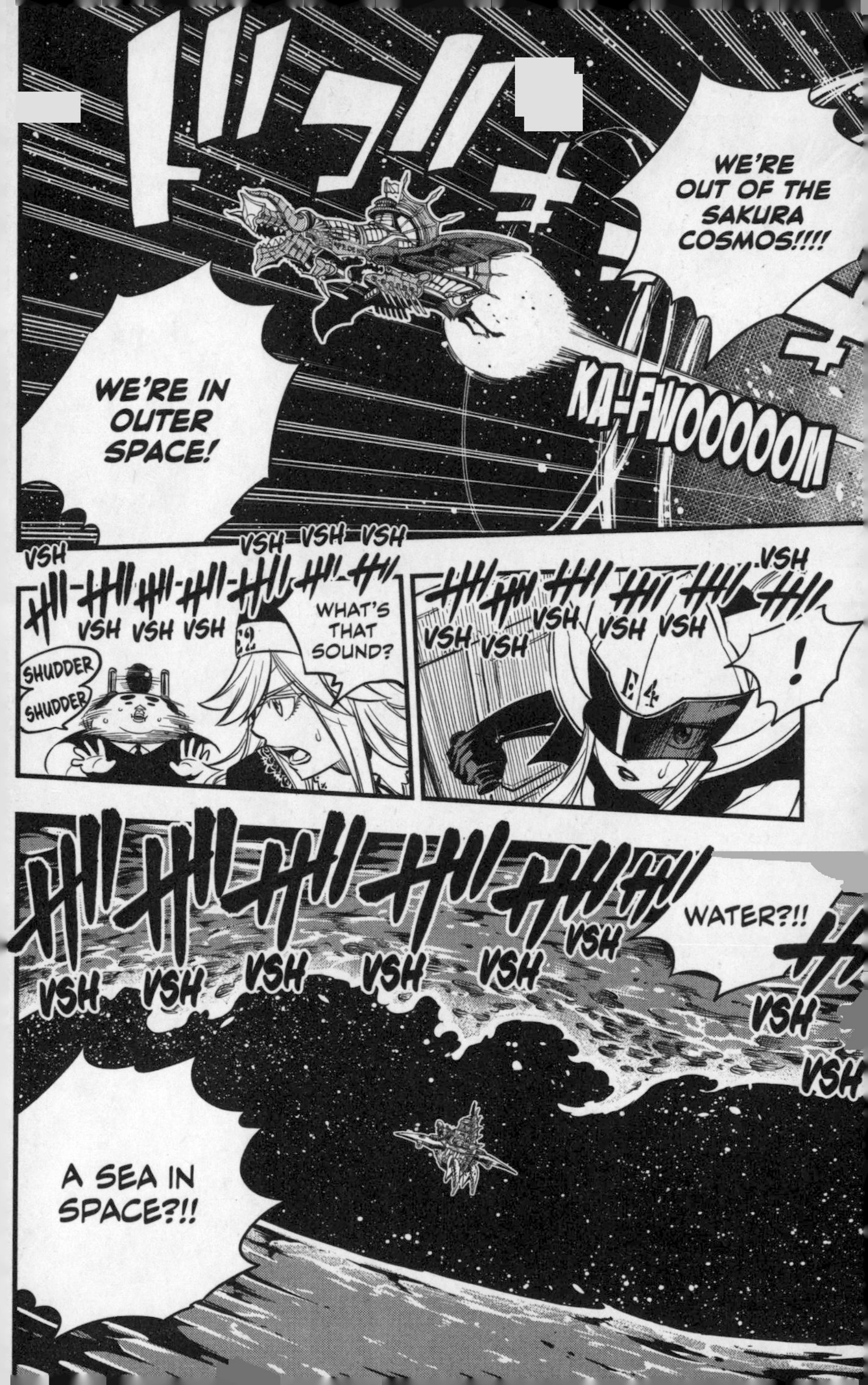
WE'RE OUT OF THE SAKURA COSMOS!!!!
KA-FWOOOOOM
WE'RE IN OUTER SPACE!
VSH VSH VSH VSH VSH VSH
!
VSH VSH VSH VSH VSH VSH VSH VSH
WHAT'S THAT SOUND?
SHUDDER SHUDDER
WATER?!!
VSH VSH
VSH VSH VSH VSH VSH VSH
A SEA IN SPACE?!!

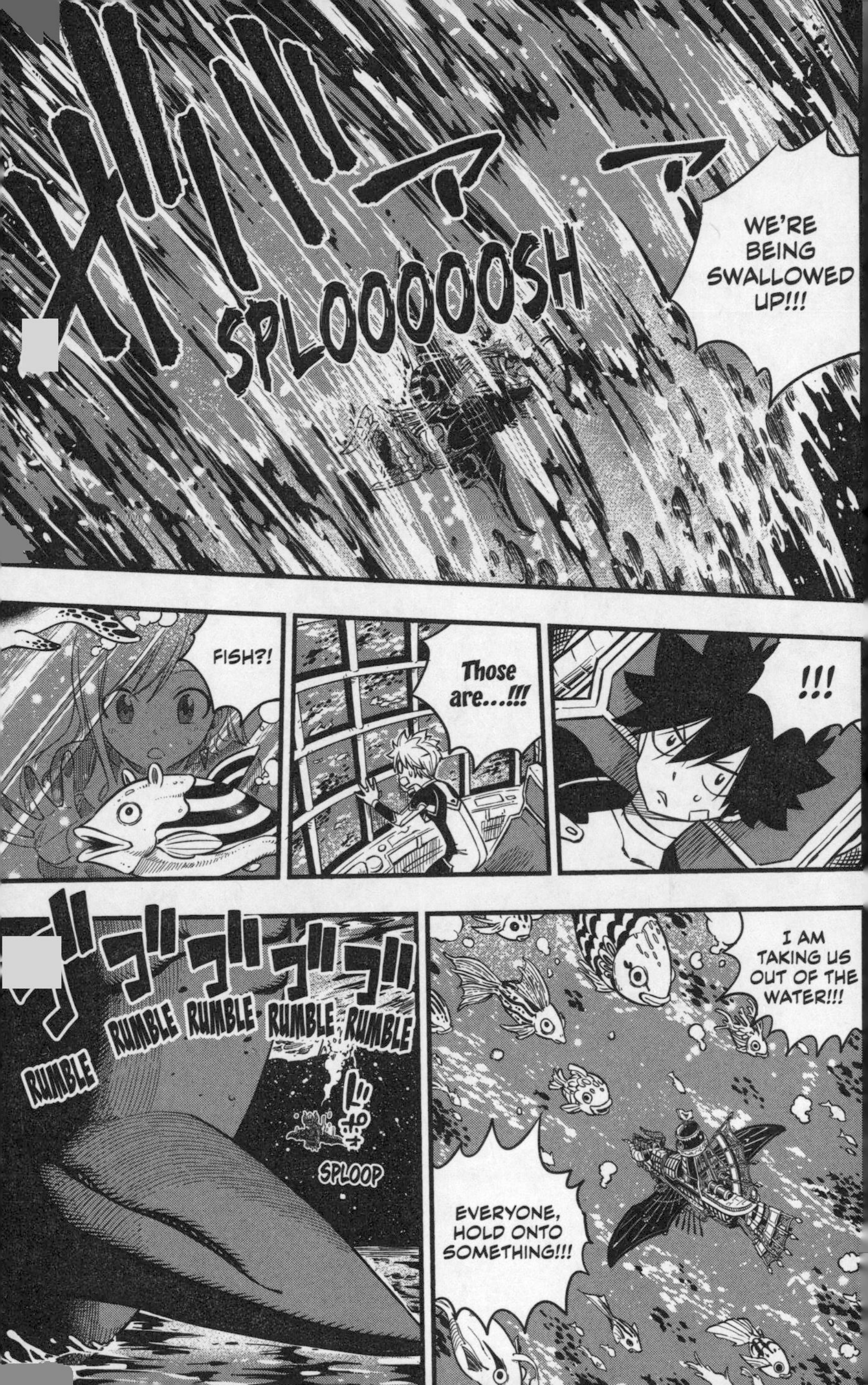
WE'RE BEING SWALLOWED UP!!!
SPLOOOOOSH
!!!
Those are...!!!
FISH?!
I AM TAKING US OUT OF THE WATER!!!
EVERYONE, HOLD ONTO SOMETHING!!!
RUMBLE RUMBLE RUMBLE RUMBLE RUMBLE
SPLOOP

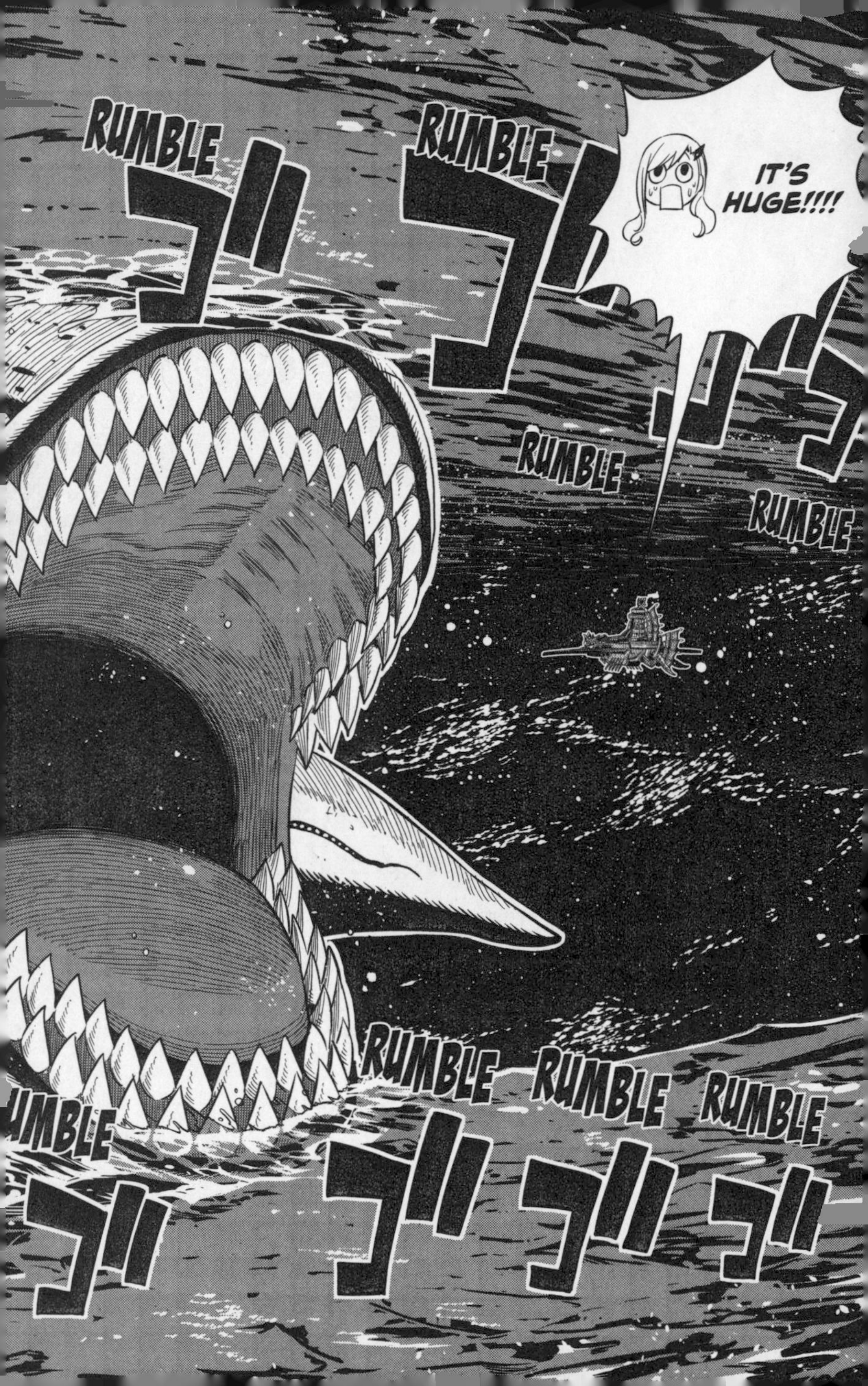
IT'S HUGE!!!!
RUMBLE
RUMBLE
RUMBLE
RUMBLE
RUMBLE
RUMBLE
RUMBLE
UMBLE

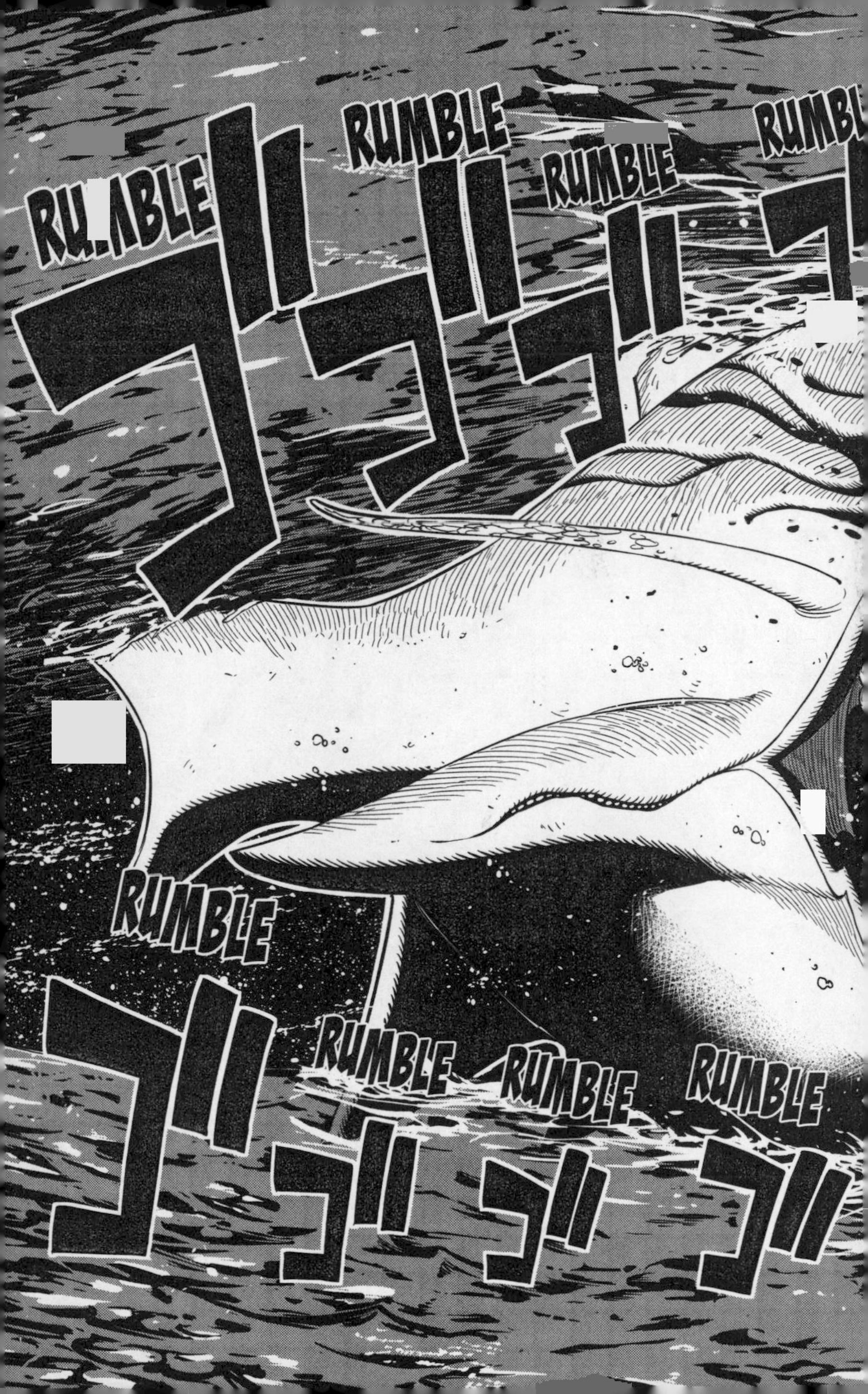
RUMBLE
RUMBLE
ゴゴゴゴ
RUMBLE
RUMBLE
RUMBLE
RUMBLE
ゴゴゴゴ

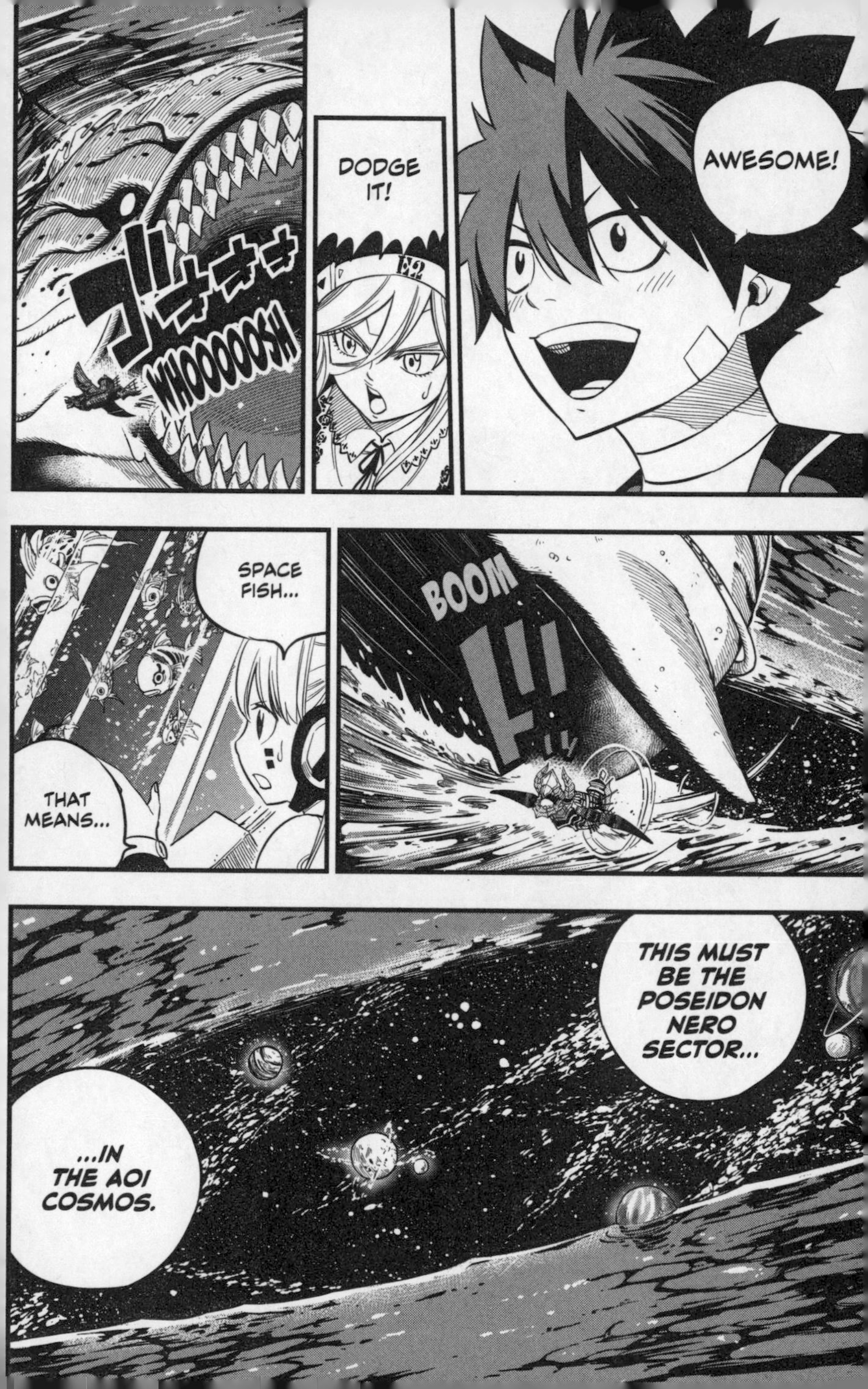
AWESOME!
DODGE IT!
WHOOOOOSH
BOOM
SPACE FISH...
THAT MEANS...
THIS MUST BE THE POSEIDON NERO SECTOR...
...IN THE AOI COSMOS.

EDENS ZERO

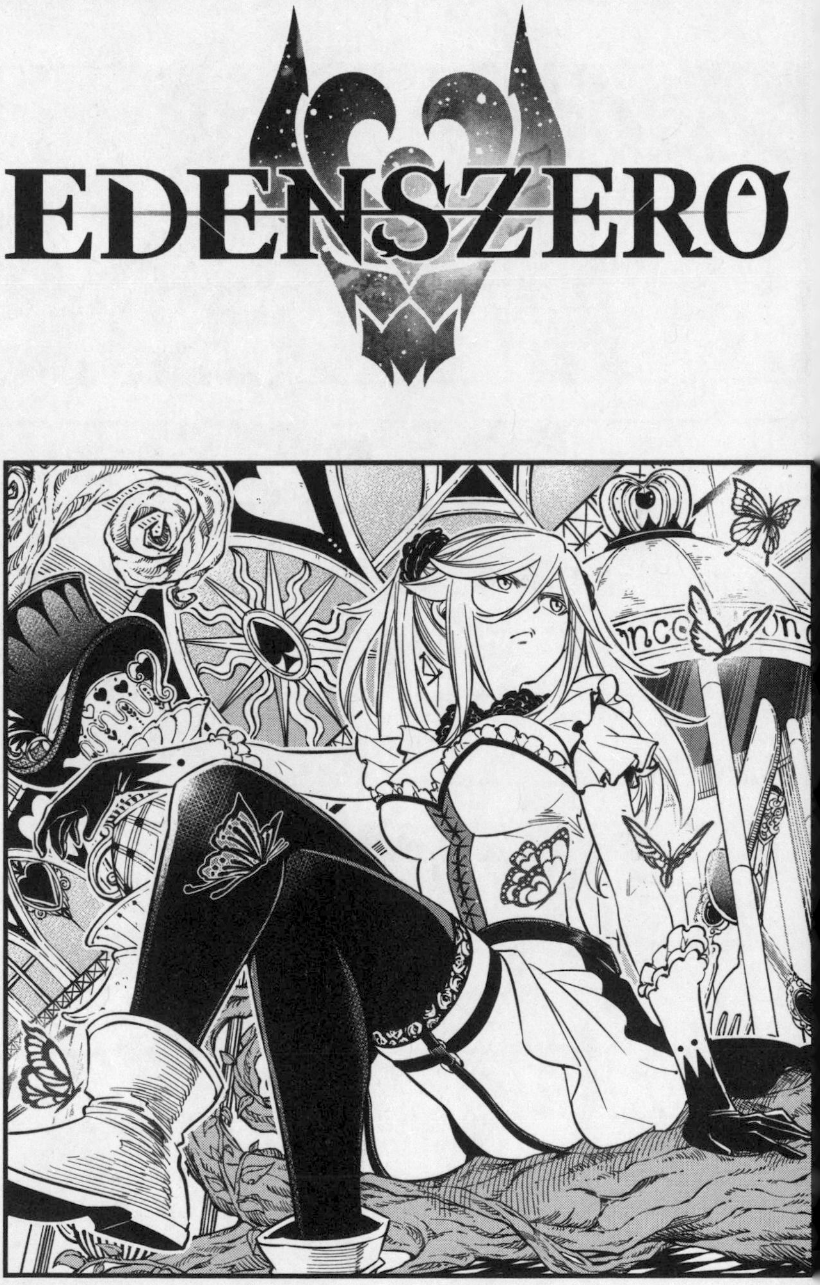

CHAPTER 106: PRAYER COUNCIL

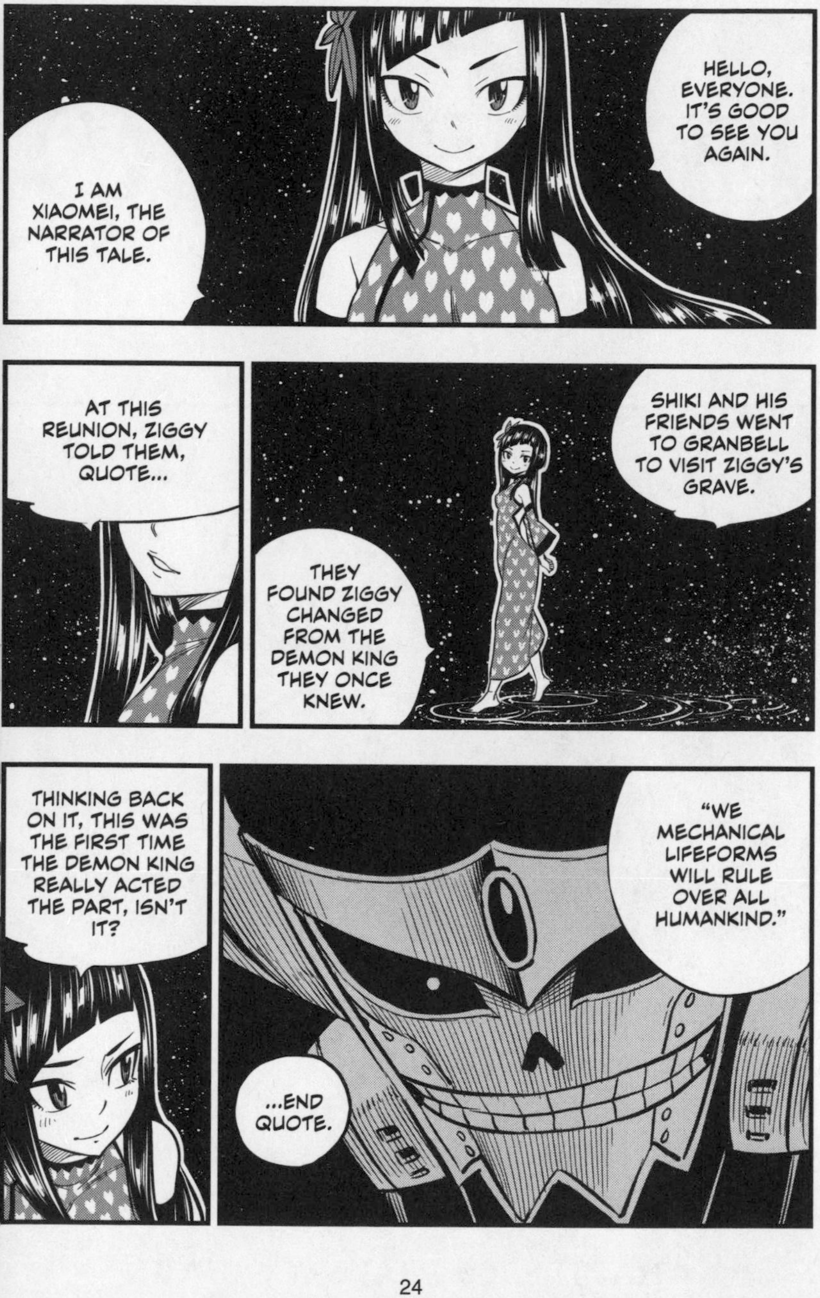
HELLO, EVERYONE. IT'S GOOD TO SEE YOU AGAIN.
I AM XIAOMEI, THE NARRATOR OF THIS TALE.
SHIKI AND HIS FRIENDS WENT TO GRANBELL TO VISIT ZIGGY'S GRAVE.
THEY FOUND ZIGGY CHANGED FROM THE DEMON KING THEY ONCE KNEW.
AT THIS REUNION, ZIGGY TOLD THEM, QUOTE...
"WE MECHANICAL LIFEFORMS WILL RULE OVER ALL HUMANKIND."
...END QUOTE.
THINKING BACK ON IT, THIS WAS THE FIRST TIME THE DEMON KING REALLY ACTED THE PART, ISN'T IT?

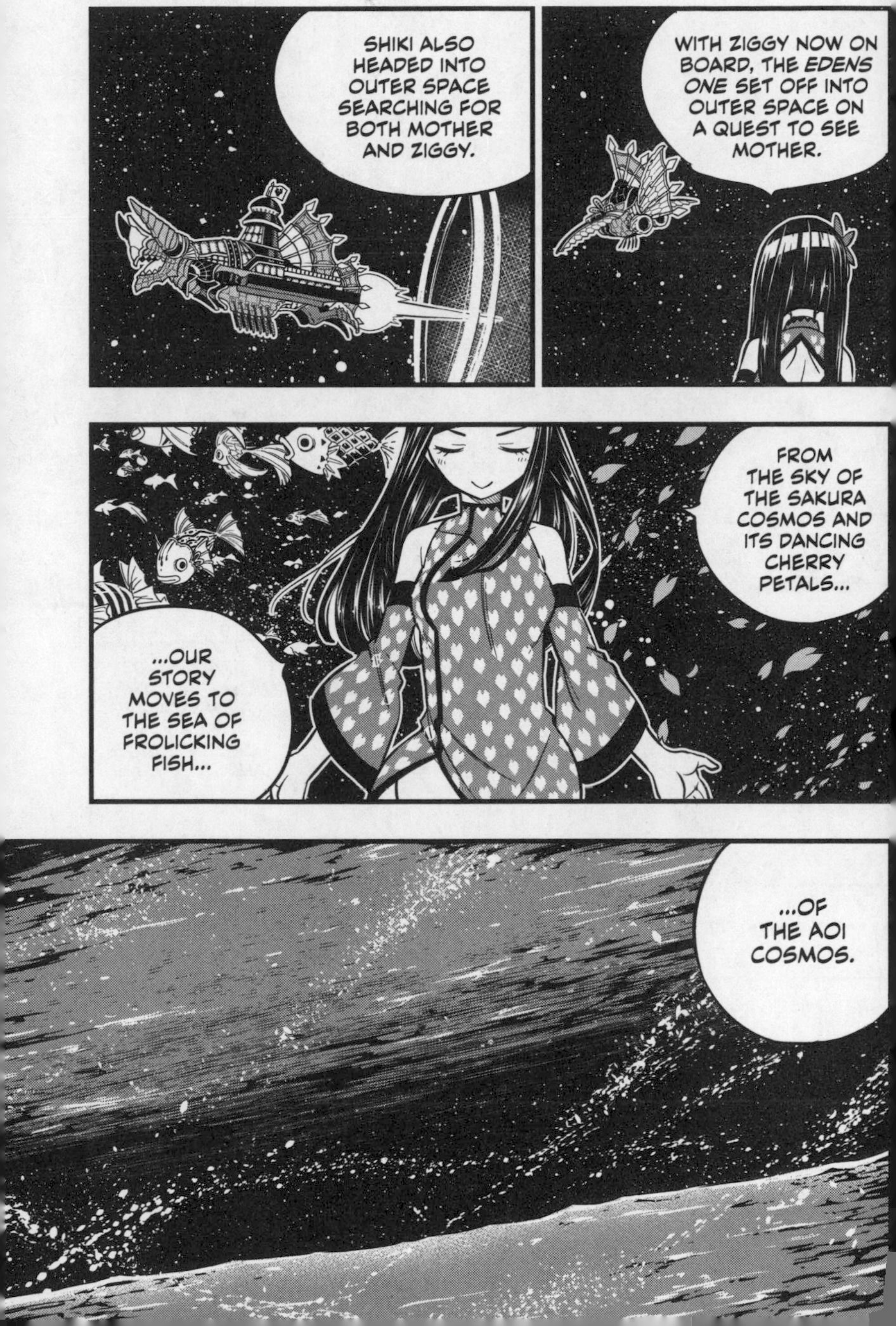
WITH ZIGGY NOW ON BOARD, THE *EDENS ONE* SET OFF INTO OUTER SPACE ON A QUEST TO SEE MOTHER.
SHIKI ALSO HEADED INTO OUTER SPACE SEARCHING FOR BOTH MOTHER AND ZIGGY.
FROM THE SKY OF THE SAKURA COSMOS AND ITS DANCING CHERRY PETALS...
...OUR STORY MOVES TO THE SEA OF FROLICKING FISH...
...OF THE AOI COSMOS.

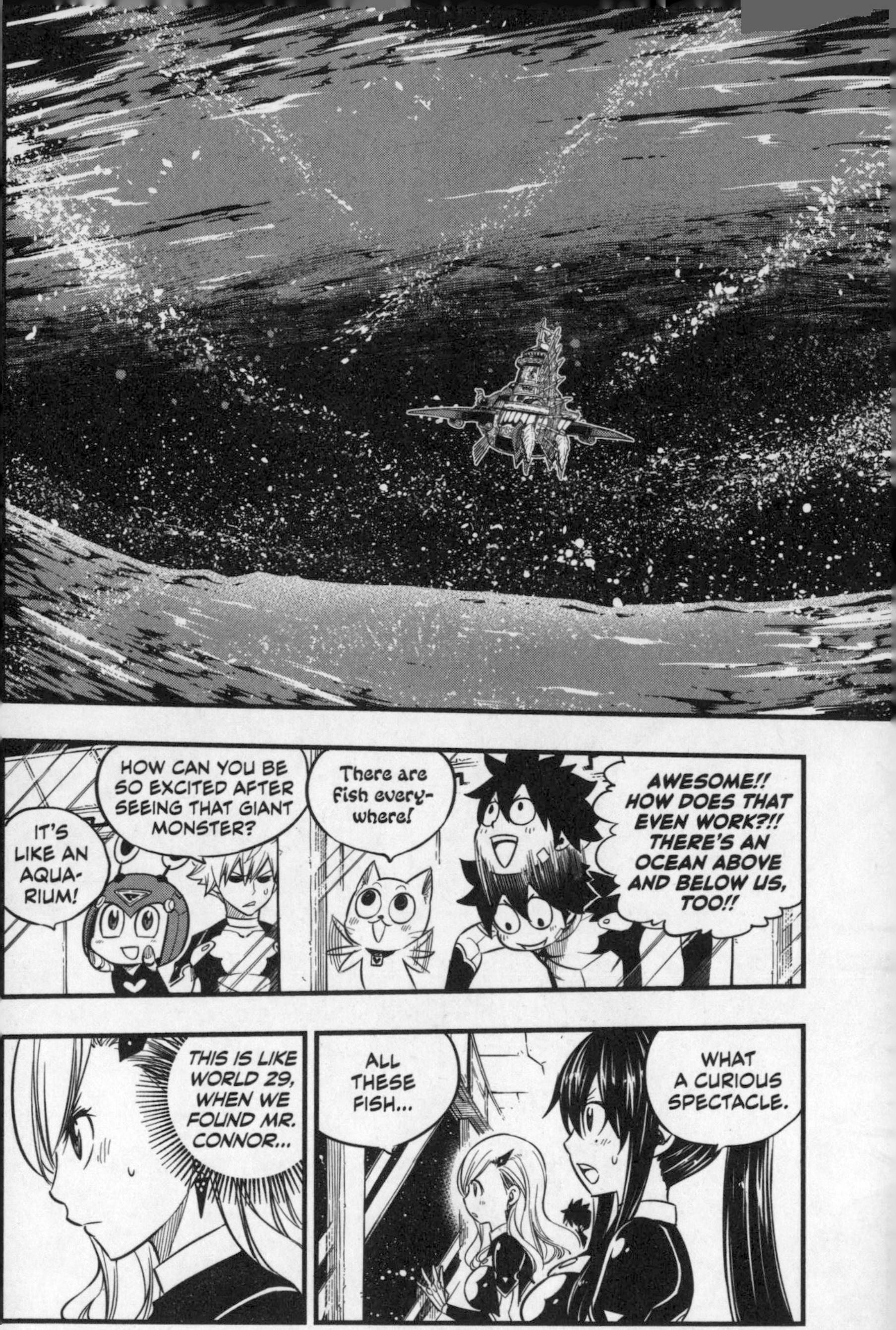
AWESOME!! HOW DOES THAT EVEN WORK?!! THERE'S AN OCEAN ABOVE AND BELOW US, TOO!!
There are fish every-where!
HOW CAN YOU BE SO EXCITED AFTER SEEING THAT GIANT MONSTER?
IT'S LIKE AN AQUA-RIUM!
WHAT A CURIOUS SPECTACLE.
ALL THESE FISH...
THIS IS LIKE WORLD 29, WHEN WE FOUND MR. CONNOR...

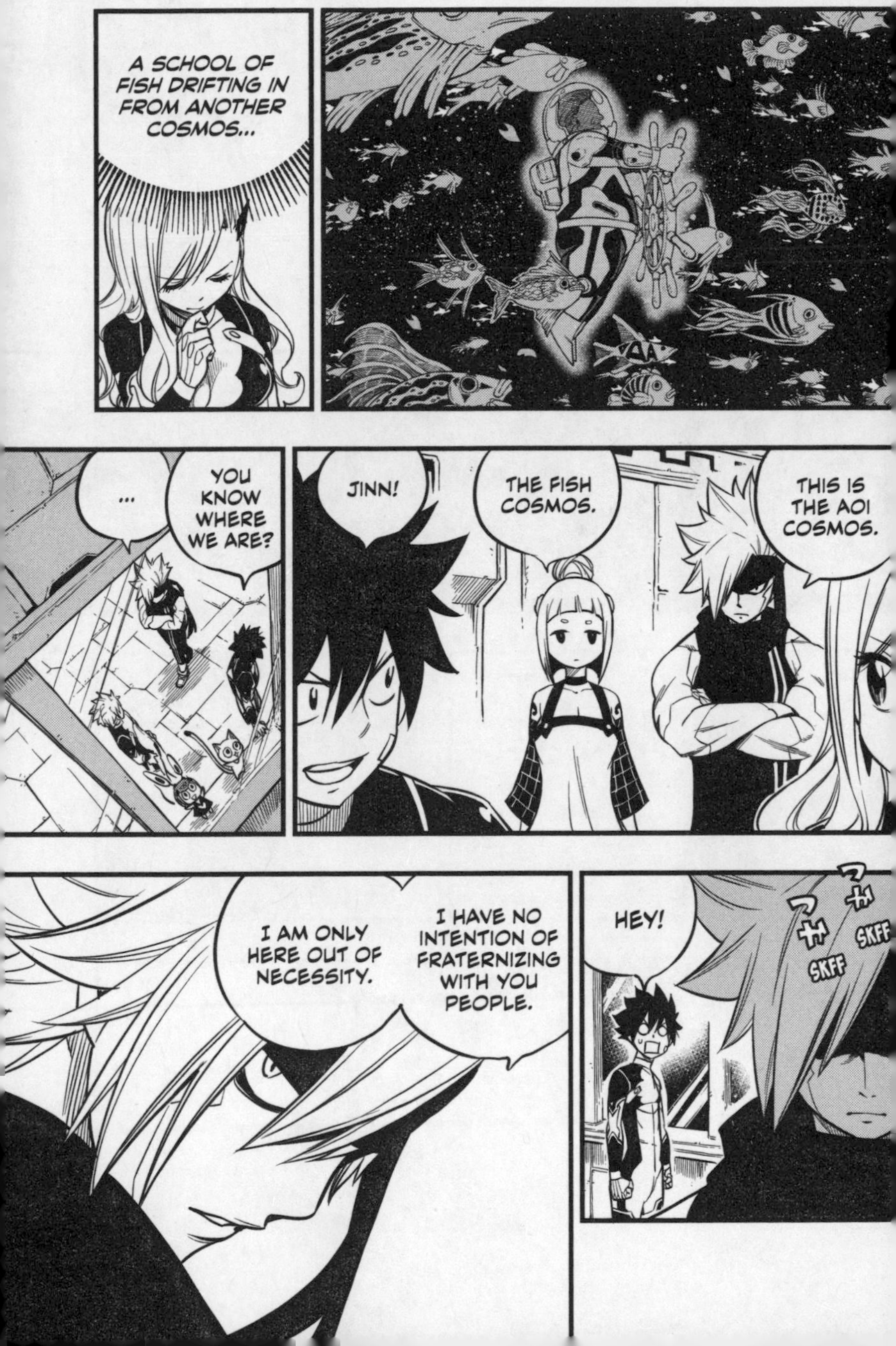
A SCHOOL OF FISH DRIFTING IN FROM ANOTHER COSMOS...
THIS IS THE AOI COSMOS.
THE FISH COSMOS.
JINN!
YOU KNOW WHERE WE ARE?
...
HEY!
SKFF
SKFF
I HAVE NO INTENTION OF FRATERNIZING WITH YOU PEOPLE.
I AM ONLY HERE OUT OF NECESSITY.

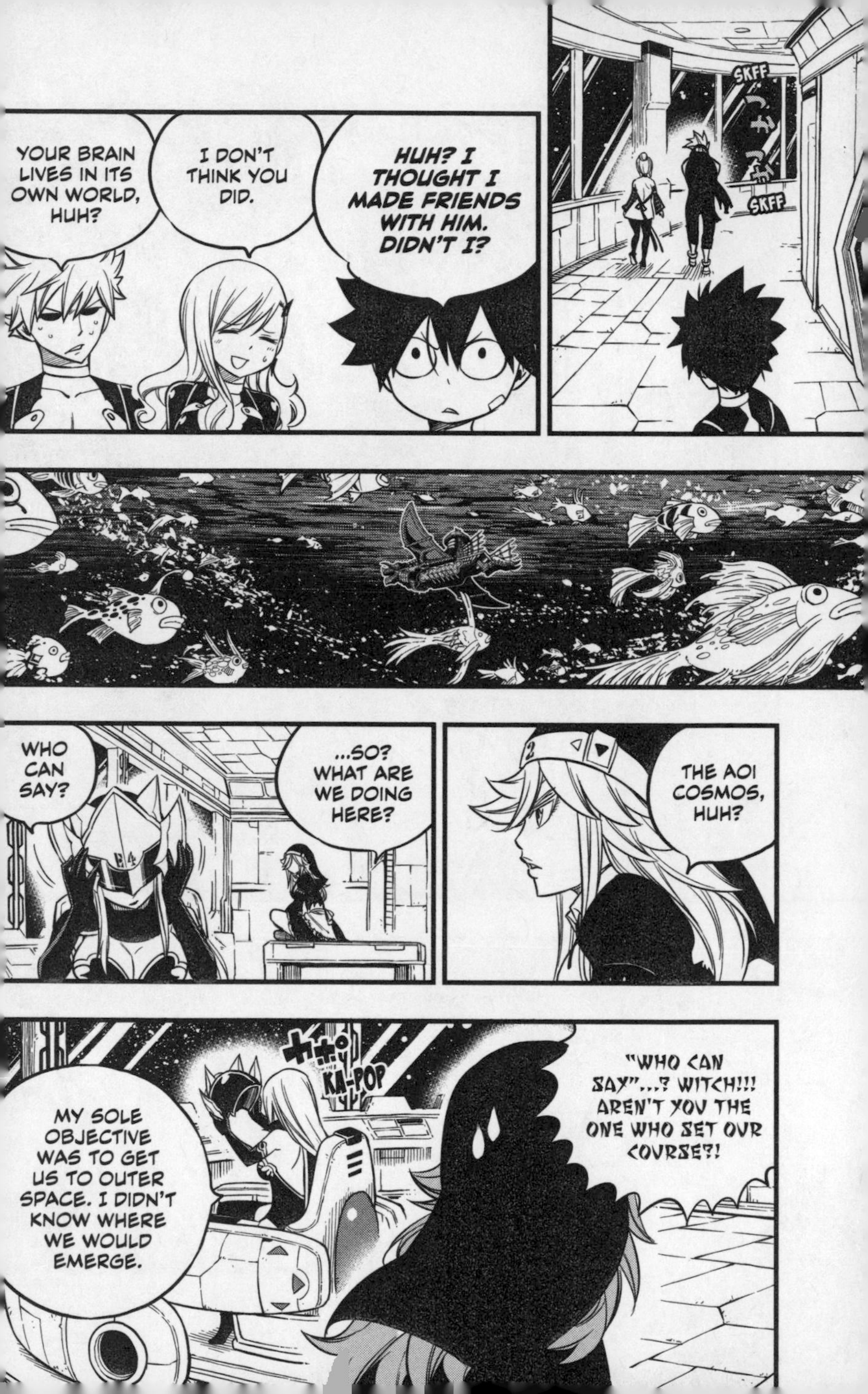
SKFF
SKFF
HUH? I THOUGHT I MADE FRIENDS WITH HIM. DIDN'T I?
I DON'T THINK YOU DID.
YOUR BRAIN LIVES IN ITS OWN WORLD, HUH?
THE AOI COSMOS, HUH?
...SO? WHAT ARE WE DOING HERE?
WHO CAN SAY?
"WHO CAN SAY"...? WITCH!!! AREN'T YOU THE ONE WHO SET OUR COURSE?!
KA-POP
MY SOLE OBJECTIVE WAS TO GET US TO OUTER SPACE. I DIDN'T KNOW WHERE WE WOULD EMERGE.

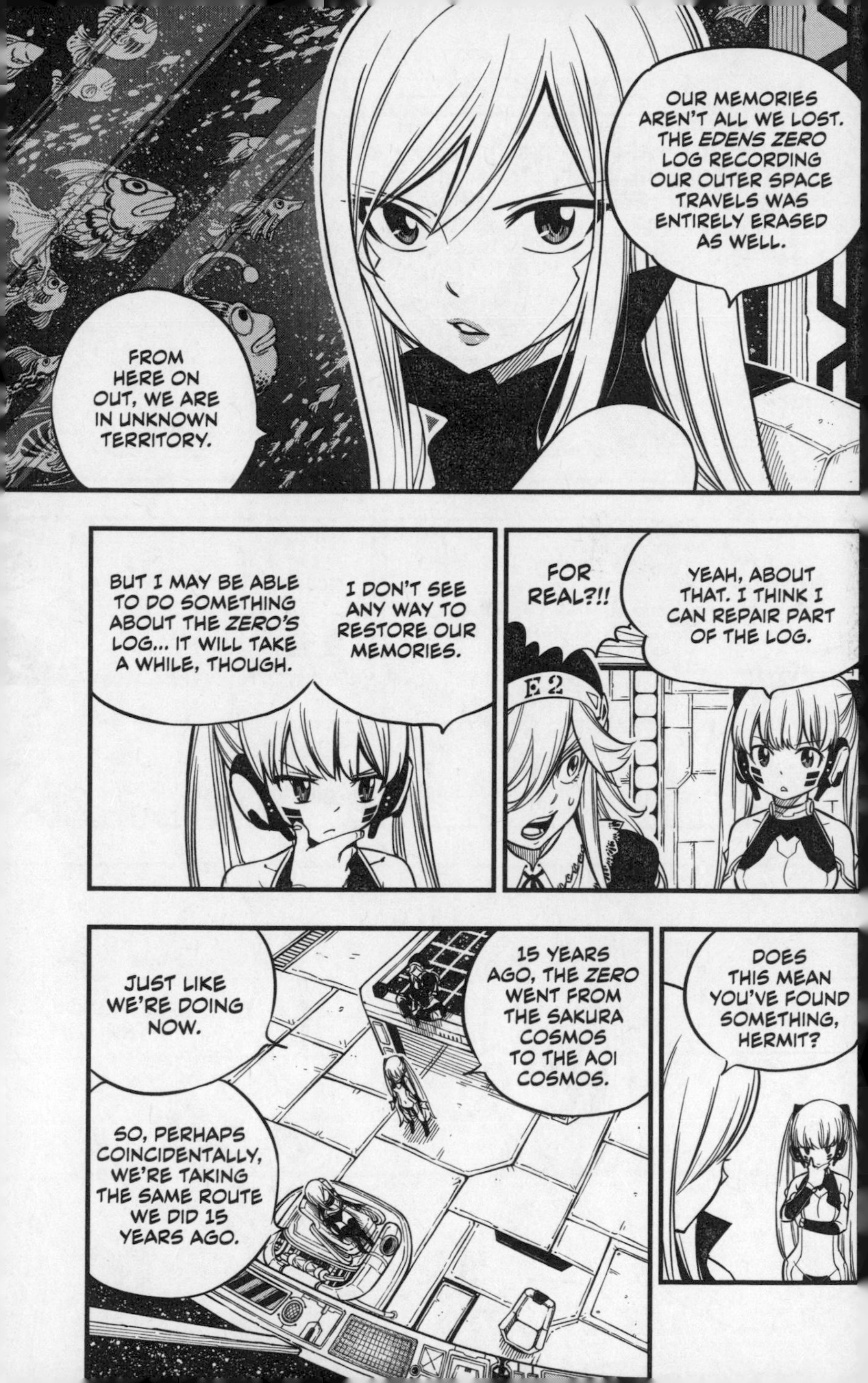
OUR MEMORIES AREN'T ALL WE LOST. THE *EDENS ZERO* LOG RECORDING OUR OUTER SPACE TRAVELS WAS ENTIRELY ERASED AS WELL.
FROM HERE ON OUT, WE ARE IN UNKNOWN TERRITORY.
YEAH, ABOUT THAT. I THINK I CAN REPAIR PART OF THE LOG.
FOR REAL?!!
E2
I DON'T SEE ANY WAY TO RESTORE OUR MEMORIES.
BUT I MAY BE ABLE TO DO SOMETHING ABOUT THE *ZERO'S* LOG... IT WILL TAKE A WHILE, THOUGH.
DOES THIS MEAN YOU'VE FOUND SOMETHING, HERMIT?
15 YEARS AGO, THE *ZERO* WENT FROM THE SAKURA COSMOS TO THE AOI COSMOS.
JUST LIKE WE'RE DOING NOW.
SO, PERHAPS COINCIDENTALLY, WE'RE TAKING THE SAME ROUTE WE DID 15 YEARS AGO.

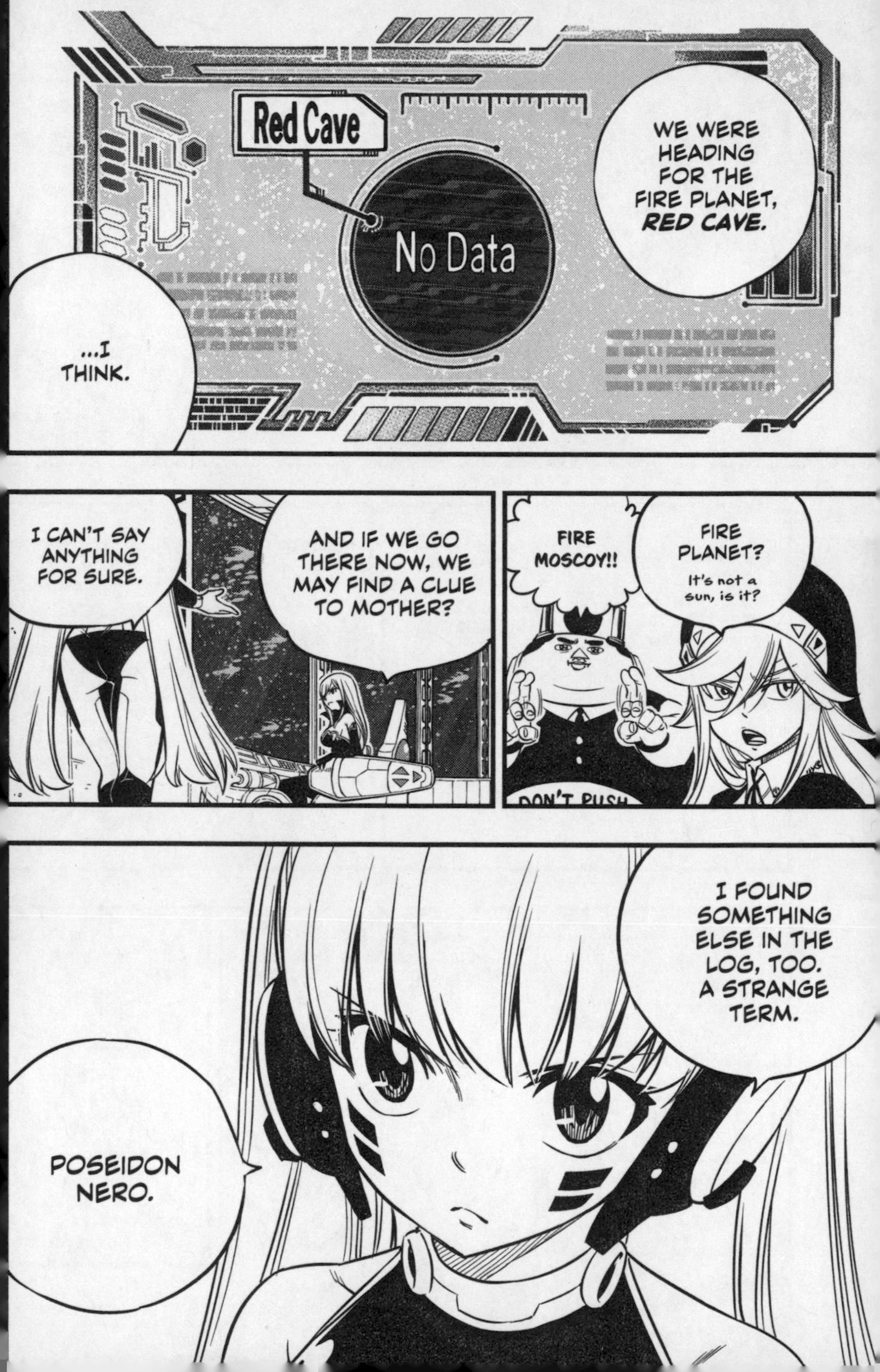
WE WERE HEADING FOR THE FIRE PLANET, RED CAVE.
Red Cave
No Data
...I THINK.
FIRE PLANET? It's not a sun, is it?
FIRE MOSCOY!!
DON'T PUSH
AND IF WE GO THERE NOW, WE MAY FIND A CLUE TO MOTHER?
I CAN'T SAY ANYTHING FOR SURE.
I FOUND SOMETHING ELSE IN THE LOG, TOO. A STRANGE TERM.
POSEIDON NERO.

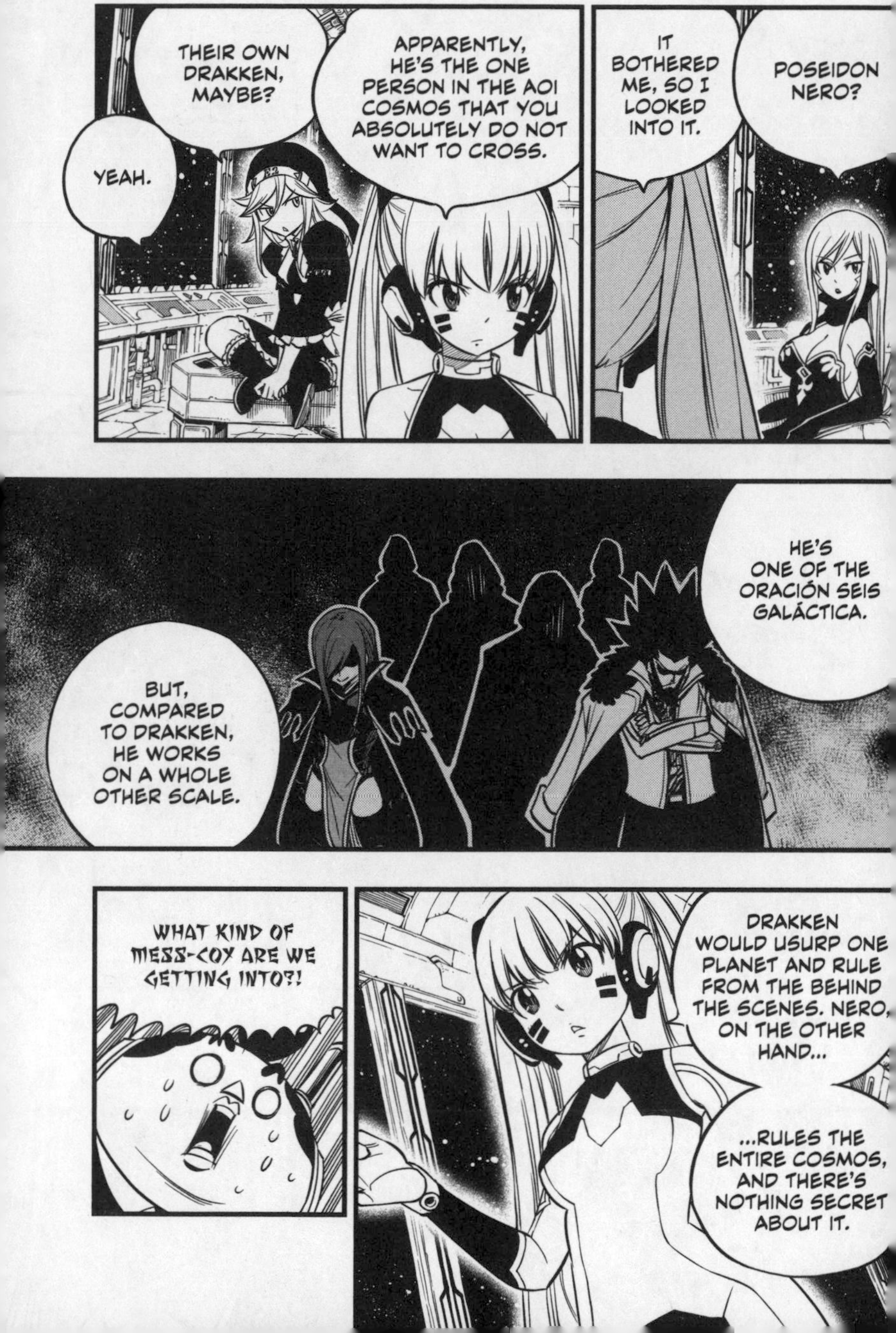
POSEIDON NERO?
IT BOTHERED ME, SO I LOOKED INTO IT.
APPARENTLY, HE'S THE ONE PERSON IN THE AOI COSMOS THAT YOU ABSOLUTELY DO NOT WANT TO CROSS.
THEIR OWN DRAKKEN, MAYBE?
YEAH.
HE'S ONE OF THE ORACIÓN SEIS GALÁCTICA.
BUT, COMPARED TO DRAKKEN, HE WORKS ON A WHOLE OTHER SCALE.
DRAKKEN WOULD USURP ONE PLANET AND RULE FROM THE BEHIND THE SCENES. NERO, ON THE OTHER HAND...
...RULES THE ENTIRE COSMOS, AND THERE'S NOTHING SECRET ABOUT IT.
WHAT KIND OF MESS-COY ARE WE GETTING INTO?!

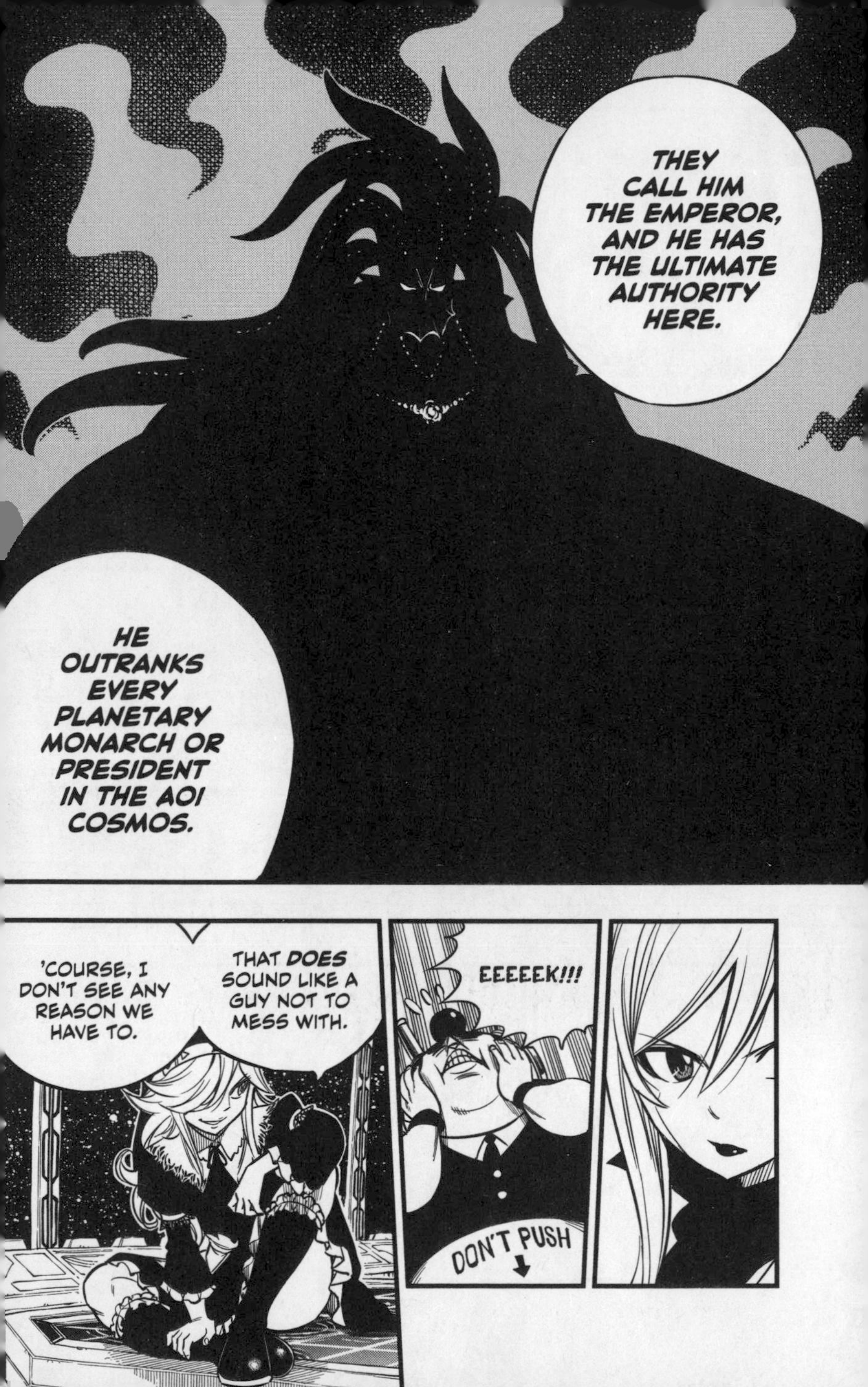
THEY CALL HIM THE EMPEROR, AND HE HAS THE ULTIMATE AUTHORITY HERE.
HE OUTRANKS EVERY PLANETARY MONARCH OR PRESIDENT IN THE AOI COSMOS.
EEEEEK!!!
DON'T PUSH
THAT DOES SOUND LIKE A GUY NOT TO MESS WITH.
'COURSE, I DON'T SEE ANY REASON WE HAVE TO.

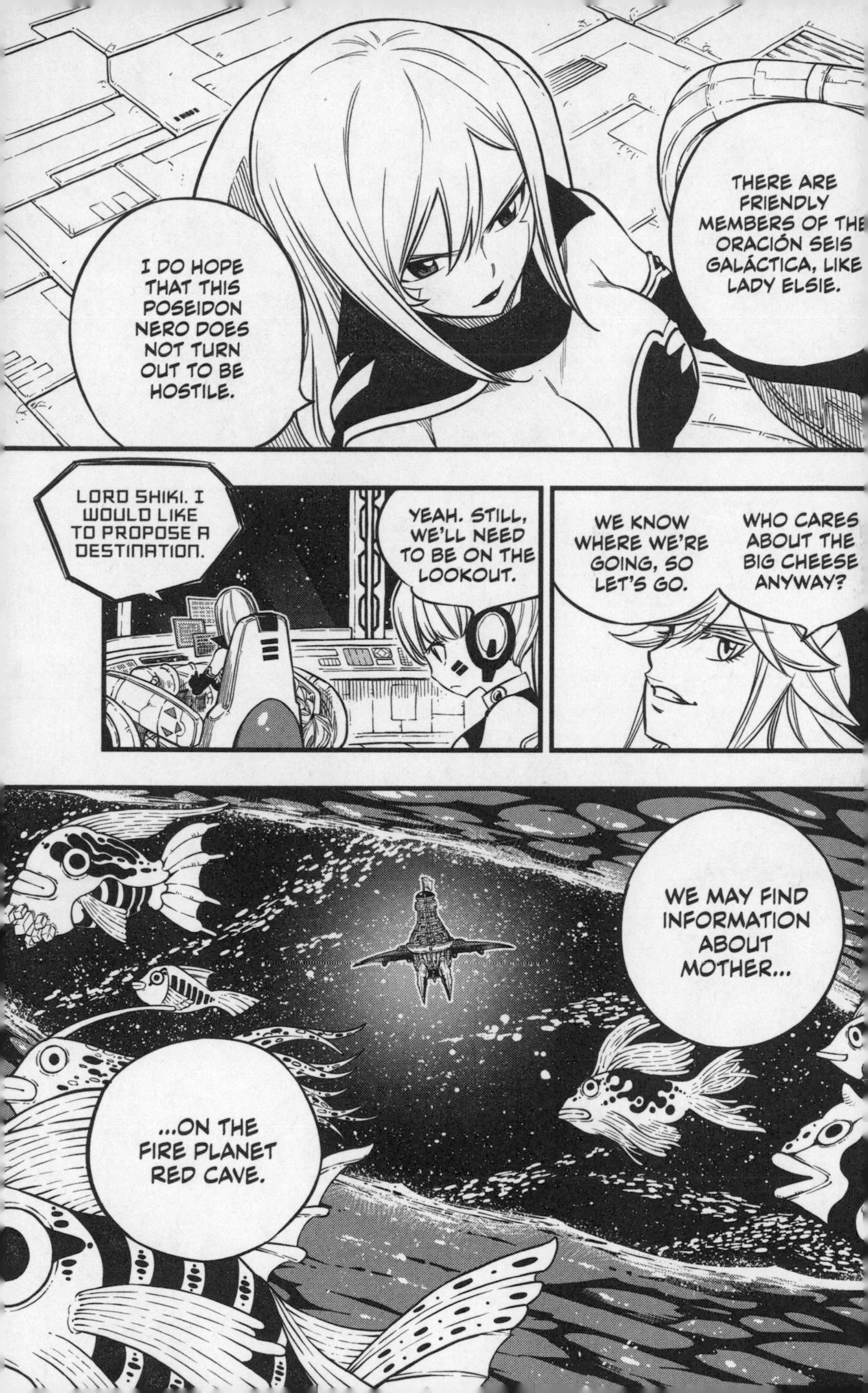
THERE ARE FRIENDLY MEMBERS OF THE ORACIÓN SEIS GALÁCTICA, LIKE LADY ELSIE.
I DO HOPE THAT THIS POSEIDON NERO DOES NOT TURN OUT TO BE HOSTILE.
WHO CARES ABOUT THE BIG CHEESE ANYWAY?
WE KNOW WHERE WE'RE GOING, SO LET'S GO.
YEAH. STILL, WE'LL NEED TO BE ON THE LOOKOUT.
LORD SHIKI. I WOULD LIKE TO PROPOSE A DESTINATION.
WE MAY FIND INFORMATION ABOUT MOTHER...
...ON THE FIRE PLANET RED CAVE.

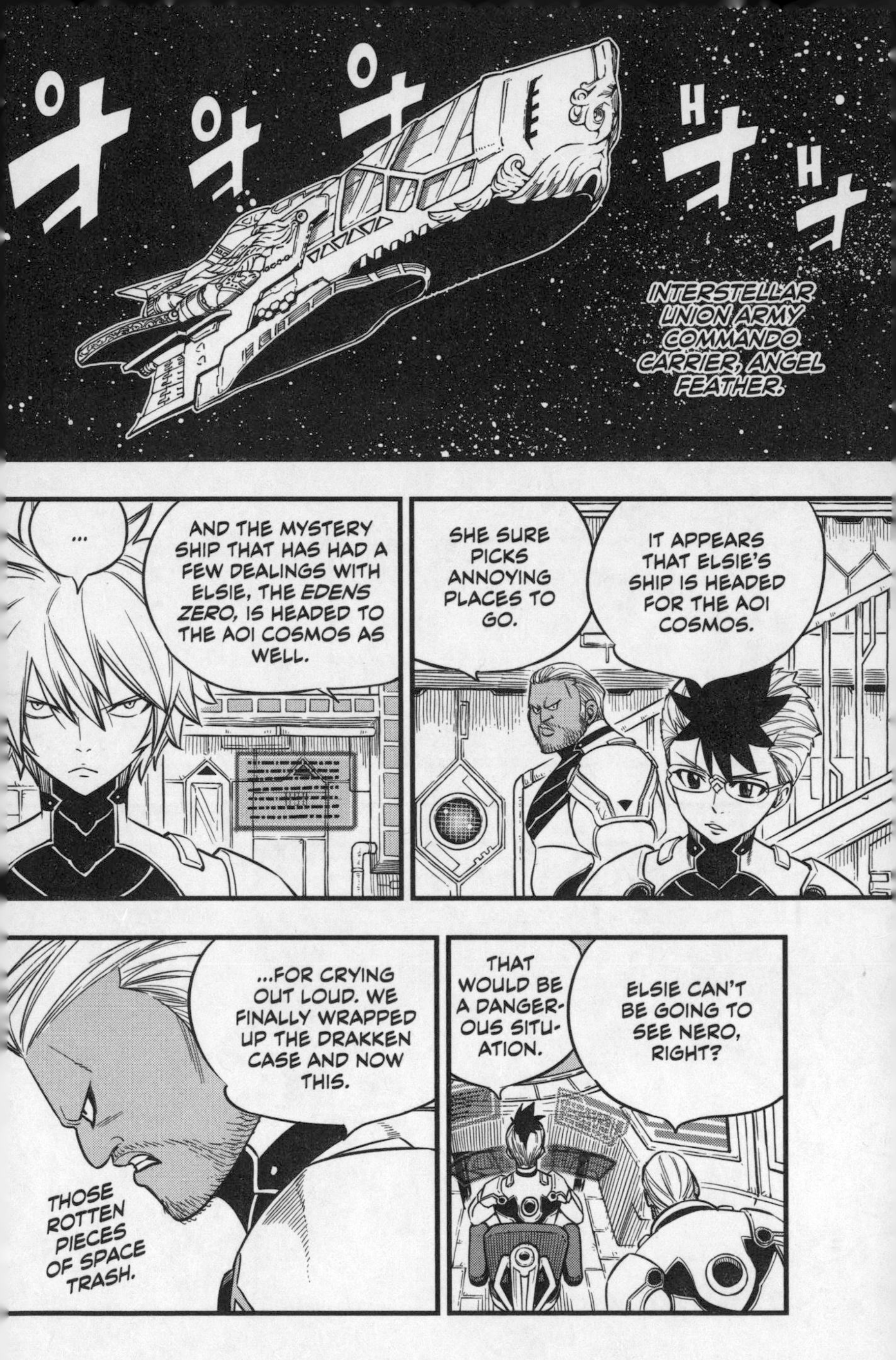
INTERSTELLAR UNION ARMY COMMANDO CARRIER, ANGEL FEATHER.
IT APPEARS THAT ELSIE'S SHIP IS HEADED FOR THE AOI COSMOS.
SHE SURE PICKS ANNOYING PLACES TO GO.
AND THE MYSTERY SHIP THAT HAS HAD A FEW DEALINGS WITH ELSIE, THE *EDENS ZERO*, IS HEADED TO THE AOI COSMOS AS WELL.
...
ELSIE CAN'T BE GOING TO SEE NERO, RIGHT?
THAT WOULD BE A DANGEROUS SITUATION.
...FOR CRYING OUT LOUD. WE FINALLY WRAPPED UP THE DRAKKEN CASE AND NOW THIS.
THOSE ROTTEN PIECES OF SPACE TRASH.

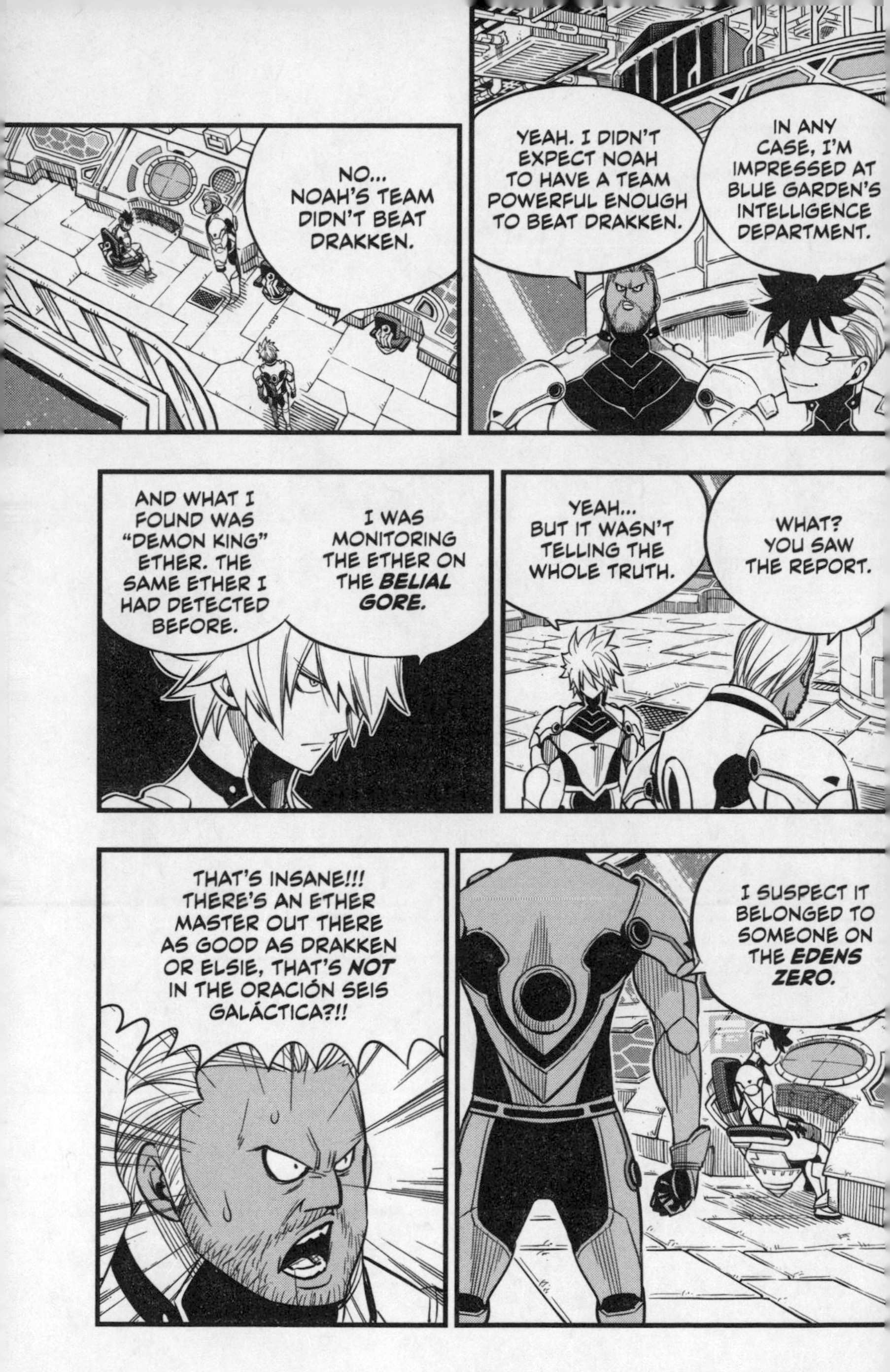
IN ANY CASE, I'M IMPRESSED AT BLUE GARDEN'S INTELLIGENCE DEPARTMENT.
YEAH. I DIDN'T EXPECT NOAH TO HAVE A TEAM POWERFUL ENOUGH TO BEAT DRAKKEN.
NO... NOAH'S TEAM DIDN'T BEAT DRAKKEN.
WHAT? YOU SAW THE REPORT.
YEAH... BUT IT WASN'T TELLING THE WHOLE TRUTH.
I WAS MONITORING THE ETHER ON THE ***BELIAL GORE.***
AND WHAT I FOUND WAS "DEMON KING" ETHER. THE SAME ETHER I HAD DETECTED BEFORE.
I SUSPECT IT BELONGED TO SOMEONE ON THE ***EDENS ZERO.***
THAT'S INSANE!!! THERE'S AN ETHER MASTER OUT THERE AS GOOD AS DRAKKEN OR ELSIE, THAT'S ***NOT*** IN THE ORACIÓN SEIS GALÁCTICA?!!

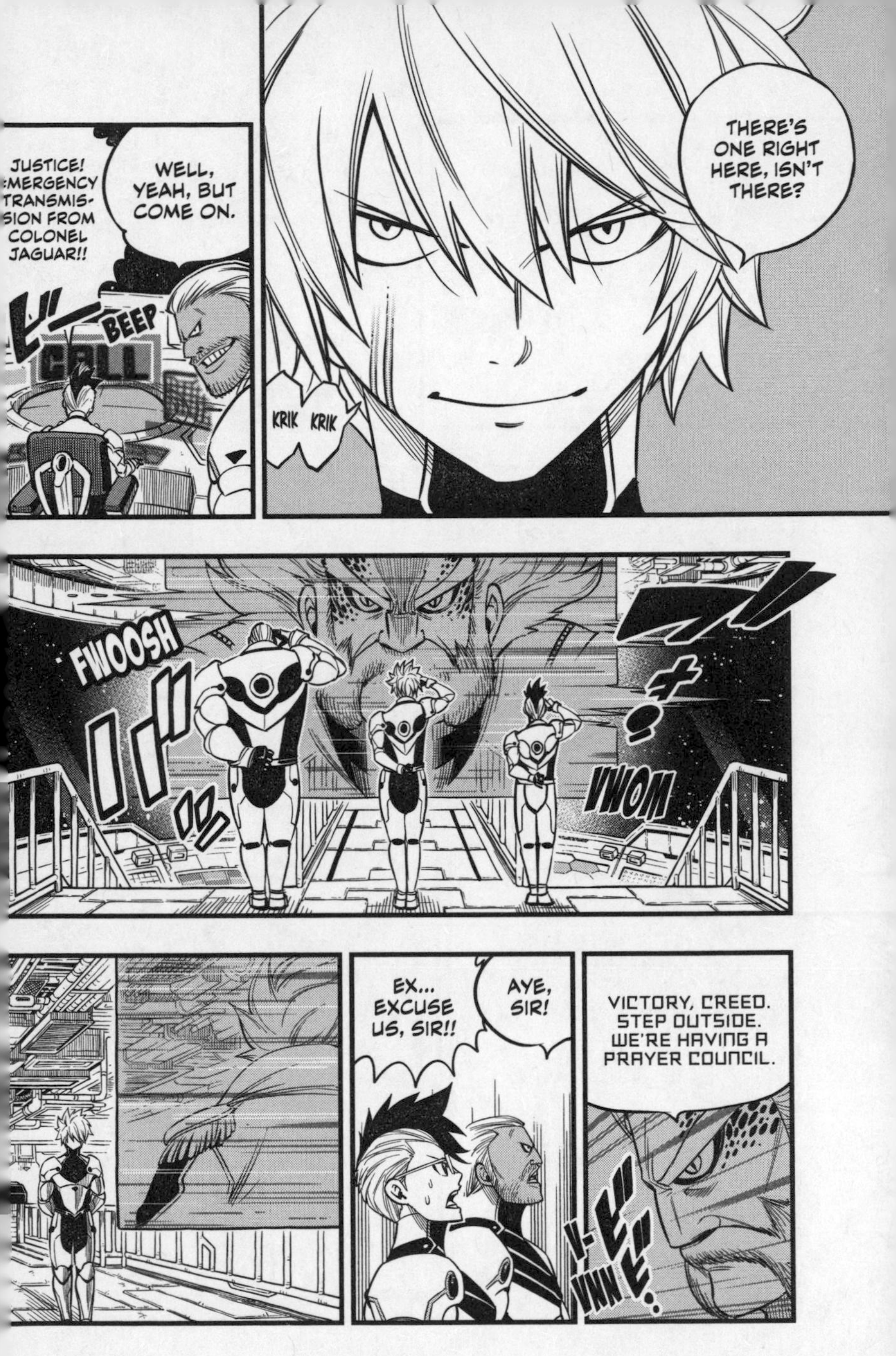

THERE'S ONE RIGHT HERE, ISN'T THERE?
KRIK KRIK
WELL, YEAH, BUT COME ON.
JUSTICE! EMERGENCY TRANSMISSION FROM COLONEL JAGUAR!!
BEEP
CALL
FWOOSH
VWOM
VICTORY, CREED. STEP OUTSIDE. WE'RE HAVING A PRAYER COUNCIL.
AYE, SIR!
EX... EXCUSE US, SIR!!

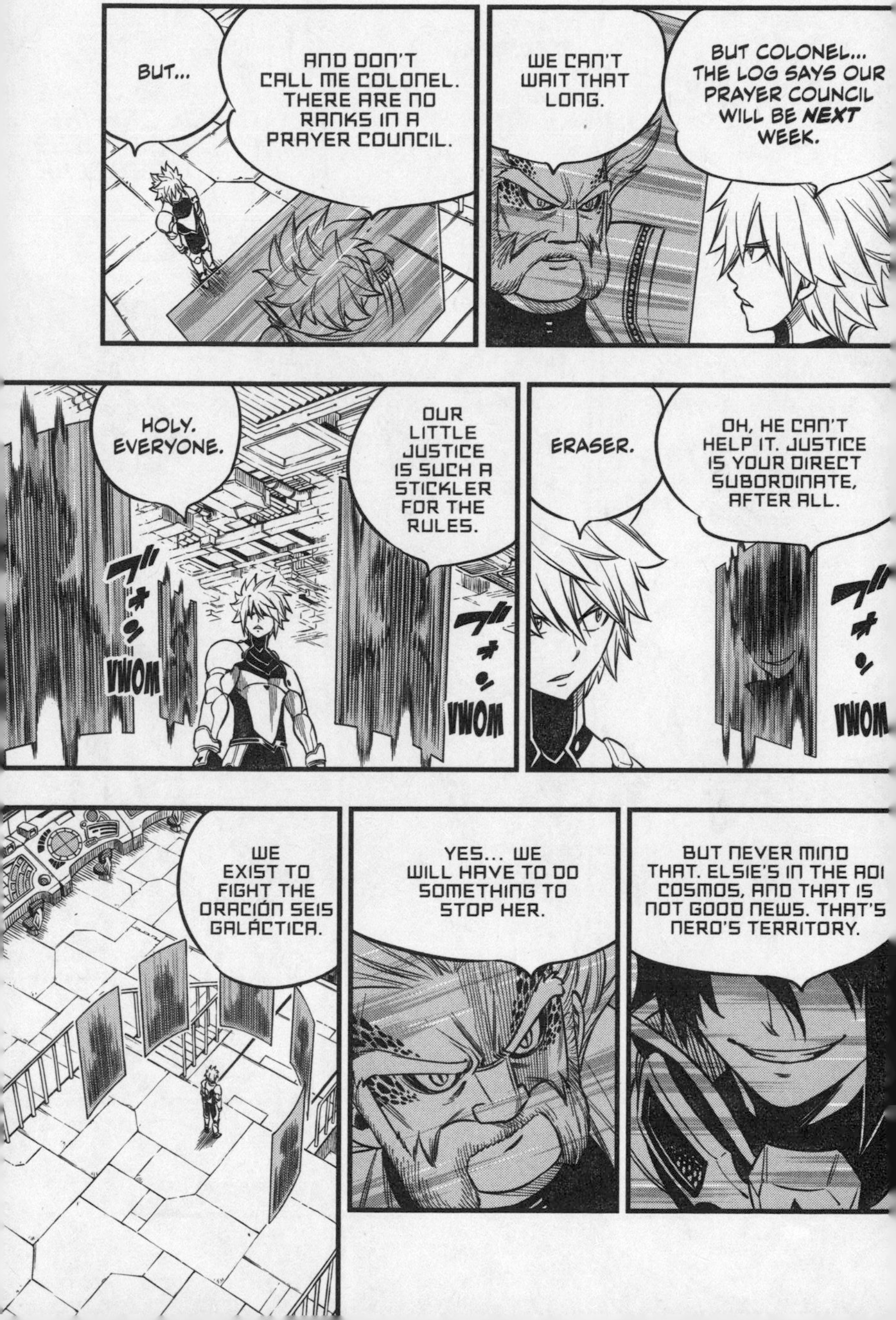
BUT COLONEL... THE LOG SAYS OUR PRAYER COUNCIL WILL BE **NEXT** WEEK.
WE CAN'T WAIT THAT LONG.
AND DON'T CALL ME COLONEL. THERE ARE NO RANKS IN A PRAYER COUNCIL.
BUT...
OH, HE CAN'T HELP IT. JUSTICE IS YOUR DIRECT SUBORDINATE, AFTER ALL.
ERASER.
VWOM
OUR LITTLE JUSTICE IS SUCH A STICKLER FOR THE RULES.
VWOM
HOLY. EVERYONE.
VWOM
BUT NEVER MIND THAT. ELSIE'S IN THE AOI COSMOS, AND THAT IS NOT GOOD NEWS. THAT'S NERO'S TERRITORY.
YES... WE WILL HAVE TO DO SOMETHING TO STOP HER.
WE EXIST TO FIGHT THE ORACIÓN SEIS GALÁCTICA.

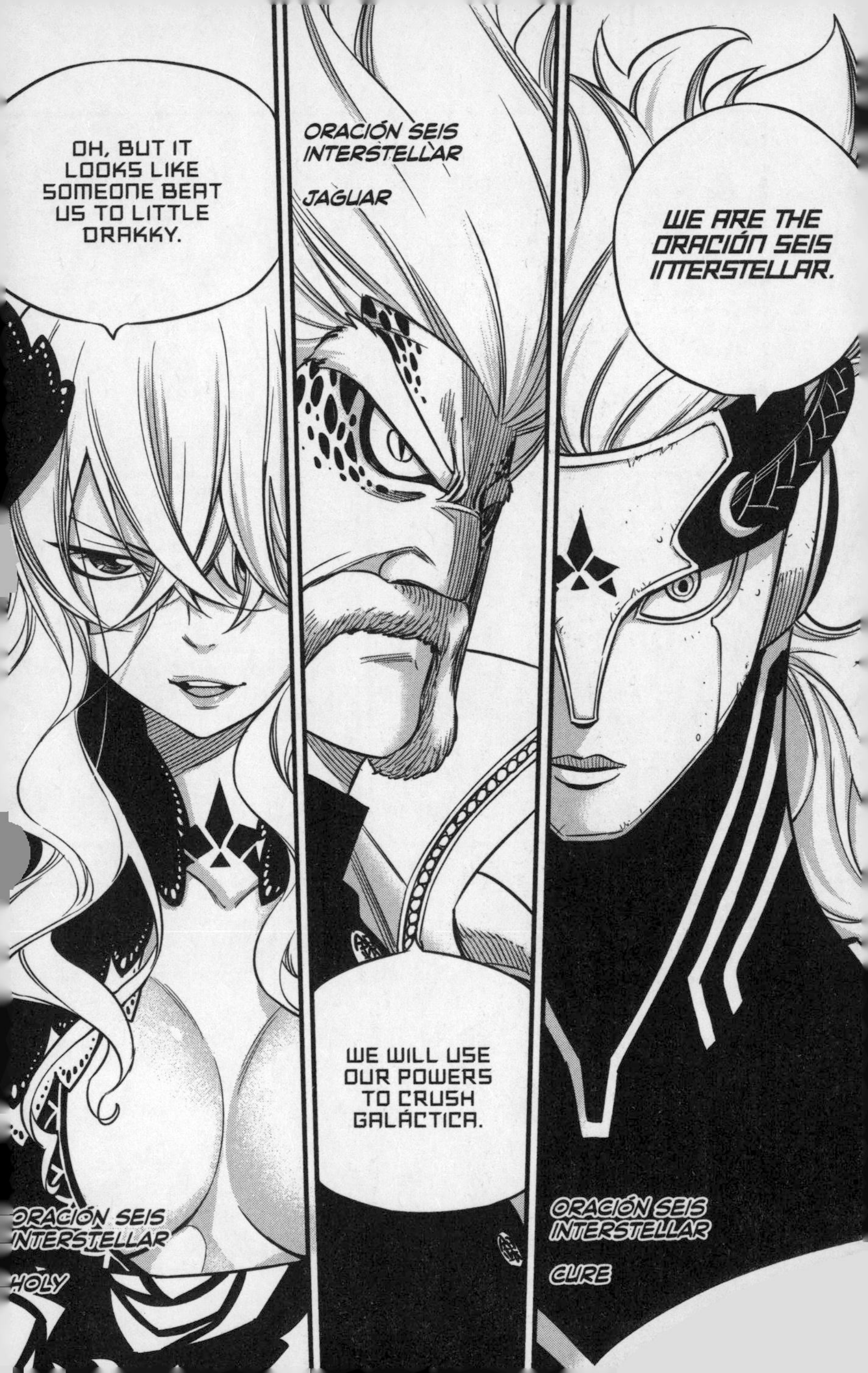
WE ARE THE ORACIÓN SEIS INTERSTELLAR.
ORACIÓN SEIS INTERSTELLAR
CURE
ORACIÓN SEIS INTERSTELLAR
JAGUAR
WE WILL USE OUR POWERS TO CRUSH GALÁCTICA.
OH, BUT IT LOOKS LIKE SOMEONE BEAT US TO LITTLE DRAKKY.
ORACIÓN SEIS INTERSTELLAR
HOLY

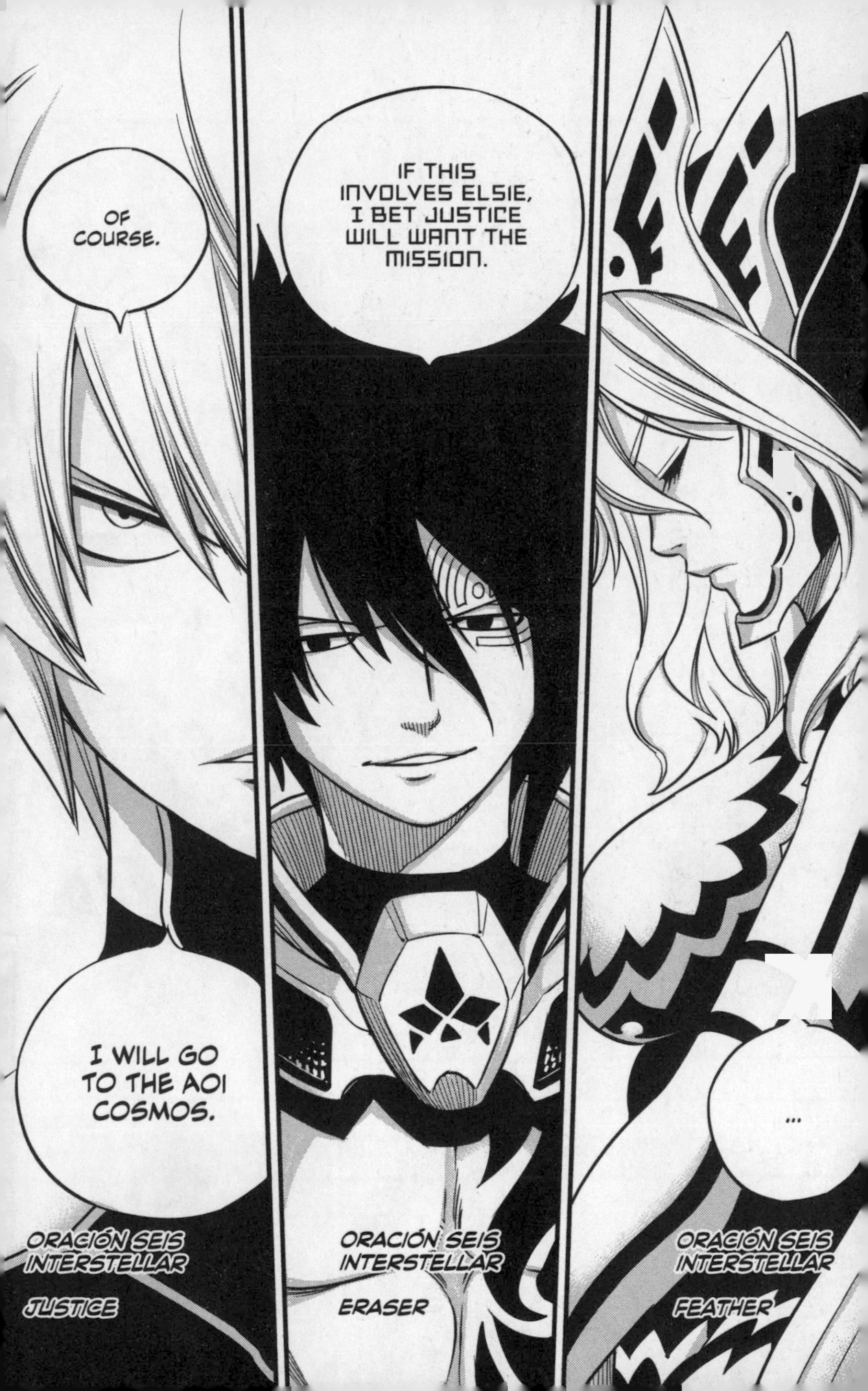
...
ORACIÓN SEIS INTERSTELLAR
FEATHER
IF THIS INVOLVES ELSIE, I BET JUSTICE WILL WANT THE MISSION.
ORACIÓN SEIS INTERSTELLAR
ERASER
OF COURSE.
I WILL GO TO THE AOI COSMOS.
ORACIÓN SEIS INTERSTELLAR
JUSTICE

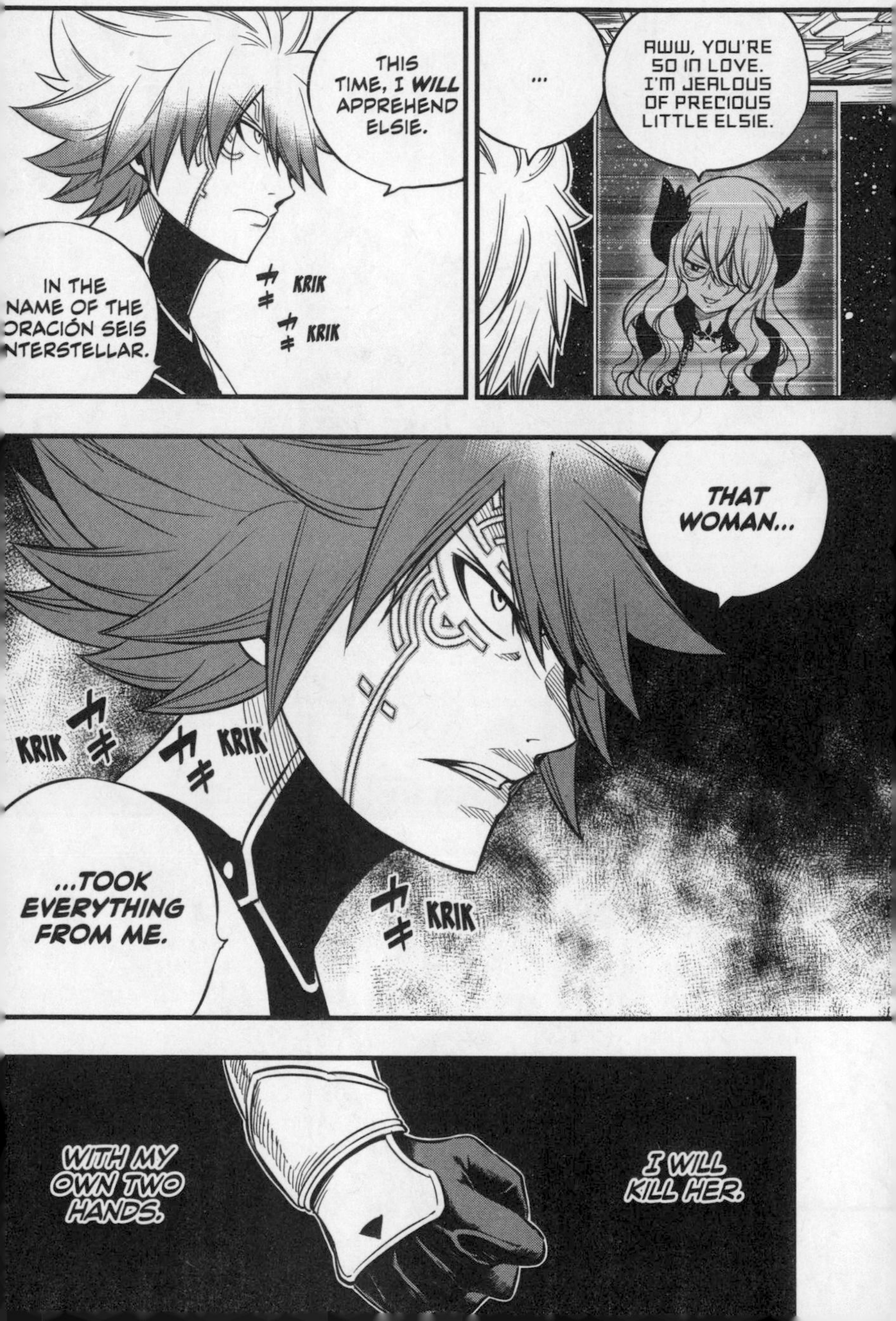
AWW, YOU'RE SO IN LOVE. I'M JEALOUS OF PRECIOUS LITTLE ELSIE.
...
THIS TIME, I WILL APPREHEND ELSIE.
KRIK
KRIK
IN THE NAME OF THE ORACIÓN SEIS NTERSTELLAR.
THAT WOMAN...
KRIK
KRIK
...TOOK EVERYTHING FROM ME.
KRIK
I WILL KILL HER.
WITH MY OWN TWO HANDS.

NOW, LET US PRAY...

LET US USE OUR SACRED POWERS...

...FOR THE PEACE OF THE COSMOS.

THE FIRE PLANET RED CAVE.

WOW...

I CAN SEE IT!!

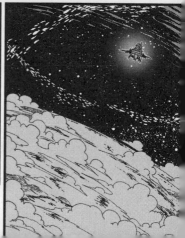

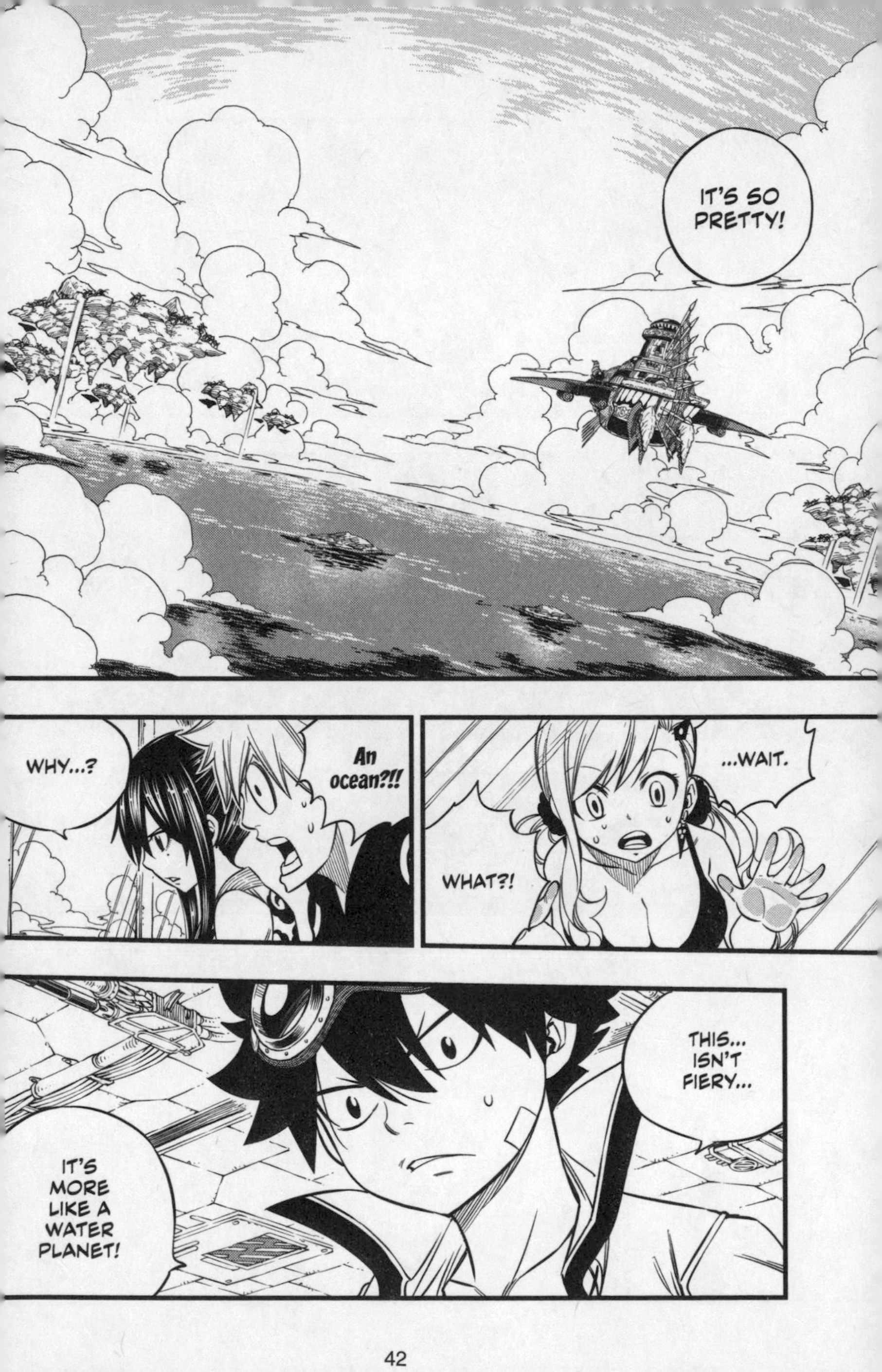
IT'S SO PRETTY!
...WAIT.
WHAT?!
An ocean?!!
WHY...?
THIS... ISN'T FIERY...
IT'S MORE LIKE A WATER PLANET!

EDENS ZERO

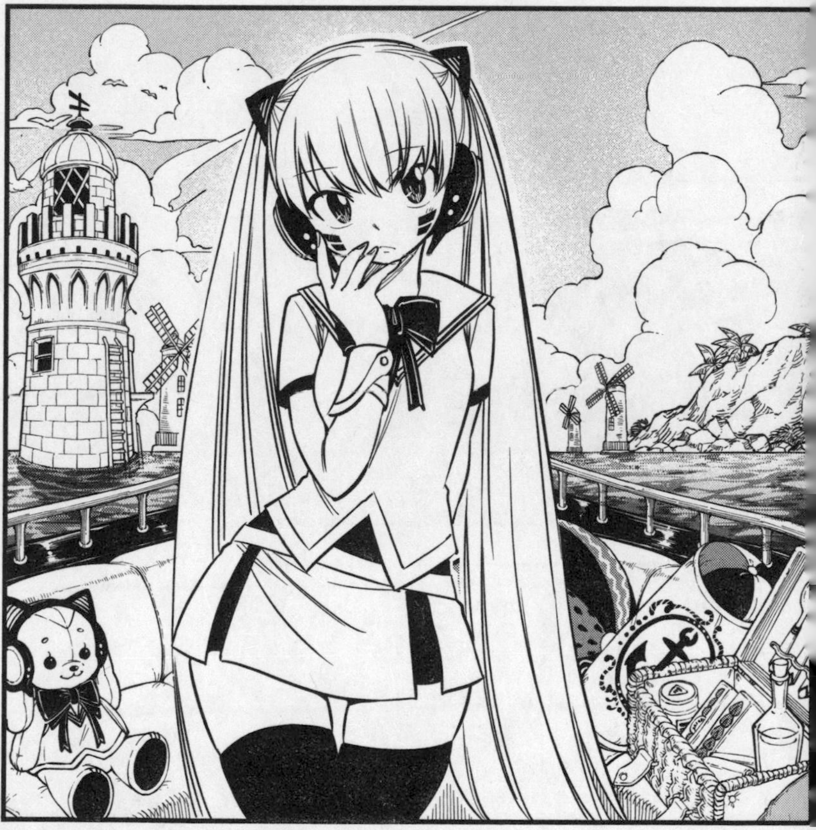

CHAPTER 107:
A PLANET WHERE STARS FALL LIKE RAIN

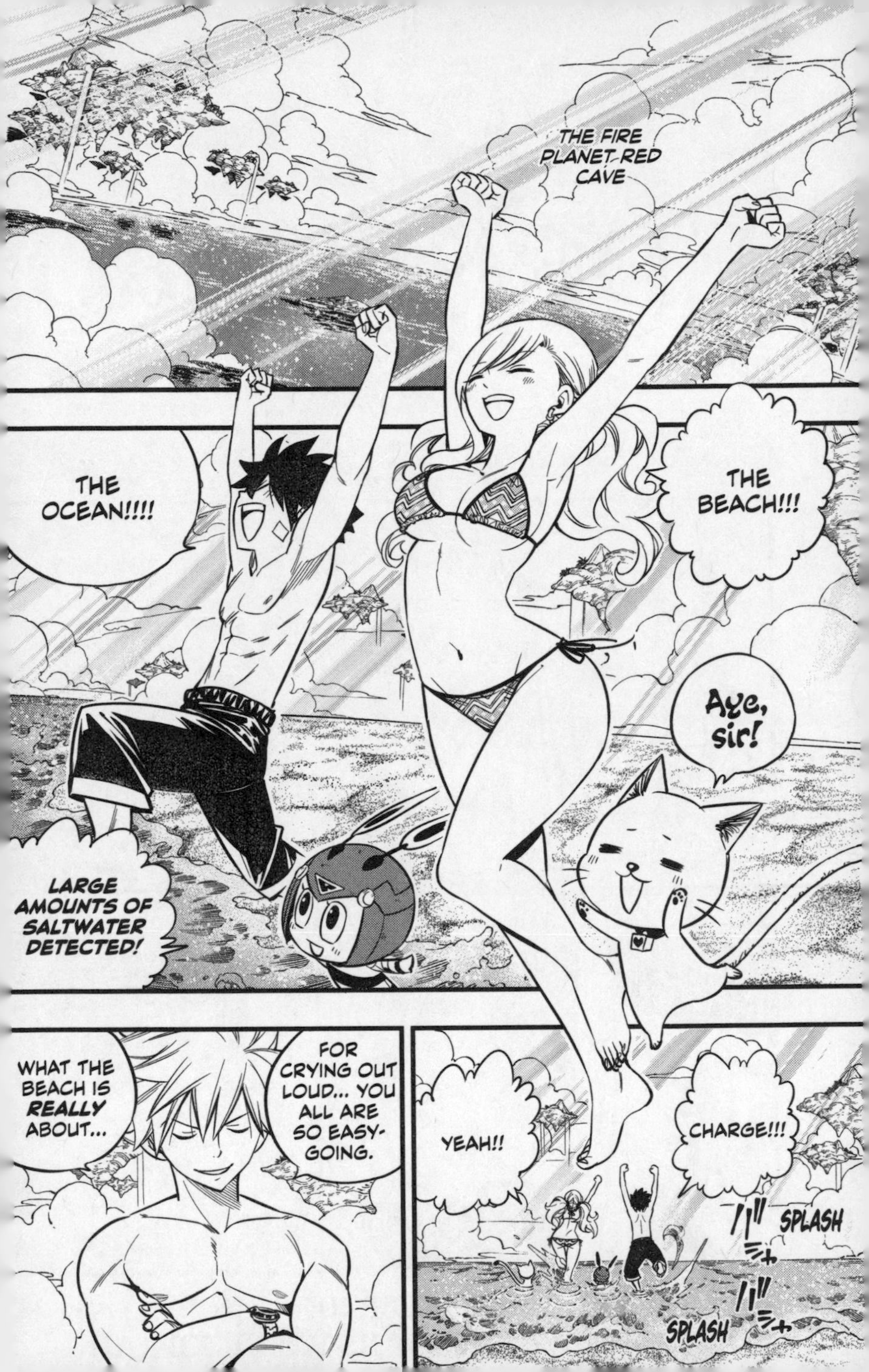
THE FIRE PLANET RED CAVE
THE BEACH!!!
THE OCEAN!!!!
Aye, sir!
LARGE AMOUNTS OF SALTWATER DETECTED!
CHARGE!!!
YEAH!!
SPLASH
SPLASH
FOR CRYING OUT LOUD... YOU ALL ARE SO EASY-GOING.
WHAT THE BEACH IS REALLY ABOUT...

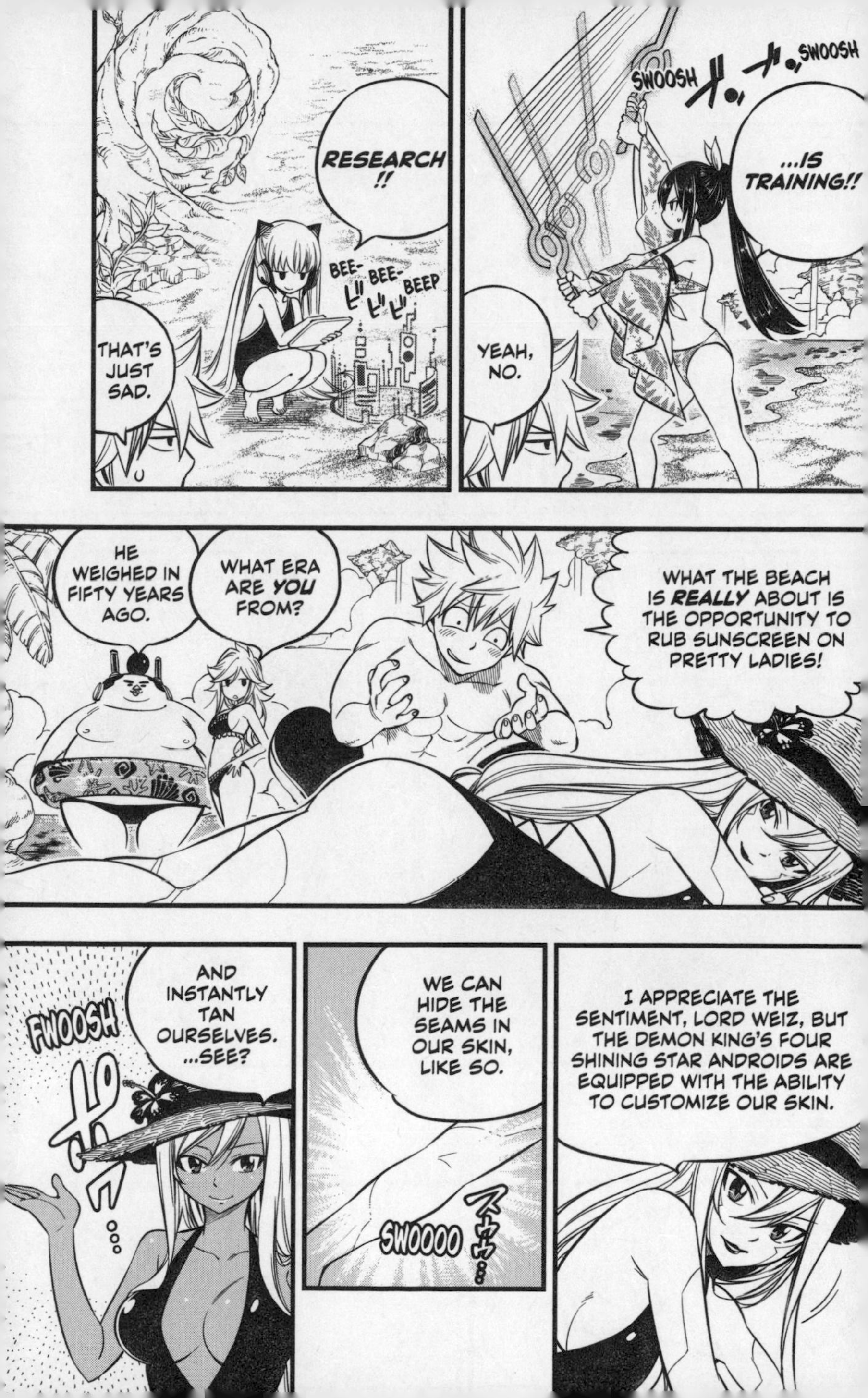
SWOOSH
SWOOSH
...IS TRAINING!!
YEAH, NO.
RESEARCH!!
BEE- BEE- BEEP
THAT'S JUST SAD.
WHAT THE BEACH IS REALLY ABOUT IS THE OPPORTUNITY TO RUB SUNSCREEN ON PRETTY LADIES!
WHAT ERA ARE YOU FROM?
HE WEIGHED IN FIFTY YEARS AGO.
I APPRECIATE THE SENTIMENT, LORD WEIZ, BUT THE DEMON KING'S FOUR SHINING STAR ANDROIDS ARE EQUIPPED WITH THE ABILITY TO CUSTOMIZE OUR SKIN.
WE CAN HIDE THE SEAMS IN OUR SKIN, LIKE SO.
SWOOOO
AND INSTANTLY TAN OURSELVES. ...SEE?
FWOOSH

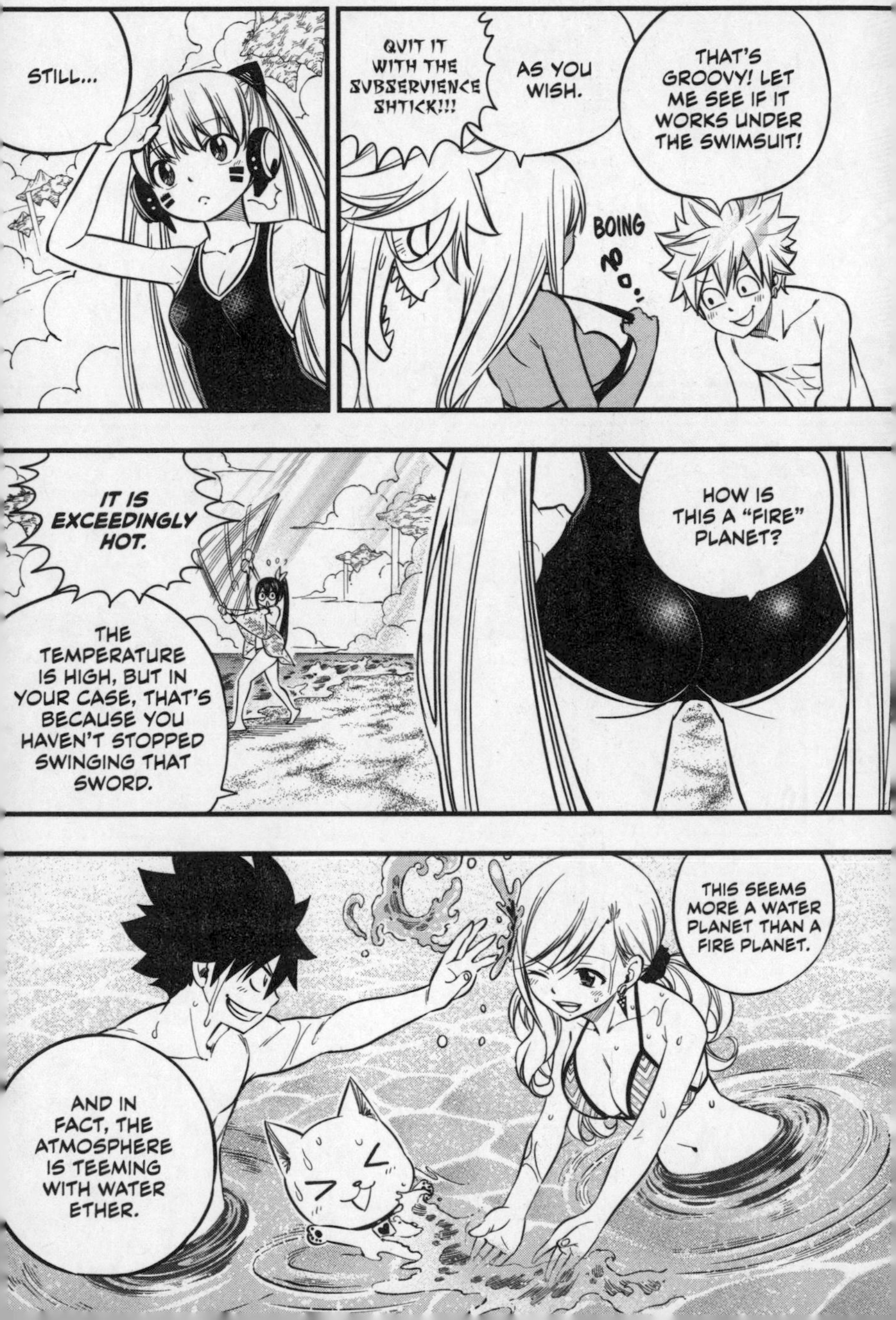
THAT'S GROOVY! LET ME SEE IF IT WORKS UNDER THE SWIMSUIT!
AS YOU WISH.
QUIT IT WITH THE SUBSERVIENCE SHTICK!!!
BOING
STILL...
HOW IS THIS A "FIRE" PLANET?
IT IS EXCEEDINGLY HOT.
THE TEMPERATURE IS HIGH, BUT IN YOUR CASE, THAT'S BECAUSE YOU HAVEN'T STOPPED SWINGING THAT SWORD.
THIS SEEMS MORE A WATER PLANET THAN A FIRE PLANET.
AND IN FACT, THE ATMOSPHERE IS TEEMING WITH WATER ETHER.

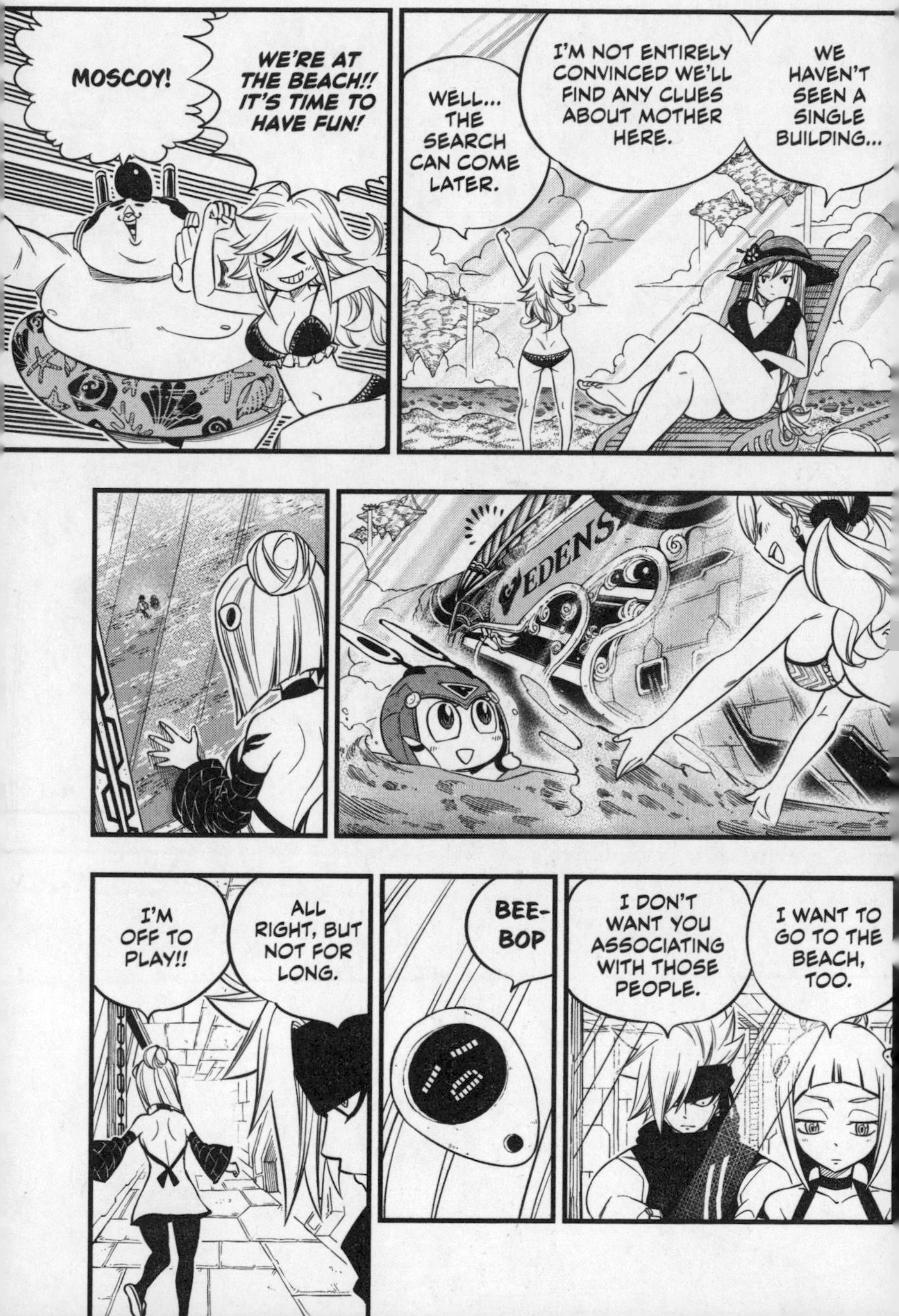
WE HAVEN'T SEEN A SINGLE BUILDING...
I'M NOT ENTIRELY CONVINCED WE'LL FIND ANY CLUES ABOUT MOTHER HERE.
WELL... THE SEARCH CAN COME LATER.
WE'RE AT THE BEACH!! IT'S TIME TO HAVE FUN!
MOSCOY!
EDENS
I WANT TO GO TO THE BEACH, TOO.
I DON'T WANT YOU ASSOCIATING WITH THOSE PEOPLE.
BEE-BOP
ALL RIGHT, BUT NOT FOR LONG.
I'M OFF TO PLAY!!

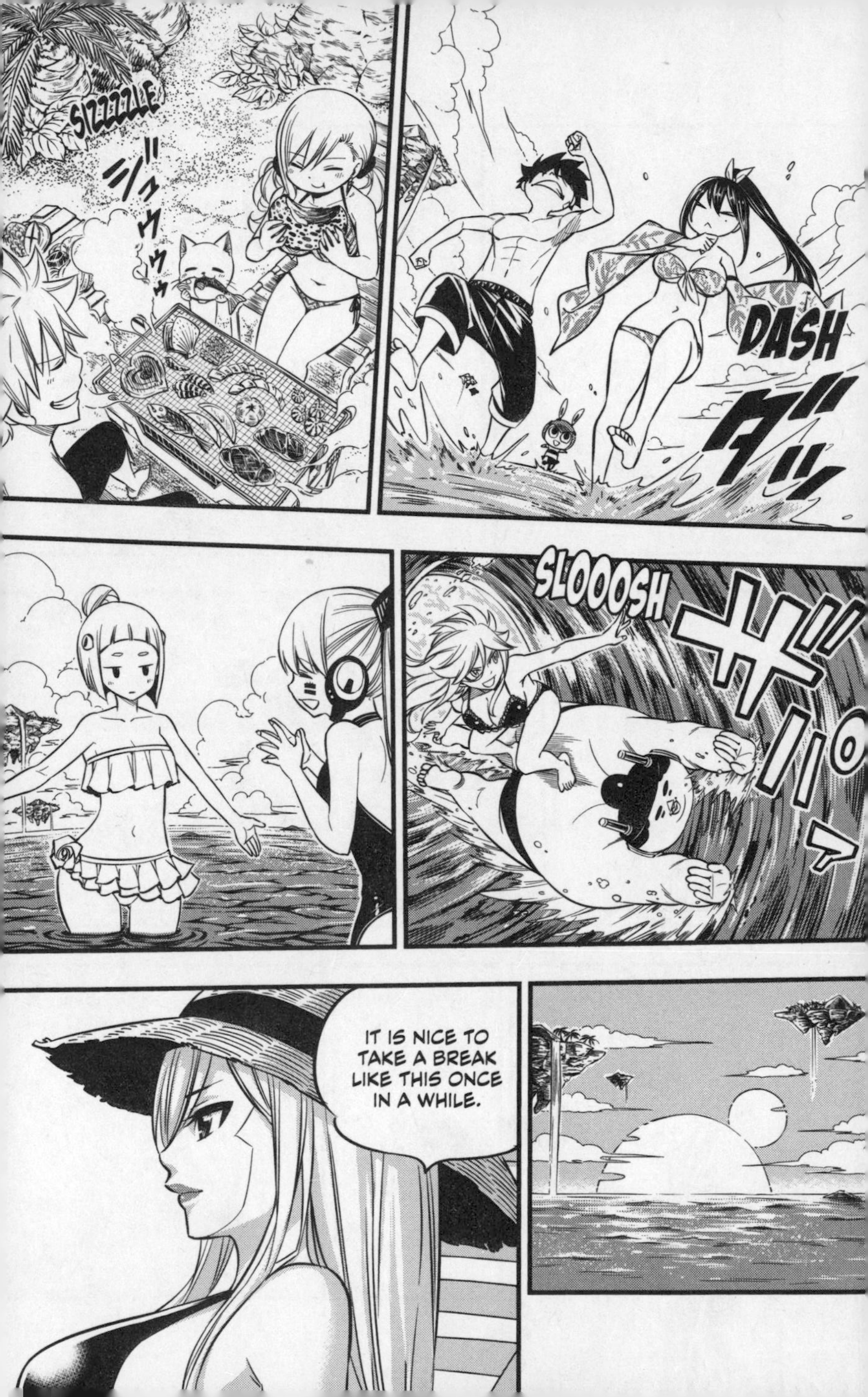
DASH
ダッ
SIZZZZZLE
ジュウウウ
SLOOOSH
IT IS NICE TO TAKE A BREAK LIKE THIS ONCE IN A WHILE.

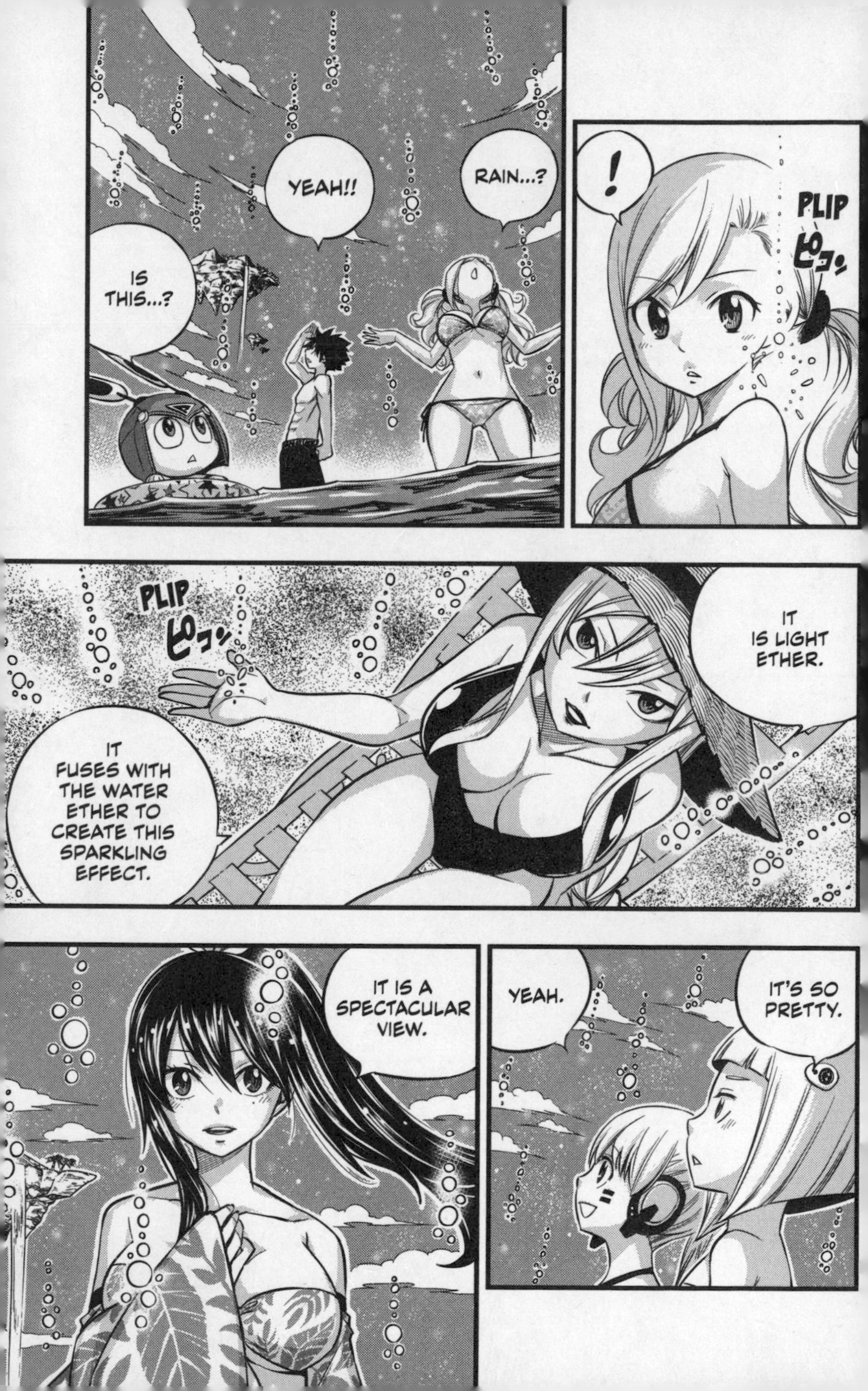
!
PLIP
ピコッ
RAIN...?
YEAH!!
IS THIS...?
IT IS LIGHT ETHER.
PLIP
ピコッ
IT FUSES WITH THE WATER ETHER TO CREATE THIS SPARKLING EFFECT.
IT'S SO PRETTY.
YEAH.
IT IS A SPECTACULAR VIEW.

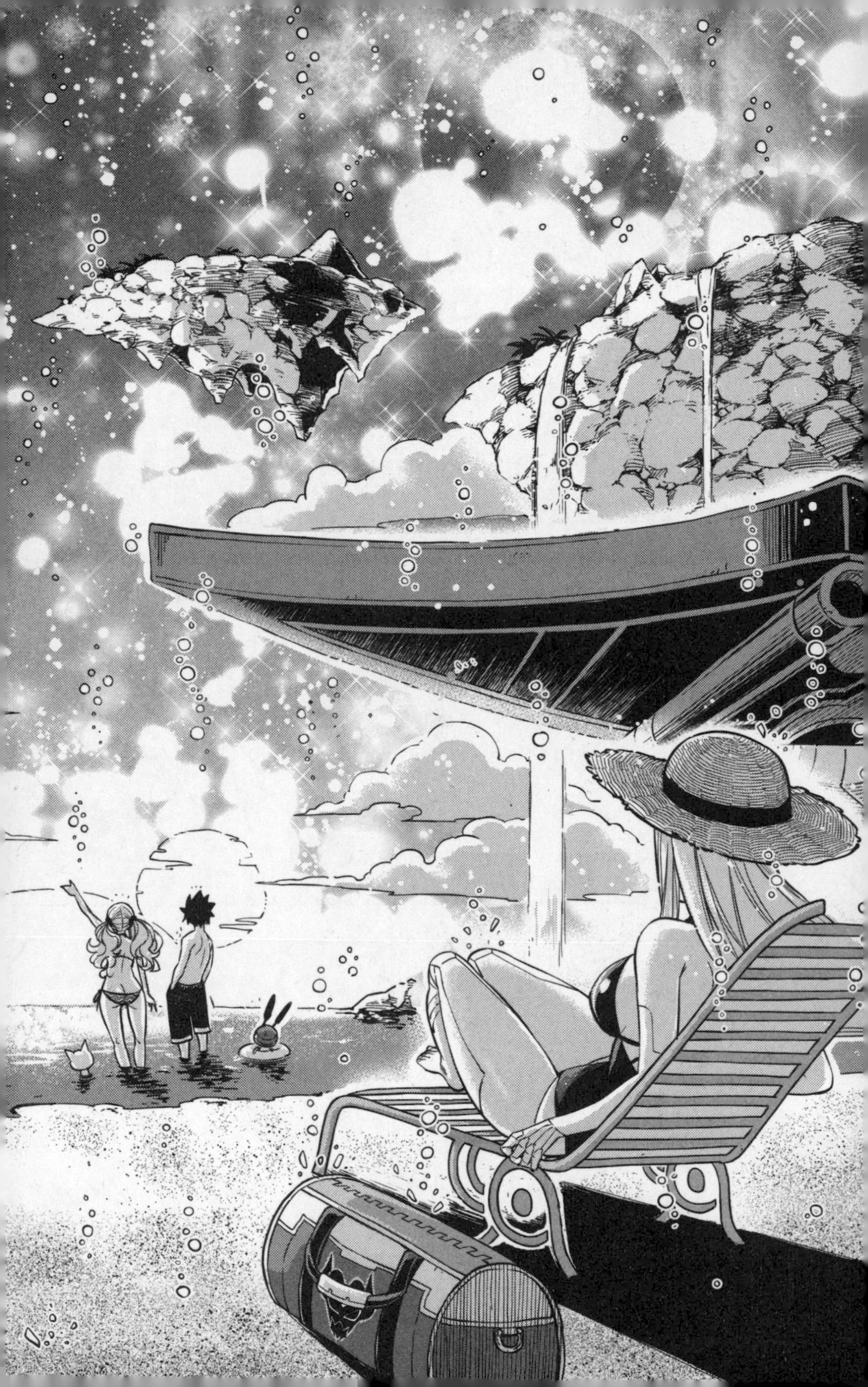

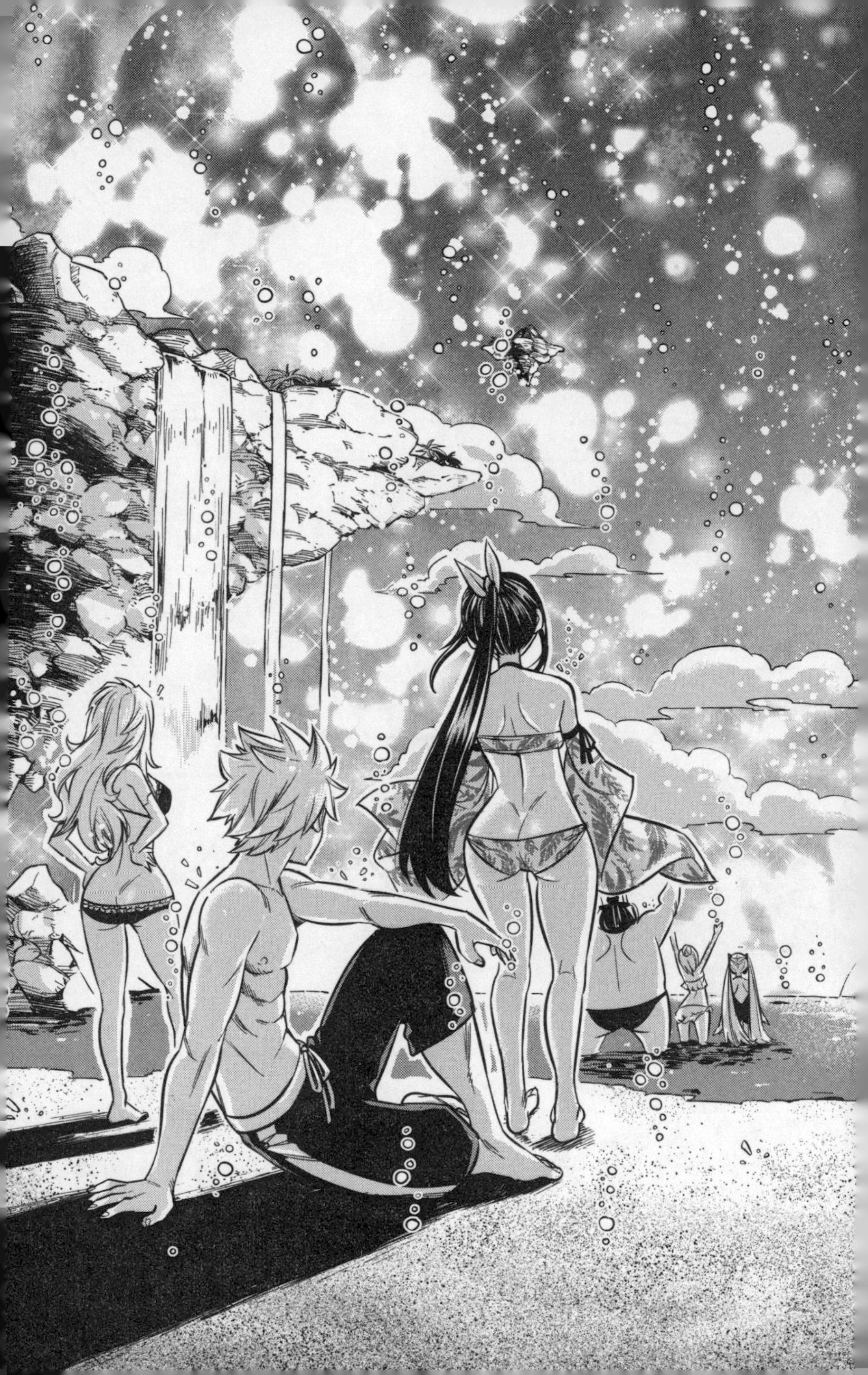

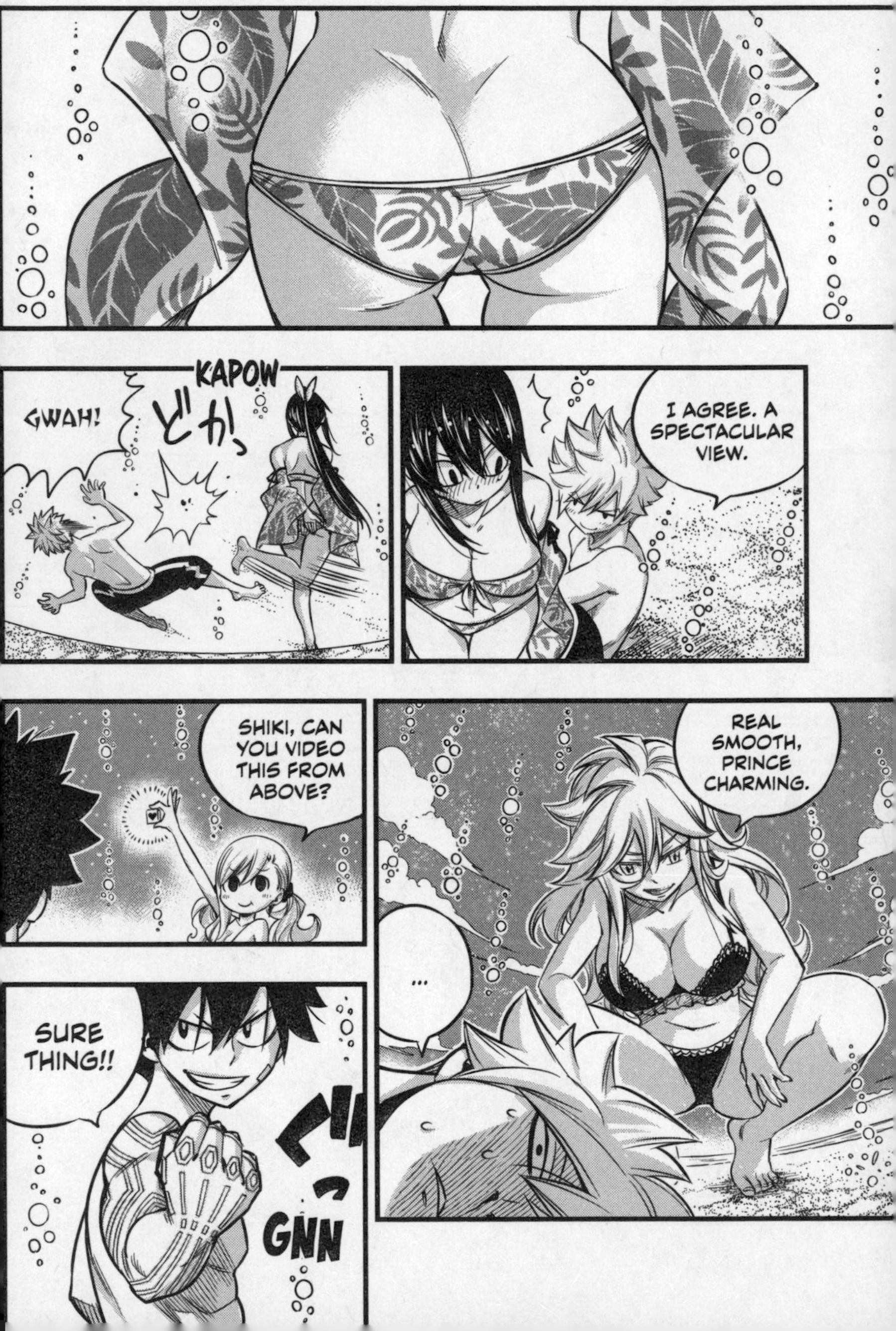
I AGREE. A SPECTACULAR VIEW.
KAPOW
どかっ
GWAH!
REAL SMOOTH, PRINCE CHARMING.
...
SHIKI, CAN YOU VIDEO THIS FROM ABOVE?
SURE THING!!
ぐっ
GNN

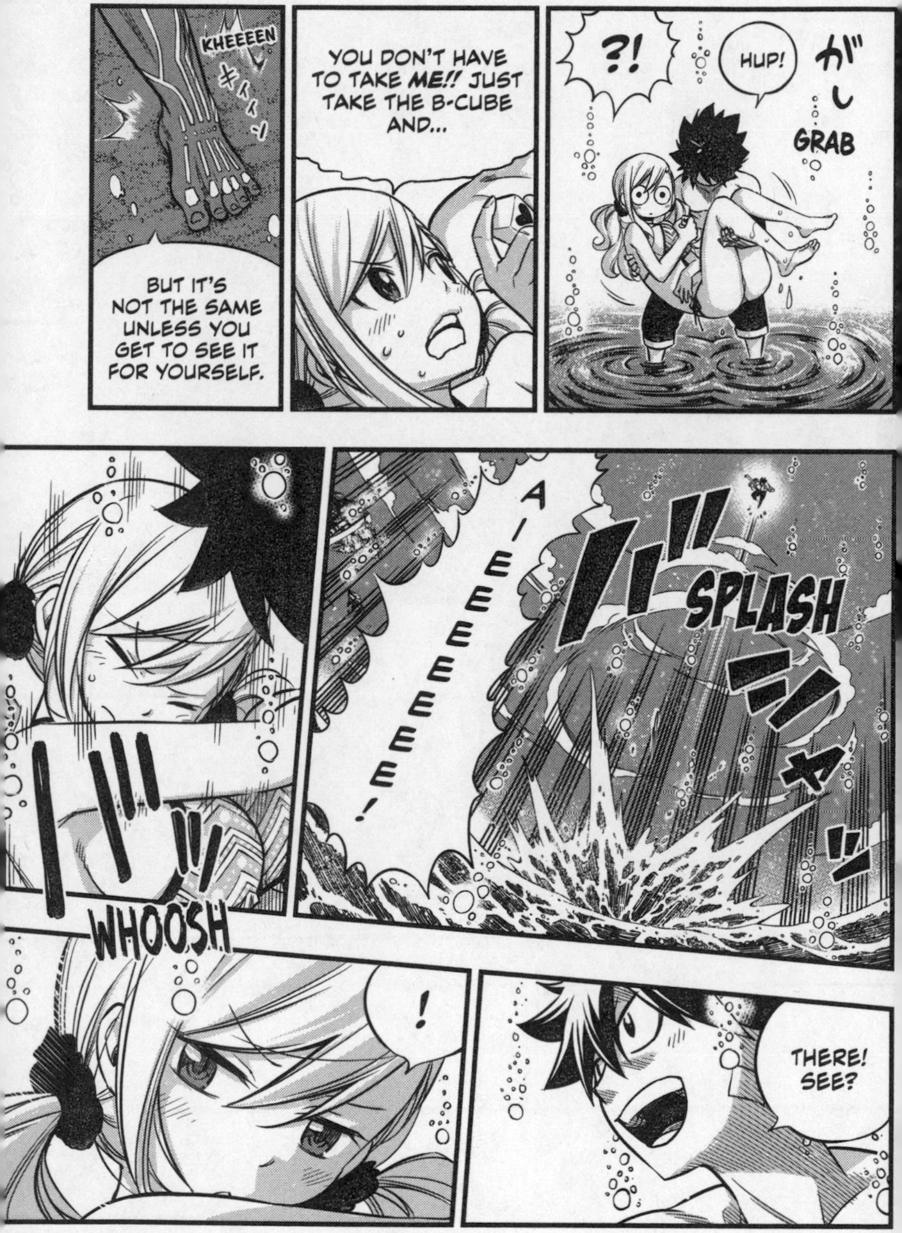
?!
HUP!
がし
GRAB
YOU DON'T HAVE TO TAKE *ME!!* JUST TAKE THE B-CUBE AND...
KHEEEEN
キィィン
BUT IT'S NOT THE SAME UNLESS YOU GET TO SEE IT FOR YOURSELF.
A-IEEEEEEEEE!
SPLASH
WHOOSH
THERE! SEE?
!

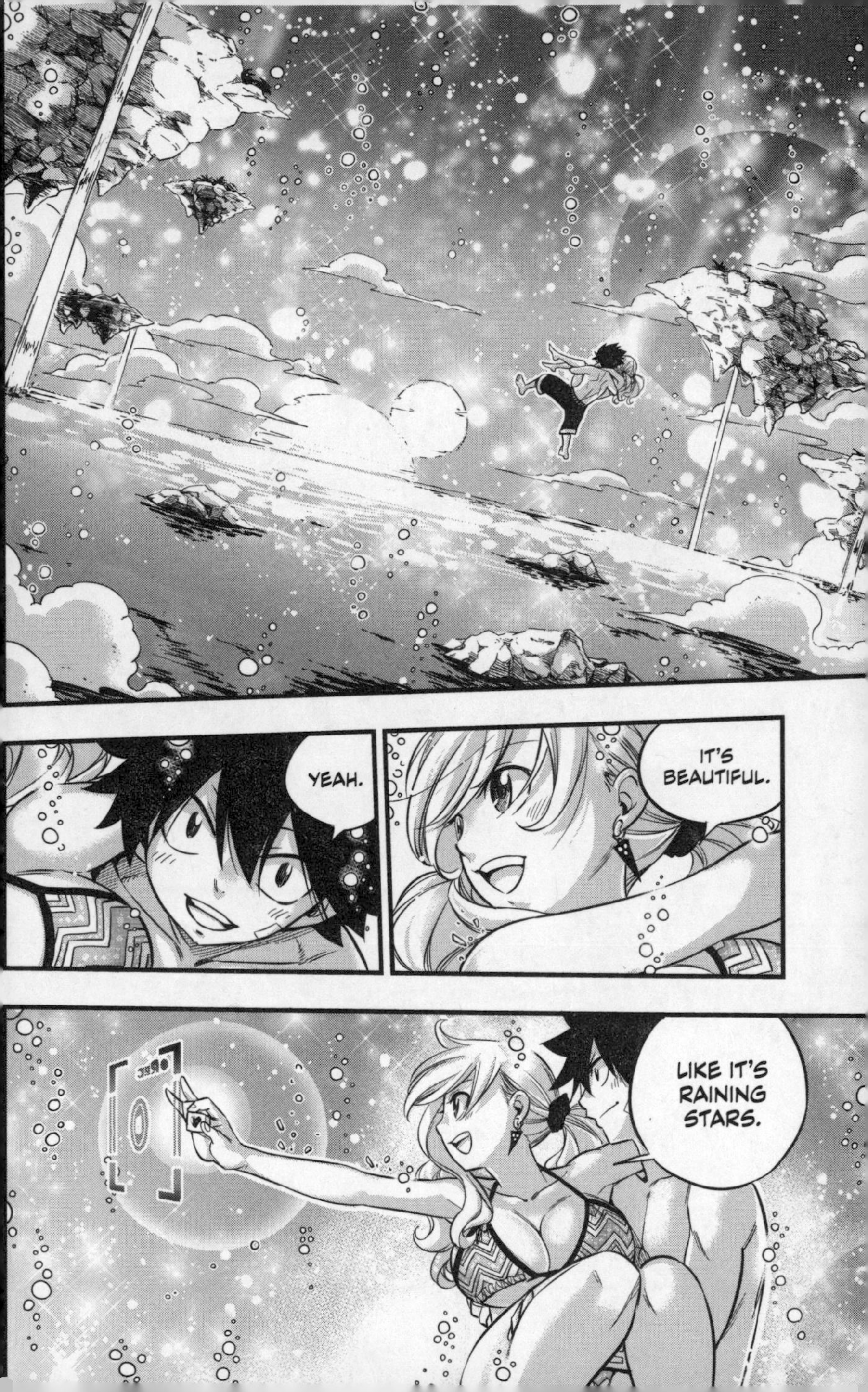
IT'S BEAUTIFUL.
YEAH.
LIKE IT'S RAINING STARS.

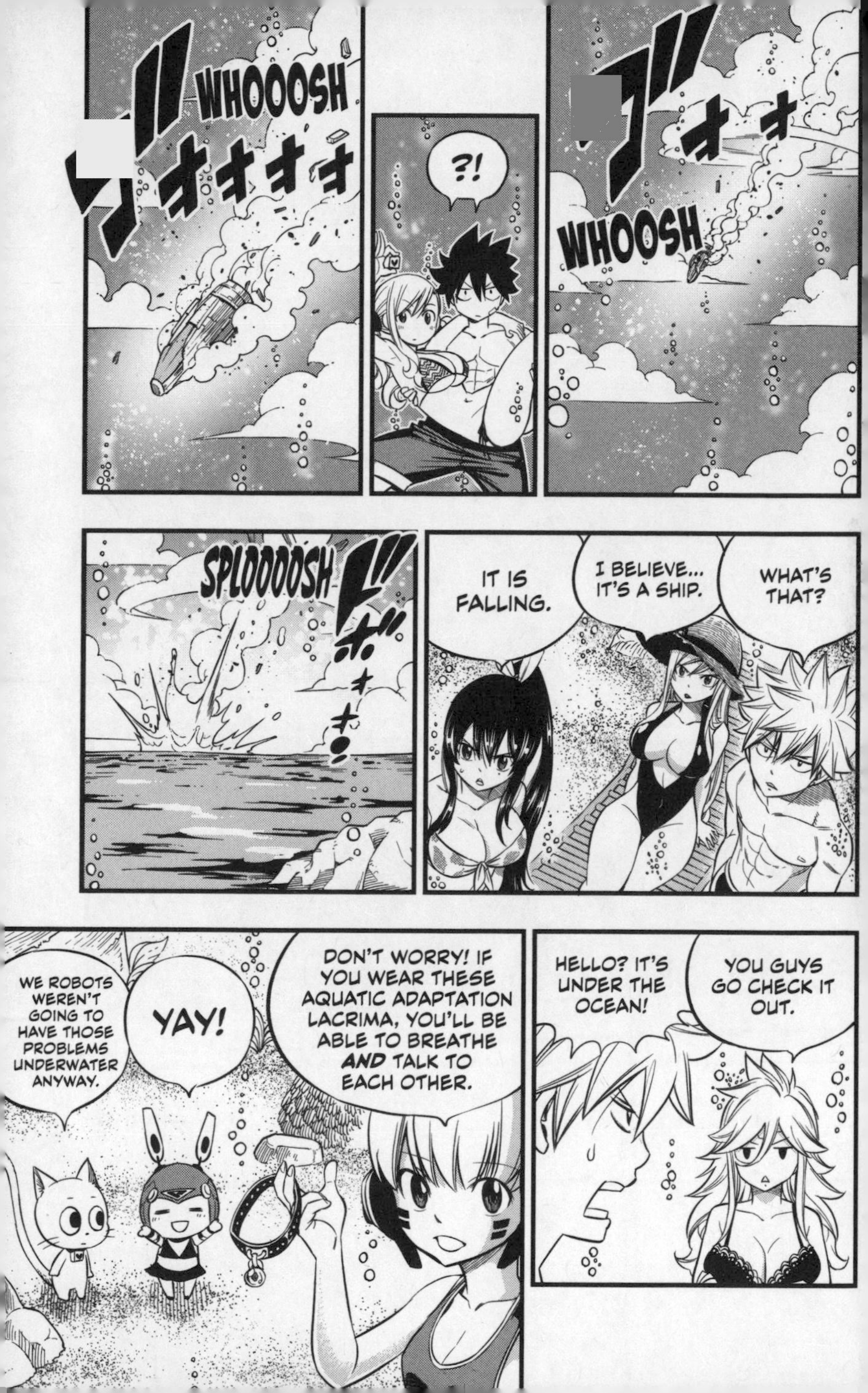
WHOOSH
?!
WHOOOSH
WHAT'S THAT?
I BELIEVE... IT'S A SHIP.
IT IS FALLING.
SPLOOOOSH
YOU GUYS GO CHECK IT OUT.
HELLO? IT'S UNDER THE OCEAN!
DON'T WORRY! IF YOU WEAR THESE AQUATIC ADAPTATION LACRIMA, YOU'LL BE ABLE TO BREATHE AND TALK TO EACH OTHER.
YAY!
WE ROBOTS WEREN'T GOING TO HAVE THOSE PROBLEMS UNDERWATER ANYWAY.

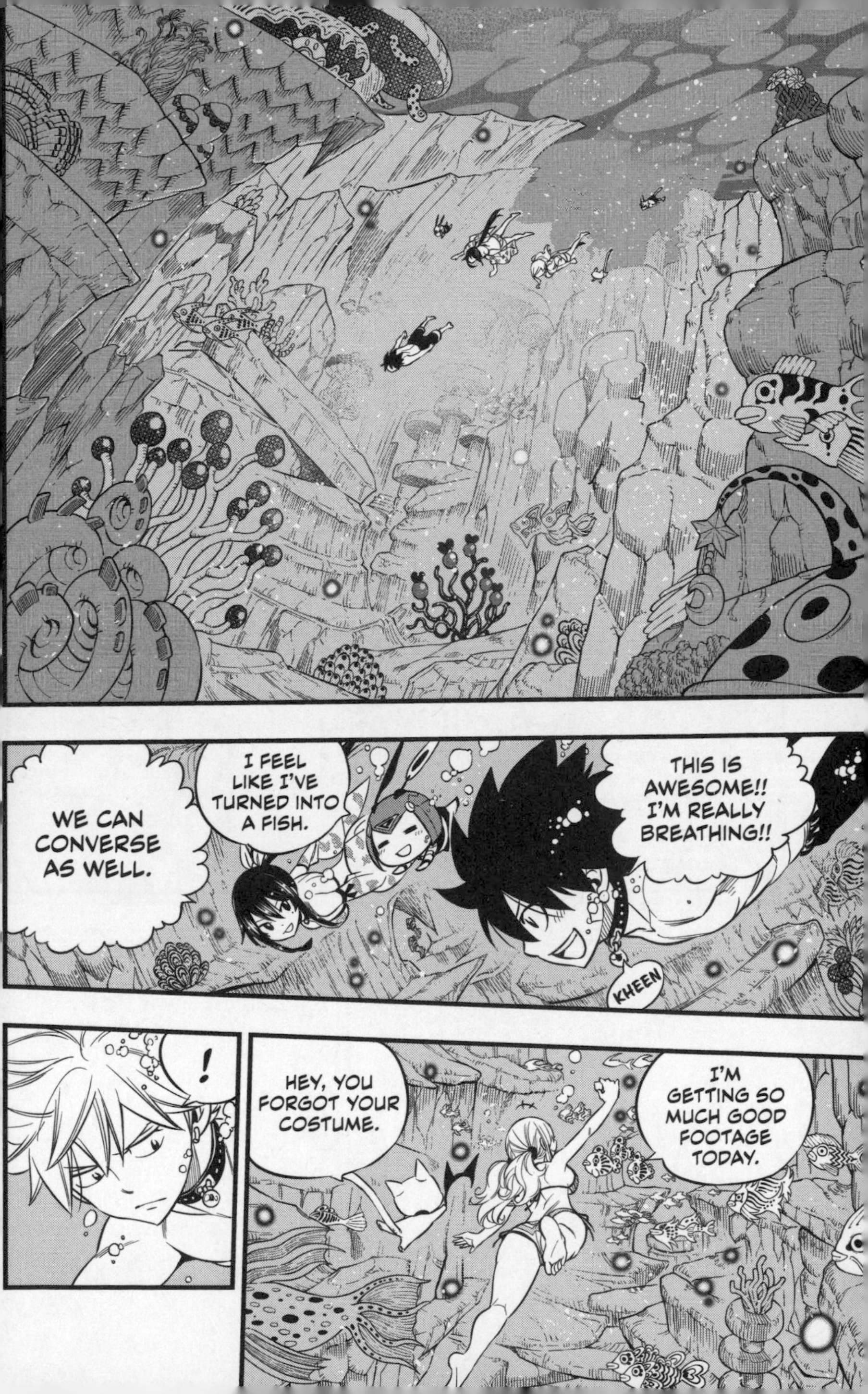
THIS IS AWESOME!! I'M REALLY BREATHING!!
KHEEN
I FEEL LIKE I'VE TURNED INTO A FISH.
WE CAN CONVERSE AS WELL.
I'M GETTING SO MUCH GOOD FOOTAGE TODAY.
HEY, YOU FORGOT YOUR COSTUME.
!

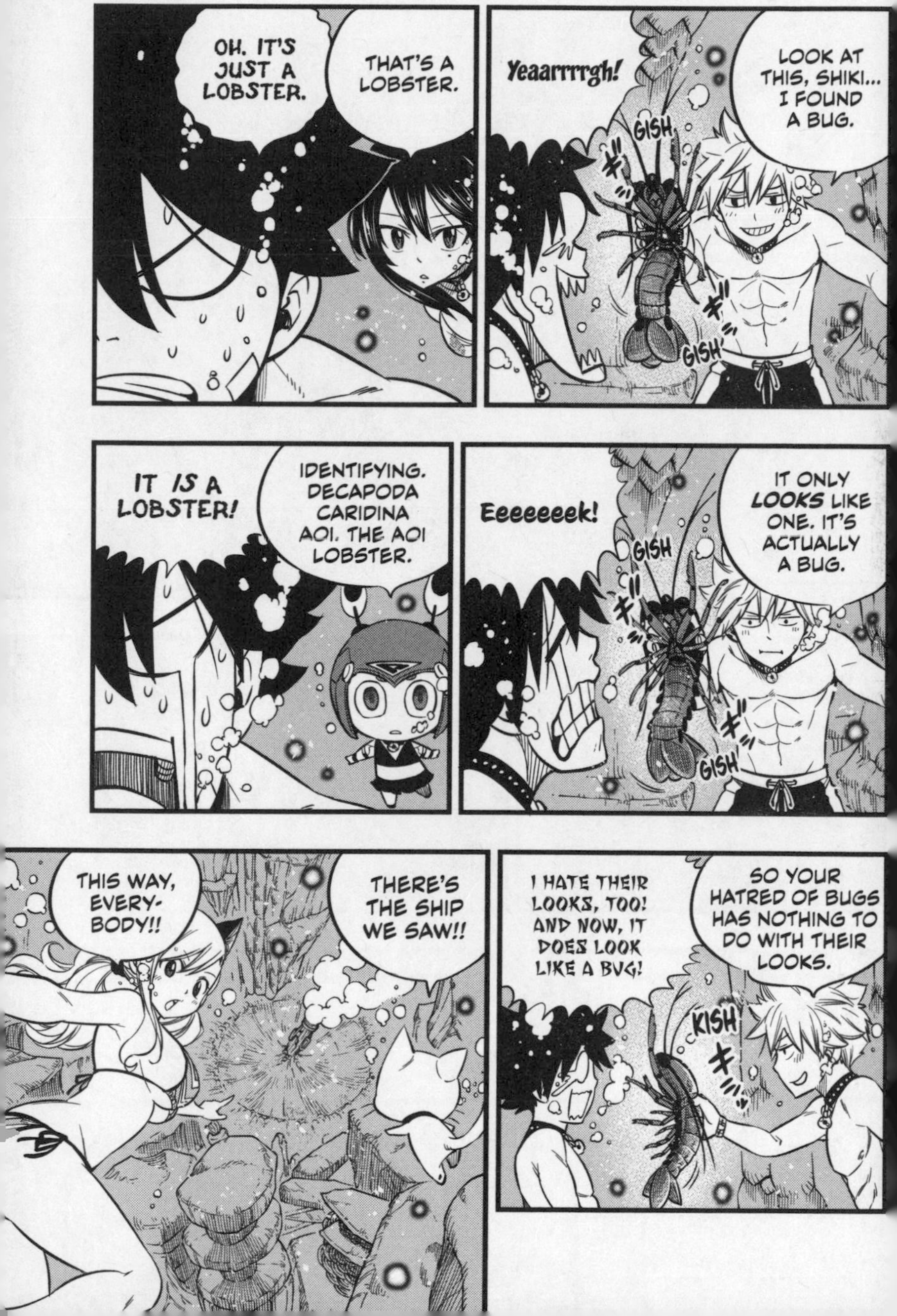
LOOK AT THIS, SHIKI... I FOUND A BUG.
Yeaarrrrgh!
GISH
GISH
THAT'S A LOBSTER.
OH. IT'S JUST A LOBSTER.
IT ONLY LOOKS LIKE ONE. IT'S ACTUALLY A BUG.
Eeeeeeek!
GISH
GISH
IDENTIFYING. DECAPODA CARIDINA AOI. THE AOI LOBSTER.
IT IS A LOBSTER!
SO YOUR HATRED OF BUGS HAS NOTHING TO DO WITH THEIR LOOKS.
I HATE THEIR LOOKS, TOO! AND NOW, IT DOES LOOK LIKE A BUG!
KISH
THERE'S THE SHIP WE SAW!!
THIS WAY, EVERYBODY!!

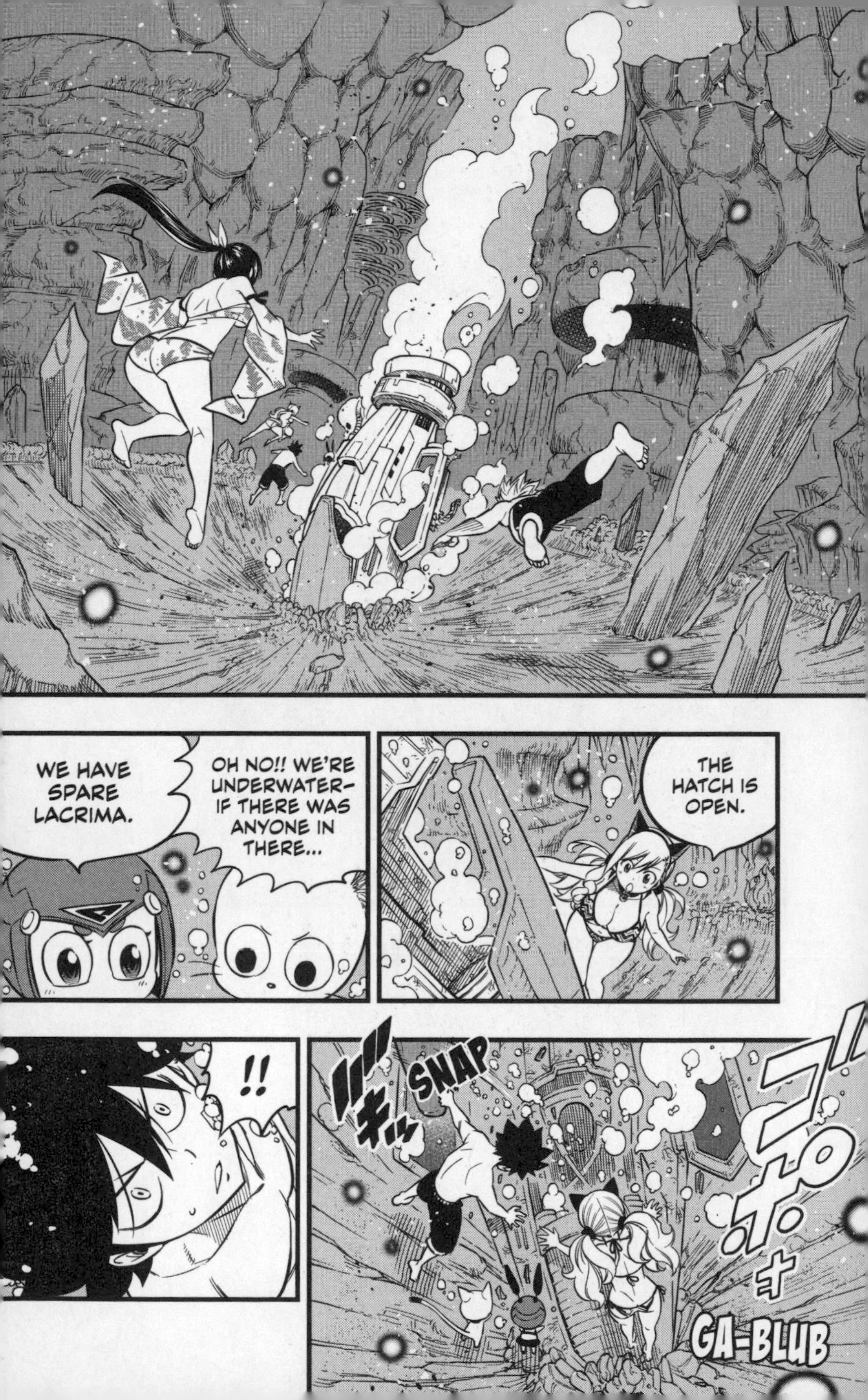
THE HATCH IS OPEN.
OH NO!! WE'RE UNDERWATER—IF THERE WAS ANYONE IN THERE...
WE HAVE SPARE LACRIMA.
ゴポォ
GA-BLUB
ギ
SNAP
!!

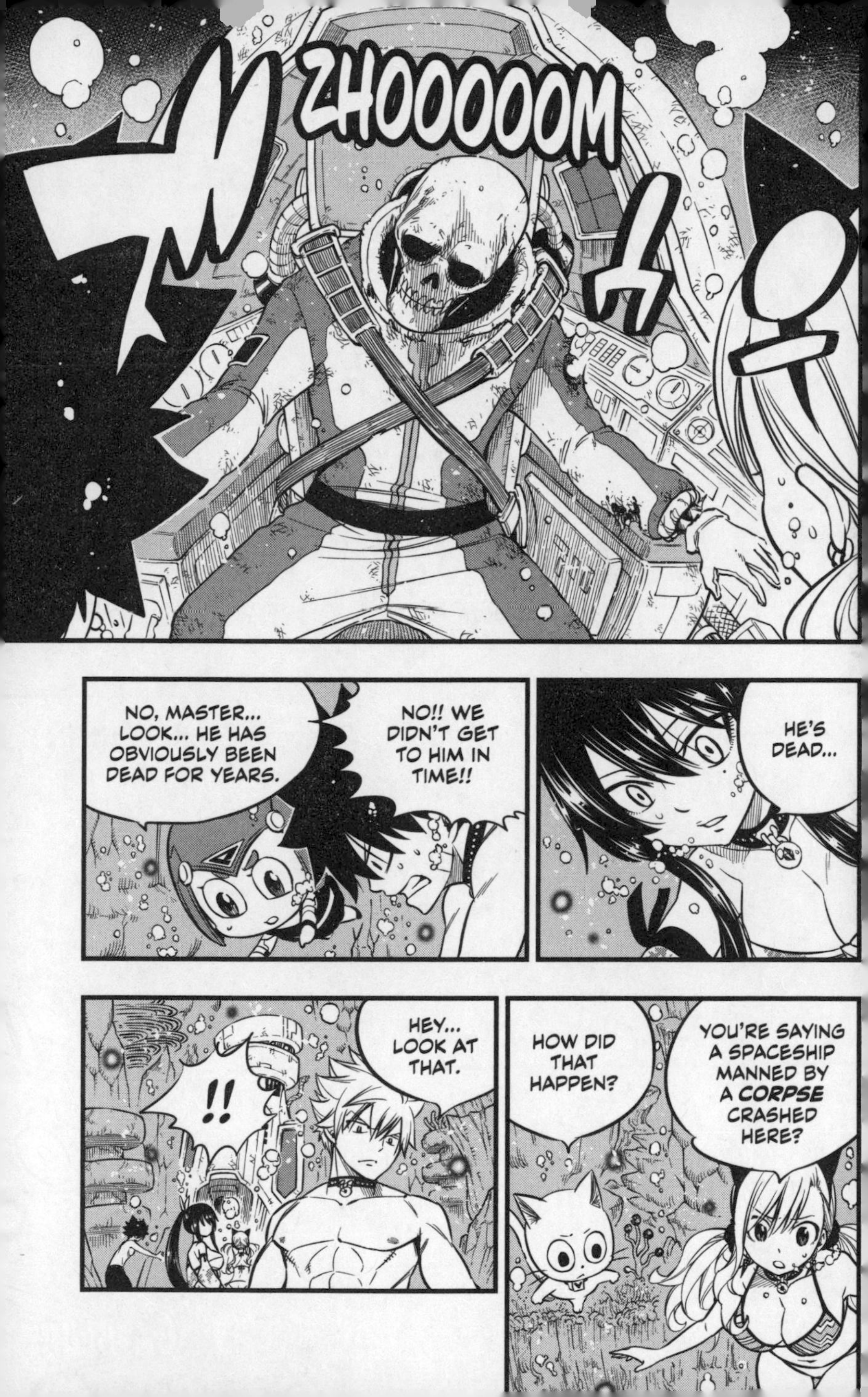
ZHOOOOOM
HE'S DEAD...
NO!! WE DIDN'T GET TO HIM IN TIME!!
NO, MASTER... LOOK... HE HAS OBVIOUSLY BEEN DEAD FOR YEARS.
YOU'RE SAYING A SPACESHIP MANNED BY A **CORPSE** CRASHED HERE?
HOW DID THAT HAPPEN?
HEY... LOOK AT THAT.
!!

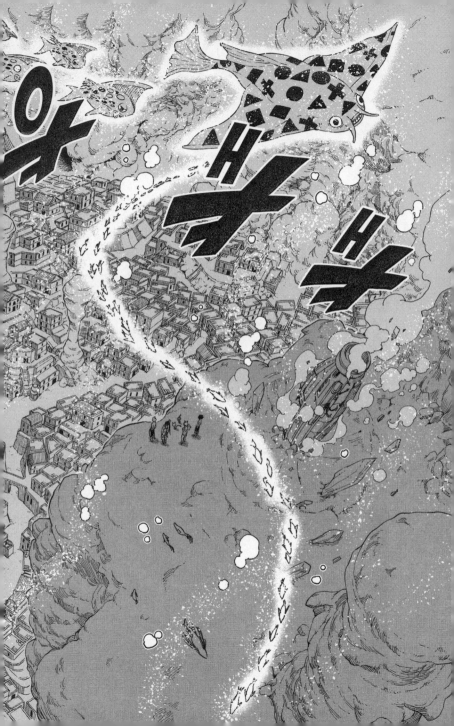

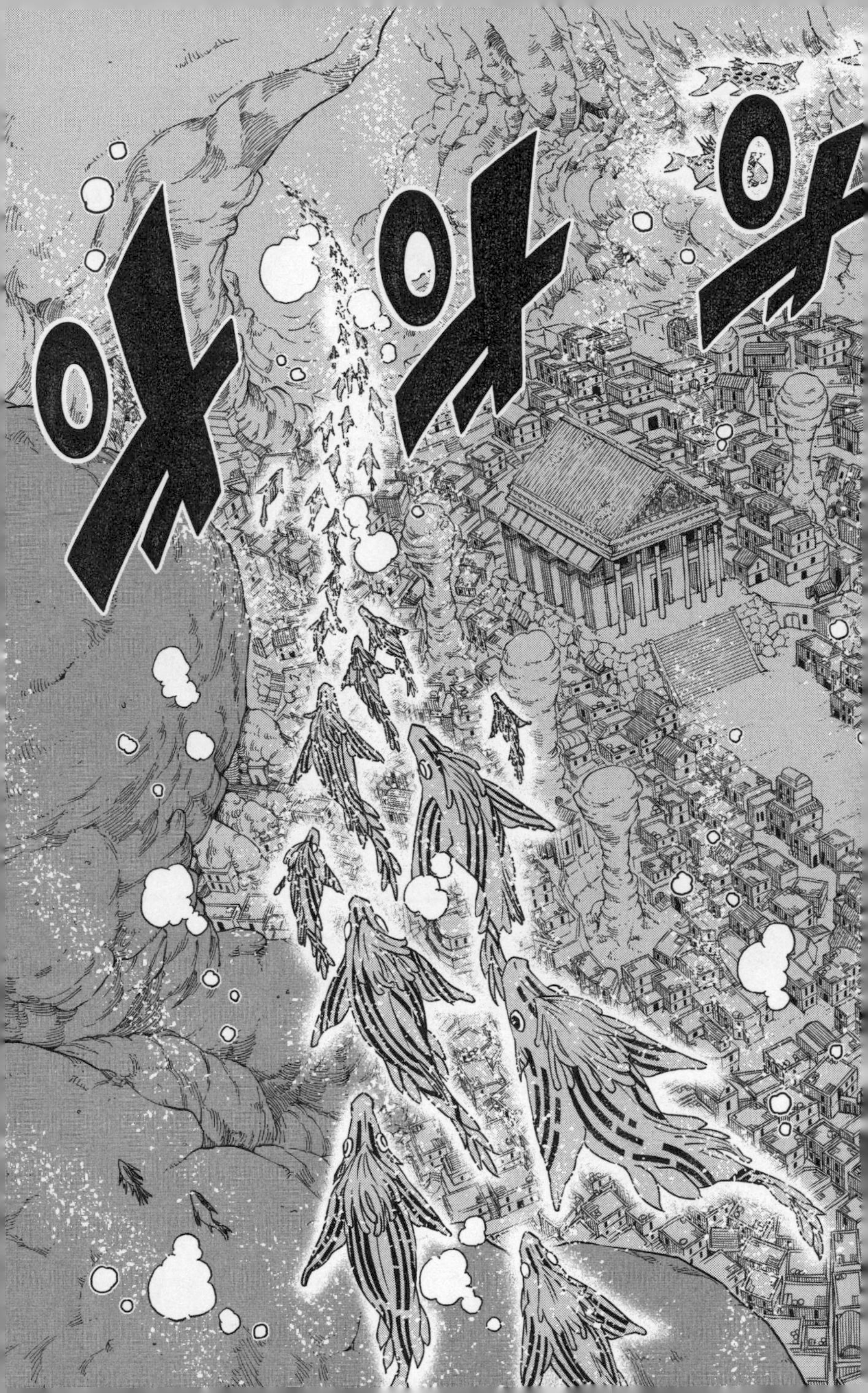

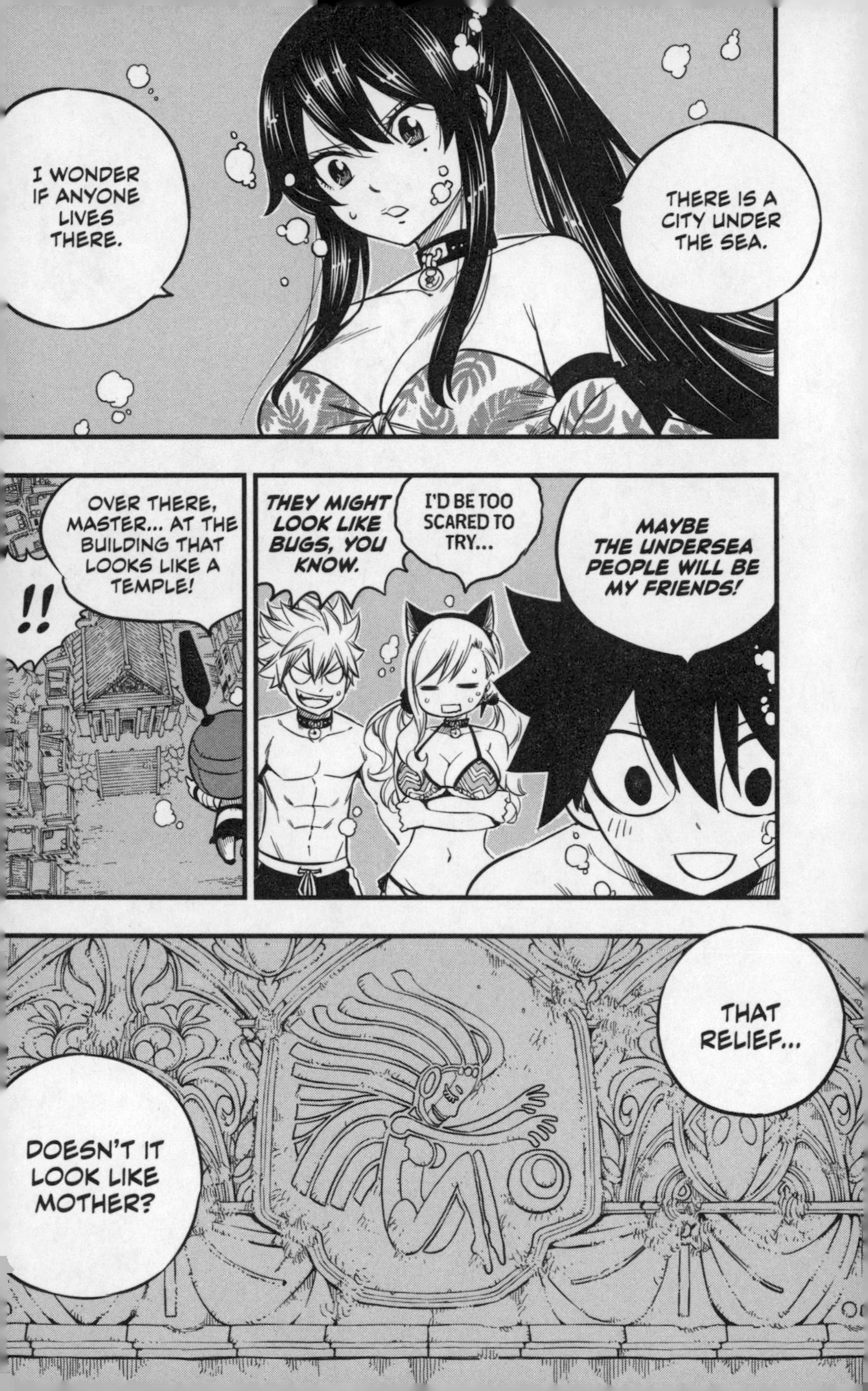
THERE IS A CITY UNDER THE SEA.
I WONDER IF ANYONE LIVES THERE.
MAYBE THE UNDERSEA PEOPLE WILL BE MY FRIENDS!
I'D BE TOO SCARED TO TRY...
THEY MIGHT LOOK LIKE BUGS, YOU KNOW.
OVER THERE, MASTER... AT THE BUILDING THAT LOOKS LIKE A TEMPLE!
!!
THAT RELIEF...
DOESN'T IT LOOK LIKE MOTHER?

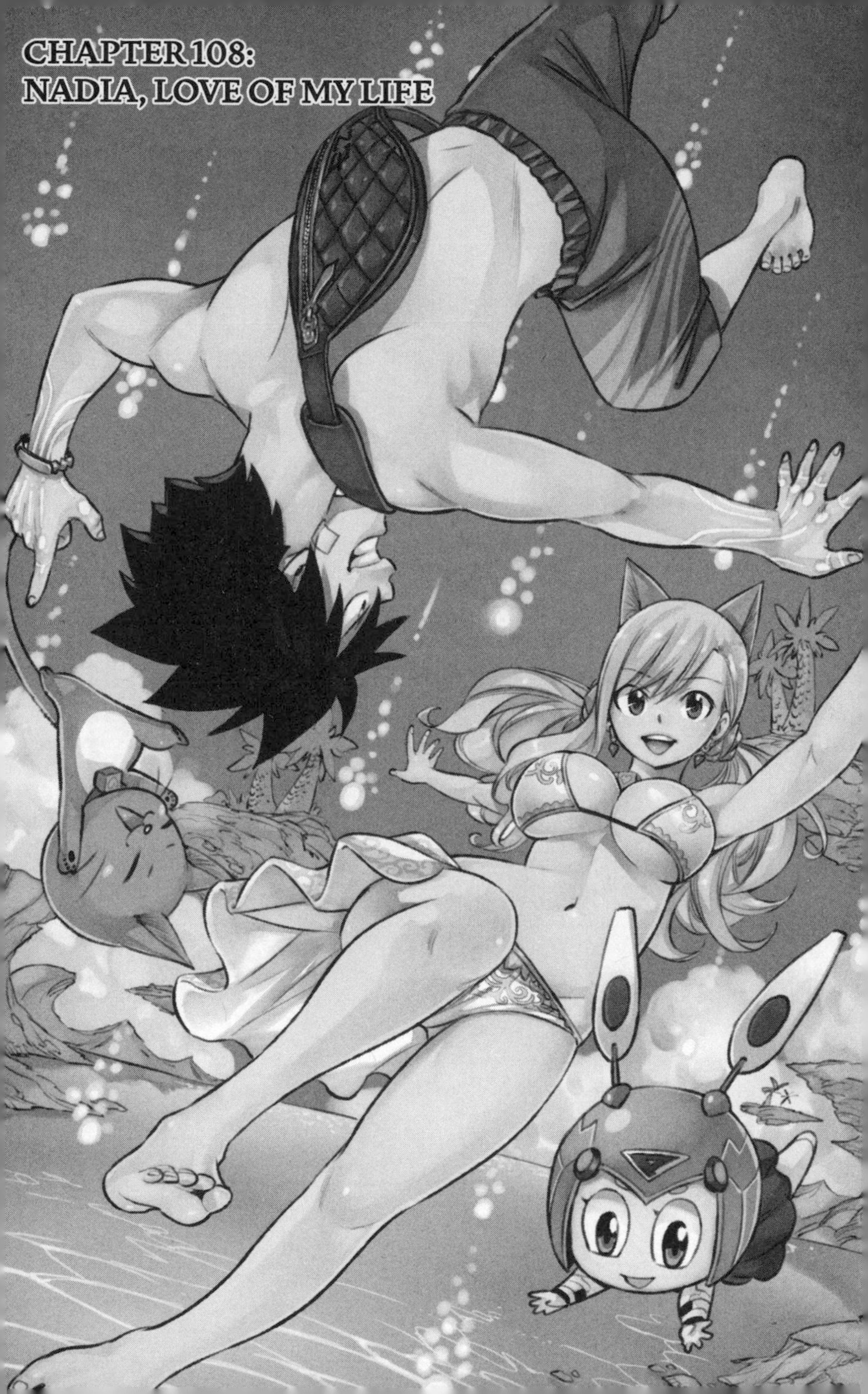
CHAPTER 108:
NADIA, LOVE OF MY LIFE

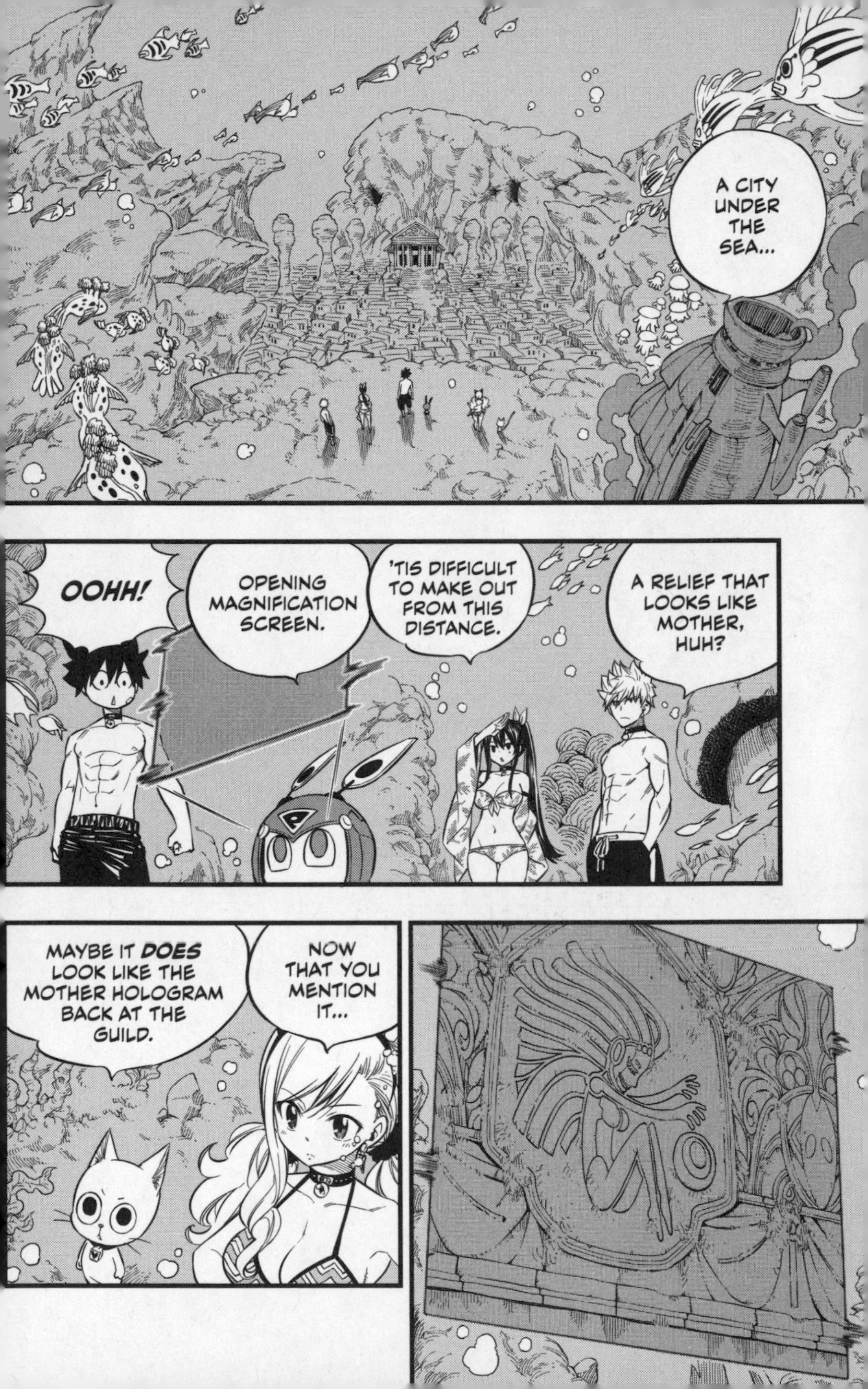
A CITY UNDER THE SEA...
A RELIEF THAT LOOKS LIKE MOTHER, HUH?
'TIS DIFFICULT TO MAKE OUT FROM THIS DISTANCE.
OPENING MAGNIFICATION SCREEN.
OOHH!
NOW THAT YOU MENTION IT...
MAYBE IT *DOES* LOOK LIKE THE MOTHER HOLOGRAM BACK AT THE GUILD.

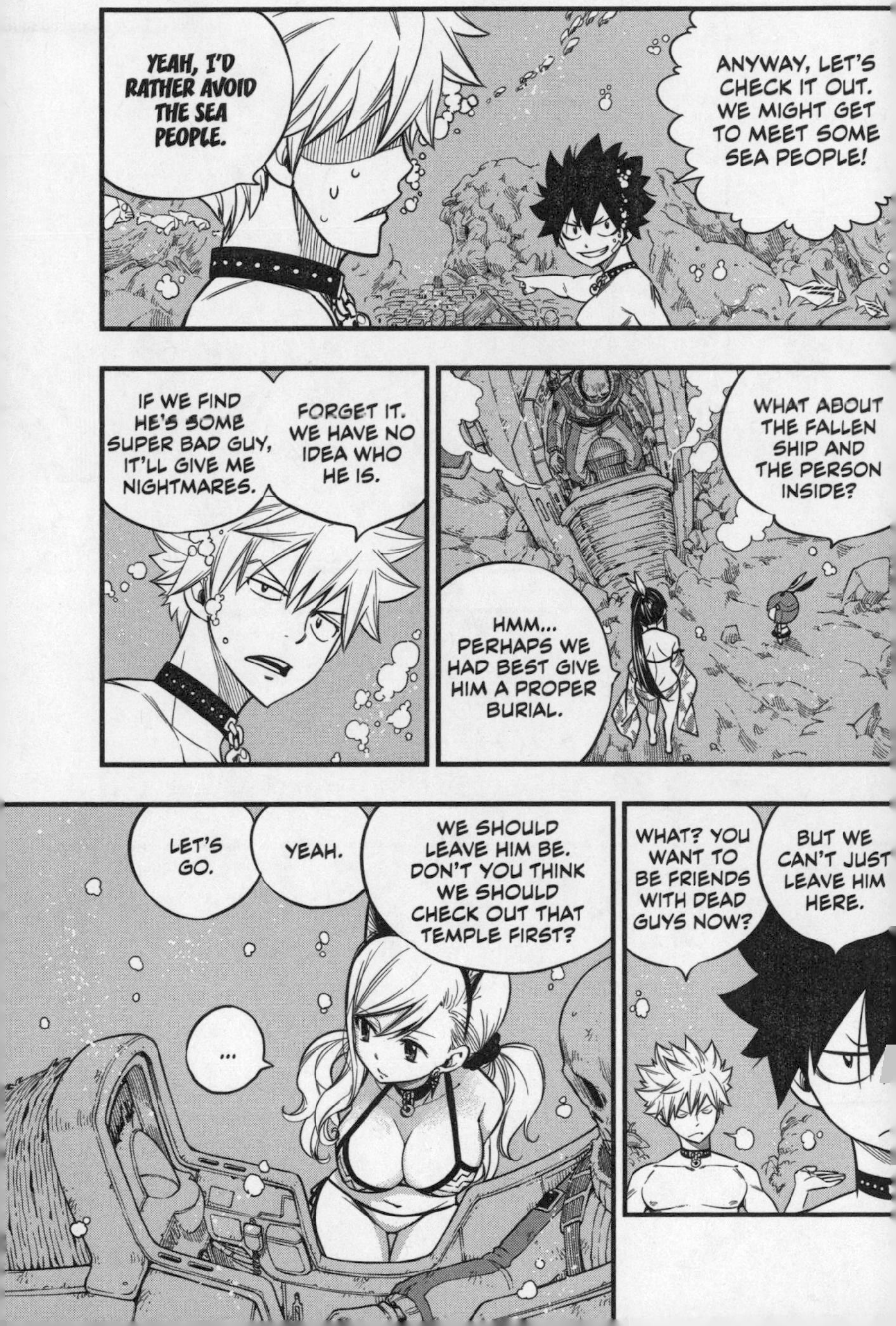
ANYWAY, LET'S CHECK IT OUT. WE MIGHT GET TO MEET SOME SEA PEOPLE!
YEAH, I'D RATHER AVOID THE SEA PEOPLE.
WHAT ABOUT THE FALLEN SHIP AND THE PERSON INSIDE?
HMM... PERHAPS WE HAD BEST GIVE HIM A PROPER BURIAL.
FORGET IT. WE HAVE NO IDEA WHO HE IS.
IF WE FIND HE'S SOME SUPER BAD GUY, IT'LL GIVE ME NIGHTMARES.
BUT WE CAN'T JUST LEAVE HIM HERE.
WHAT? YOU WANT TO BE FRIENDS WITH DEAD GUYS NOW?
WE SHOULD LEAVE HIM BE. DON'T YOU THINK WE SHOULD CHECK OUT THAT TEMPLE FIRST?
YEAH.
LET'S GO.
...

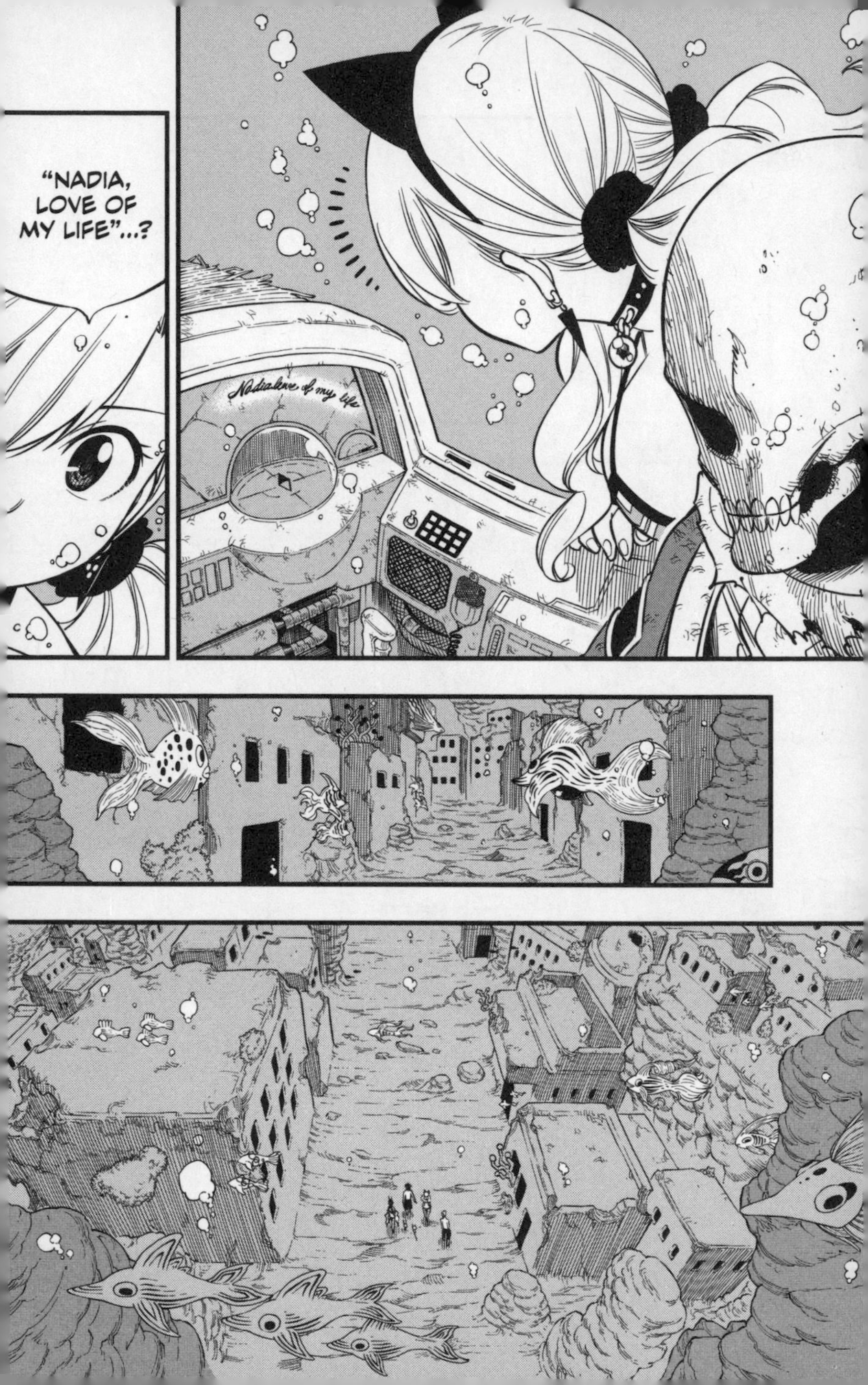
"NADIA, LOVE OF MY LIFE"...?
Nadia, love of my life

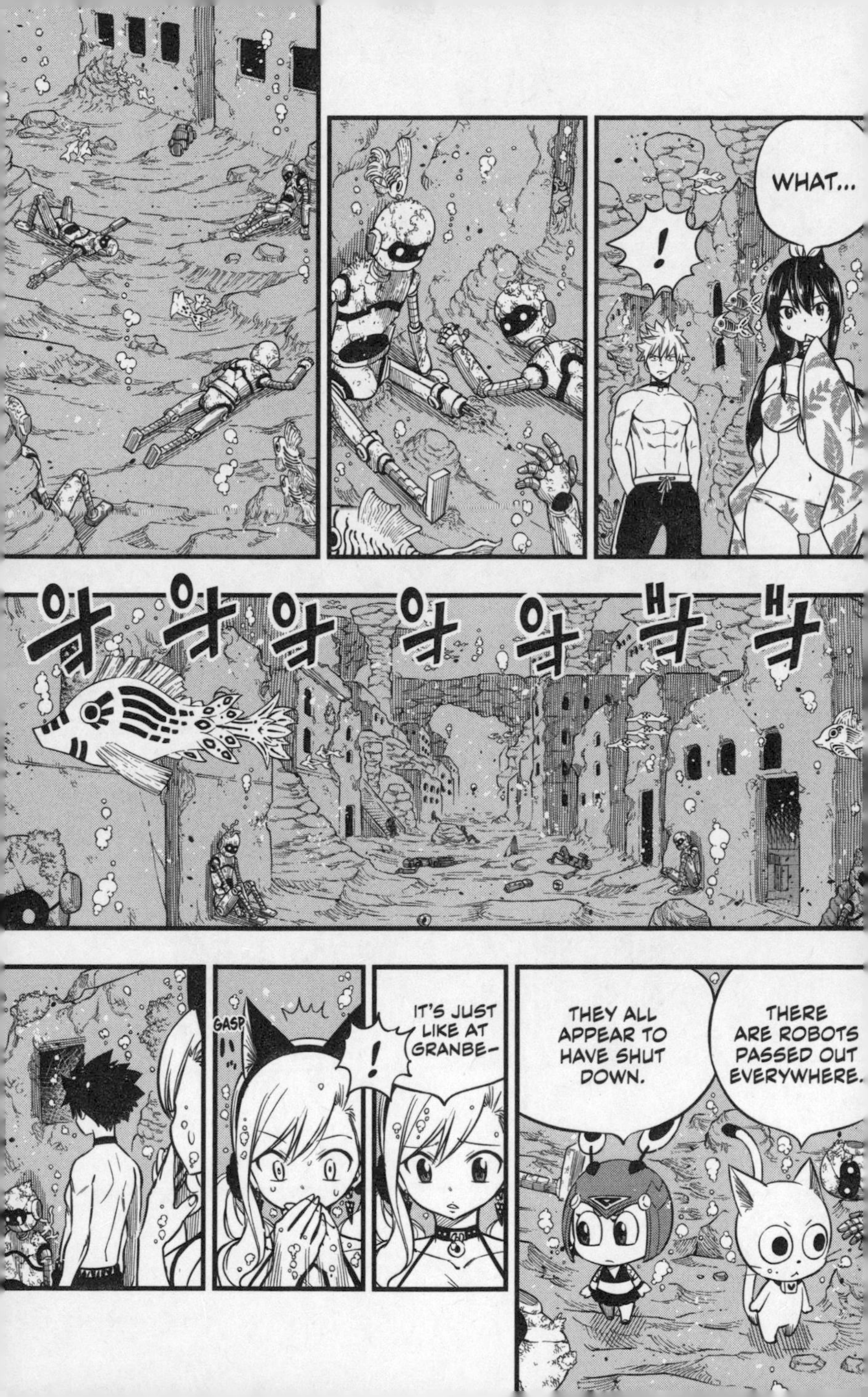
WHAT...
!
OOOOOHH
THERE ARE ROBOTS PASSED OUT EVERYWHERE.
THEY ALL APPEAR TO HAVE SHUT DOWN.
IT'S JUST LIKE AT GRANBE–
!
GASP

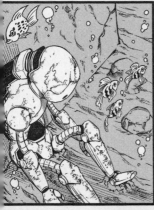

I WONDER WHAT HAP-PENED.

KA-FWOOM

SWOOO スゥ～

LET'S GO TO THE TEM-PLE.

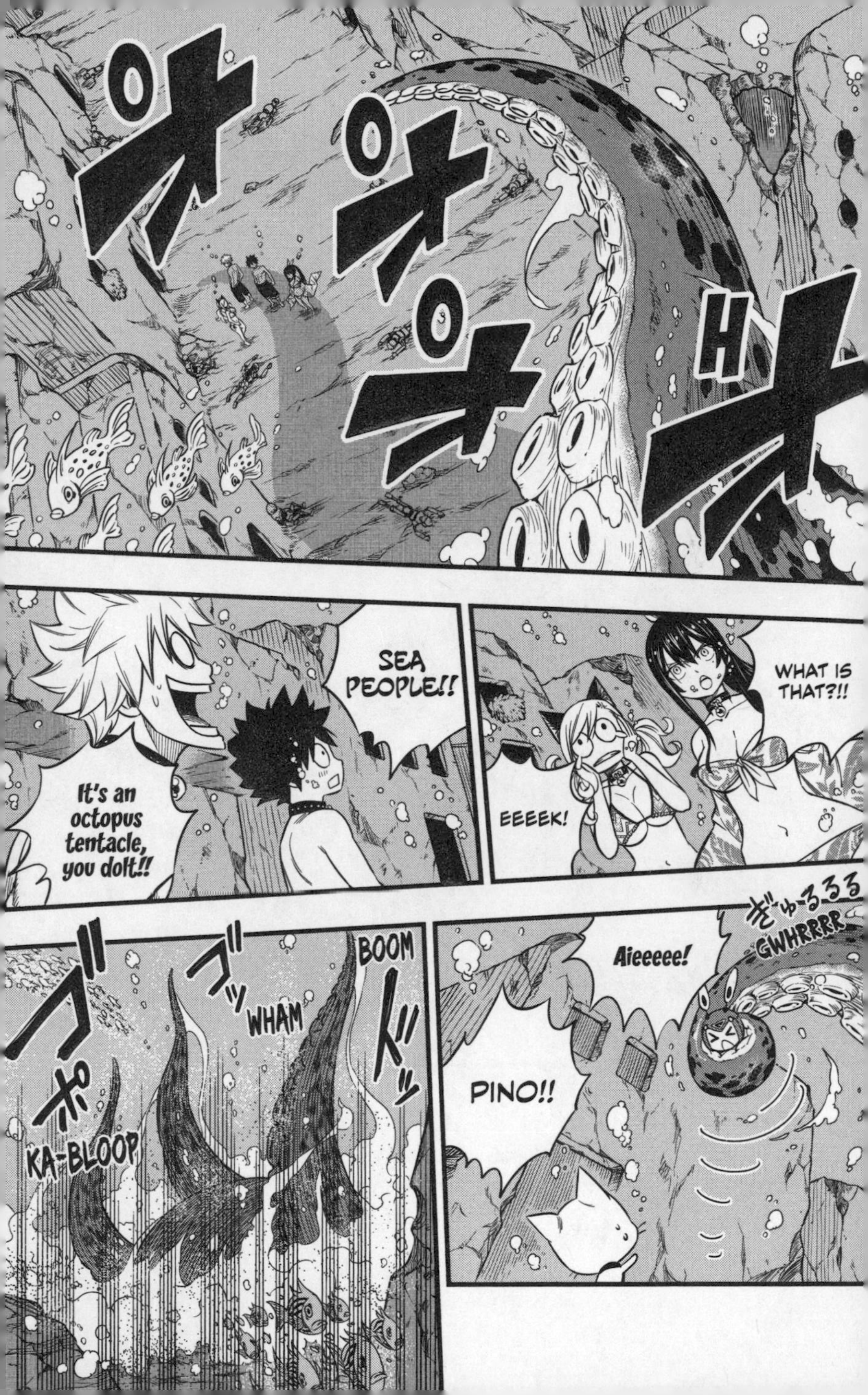
WHAT IS THAT?!!
EEEEK!
SEA PEOPLE!!
It's an octopus tentacle, you dolt!!
ぎゅるるる
GWHRRRR
Aieeeee!
PINO!!
BOOM
WHAM
KA-BLOOP

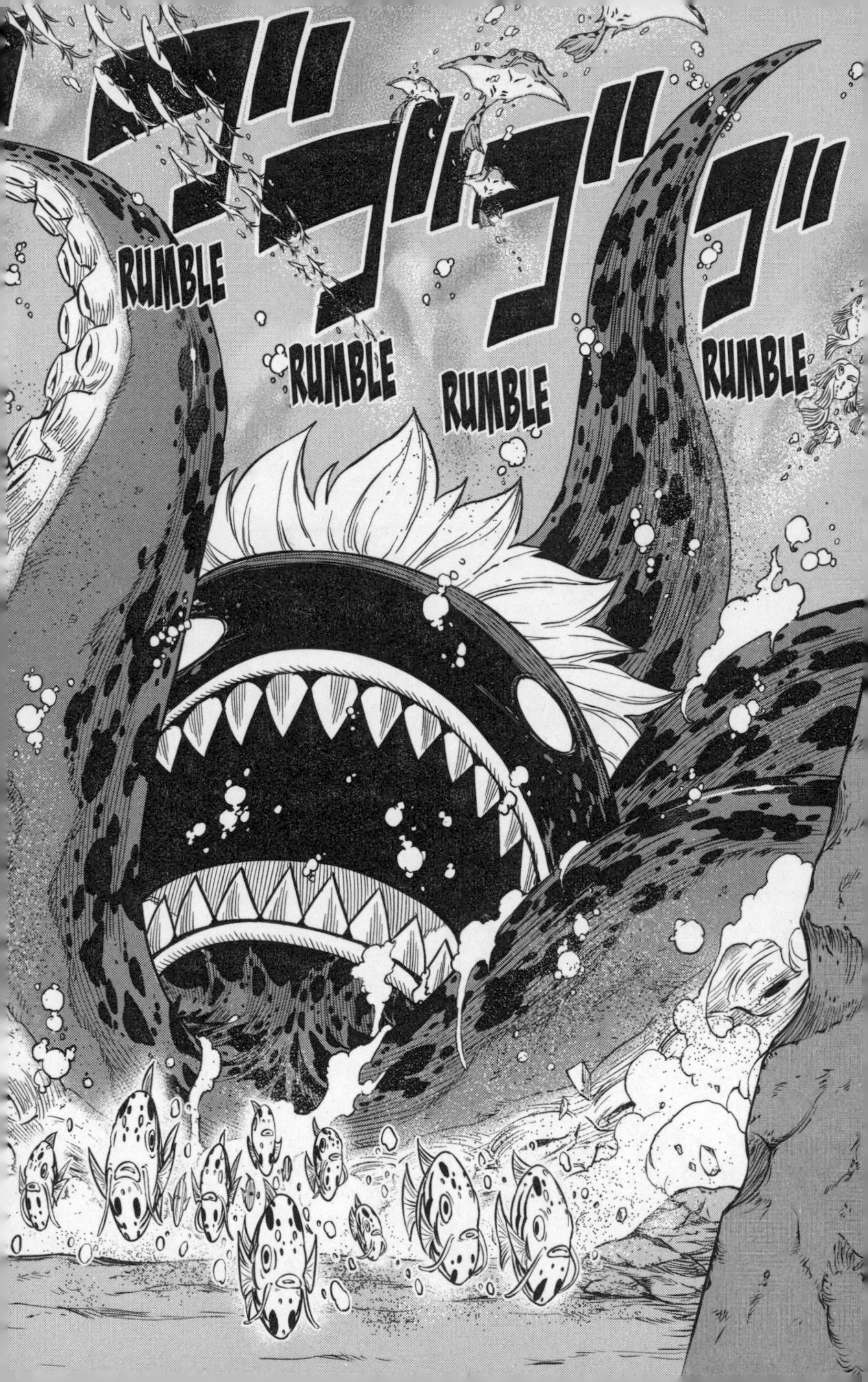
RUMBLE
RUMBLE
RUMBLE
RUMBLE

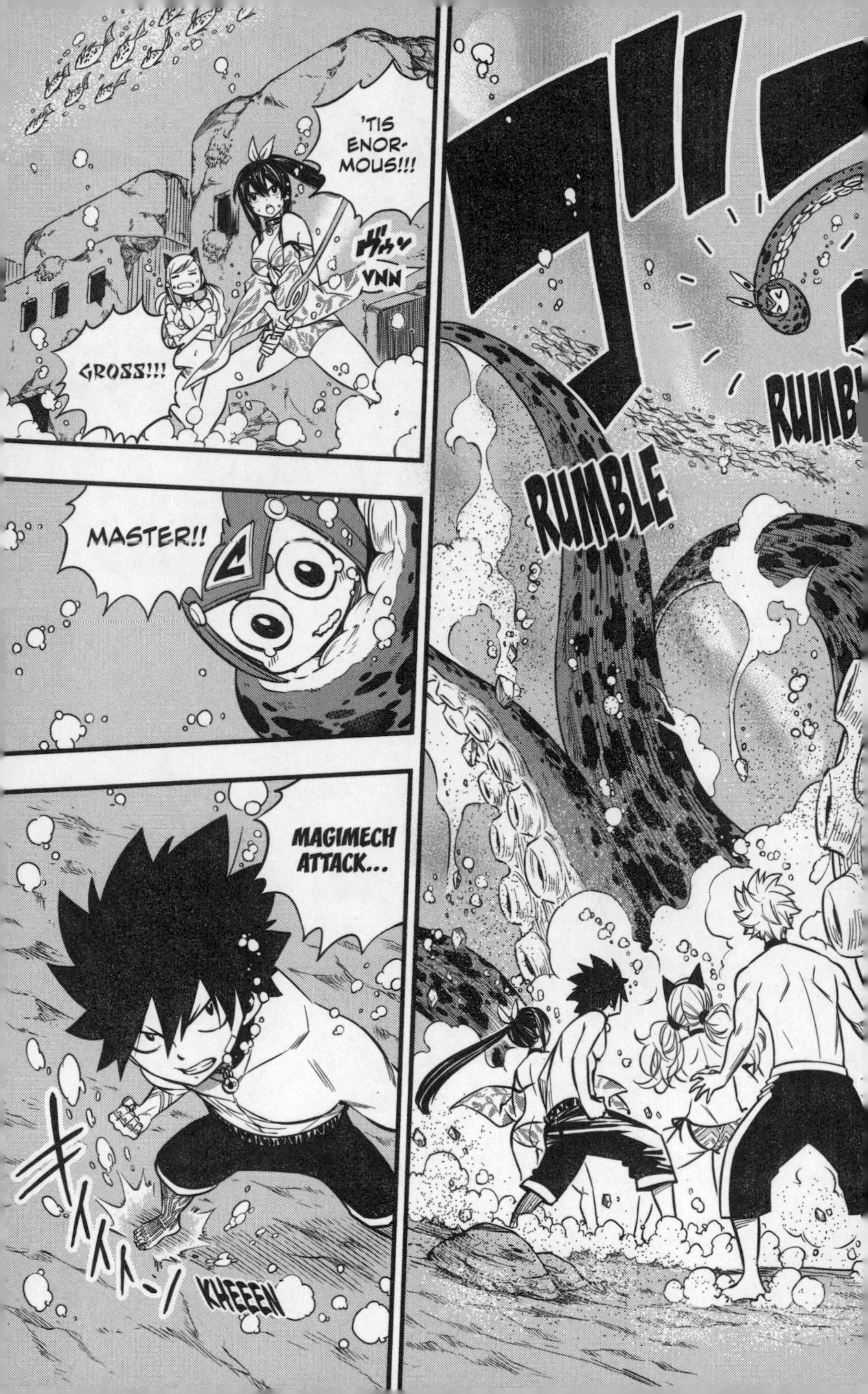
RUMBLE
RUMBLE
'TIS ENORMOUS!!!
ヴゥン
VNN
GROSS!!!
MASTER!!
MAGIMECH ATTACK...
KHEEEN

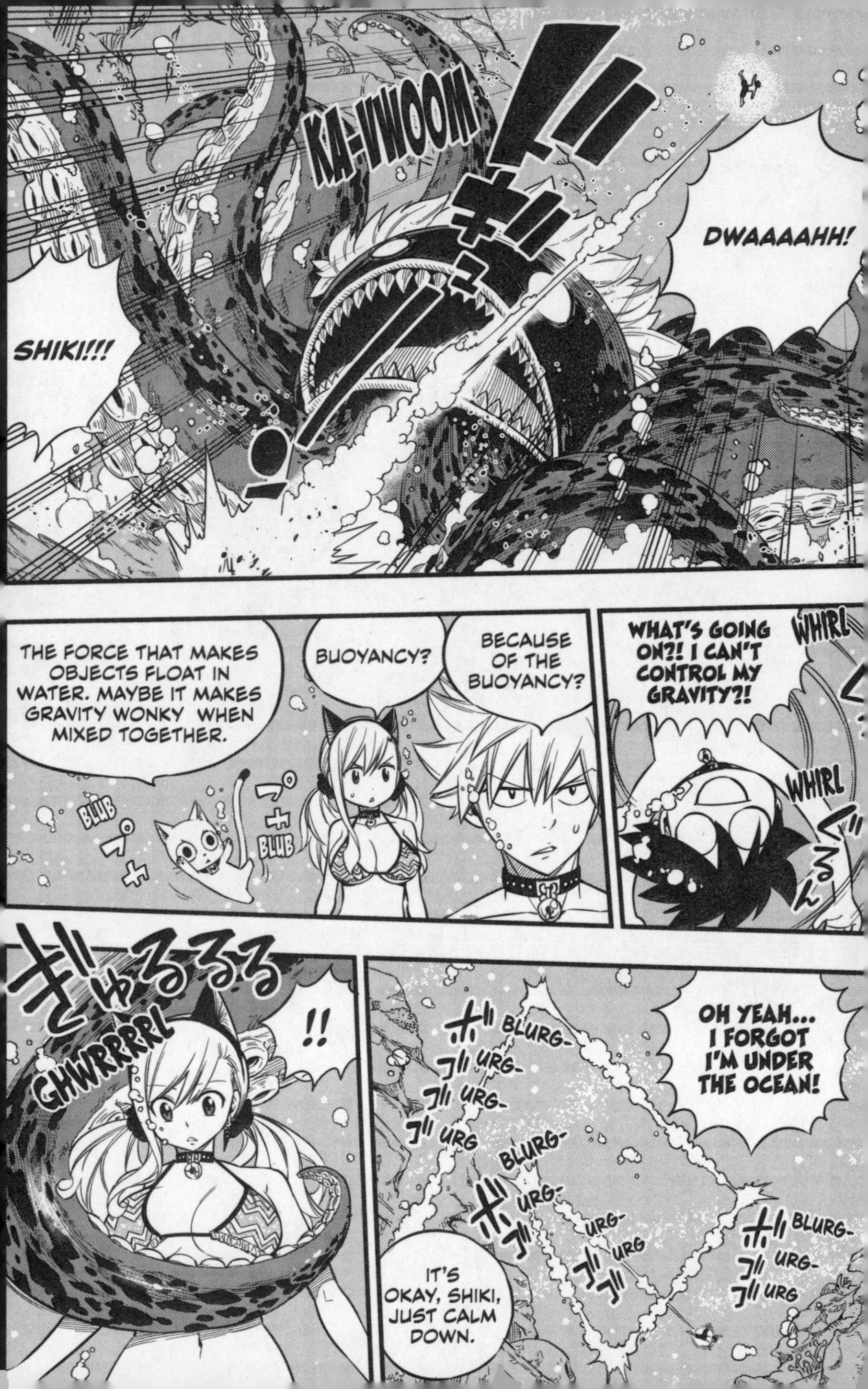
DWAAAAHH!
KA-VWOOM
SHIKI!!!
WHAT'S GOING ON?! I CAN'T CONTROL MY GRAVITY?!
WHIRL
WHIRL
BECAUSE OF THE BUOYANCY?
BUOYANCY?
THE FORCE THAT MAKES OBJECTS FLOAT IN WATER. MAYBE IT MAKES GRAVITY WONKY WHEN MIXED TOGETHER.
BLUB
BLUB
OH YEAH... I FORGOT I'M UNDER THE OCEAN!
BLURG-
URG-
URG-
URG
BLURG-
URG-
URG-
URG
BLURG-
URG-
URG
IT'S OKAY, SHIKI, JUST CALM DOWN.
!!
ぎゅるるる
GHWRRRR!

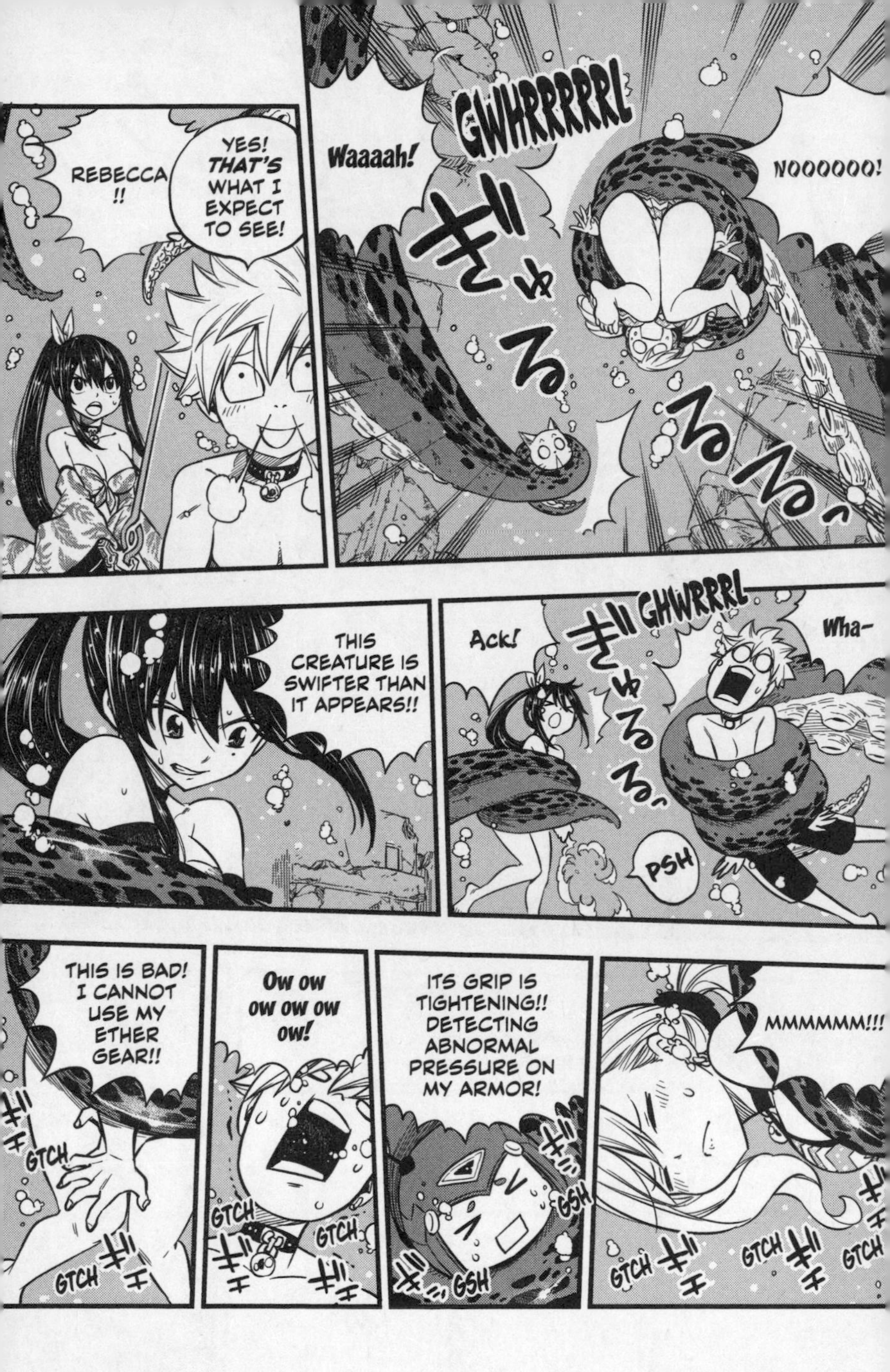
NOOOOOO!
GWHRRRRRL
Waaaah!
ぎゅるるる
YES! THAT'S WHAT I EXPECT TO SEE!
REBECCA!!
Wha-
GHWRRRL
ぎゅるるる
Ack!
PSH
THIS CREATURE IS SWIFTER THAN IT APPEARS!!
MMMMMM!!!
GTCH
GTCH
GTCH
ITS GRIP IS TIGHTENING!! DETECTING ABNORMAL PRESSURE ON MY ARMOR!
GSH
GSH
Ow ow ow ow ow ow!
GTCH
GTCH
THIS IS BAD! I CANNOT USE MY ETHER GEAR!!
GTCH
GTCH

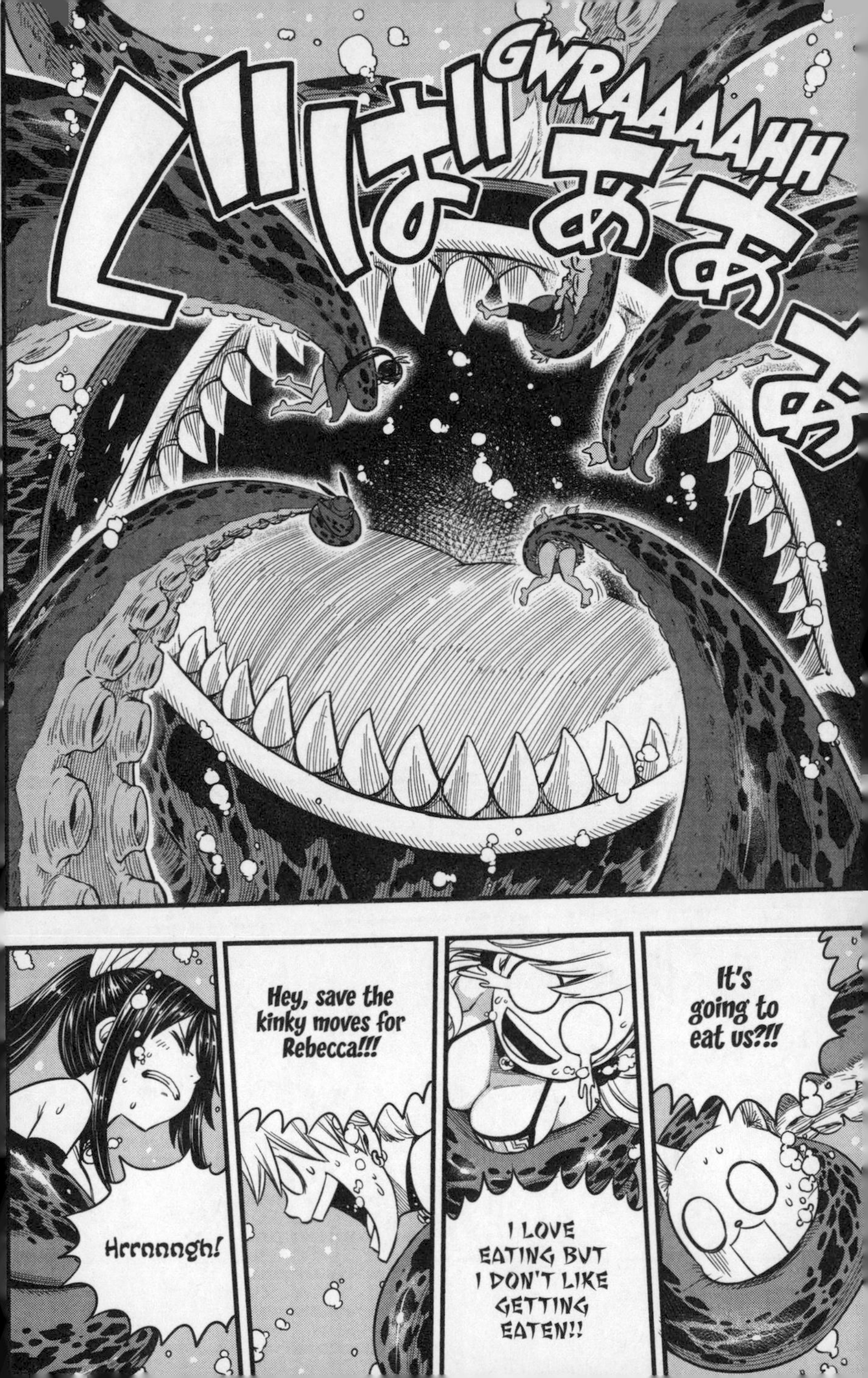
GWRAAAAAHH
It's going to eat us?!!
I LOVE EATING BUT I DON'T LIKE GETTING EATEN!!
Hey, save the kinky moves for Rebecca!!!
Hrrnnngh!

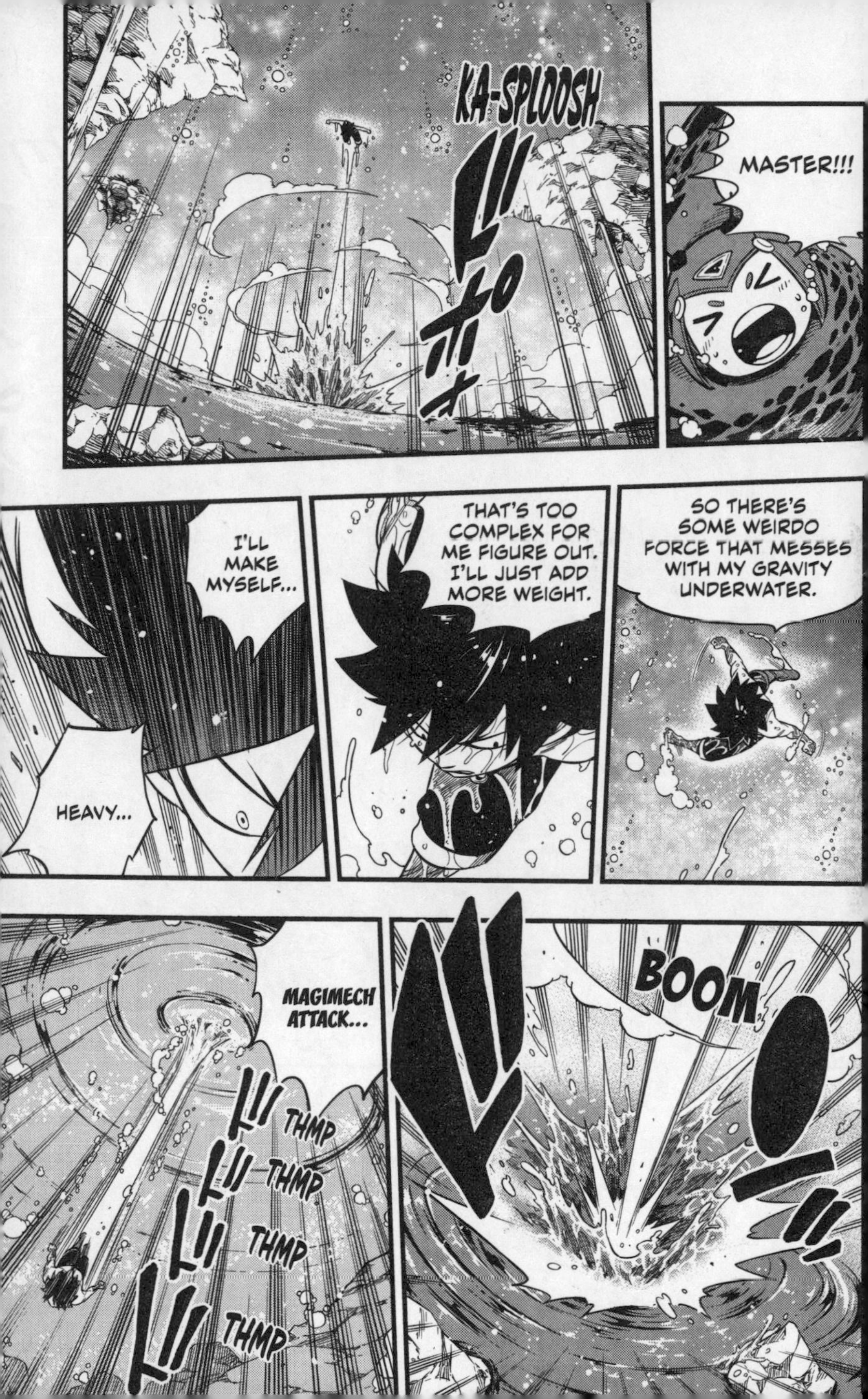
MASTER!!!
KA-SPLOOSH
SO THERE'S SOME WEIRDO FORCE THAT MESSES WITH MY GRAVITY UNDERWATER.
THAT'S TOO COMPLEX FOR ME FIGURE OUT. I'LL JUST ADD MORE WEIGHT.
I'LL MAKE MYSELF...
HEAVY...
BOOM
MAGIMECH ATTACK...
THMP
THMP
THMP
THMP

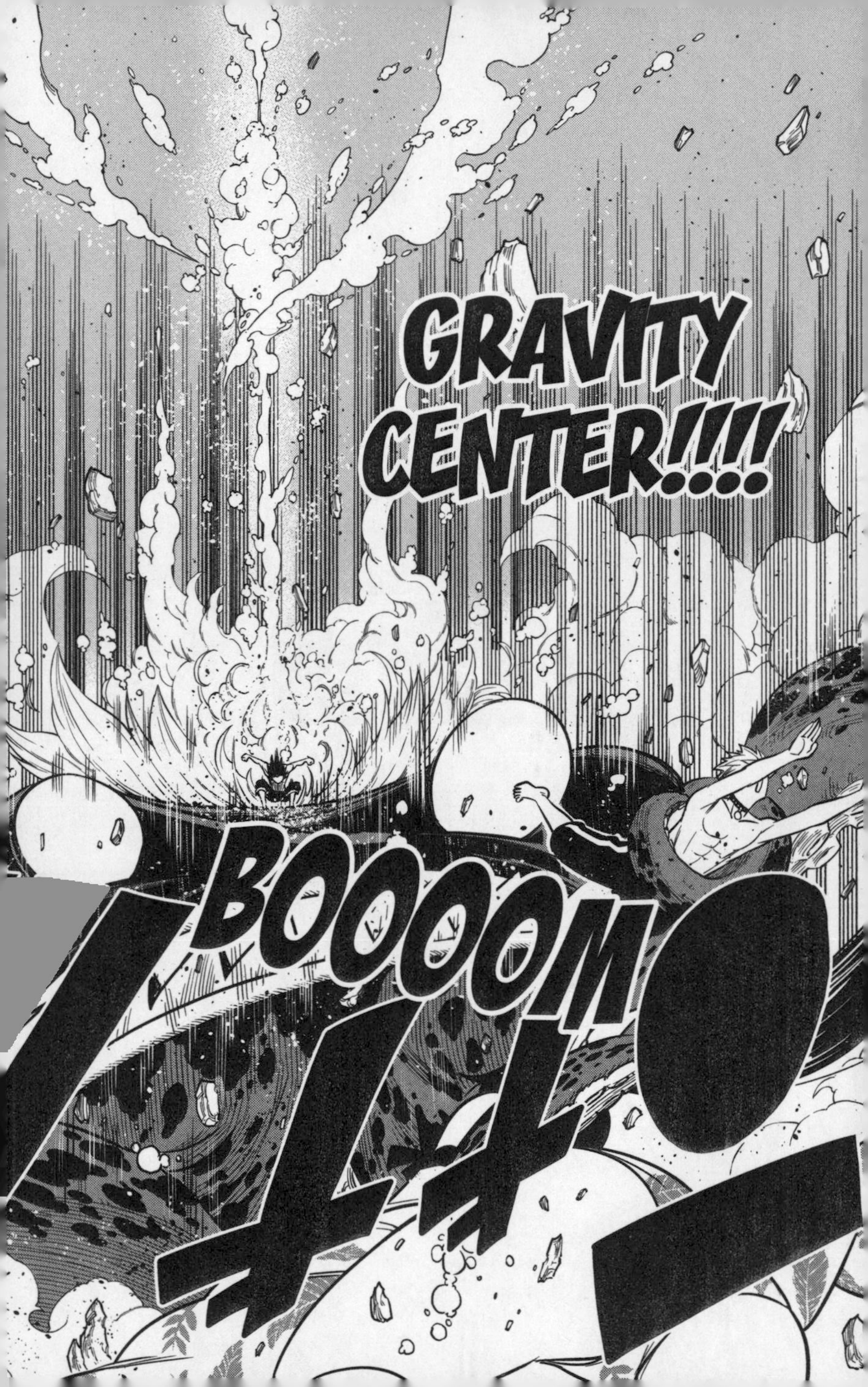
GRAVITY CENTER!!!!
BOOOOM

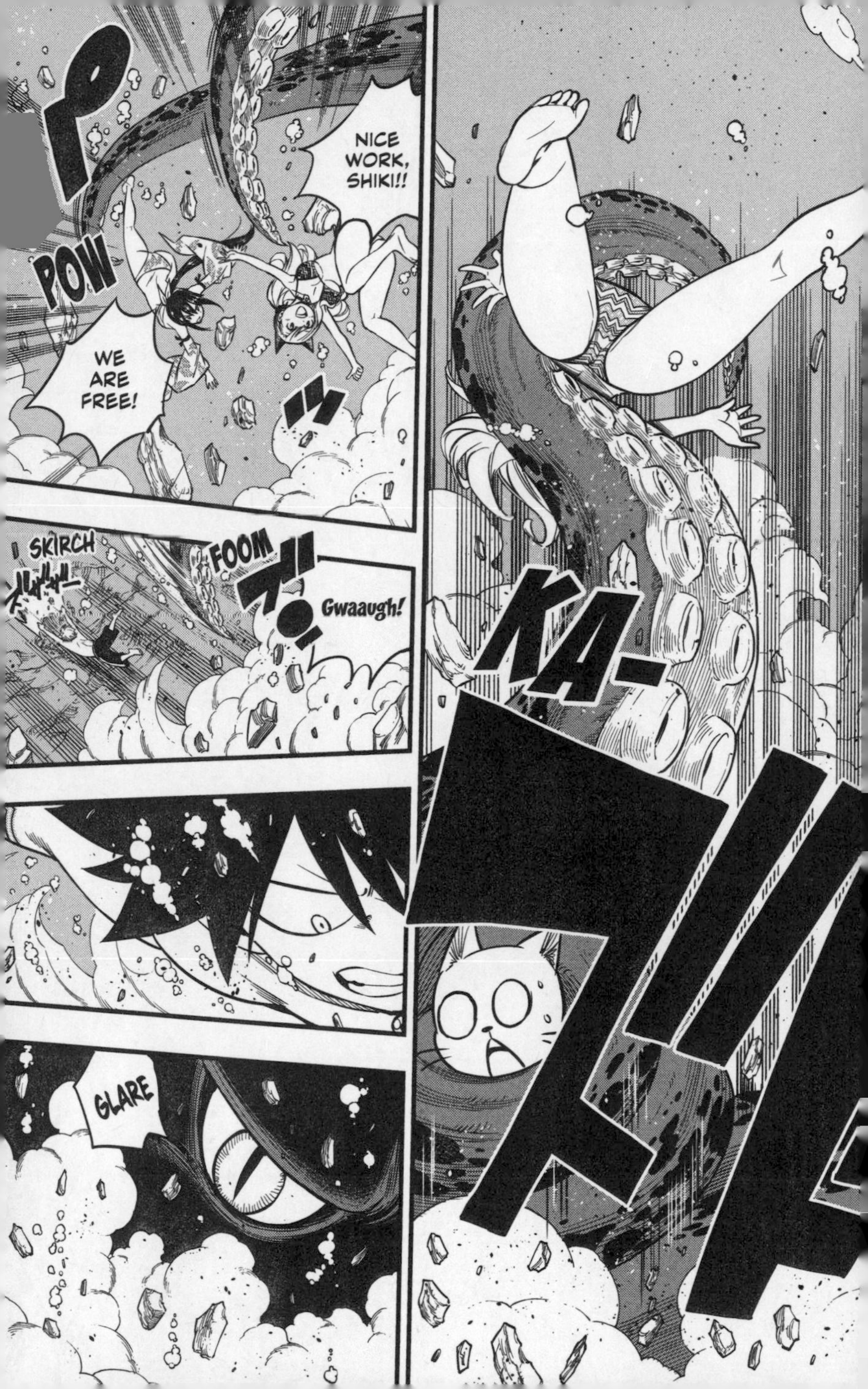
KA-
NICE WORK, SHIKI!!
POP
POW
WE ARE FREE!
FOOM
Gwaaugh!
SKIRCH
GLARE

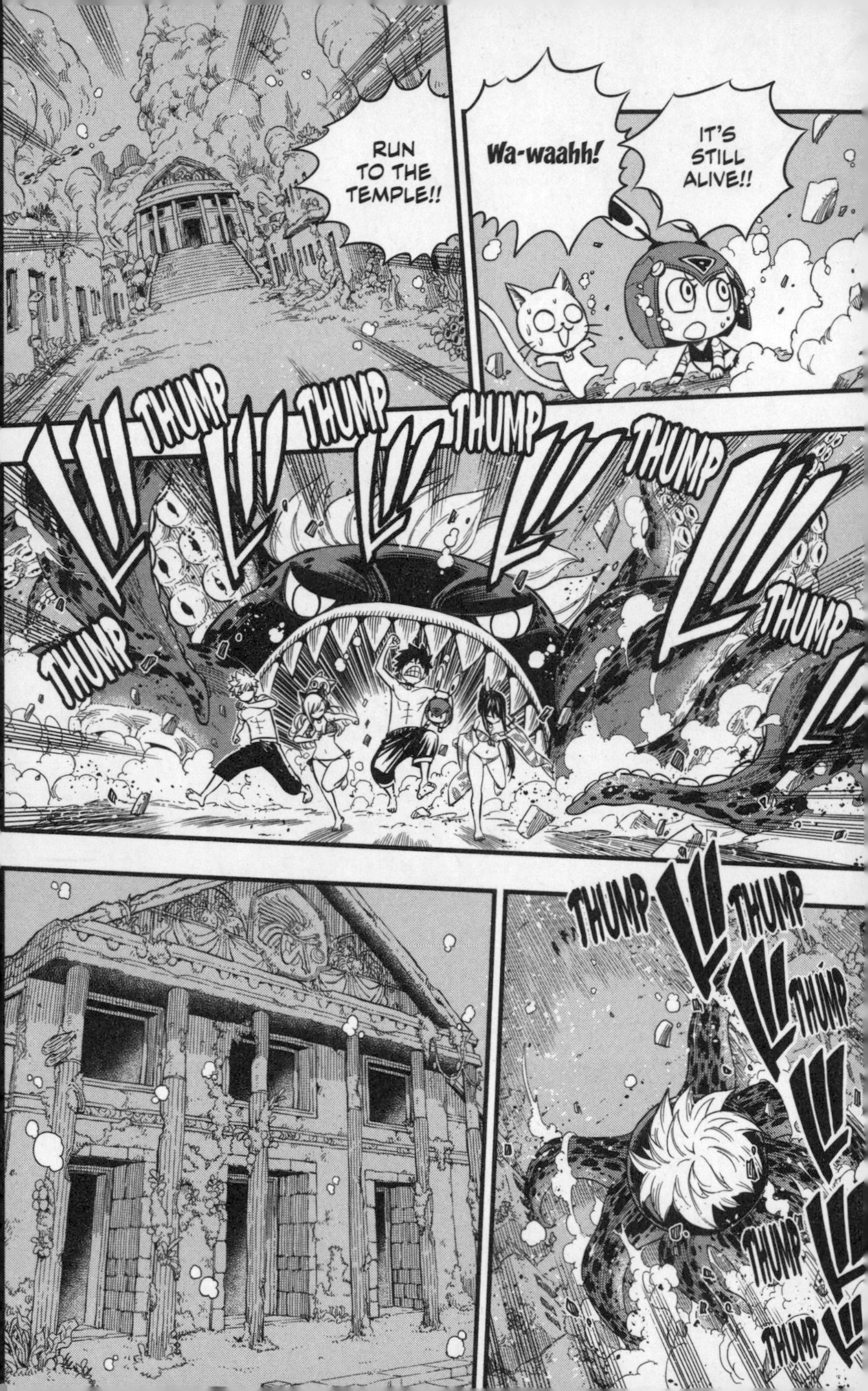
Wa-waahh!
IT'S STILL ALIVE!!
RUN TO THE TEMPLE!!
THUMP
THUMP
THUMP
THUMP
THUMP
THUMP
THUMP
THUMP
THUMP
THUMP
THUMP

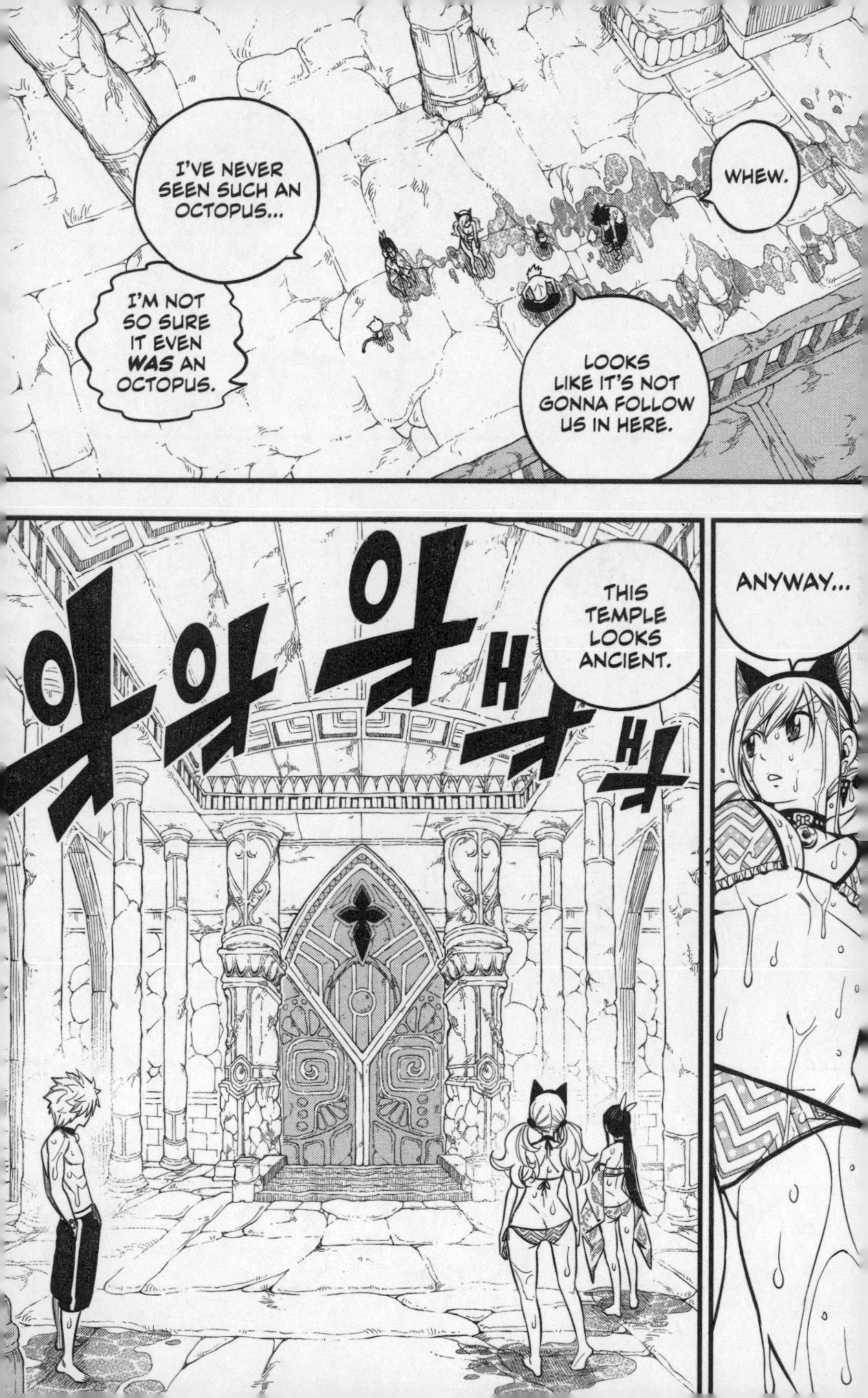
WHEW.
LOOKS LIKE IT'S NOT GONNA FOLLOW US IN HERE.
I'VE NEVER SEEN SUCH AN OCTOPUS...
I'M NOT SO SURE IT EVEN **WAS** AN OCTOPUS.
ANYWAY...
THIS TEMPLE LOOKS ANCIENT.

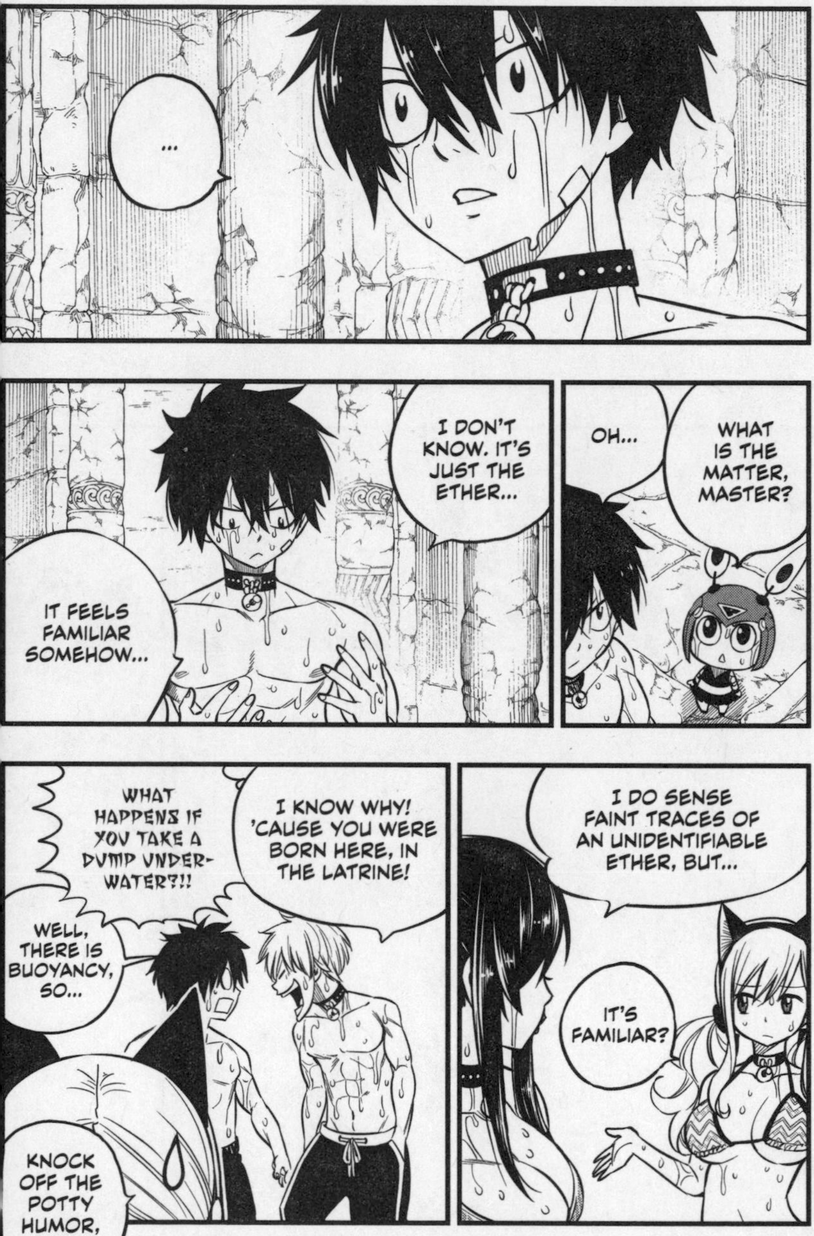
...
WHAT IS THE MATTER, MASTER?
OH...
I DON'T KNOW. IT'S JUST THE ETHER...
IT FEELS FAMILIAR SOMEHOW...
I DO SENSE FAINT TRACES OF AN UNIDENTIFIABLE ETHER, BUT...
IT'S FAMILIAR?
I KNOW WHY! 'CAUSE YOU WERE BORN HERE, IN THE LATRINE!
WHAT HAPPENS IF YOU TAKE A DUMP UNDER-WATER?!!
WELL, THERE IS BUOYANCY, SO...
KNOCK OFF THE POTTY HUMOR, OKAY?

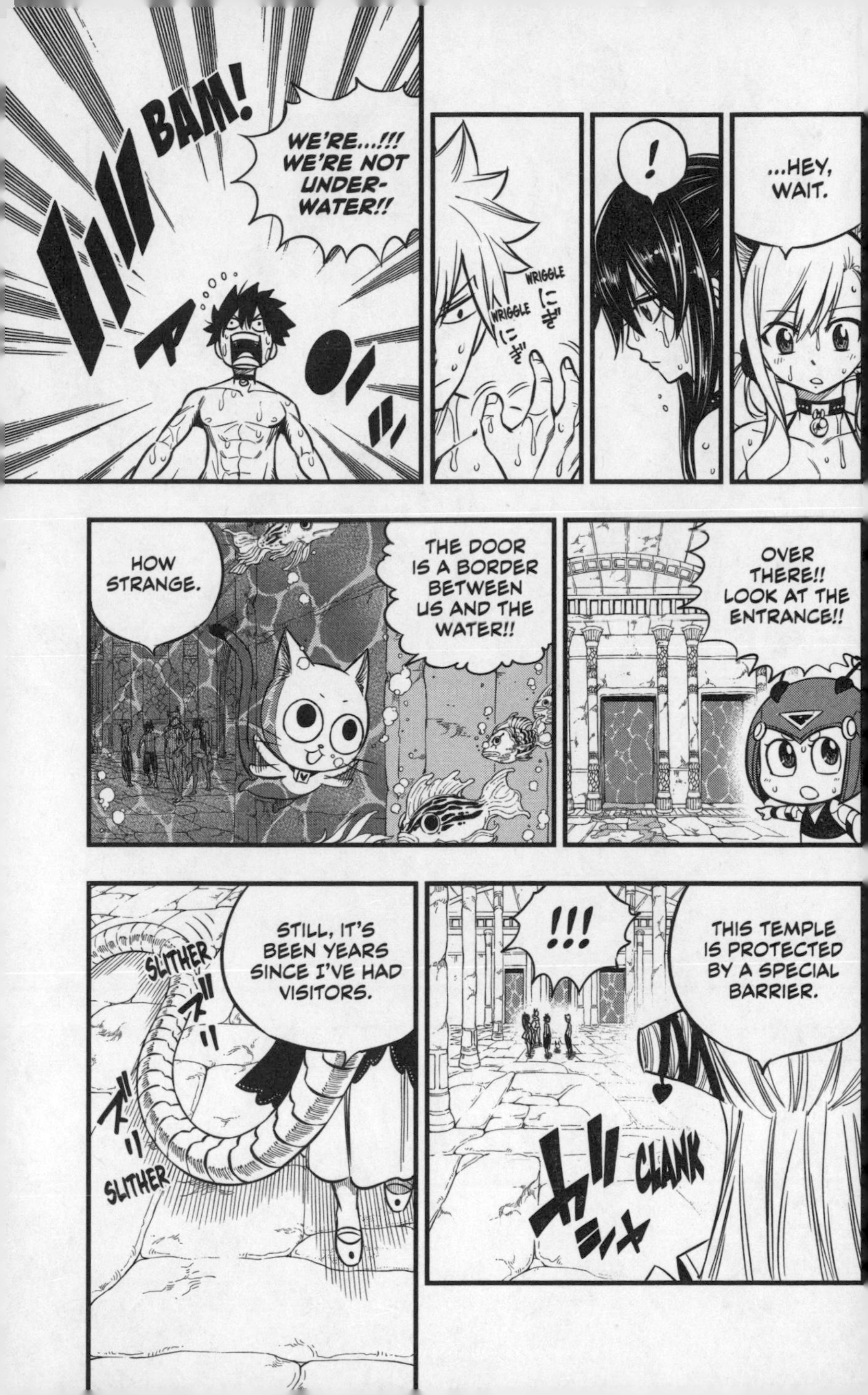
...HEY, WAIT.
!
WRIGGLE
にぎ
WRIGGLE
にぎ
BAM!
WE'RE...!!! WE'RE NOT UNDER-WATER!!
OVER THERE!! LOOK AT THE ENTRANCE!!
THE DOOR IS A BORDER BETWEEN US AND THE WATER!!
HOW STRANGE.
THIS TEMPLE IS PROTECTED BY A SPECIAL BARRIER.
!!!
CLANK
STILL, IT'S BEEN YEARS SINCE I'VE HAD VISITORS.
SLITHER
SLITHER

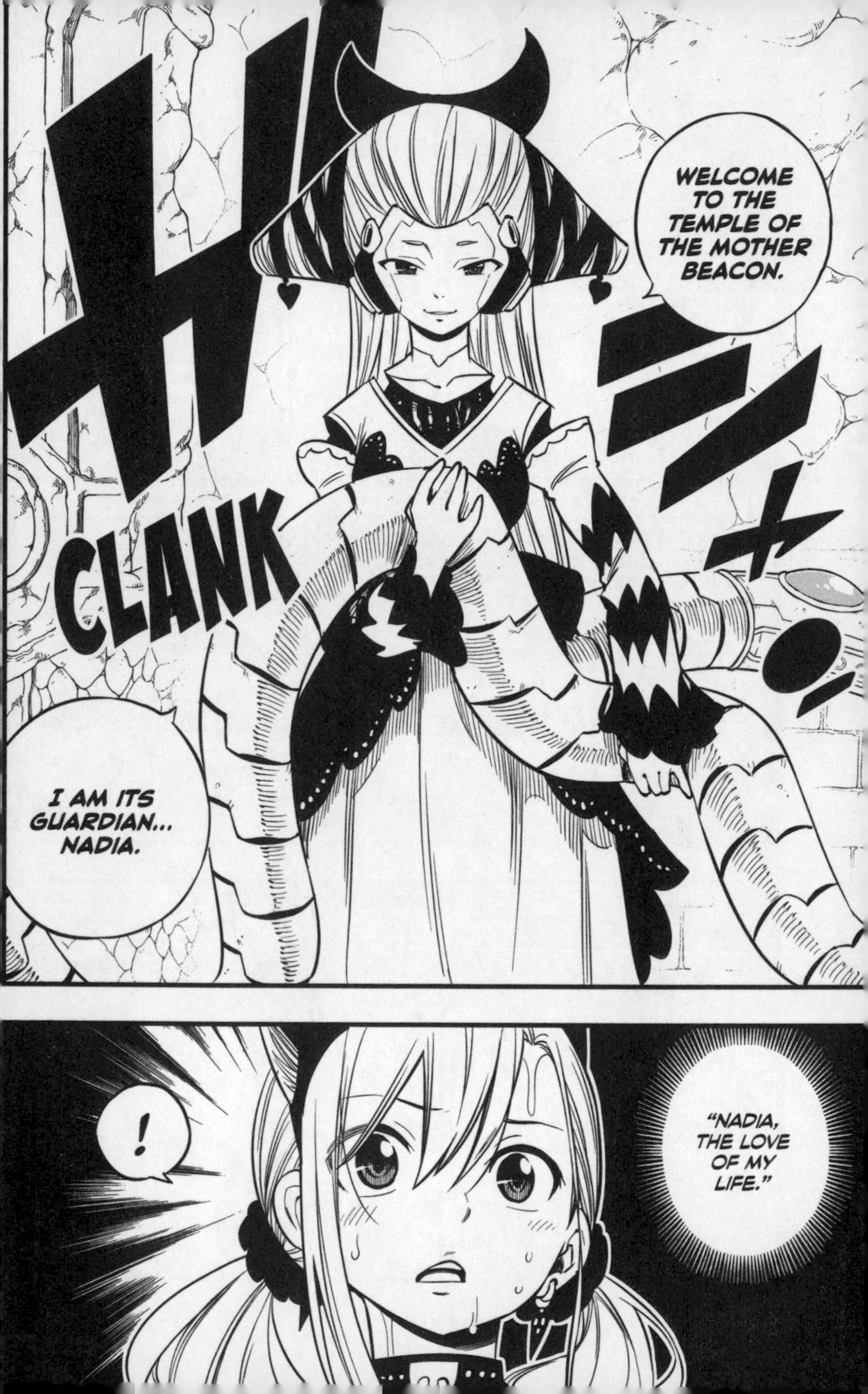
WELCOME TO THE TEMPLE OF THE MOTHER BEACON.
CLANK
I AM ITS GUARDIAN... NADIA.
"NADIA, THE LOVE OF MY LIFE."
!

EDENS ZERO

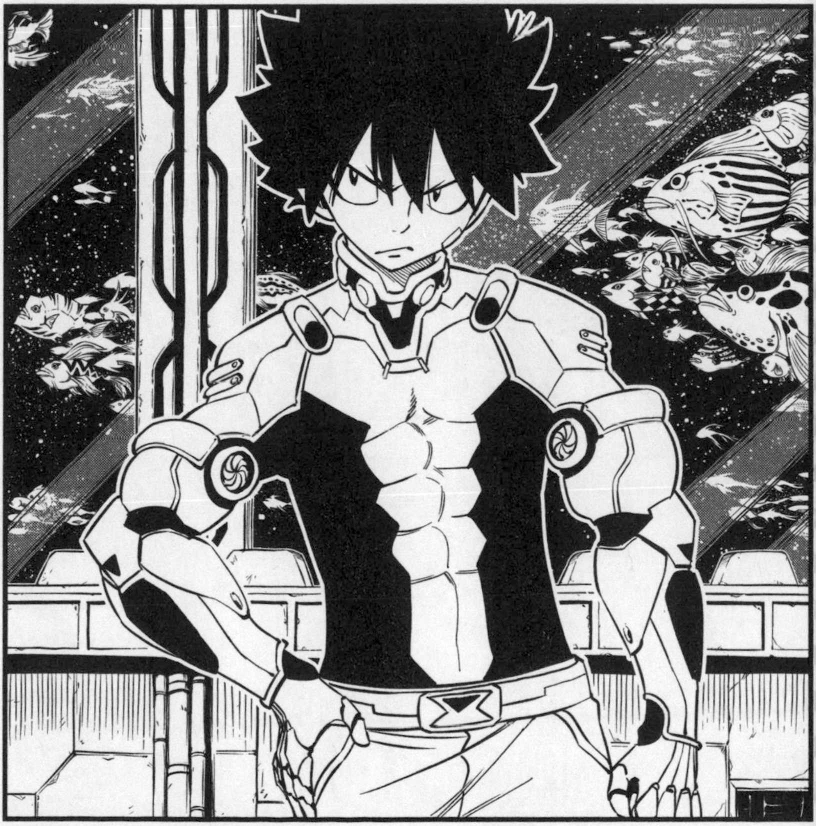

CHAPTER 109: RED CAVE

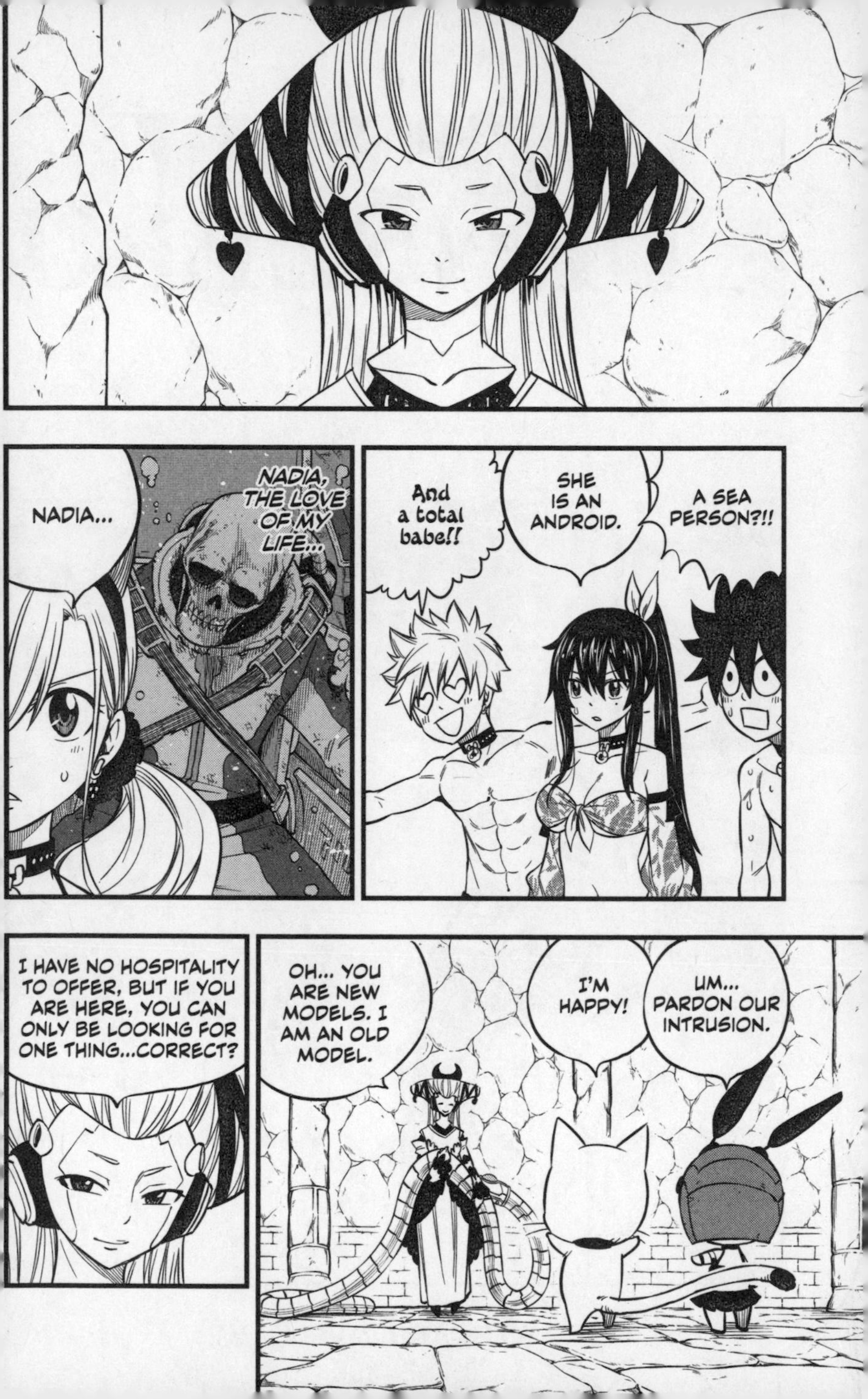
A SEA PERSON?!!
SHE IS AN ANDROID.
And a total babe!!
NADIA, THE LOVE OF MY LIFE...
NADIA...
UM... PARDON OUR INTRUSION.
I'M HAPPY!
OH... YOU ARE NEW MODELS. I AM AN OLD MODEL.
I HAVE NO HOSPITALITY TO OFFER, BUT IF YOU ARE HERE, YOU CAN ONLY BE LOOKING FOR ONE THING...CORRECT?

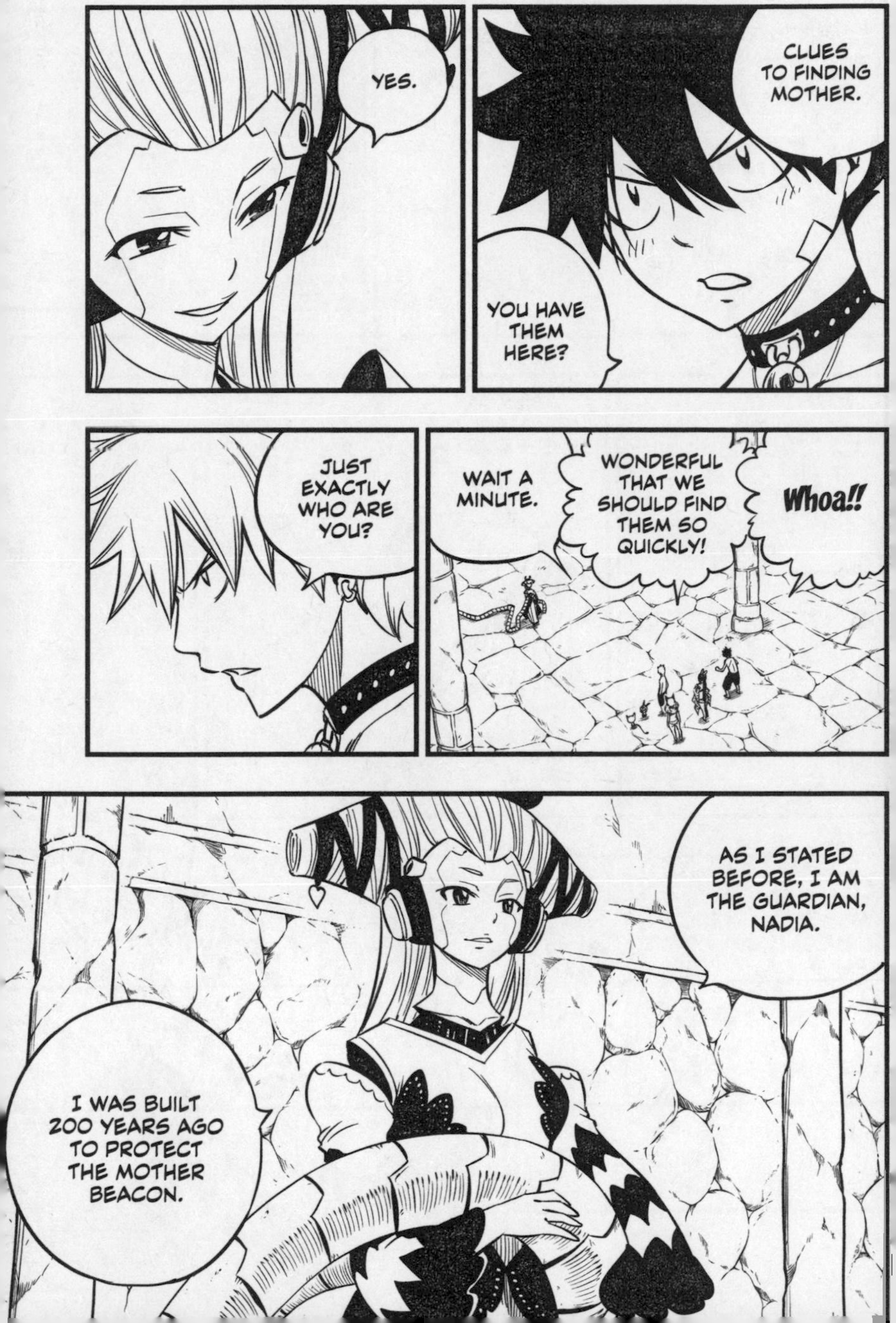
CLUES TO FINDING MOTHER.
YOU HAVE THEM HERE?
YES.
Whoa!!
WONDERFUL THAT WE SHOULD FIND THEM SO QUICKLY!
WAIT A MINUTE.
JUST EXACTLY WHO ARE YOU?
AS I STATED BEFORE, I AM THE GUARDIAN, NADIA.
I WAS BUILT 200 YEARS AGO TO PROTECT THE MOTHER BEACON.

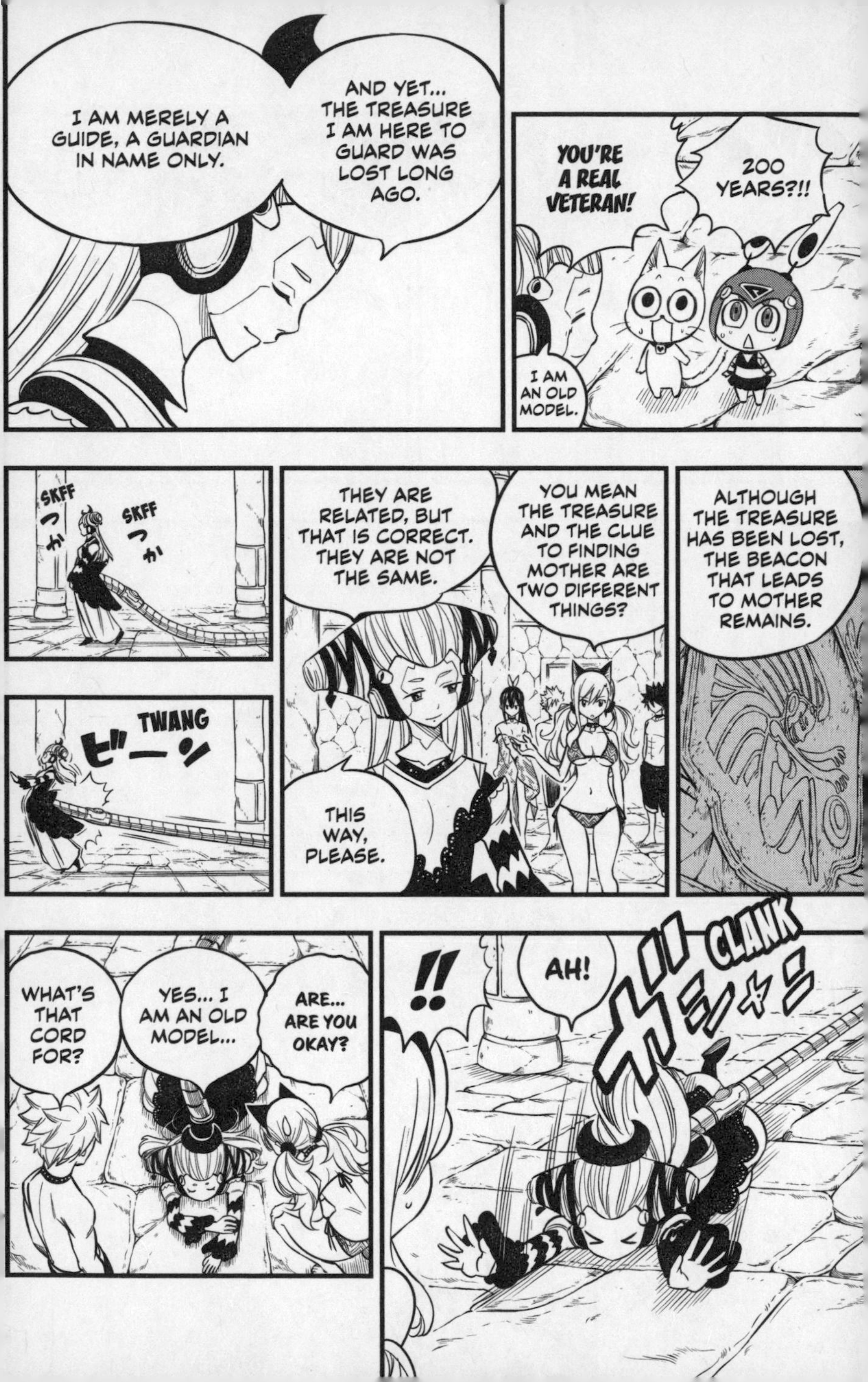
200 YEARS?!!
YOU'RE A REAL VETERAN!
I AM AN OLD MODEL.
AND YET... THE TREASURE I AM HERE TO GUARD WAS LOST LONG AGO.
I AM MERELY A GUIDE, A GUARDIAN IN NAME ONLY.
ALTHOUGH THE TREASURE HAS BEEN LOST, THE BEACON THAT LEADS TO MOTHER REMAINS.
YOU MEAN THE TREASURE AND THE CLUE TO FINDING MOTHER ARE TWO DIFFERENT THINGS?
THEY ARE RELATED, BUT THAT IS CORRECT. THEY ARE NOT THE SAME.
THIS WAY, PLEASE.
SKFF
つか
SKFF
つか
TWANG
CLANK
AH!
!!
ARE... ARE YOU OKAY?
YES... I AM AN OLD MODEL...
WHAT'S THAT CORD FOR?

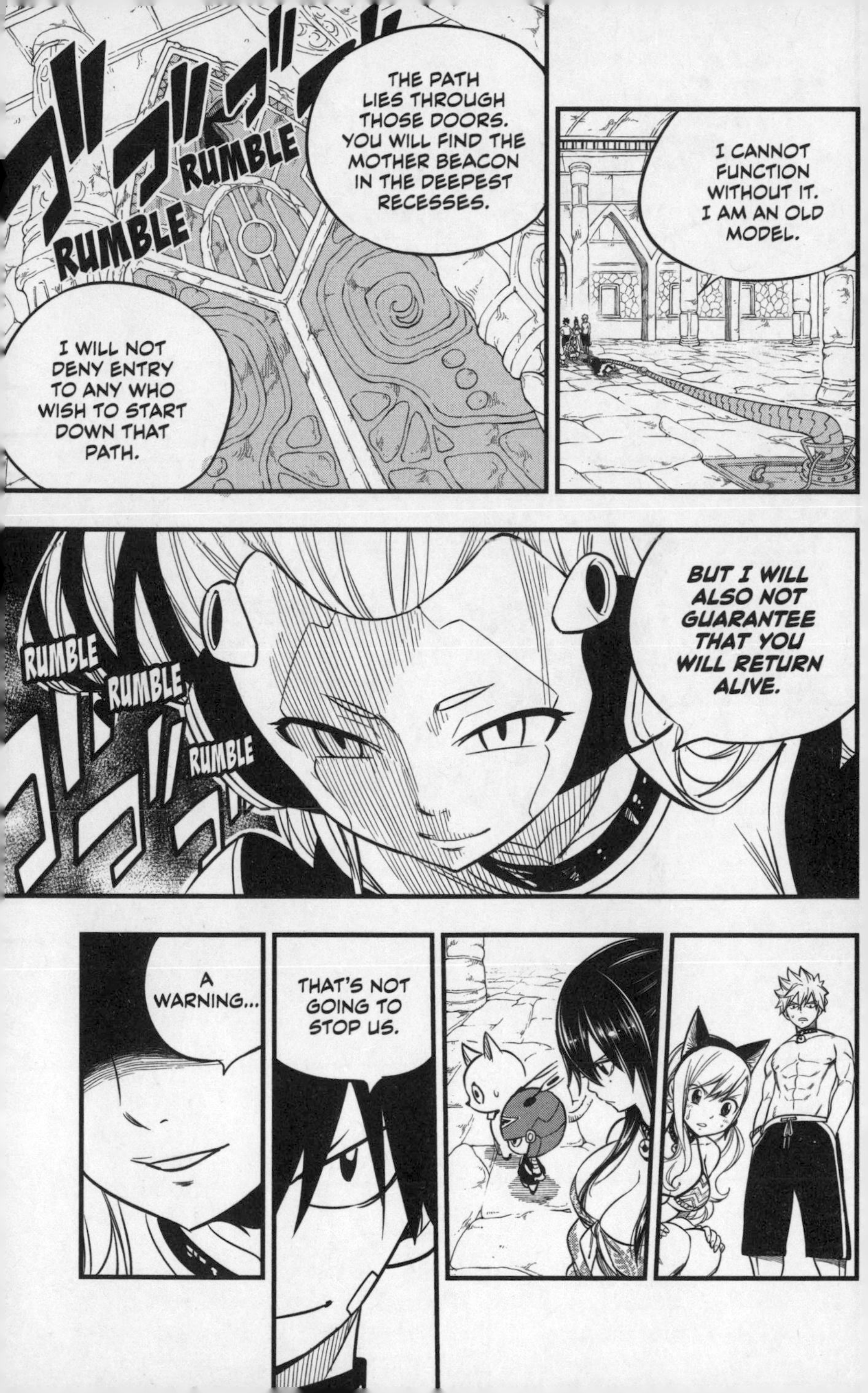

I CANNOT FUNCTION WITHOUT IT. I AM AN OLD MODEL.
THE PATH LIES THROUGH THOSE DOORS. YOU WILL FIND THE MOTHER BEACON IN THE DEEPEST RECESSES.
RUMBLE
RUMBLE
I WILL NOT DENY ENTRY TO ANY WHO WISH TO START DOWN THAT PATH.
BUT I WILL ALSO NOT GUARANTEE THAT YOU WILL RETURN ALIVE.
RUMBLE
RUMBLE
RUMBLE
THAT'S NOT GOING TO STOP US.
A WARNING...

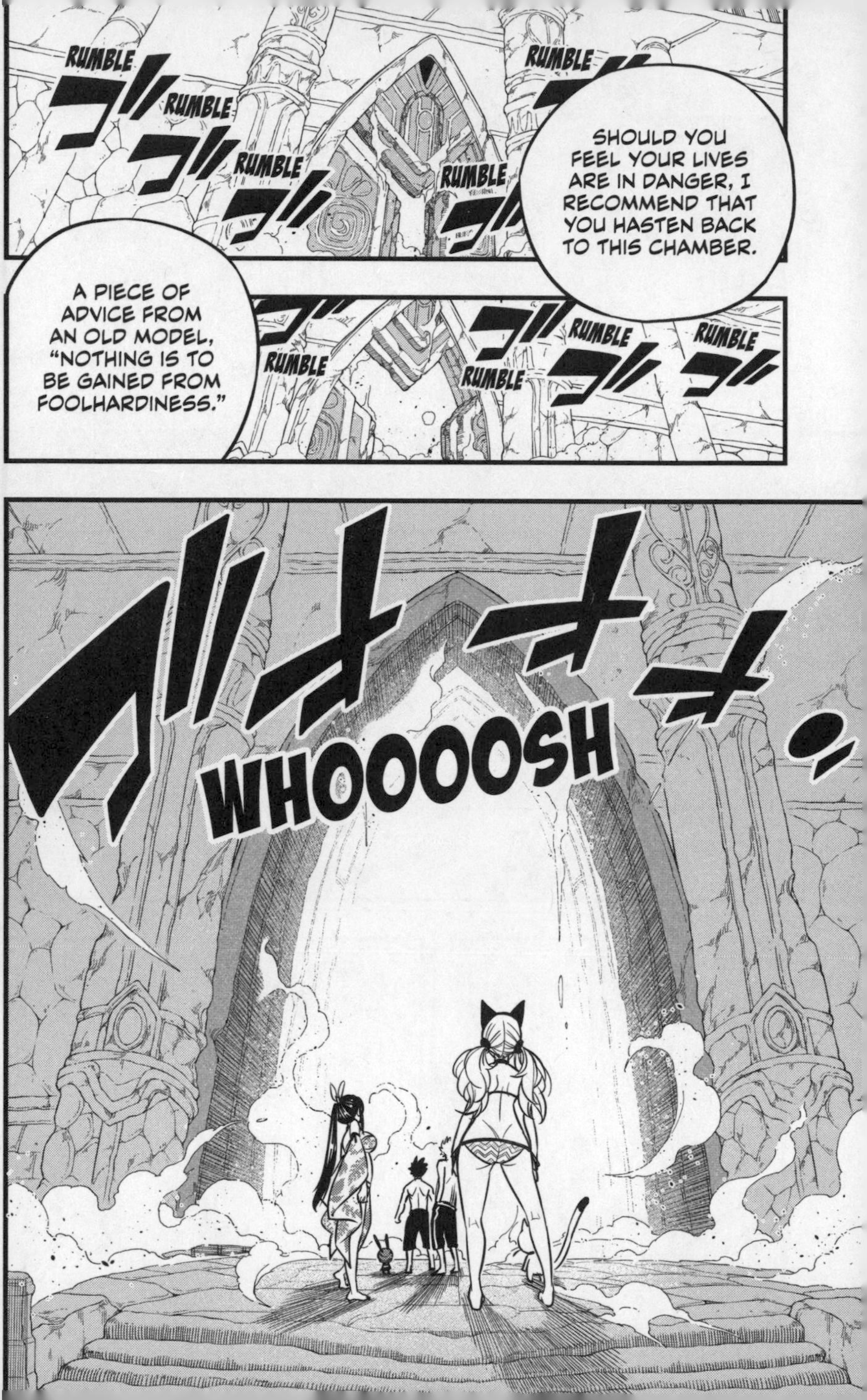
RUMBLE
RUMBLE
RUMBLE
RUMBLE
RUMBLE
SHOULD YOU FEEL YOUR LIVES ARE IN DANGER, I RECOMMEND THAT YOU HASTEN BACK TO THIS CHAMBER.
RUMBLE
RUMBLE
RUMBLE
RUMBLE
A PIECE OF ADVICE FROM AN OLD MODEL, "NOTHING IS TO BE GAINED FROM FOOLHARDINESS."
WHOOOOSH

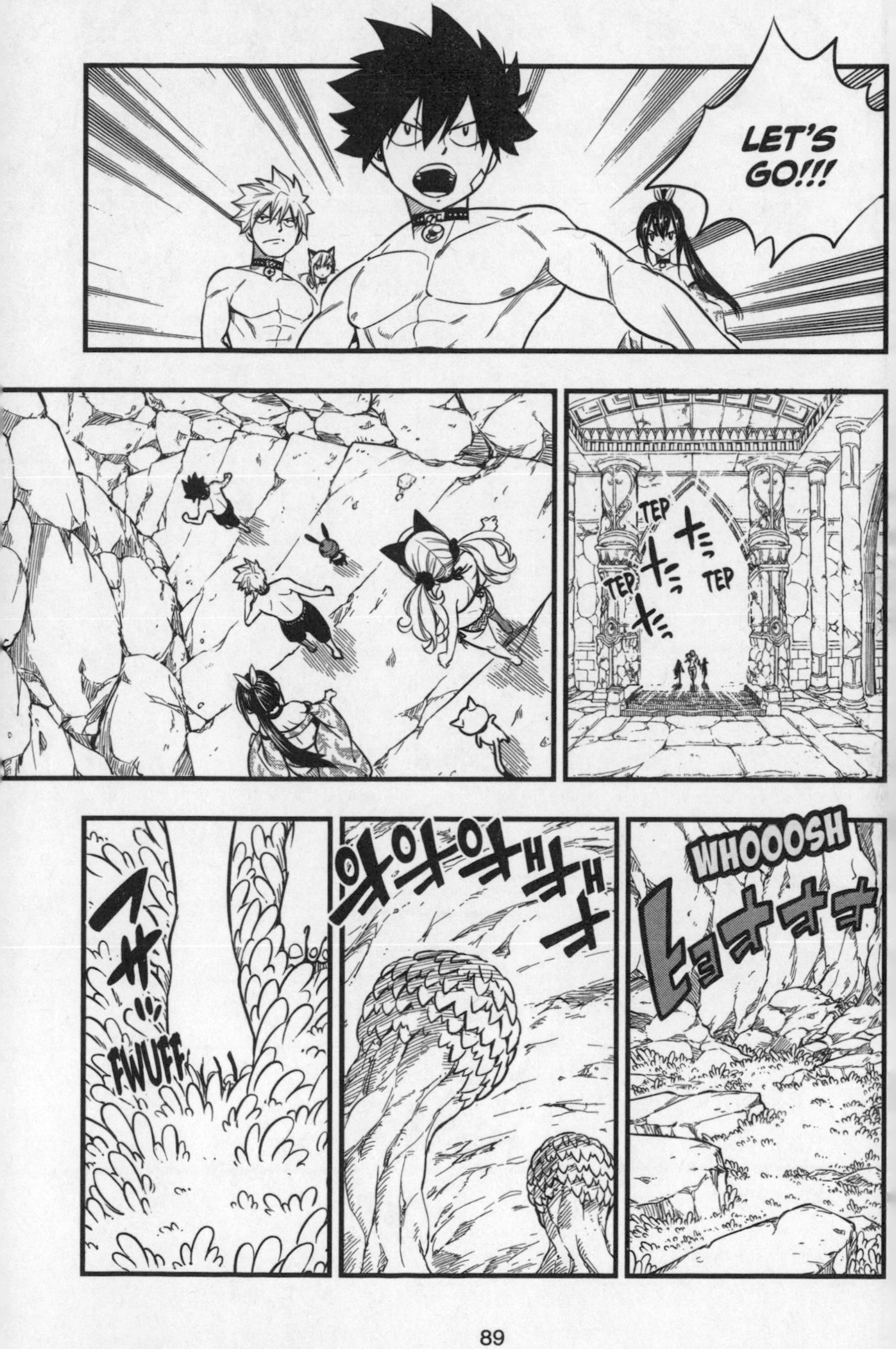

LET'S GO!!!
TEP
TEP
TEP
WHOOOSH
FWUFF

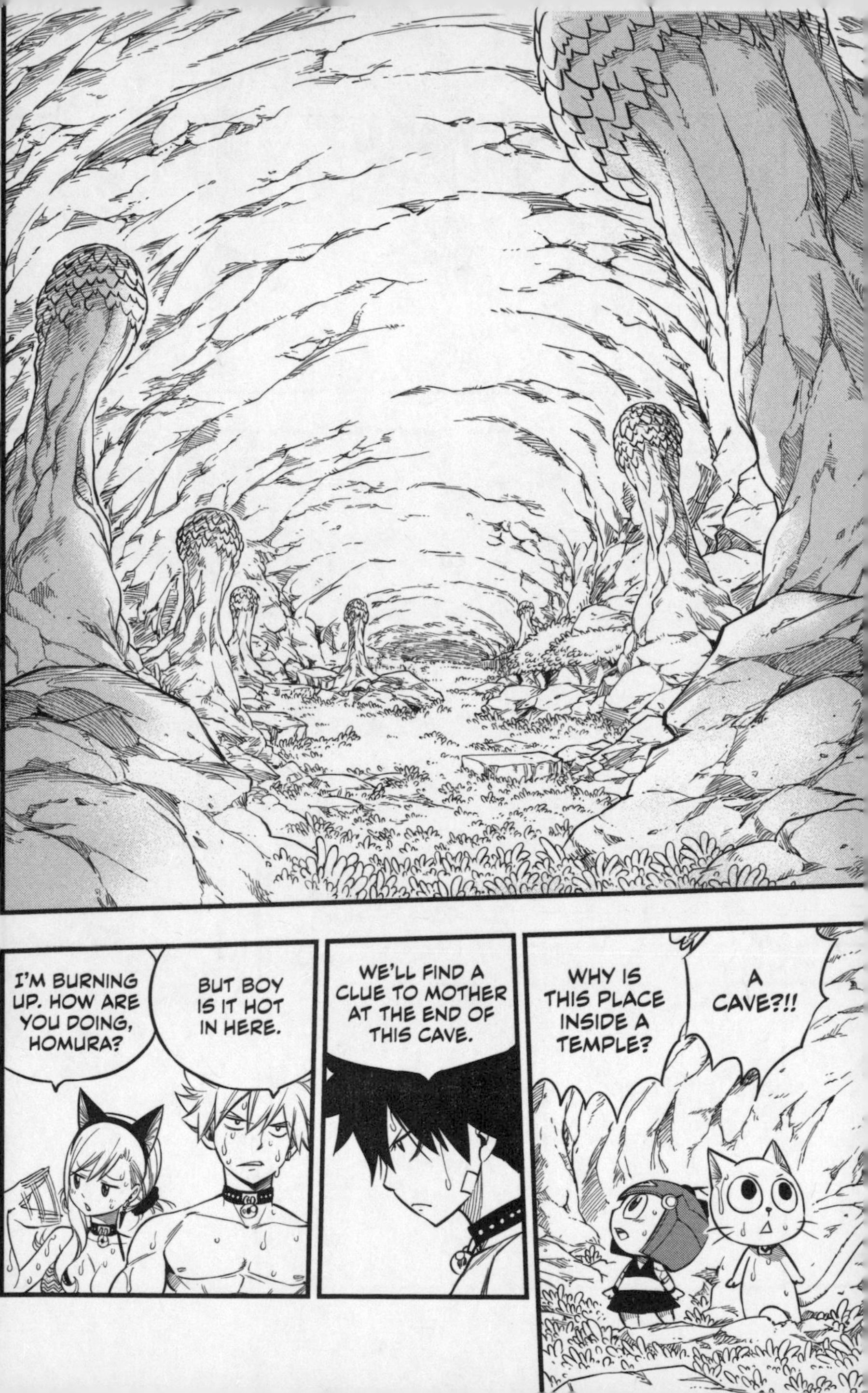
A CAVE?!!
WHY IS THIS PLACE INSIDE A TEMPLE?
WE'LL FIND A CLUE TO MOTHER AT THE END OF THIS CAVE.
BUT BOY IS IT HOT IN HERE.
I'M BURNING UP. HOW ARE YOU DOING, HOMURA?

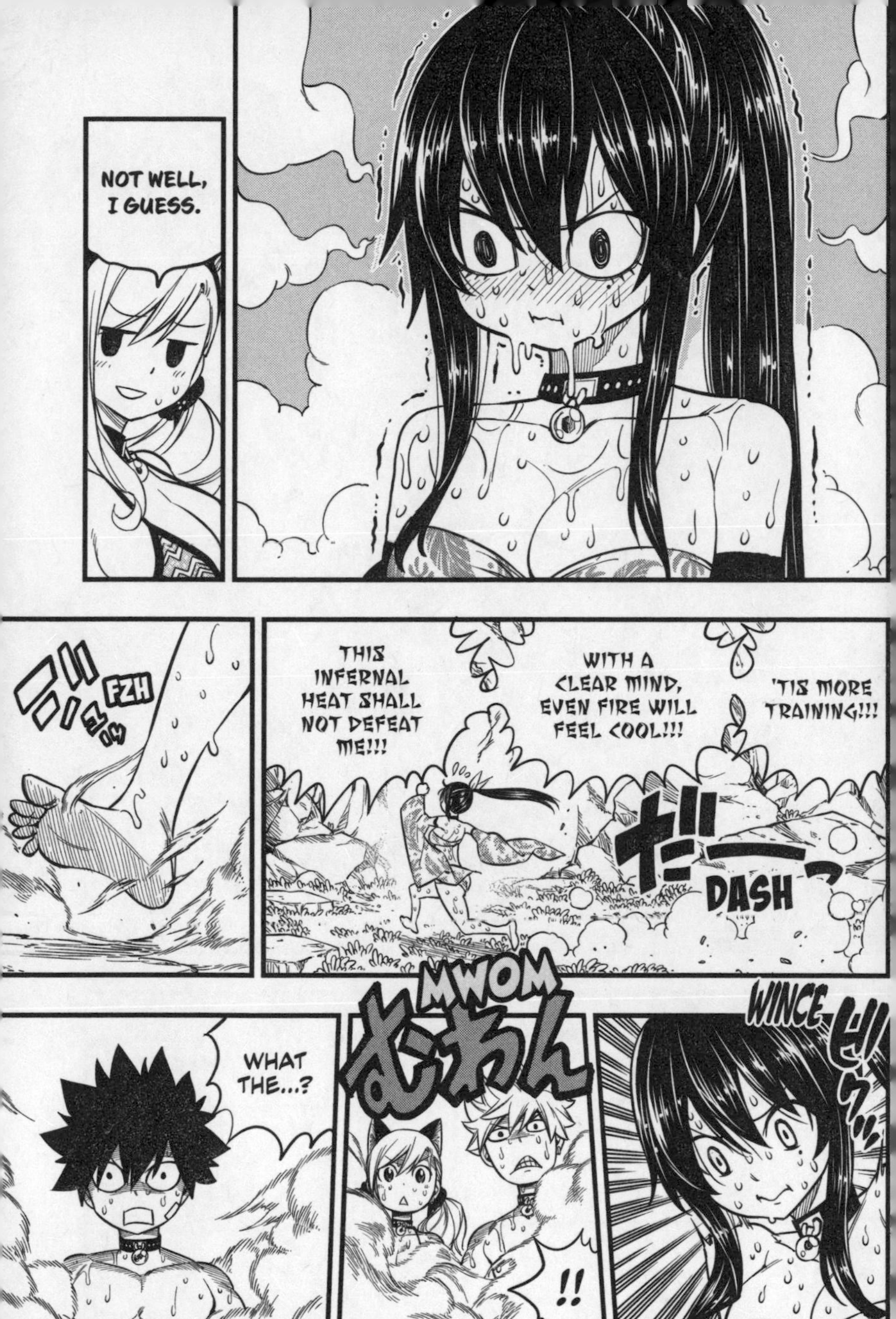
NOT WELL, I GUESS.
'TIS MORE TRAINING!!!
WITH A CLEAR MIND, EVEN FIRE WILL FEEL COOL!!!
THIS INFERNAL HEAT SHALL NOT DEFEAT ME!!!
DASH
FZH
WINCE
MWOM
!!
WHAT THE...?

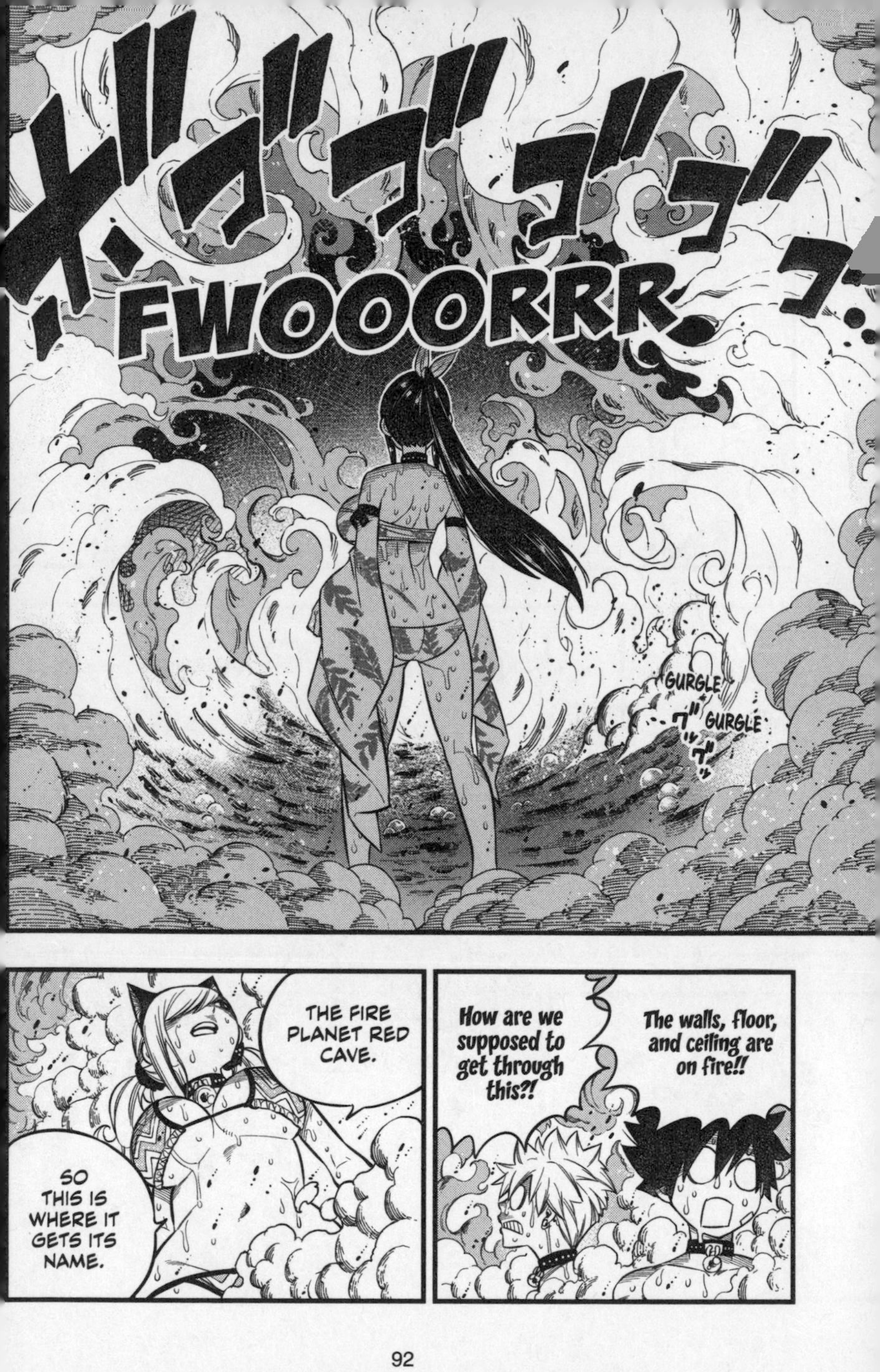
FWOOORRR...
GURGLE
GURGLE
The walls, floor, and ceiling are on fire!!
How are we supposed to get through this?!
THE FIRE PLANET RED CAVE.
SO THIS IS WHERE IT GETS ITS NAME.

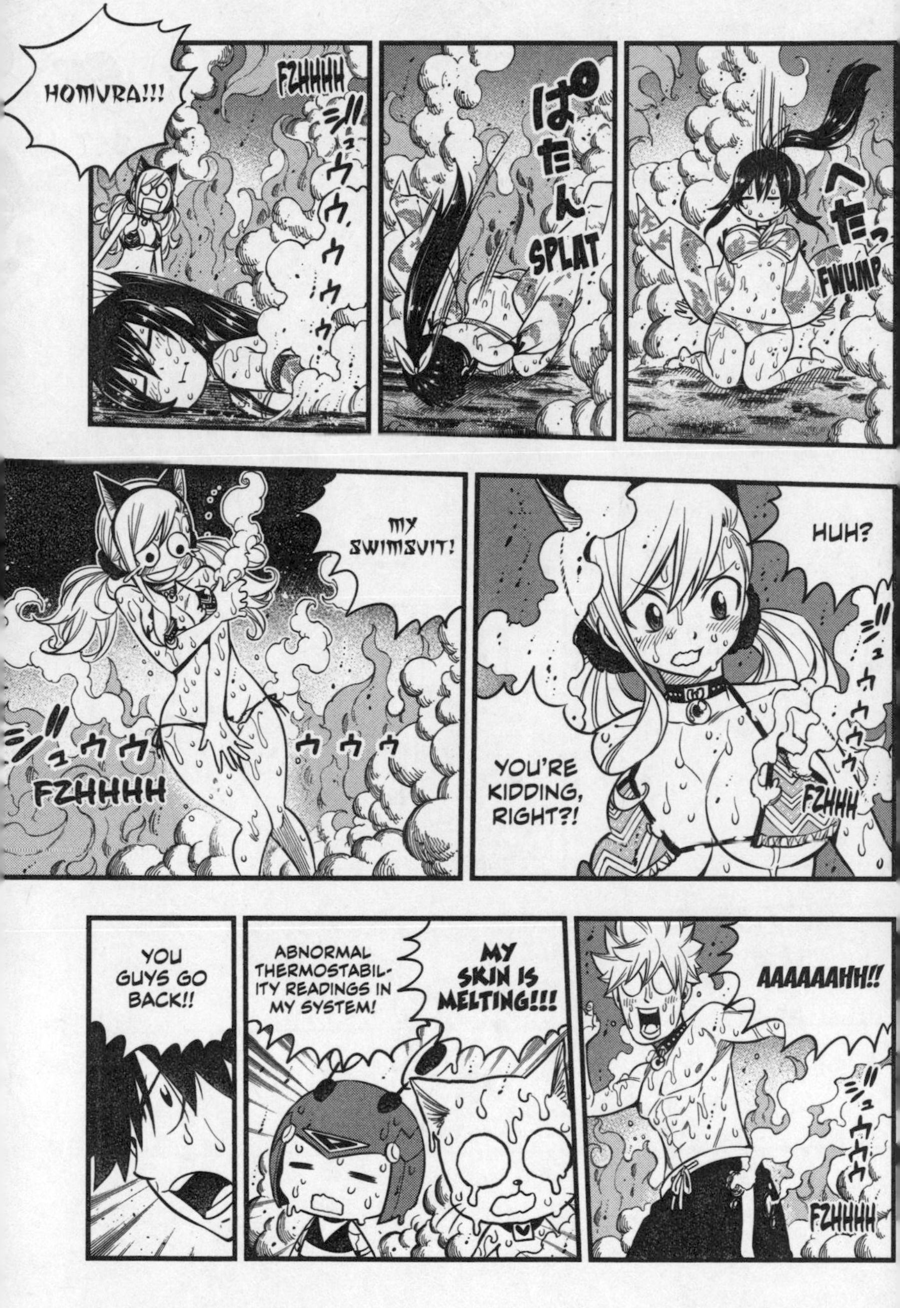
へたっ
FWUMP
ぱたん
SPLAT
HOMURA!!!
FZHHHH
ジュウウウウウ
HUH?
ジュウウウウ
YOU'RE KIDDING, RIGHT?!
FZHHH
MY SWIMSUIT!
ウウウ
ジュウウ
FZHHHH
AAAAAAHH!!
ジュウウ
FZHHHH
MY SKIN IS MELTING!!!
ABNORMAL THERMOSTABILITY READINGS IN MY SYSTEM!
YOU GUYS GO BACK!!

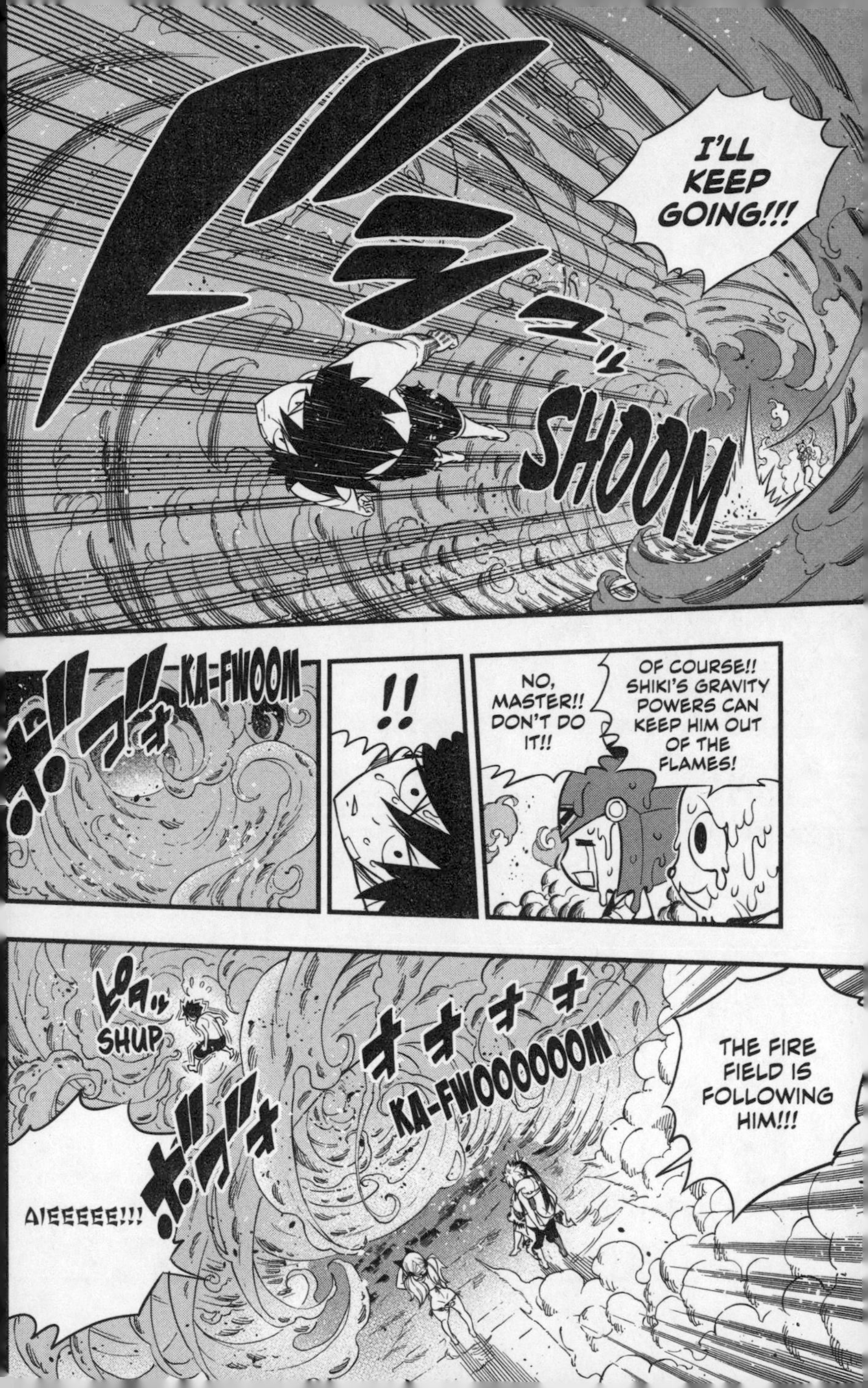
I'LL KEEP GOING!!!
SHOOM
OF COURSE!! SHIKI'S GRAVITY POWERS CAN KEEP HIM OUT OF THE FLAMES!
NO, MASTER!! DON'T DO IT!!
!!
KA-FWOOM
THE FIRE FIELD IS FOLLOWING HIM!!!
KA-FWOOOOOOM
SHUP
AIEEEEE!!!

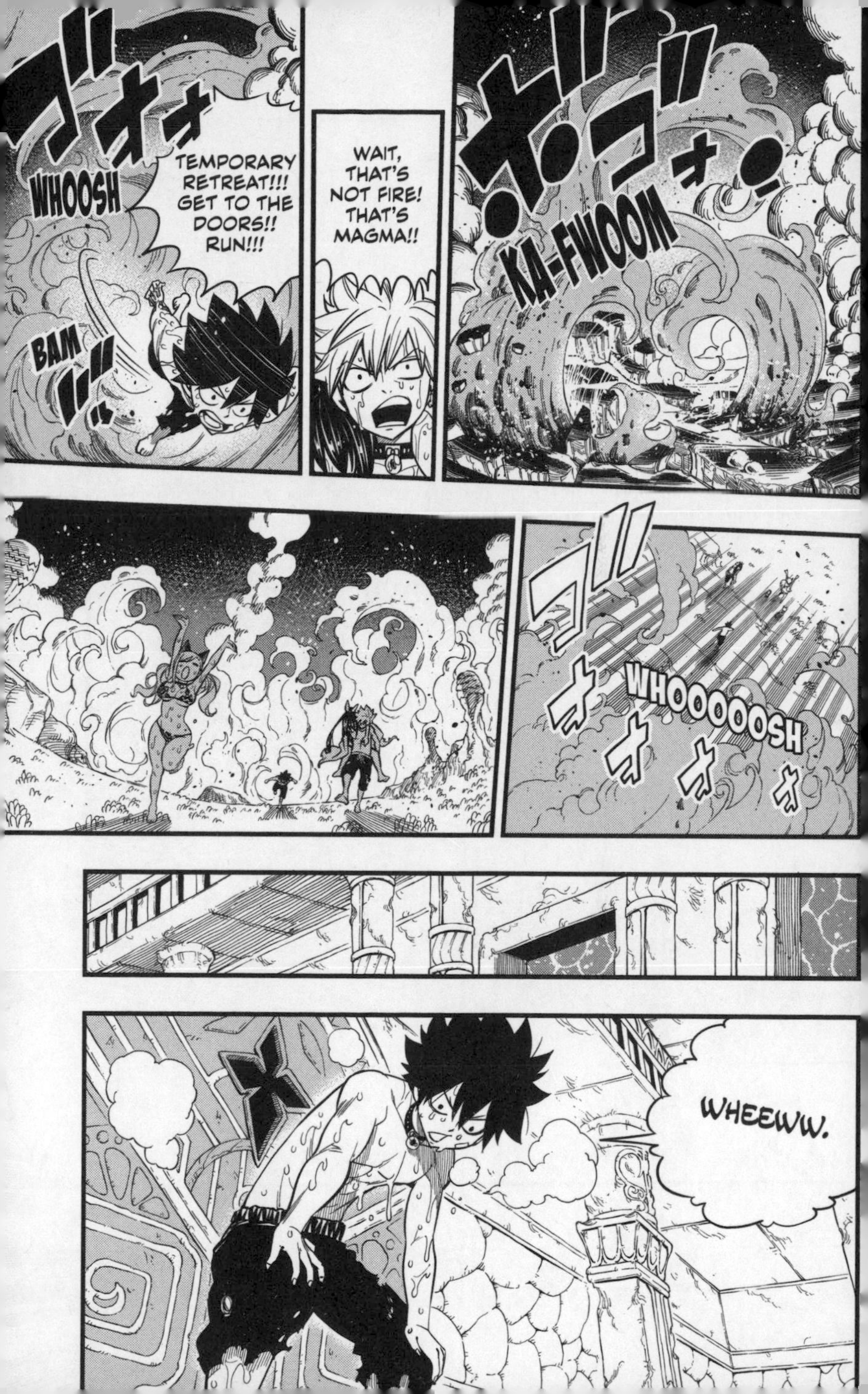
KA-FWOOM
WAIT, THAT'S NOT FIRE! THAT'S MAGMA!!
TEMPORARY RETREAT!!! GET TO THE DOORS!! RUN!!!
WHOOSH
BAM
WHOOOOOOSH
WHEEWW.

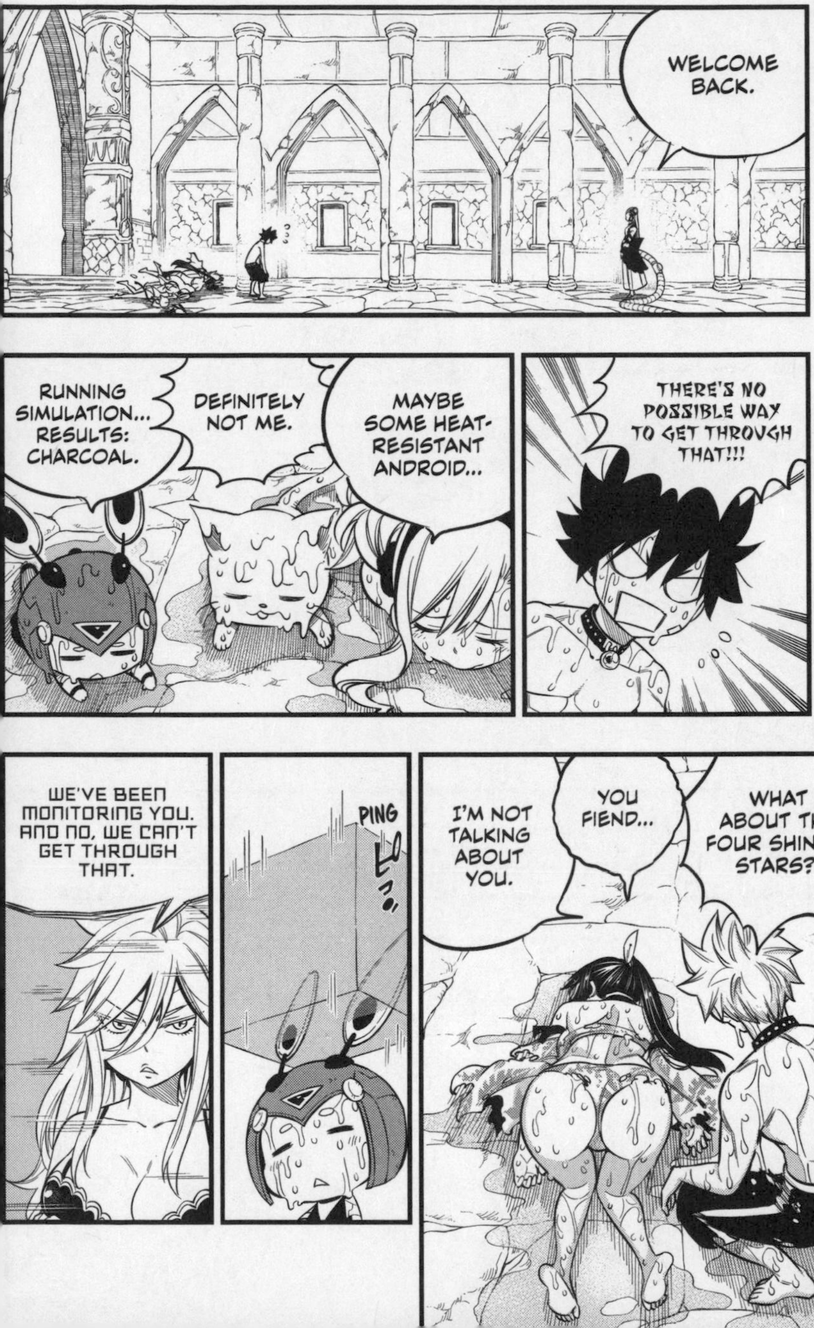
WELCOME BACK.
THERE'S NO POSSIBLE WAY TO GET THROUGH THAT!!!
MAYBE SOME HEAT-RESISTANT ANDROID...
DEFINITELY NOT ME.
RUNNING SIMULATION... RESULTS: CHARCOAL.
WHAT ABOUT THE FOUR SHINING STARS?!
YOU FIEND...
I'M NOT TALKING ABOUT YOU.
PING
WE'VE BEEN MONITORING YOU. AND NO, WE CAN'T GET THROUGH THAT.

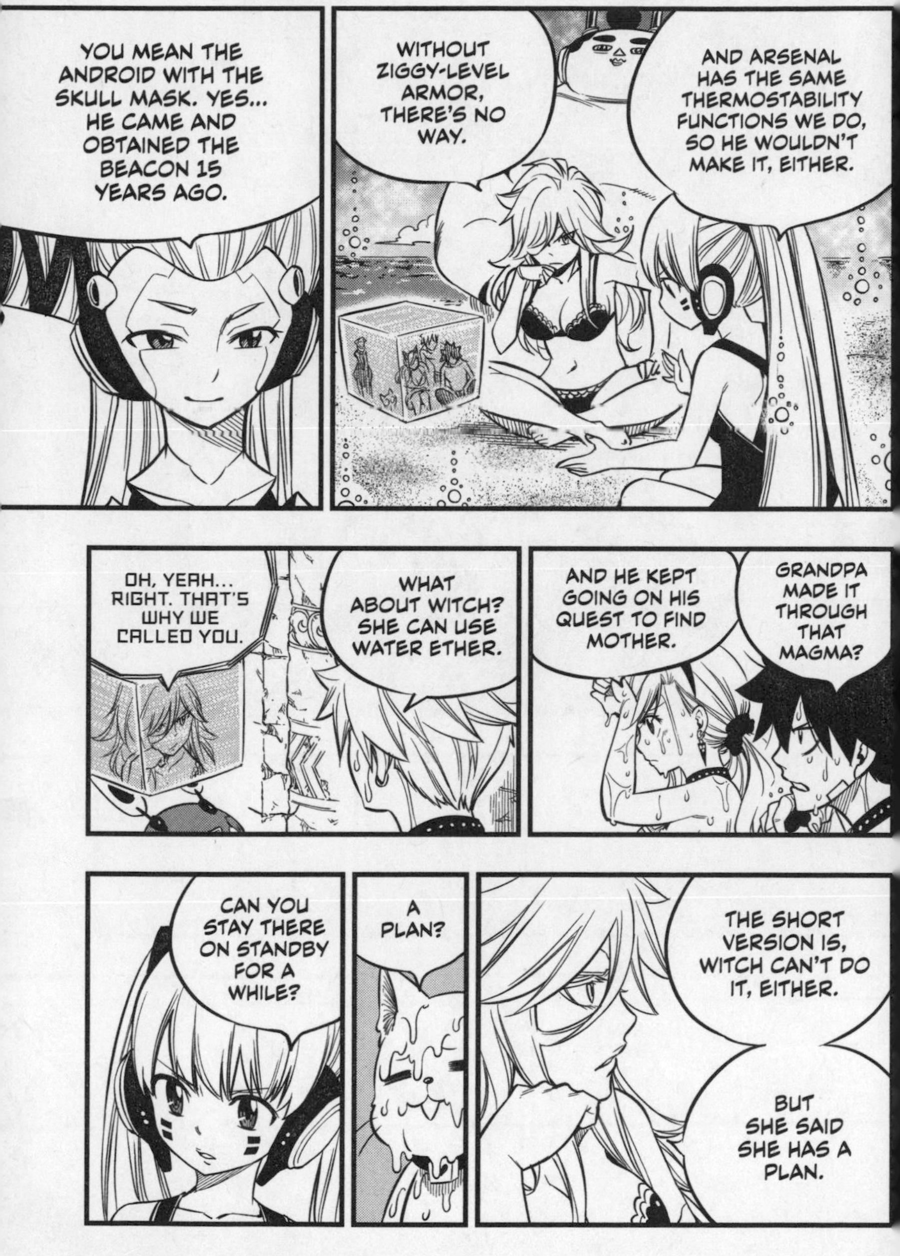
AND ARSENAL HAS THE SAME THERMOSTABILITY FUNCTIONS WE DO, SO HE WOULDN'T MAKE IT, EITHER.
WITHOUT ZIGGY-LEVEL ARMOR, THERE'S NO WAY.
YOU MEAN THE ANDROID WITH THE SKULL MASK. YES... HE CAME AND OBTAINED THE BEACON 15 YEARS AGO.
GRANDPA MADE IT THROUGH THAT MAGMA?
AND HE KEPT GOING ON HIS QUEST TO FIND MOTHER.
WHAT ABOUT WITCH? SHE CAN USE WATER ETHER.
OH, YEAH... RIGHT. THAT'S WHY WE CALLED YOU.
THE SHORT VERSION IS, WITCH CAN'T DO IT, EITHER.
BUT SHE SAID SHE HAS A PLAN.
A PLAN?
CAN YOU STAY THERE ON STANDBY FOR A WHILE?

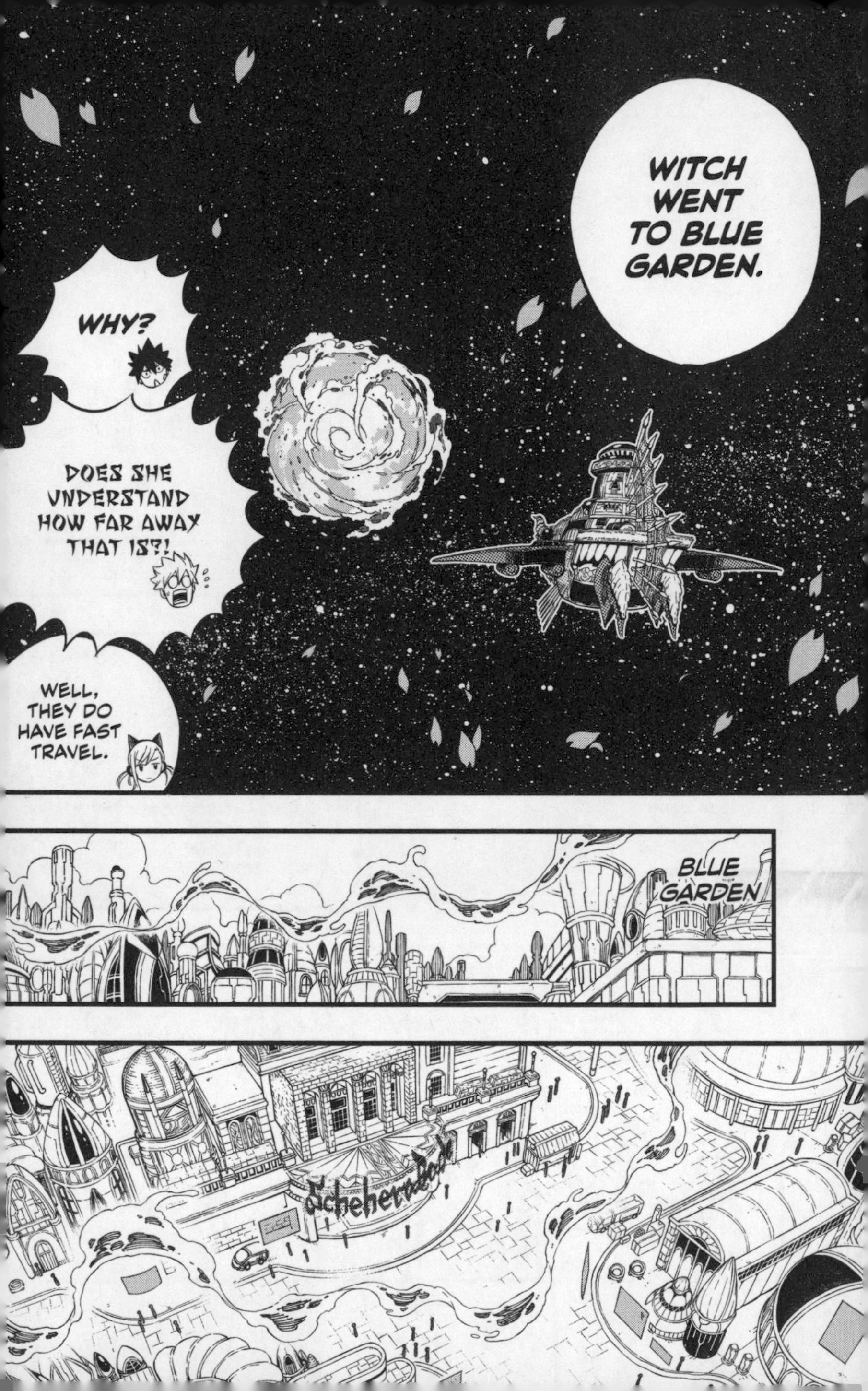
WITCH WENT TO BLUE GARDEN.
WHY?
DOES SHE UNDERSTAND HOW FAR AWAY THAT IS?!
WELL, THEY DO HAVE FAST TRAVEL.
BLUE GARDEN
Scheherazade

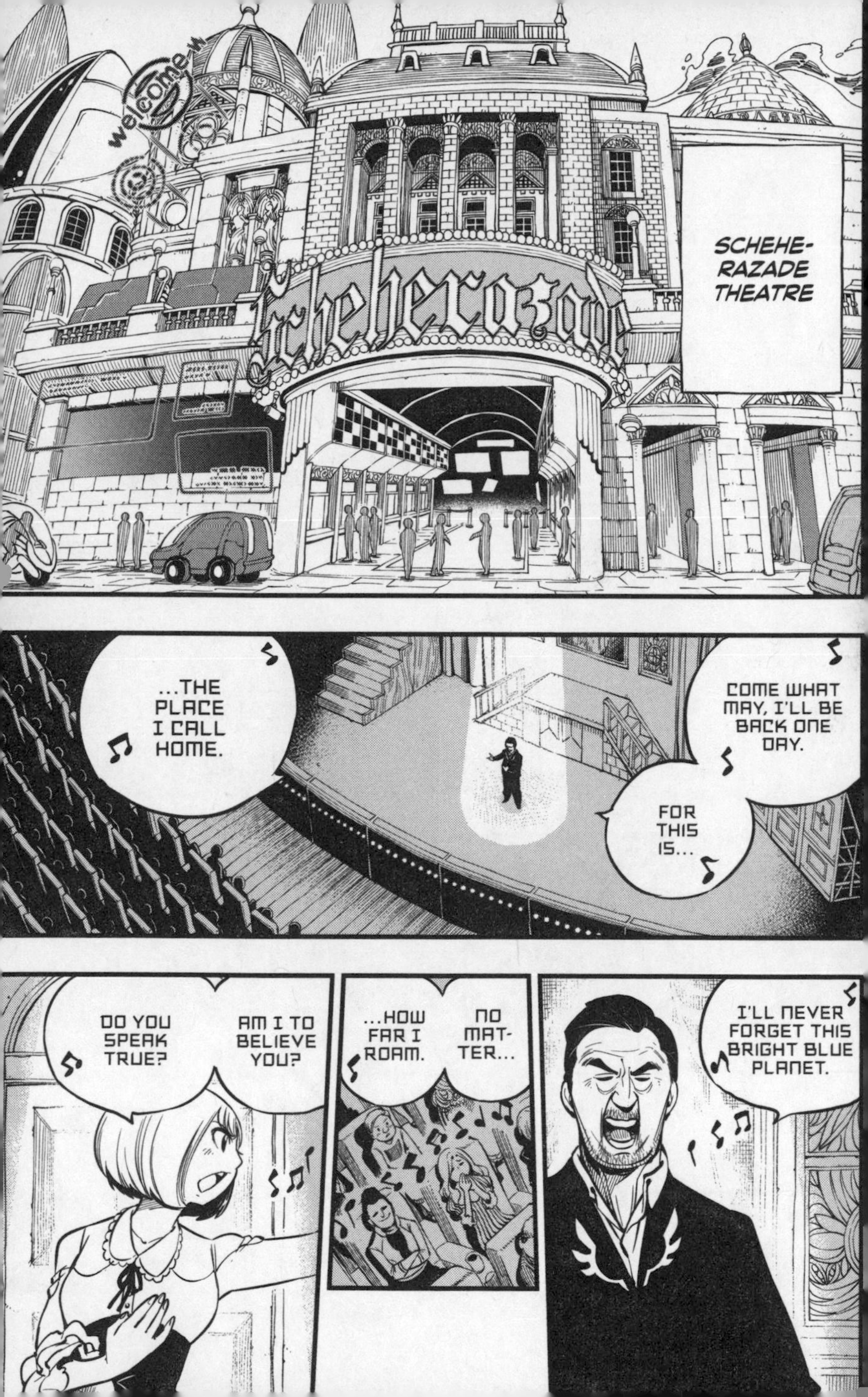
SCHEHE-RAZADE THEATRE
welcome~!!
Scheherazade
COME WHAT MAY, I'LL BE BACK ONE DAY.
FOR THIS IS...
...THE PLACE I CALL HOME.
I'LL NEVER FORGET THIS BRIGHT BLUE PLANET.
NO MAT-TER...
...HOW FAR I ROAM.
AM I TO BELIEVE YOU?
DO YOU SPEAK TRUE?

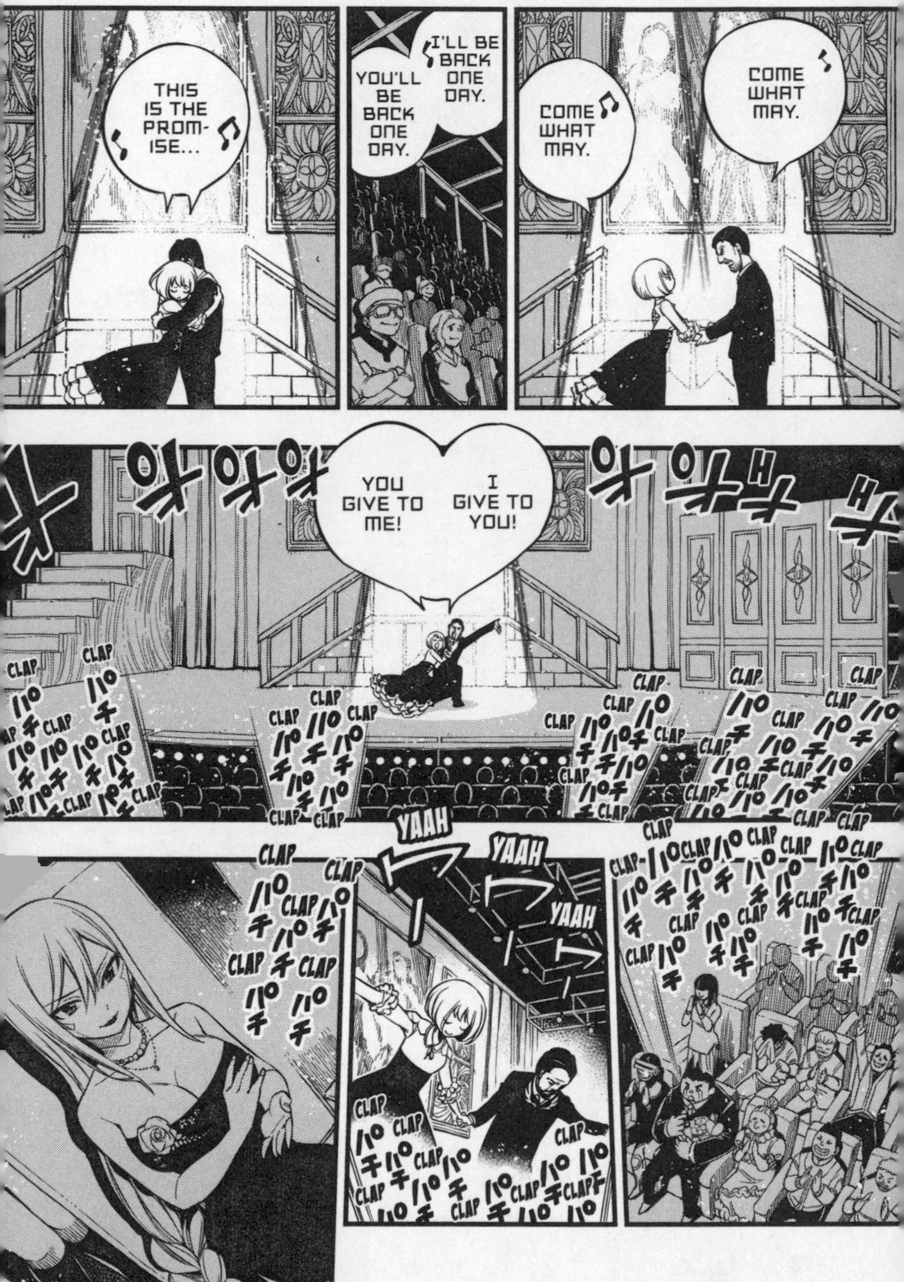
COME WHAT MAY.
COME WHAT MAY.
I'LL BE BACK ONE DAY.
YOU'LL BE BACK ONE DAY.
THIS IS THE PROMISE...
I GIVE TO YOU!
YOU GIVE TO ME!
CLAP
パチ
CLAP
パチ
YAAH
YAAH
YAAH
CLAP
パチ
CLAP
パチ

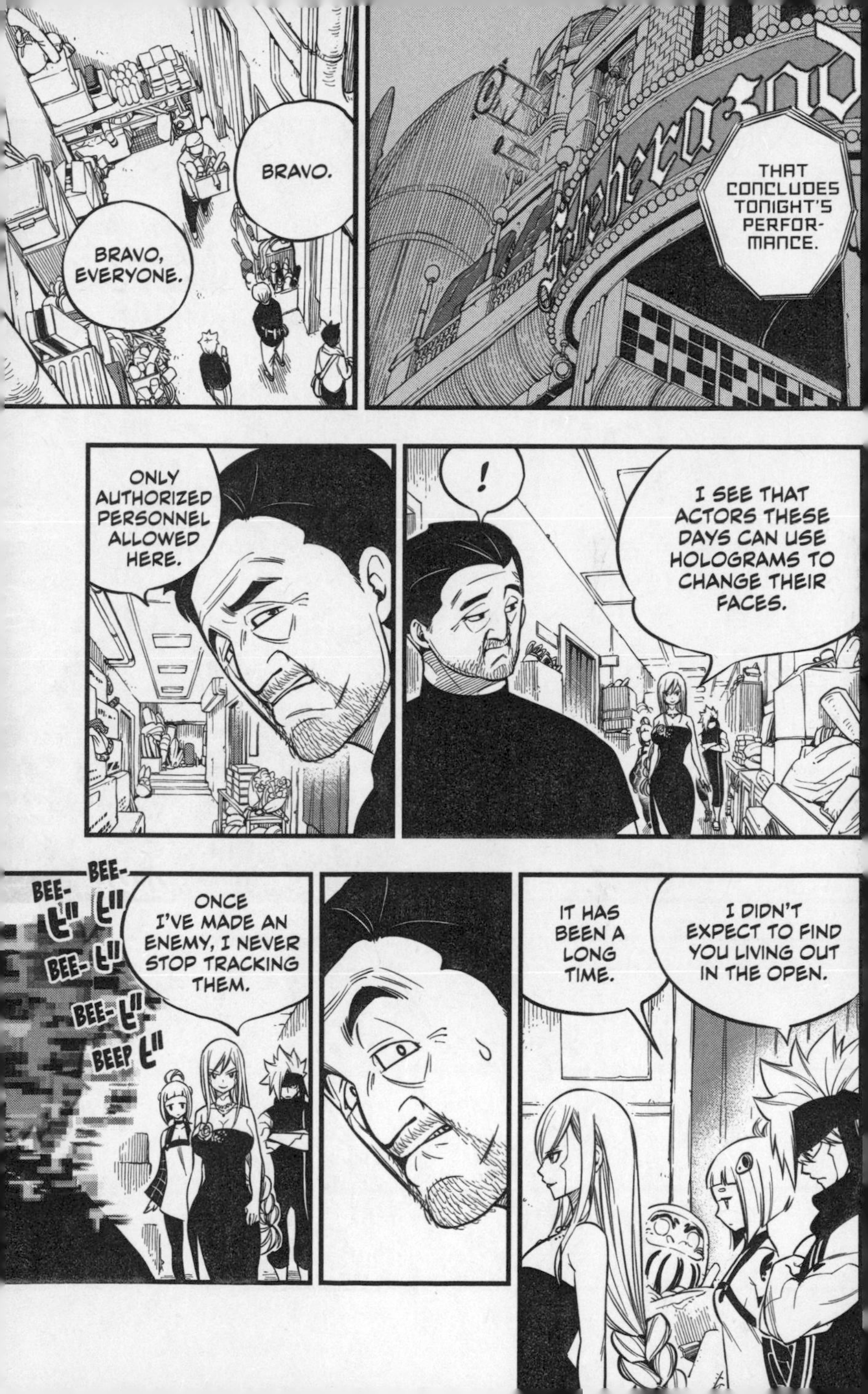
THAT CONCLUDES TONIGHT'S PERFOR-MANCE.
BRAVO.
BRAVO, EVERYONE.
I SEE THAT ACTORS THESE DAYS CAN USE HOLOGRAMS TO CHANGE THEIR FACES.
!
ONLY AUTHORIZED PERSONNEL ALLOWED HERE.
I DIDN'T EXPECT TO FIND YOU LIVING OUT IN THE OPEN.
IT HAS BEEN A LONG TIME.
ONCE I'VE MADE AN ENEMY, I NEVER STOP TRACKING THEM.
BEE-
BEE-
BEE-
BEE-
BEEP

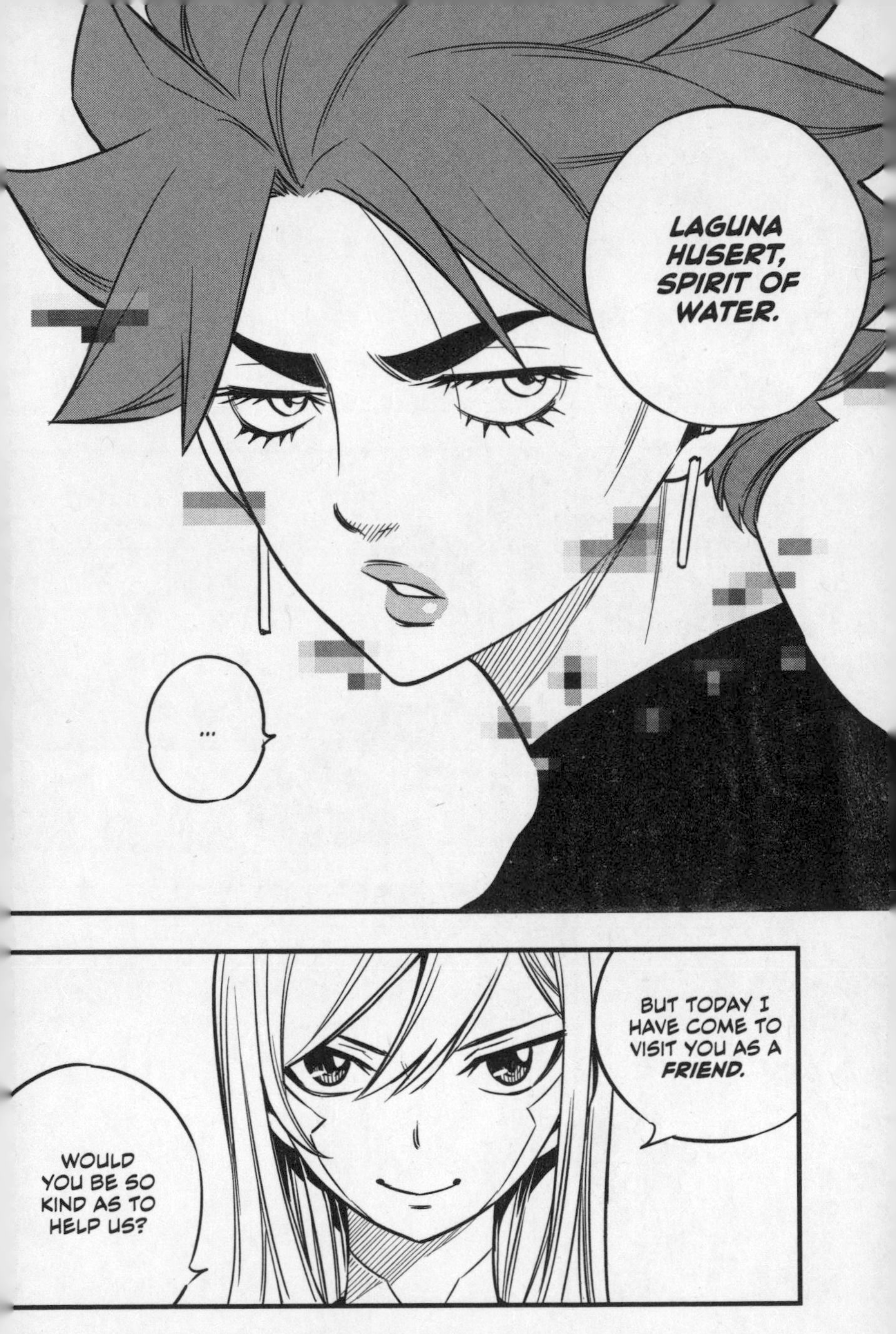
LAGUNA HUSERT, SPIRIT OF WATER.
...
BUT TODAY I HAVE COME TO VISIT YOU AS A FRIEND.
WOULD YOU BE SO KIND AS TO HELP US?

EDENS ZERO

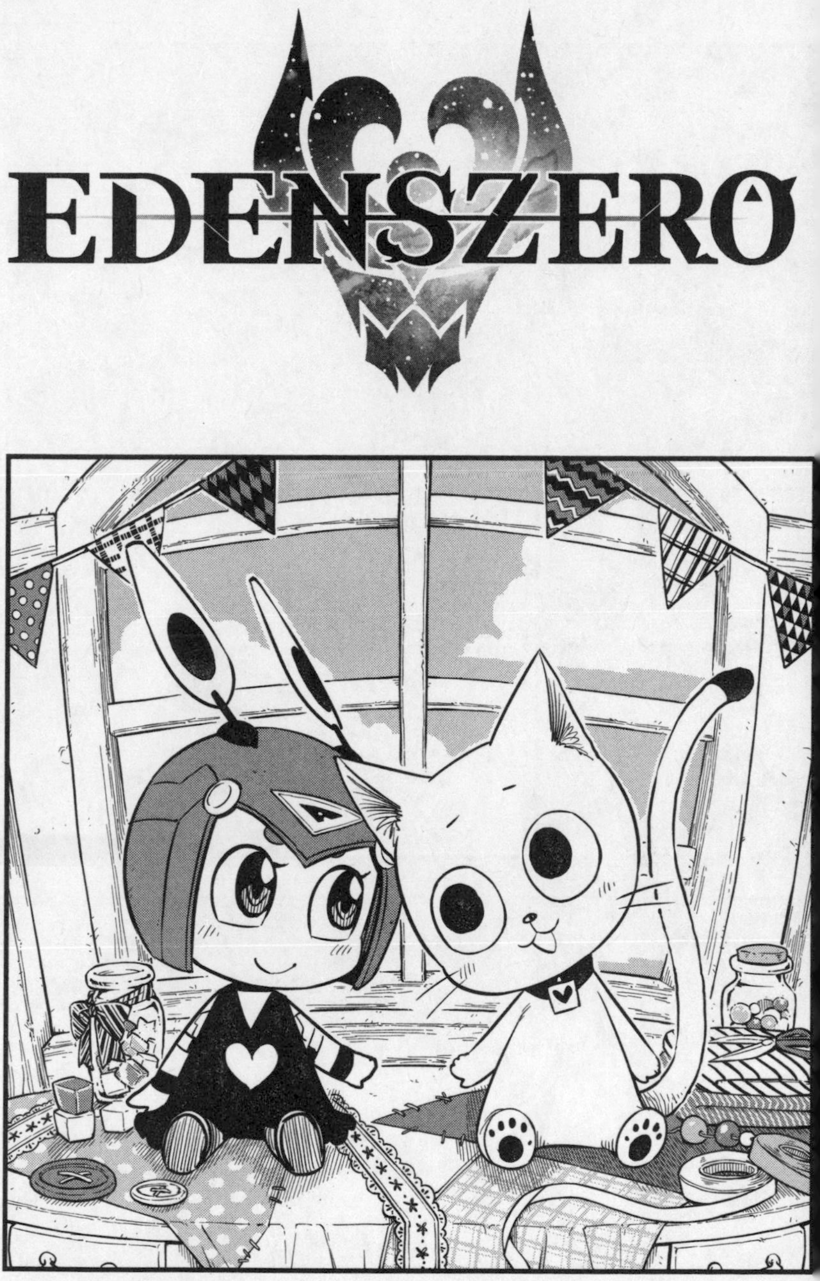

CHAPTER 110: A ROBOT IN LOVE

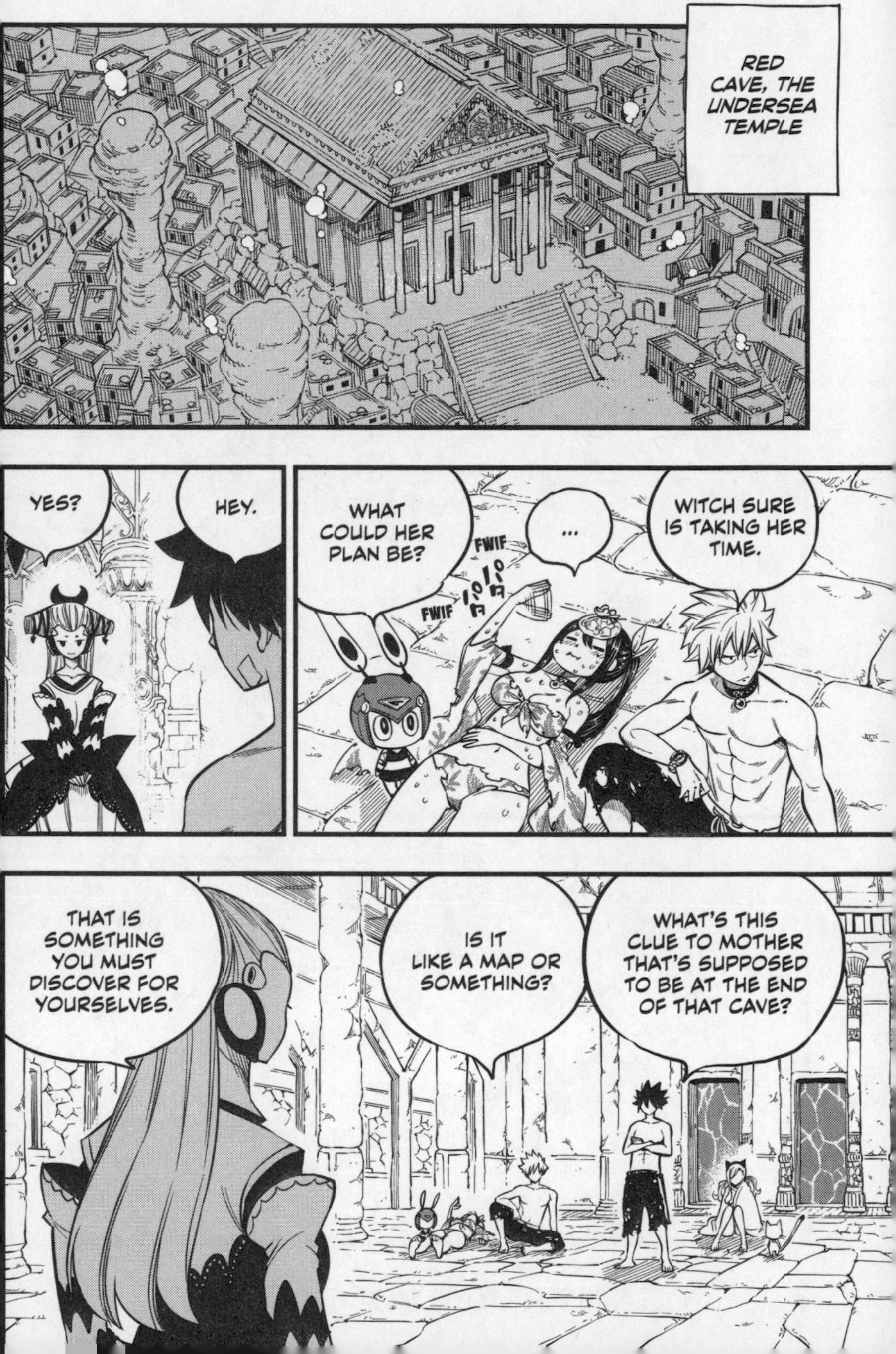
RED CAVE, THE UNDERSEA TEMPLE
WITCH SURE IS TAKING HER TIME.
...
WHAT COULD HER PLAN BE?
FWIF
FWIF
HEY.
YES?
WHAT'S THIS CLUE TO MOTHER THAT'S SUPPOSED TO BE AT THE END OF THAT CAVE?
IS IT LIKE A MAP OR SOMETHING?
THAT IS SOMETHING YOU MUST DISCOVER FOR YOURSELVES.

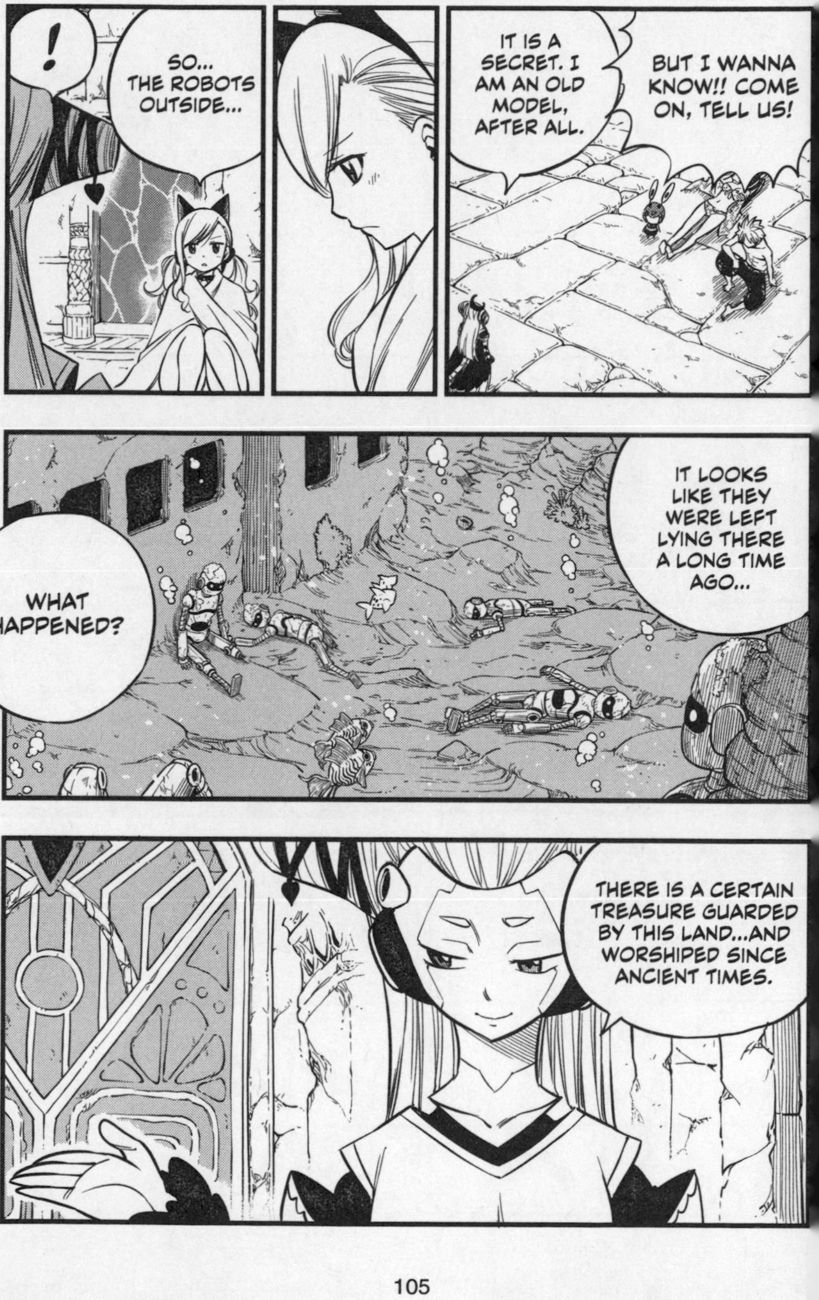
BUT I WANNA KNOW!! COME ON, TELL US!
IT IS A SECRET. I AM AN OLD MODEL, AFTER ALL.
SO... THE ROBOTS OUTSIDE...
!
IT LOOKS LIKE THEY WERE LEFT LYING THERE A LONG TIME AGO...
WHAT HAPPENED?
THERE IS A CERTAIN TREASURE GUARDED BY THIS LAND...AND WORSHIPED SINCE ANCIENT TIMES.

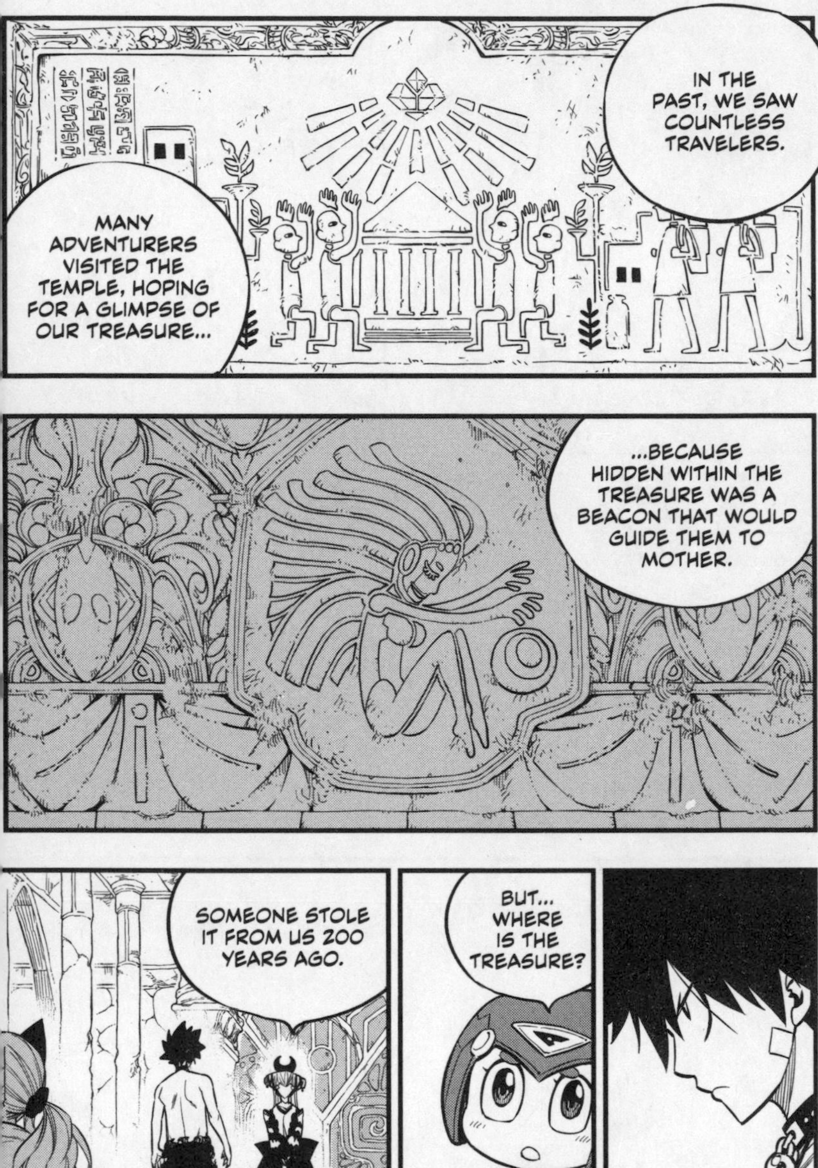
IN THE PAST, WE SAW COUNTLESS TRAVELERS.
MANY ADVENTURERS VISITED THE TEMPLE, HOPING FOR A GLIMPSE OF OUR TREASURE...
...BECAUSE HIDDEN WITHIN THE TREASURE WAS A BEACON THAT WOULD GUIDE THEM TO MOTHER.
BUT... WHERE IS THE TREASURE?
SOMEONE STOLE IT FROM US 200 YEARS AGO.

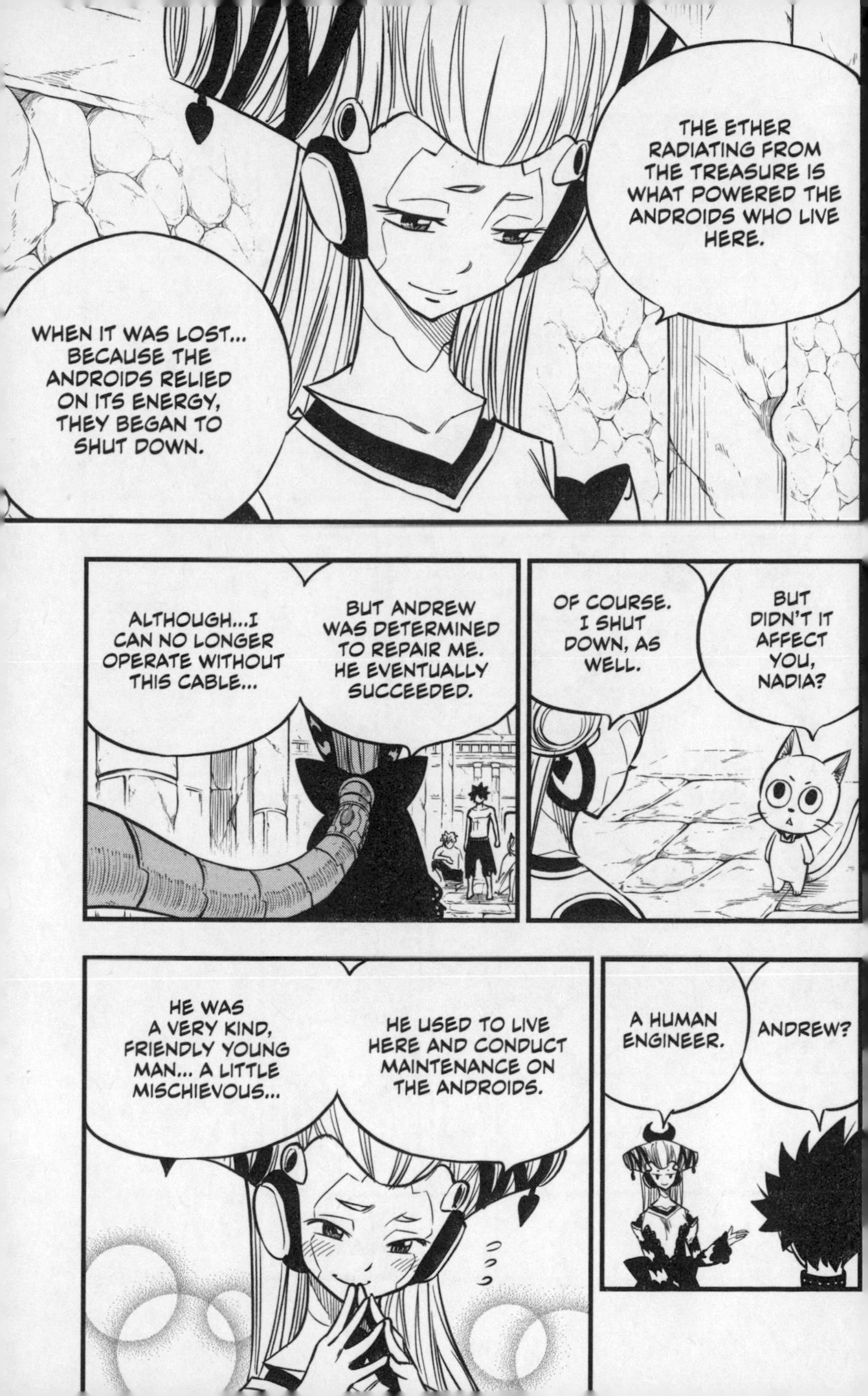
THE ETHER RADIATING FROM THE TREASURE IS WHAT POWERED THE ANDROIDS WHO LIVE HERE.
WHEN IT WAS LOST... BECAUSE THE ANDROIDS RELIED ON ITS ENERGY, THEY BEGAN TO SHUT DOWN.
BUT DIDN'T IT AFFECT YOU, NADIA?
OF COURSE. I SHUT DOWN, AS WELL.
BUT ANDREW WAS DETERMINED TO REPAIR ME. HE EVENTUALLY SUCCEEDED.
ALTHOUGH...I CAN NO LONGER OPERATE WITHOUT THIS CABLE...
ANDREW?
A HUMAN ENGINEER.
HE USED TO LIVE HERE AND CONDUCT MAINTENANCE ON THE ANDROIDS.
HE WAS A VERY KIND, FRIENDLY YOUNG MAN... A LITTLE MISCHIEVOUS...

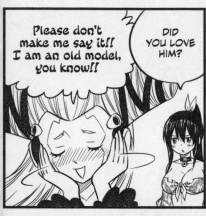

...
SPARKLE
SPARKLE
DID YOU LOVE HIM?
Please don't make me say it!! I am an old model, you know!!
A HUMAN AND AN ANDROID IN LOVE?
I SEE NOTHING WRONG WITH IT.
FINE. I'M FROM 50 YEARS AGO. I DON'T GET YOU YOUNG PEOPLE THESE DAYS.
SHE'S OLDER THAN YOU.
I am an old model! ♡
NADIA, LOVE OF MY LIFE.
Nadia love of my life
SO...WHAT HAPPENED TO ANDREW...?
HE SAID HE WOULD RETRIEVE THE TREASURE... AND HE LEFT OUR WORLD.

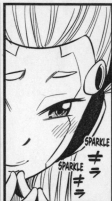

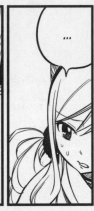

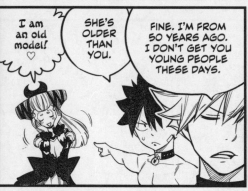

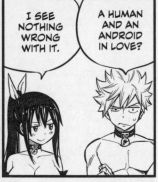

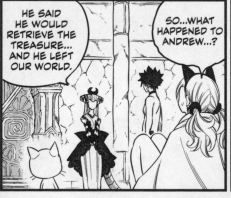

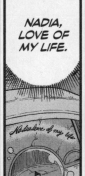

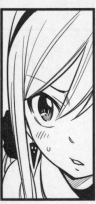

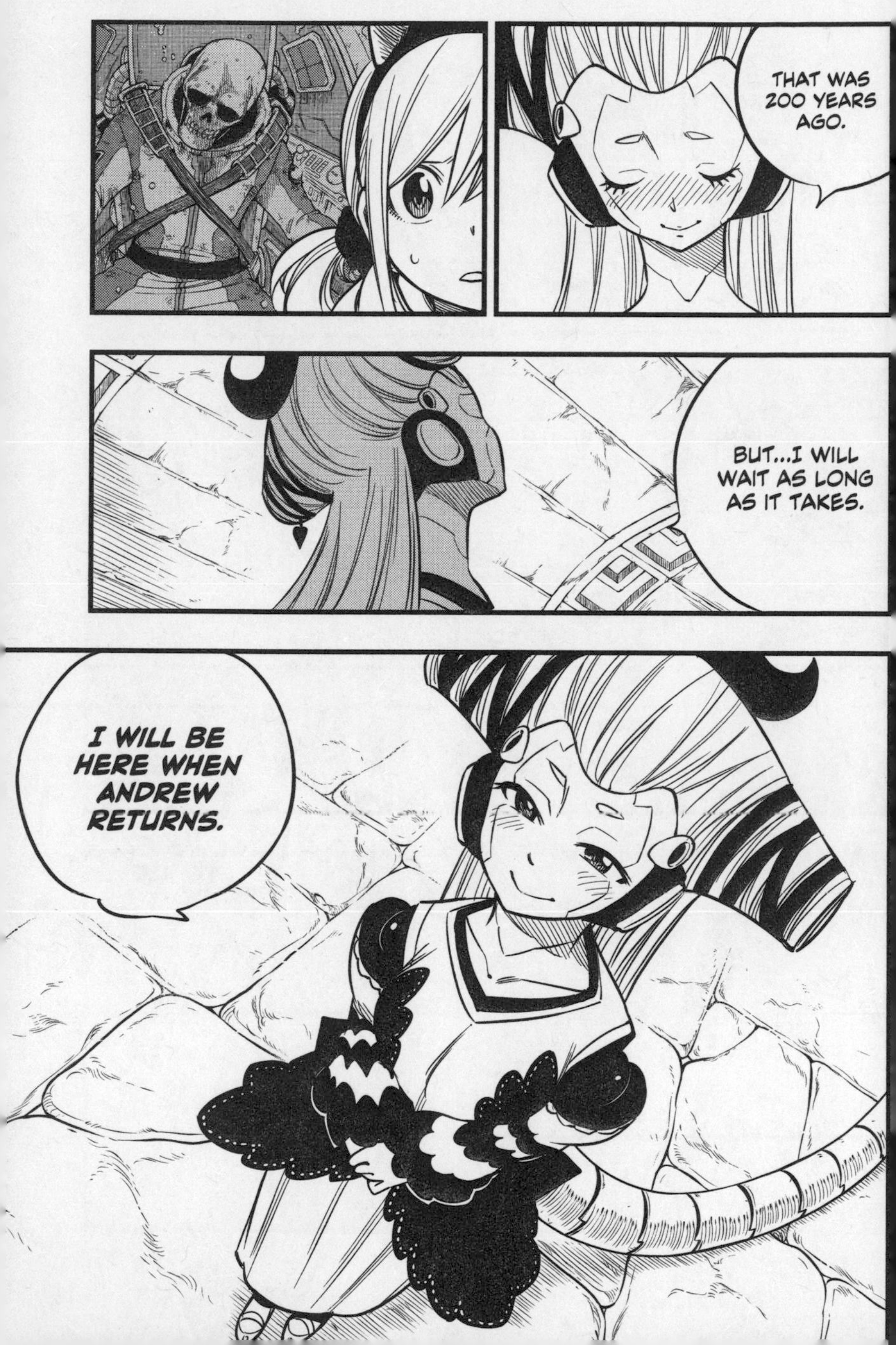
THAT WAS 200 YEARS AGO.
BUT...I WILL WAIT AS LONG AS IT TAKES.
I WILL BE HERE WHEN ANDREW RETURNS.

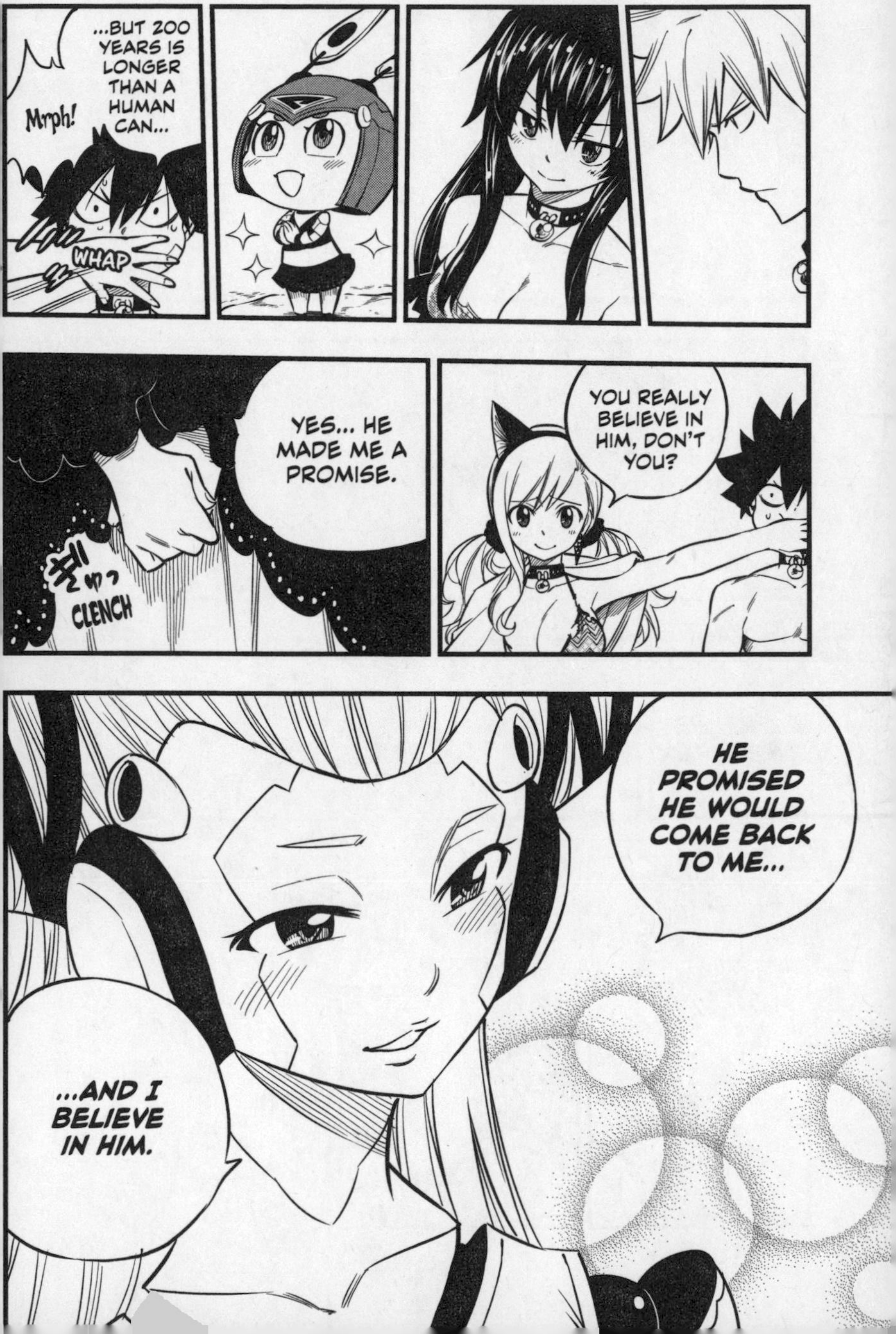
...BUT 200 YEARS IS LONGER THAN A HUMAN CAN...
Mrph!
WHAP
YOU REALLY BELIEVE IN HIM, DON'T YOU?
YES... HE MADE ME A PROMISE.
CLENCH
HE PROMISED HE WOULD COME BACK TO ME...
...AND I BELIEVE IN HIM.

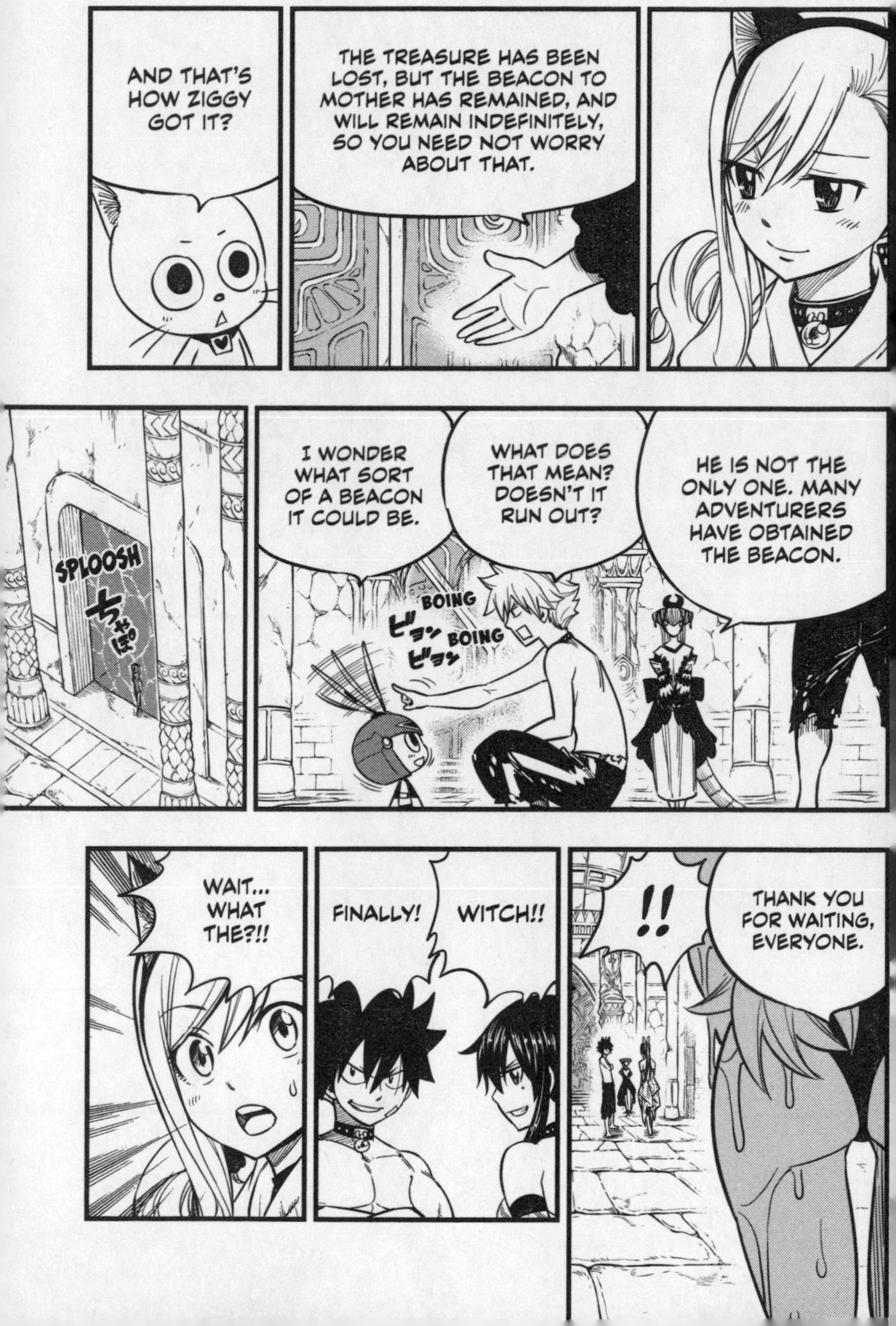
THE TREASURE HAS BEEN LOST, BUT THE BEACON TO MOTHER HAS REMAINED, AND WILL REMAIN INDEFINITELY, SO YOU NEED NOT WORRY ABOUT THAT.
AND THAT'S HOW ZIGGY GOT IT?
HE IS NOT THE ONLY ONE. MANY ADVENTURERS HAVE OBTAINED THE BEACON.
WHAT DOES THAT MEAN? DOESN'T IT RUN OUT?
I WONDER WHAT SORT OF A BEACON IT COULD BE.
BOING
ビョン
BOING
ビョン
SPLOOSH
ちゃぽ
THANK YOU FOR WAITING, EVERYONE.
!!
WITCH!!
FINALLY!
WAIT... WHAT THE?!!

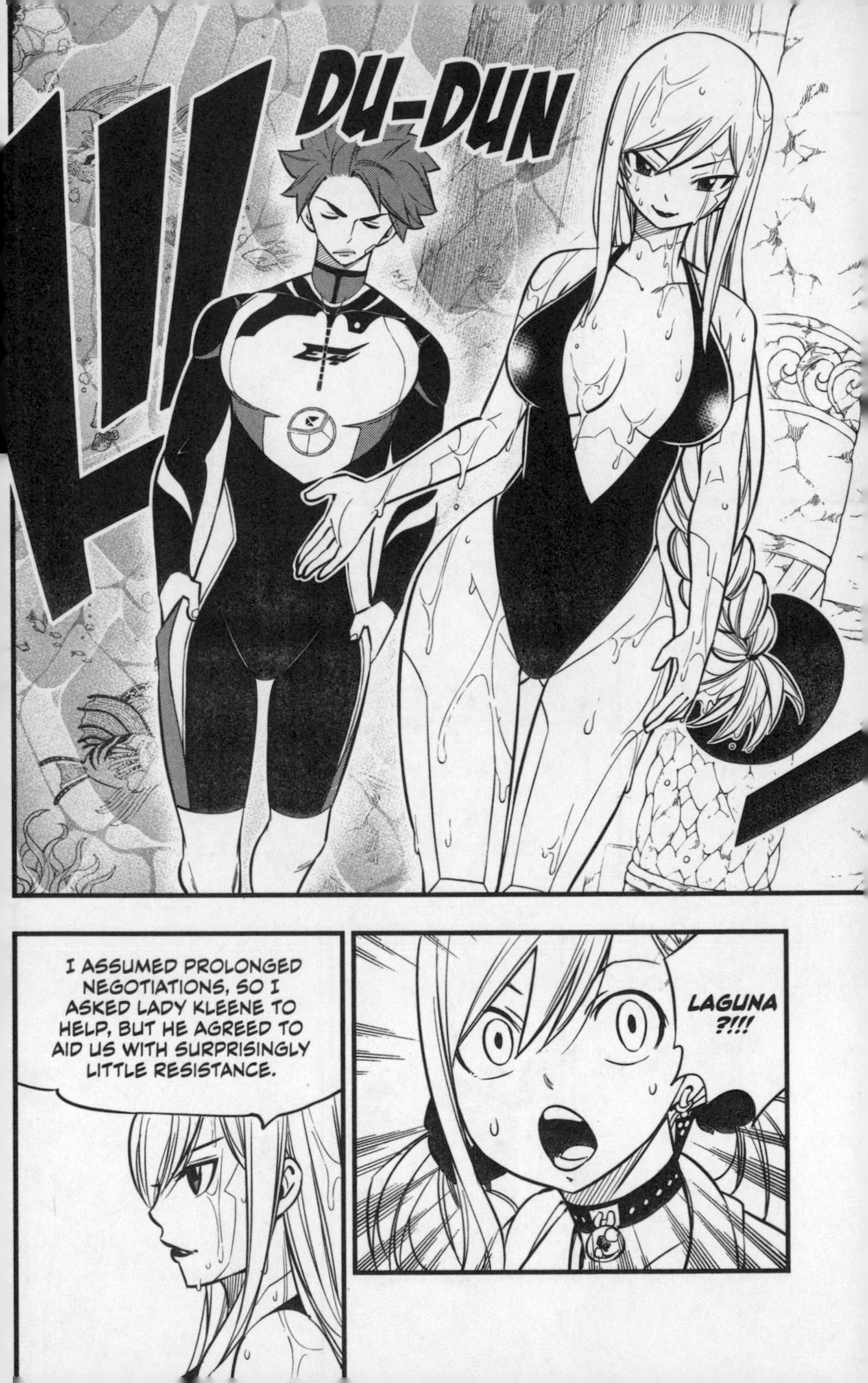
DU-DUN
LAGUNA ?!!!
I ASSUMED PROLONGED NEGOTIATIONS, SO I ASKED LADY KLEENE TO HELP, BUT HE AGREED TO AID US WITH SURPRISINGLY LITTLE RESISTANCE.

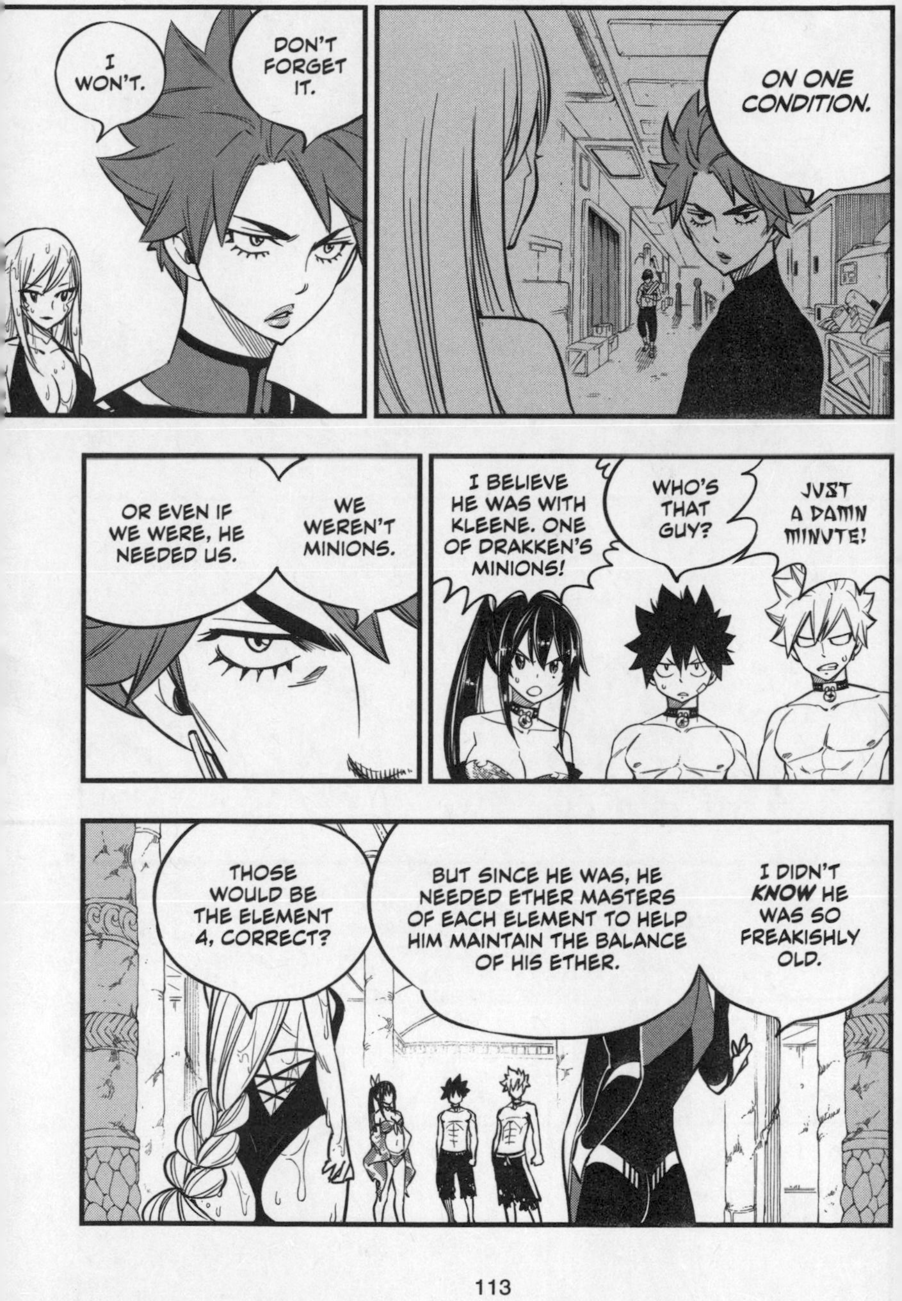
ON ONE CONDITION.
DON'T FORGET IT.
I WON'T.
JUST A DAMN MINUTE!
WHO'S THAT GUY?
I BELIEVE HE WAS WITH KLEENE. ONE OF DRAKKEN'S MINIONS!
WE WEREN'T MINIONS.
OR EVEN IF WE WERE, HE NEEDED US.
I DIDN'T *KNOW* HE WAS SO FREAKISHLY OLD.
BUT SINCE HE WAS, HE NEEDED ETHER MASTERS OF EACH ELEMENT TO HELP HIM MAINTAIN THE BALANCE OF HIS ETHER.
THOSE WOULD BE THE ELEMENT 4, CORRECT?

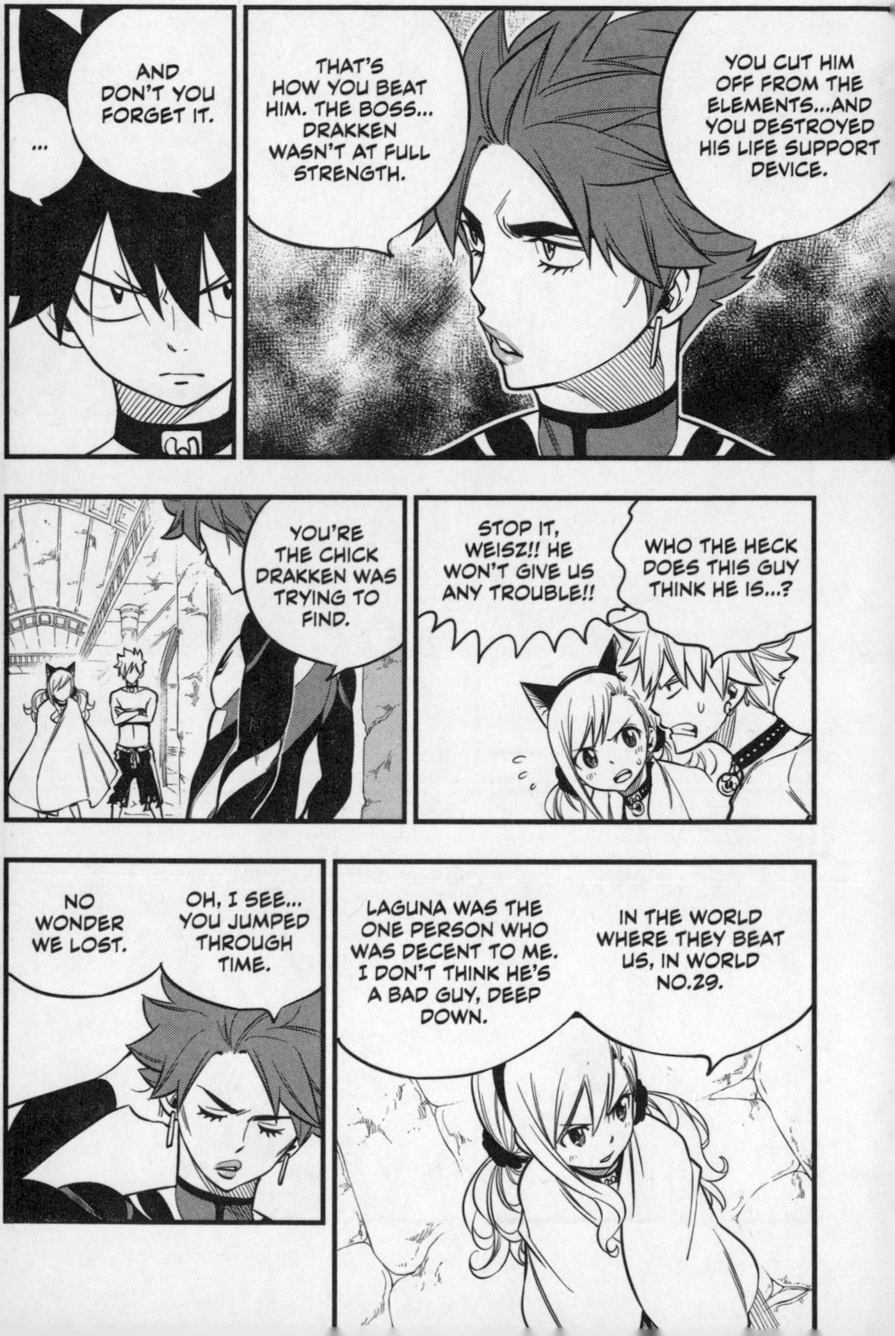
YOU CUT HIM OFF FROM THE ELEMENTS...AND YOU DESTROYED HIS LIFE SUPPORT DEVICE.
THAT'S HOW YOU BEAT HIM. THE BOSS... DRAKKEN WASN'T AT FULL STRENGTH.
AND DON'T YOU FORGET IT.
...
WHO THE HECK DOES THIS GUY THINK HE IS...?
STOP IT, WEISZ!! HE WON'T GIVE US ANY TROUBLE!!
YOU'RE THE CHICK DRAKKEN WAS TRYING TO FIND.
IN THE WORLD WHERE THEY BEAT US, IN WORLD NO.29.
LAGUNA WAS THE ONE PERSON WHO WAS DECENT TO ME. I DON'T THINK HE'S A BAD GUY, DEEP DOWN.
OH, I SEE... YOU JUMPED THROUGH TIME.
NO WONDER WE LOST.

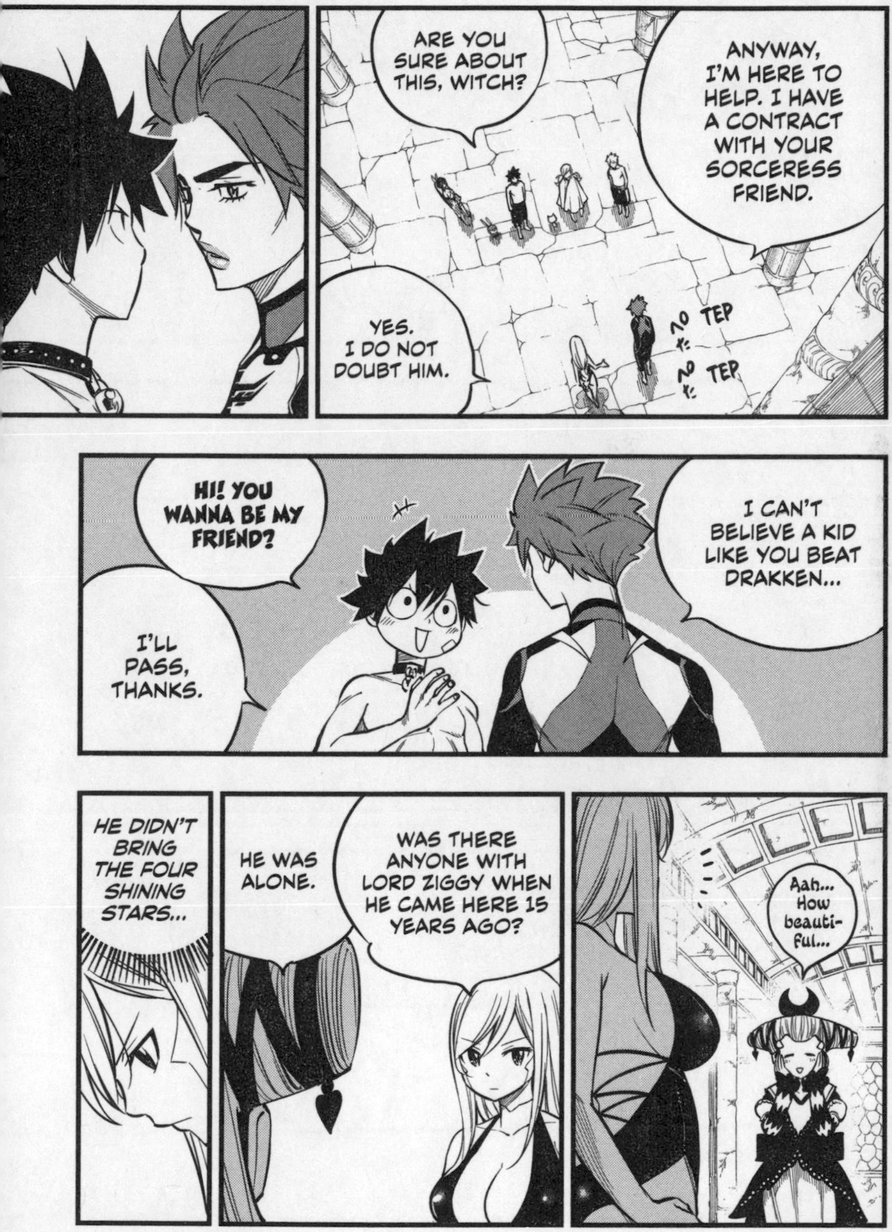
ANYWAY, I'M HERE TO HELP. I HAVE A CONTRACT WITH YOUR SORCERESS FRIEND.
ARE YOU SURE ABOUT THIS, WITCH?
TEP
TEP
YES. I DO NOT DOUBT HIM.
I CAN'T BELIEVE A KID LIKE YOU BEAT DRAKKEN...
HI! YOU WANNA BE MY FRIEND?
I'LL PASS, THANKS.
Aah... How beautiful...
...
WAS THERE ANYONE WITH LORD ZIGGY WHEN HE CAME HERE 15 YEARS AGO?
HE WAS ALONE.
HE DIDN'T BRING THE FOUR SHINING STARS...

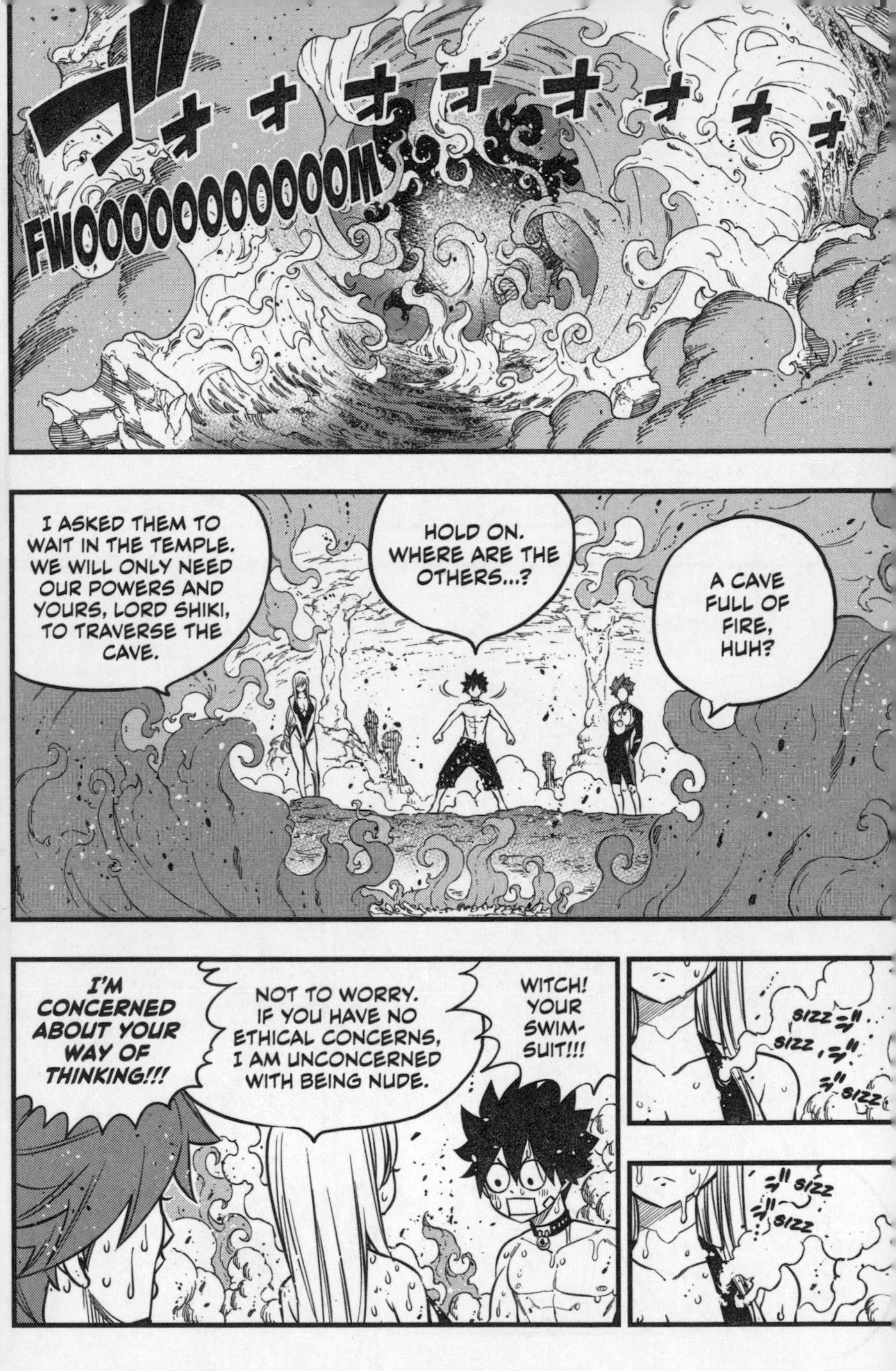
FWOOOOOOOOOOM
A CAVE FULL OF FIRE, HUH?
HOLD ON. WHERE ARE THE OTHERS...?
I ASKED THEM TO WAIT IN THE TEMPLE. WE WILL ONLY NEED OUR POWERS AND YOURS, LORD SHIKI, TO TRAVERSE THE CAVE.
SIZZ
SIZZ
SIZZ
SIZZ
SIZZ
WITCH! YOUR SWIM-SUIT!!!
NOT TO WORRY. IF YOU HAVE NO ETHICAL CONCERNS, I AM UNCONCERNED WITH BEING NUDE.
I'M CONCERNED ABOUT YOUR WAY OF THINKING!!!

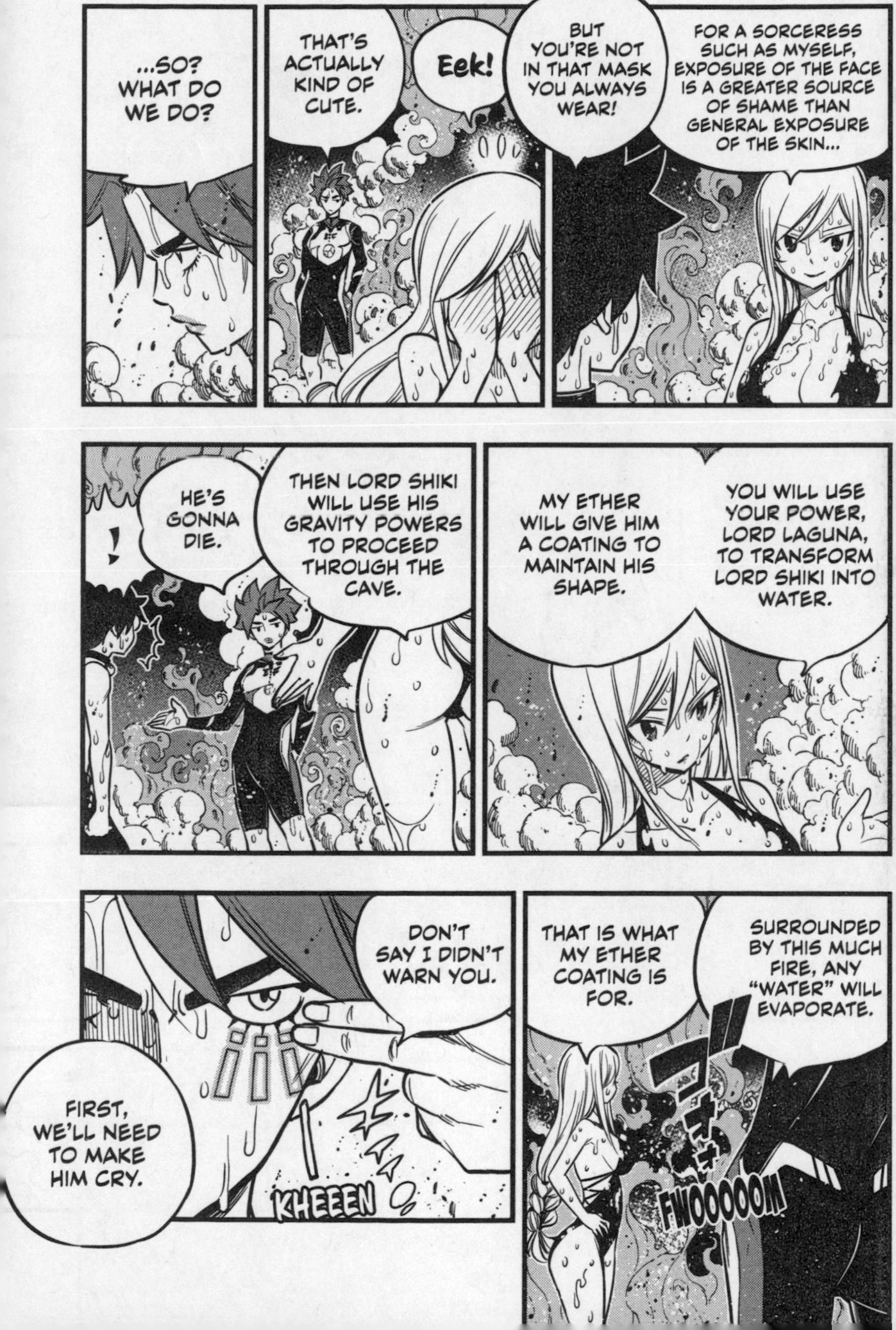
FOR A SORCERESS SUCH AS MYSELF, EXPOSURE OF THE FACE IS A GREATER SOURCE OF SHAME THAN GENERAL EXPOSURE OF THE SKIN...
BUT YOU'RE NOT IN THAT MASK YOU ALWAYS WEAR!
Eek!
THAT'S ACTUALLY KIND OF CUTE.
...SO? WHAT DO WE DO?
YOU WILL USE YOUR POWER, LORD LAGUNA, TO TRANSFORM LORD SHIKI INTO WATER.
MY ETHER WILL GIVE HIM A COATING TO MAINTAIN HIS SHAPE.
THEN LORD SHIKI WILL USE HIS GRAVITY POWERS TO PROCEED THROUGH THE CAVE.
HE'S GONNA DIE.
!
SURROUNDED BY THIS MUCH FIRE, ANY "WATER" WILL EVAPORATE.
THAT IS WHAT MY ETHER COATING IS FOR.
FWOOOOOM
DON'T SAY I DIDN'T WARN YOU.
KHEEEN
FIRST, WE'LL NEED TO MAKE HIM CRY.

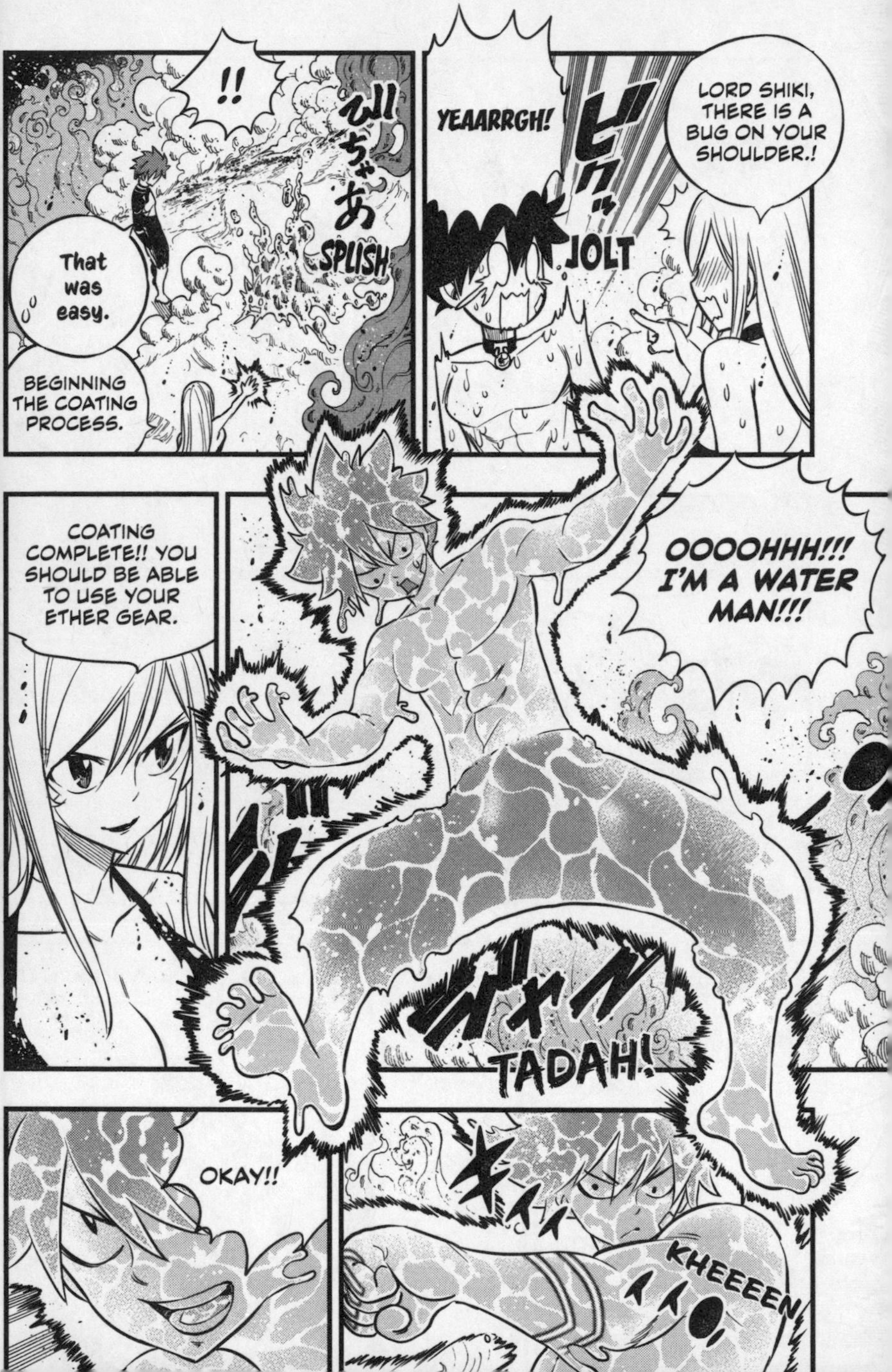
LORD SHIKI, THERE IS A BUG ON YOUR SHOULDER.!
ビクッ
JOLT
YEAARRGH!
!!
びちゃあ
SPLISH
That was easy.
BEGINNING THE COATING PROCESS.
OOOOHHH!!! I'M A WATER MAN!!!
TADAH!
COATING COMPLETE!! YOU SHOULD BE ABLE TO USE YOUR ETHER GEAR.
KHEEEEN
OKAY!!

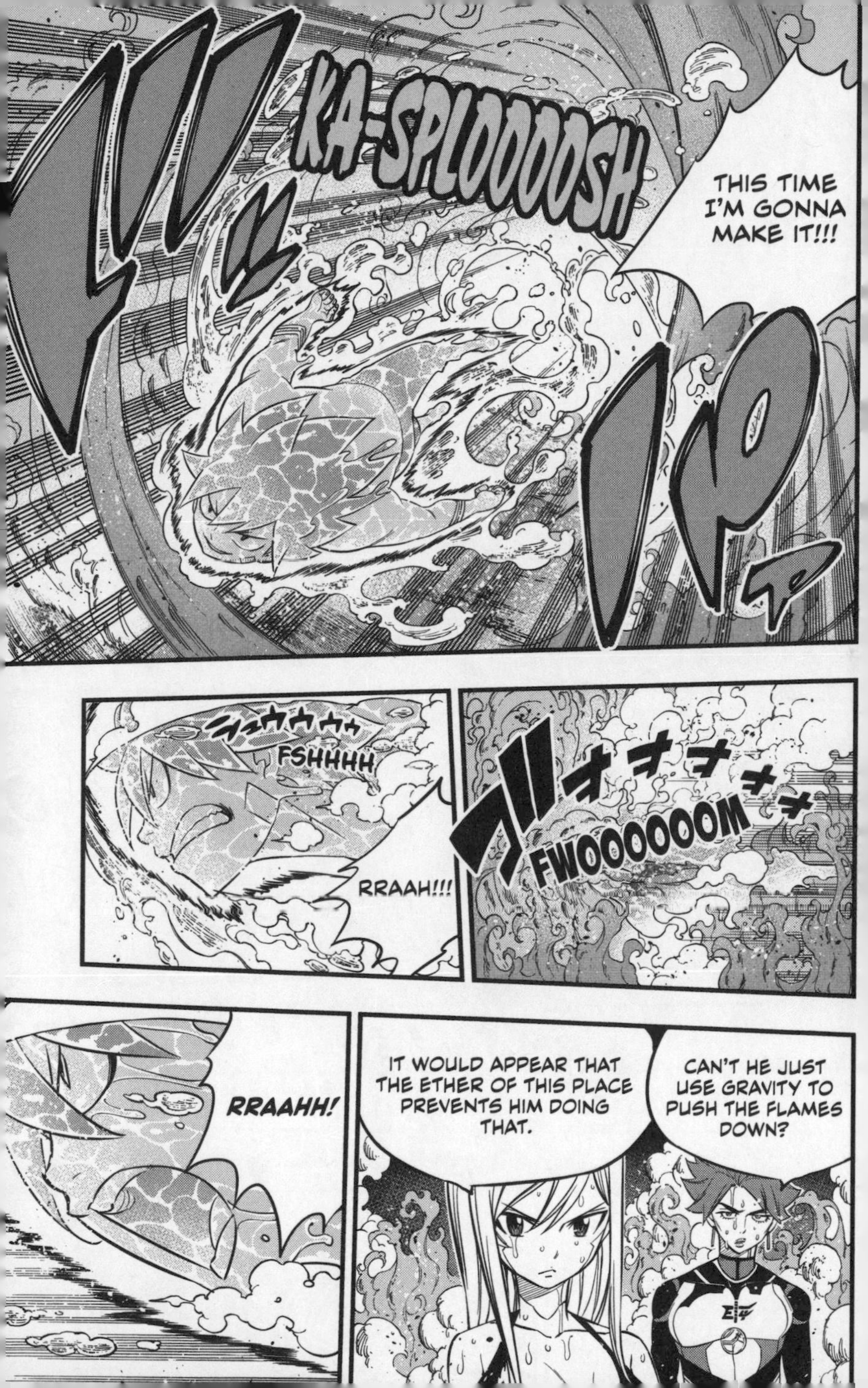
THIS TIME I'M GONNA MAKE IT!!!
KA-SPLOOOOOSH
FWOOOOOOM
FSHHHHH
RRAAH!!!
CAN'T HE JUST USE GRAVITY TO PUSH THE FLAMES DOWN?
IT WOULD APPEAR THAT THE ETHER OF THIS PLACE PREVENTS HIM DOING THAT.
RRAAHH!

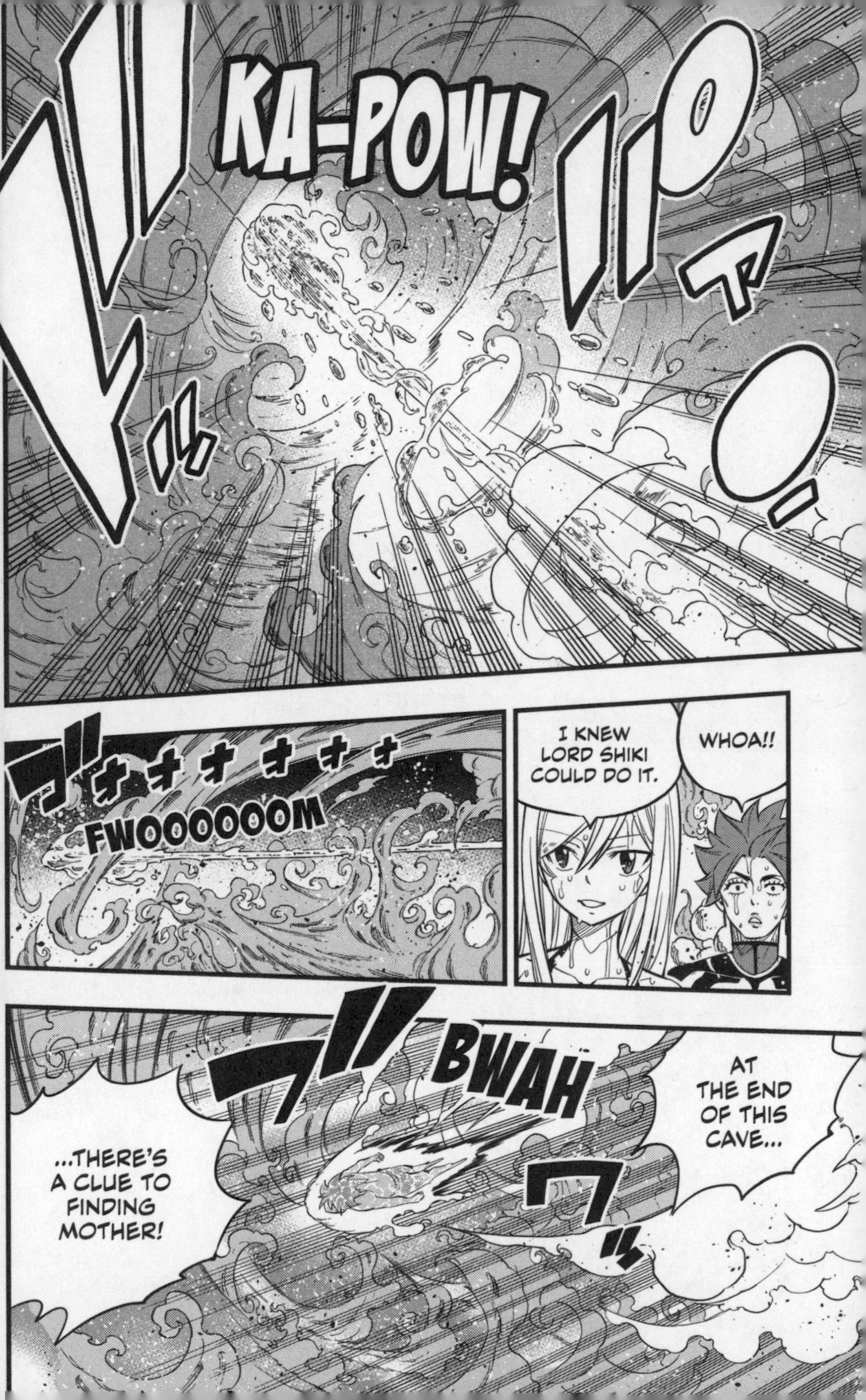
KA-POW!
WHOA!!
I KNEW LORD SHIKI COULD DO IT.
FWOOOOOOM
BWAH
AT THE END OF THIS CAVE...
...THERE'S A CLUE TO FINDING MOTHER!

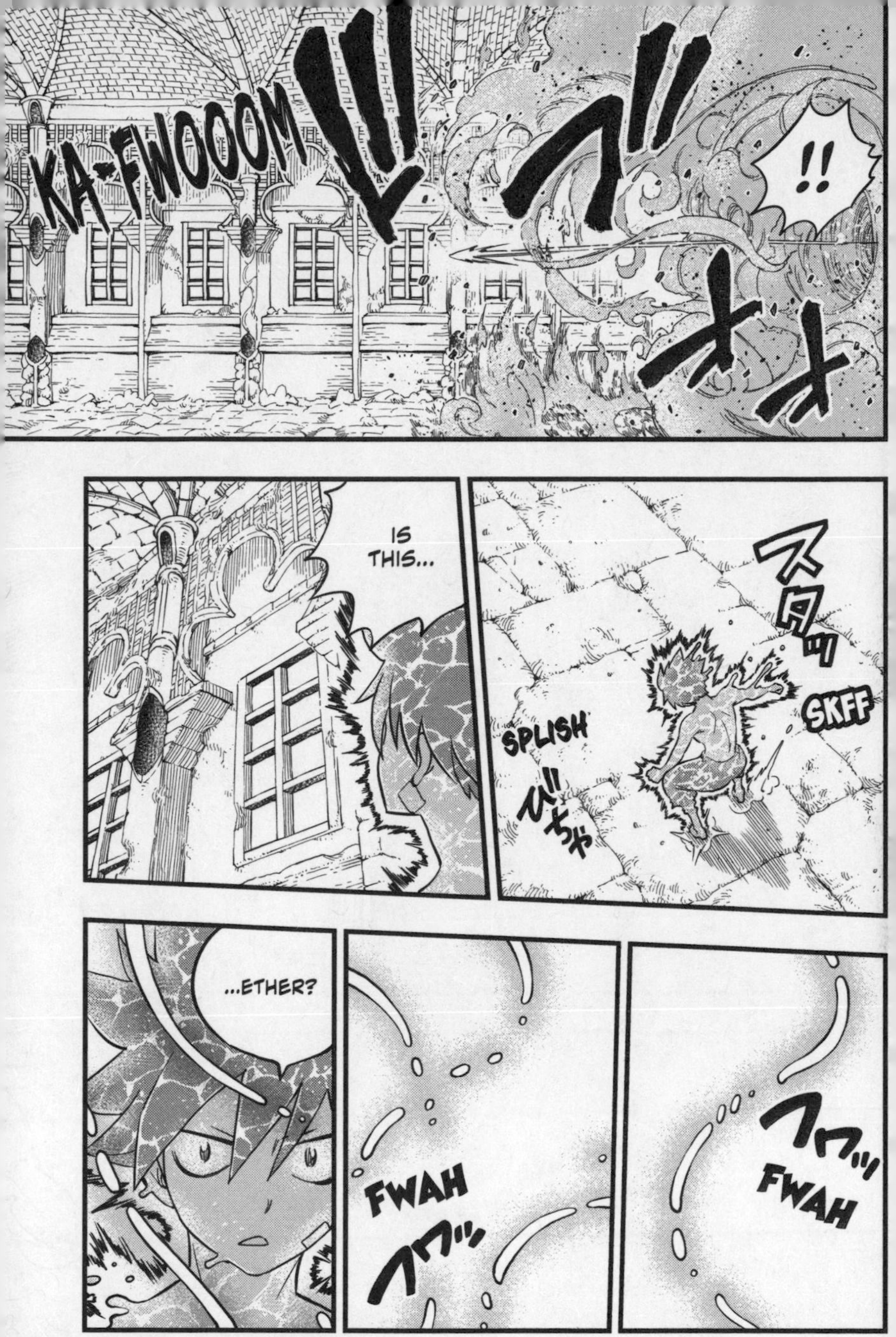

!!
KA-FWOOM!!!
スタッ
SKFF
SPLISH
びちゃ
IS THIS...
ふわッ
FWAH
FWAH
ふわッ
...ETHER?

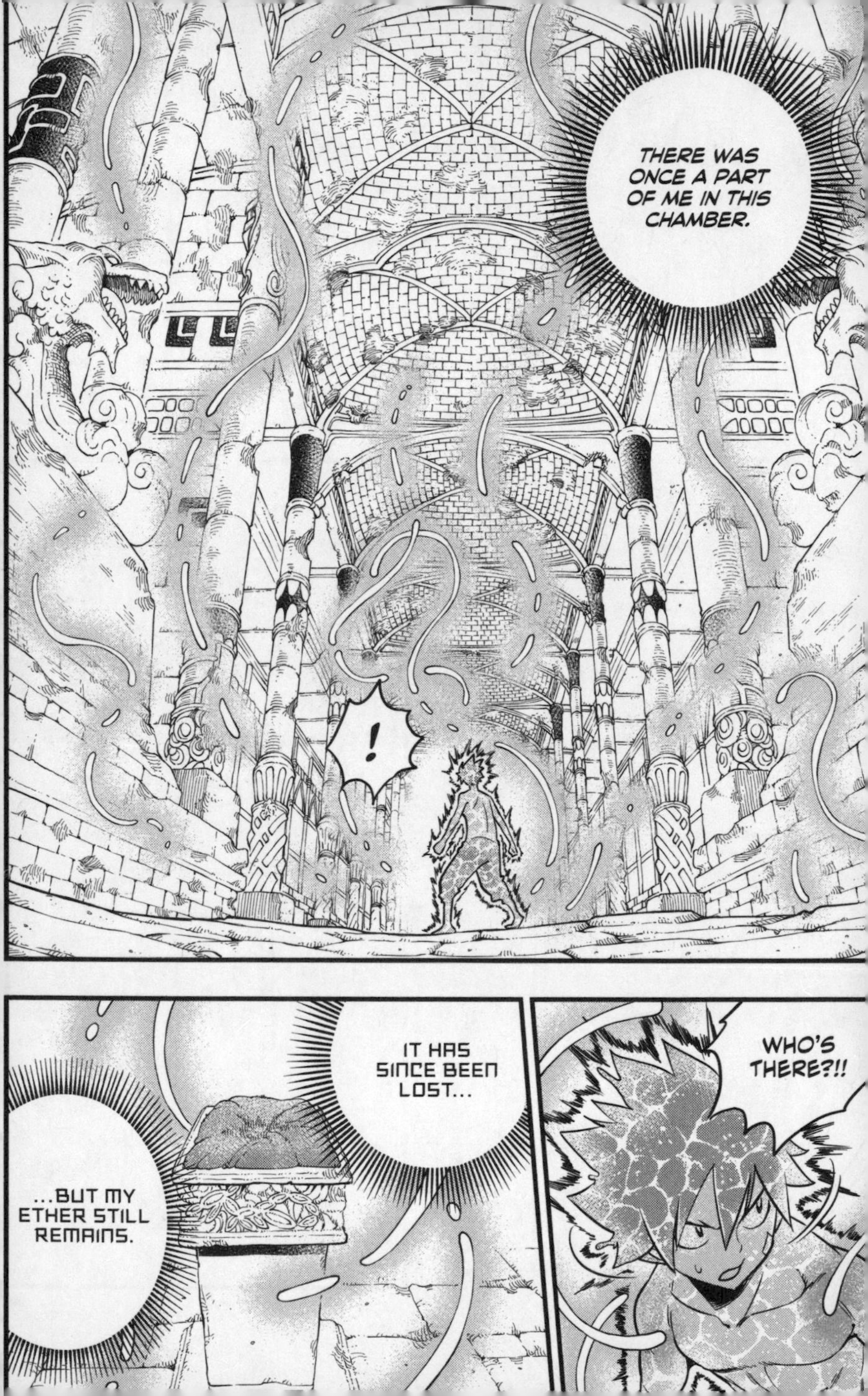
THERE WAS ONCE A PART OF ME IN THIS CHAMBER.
!
WHO'S THERE?!!
IT HAS SINCE BEEN LOST...
...BUT MY ETHER STILL REMAINS.

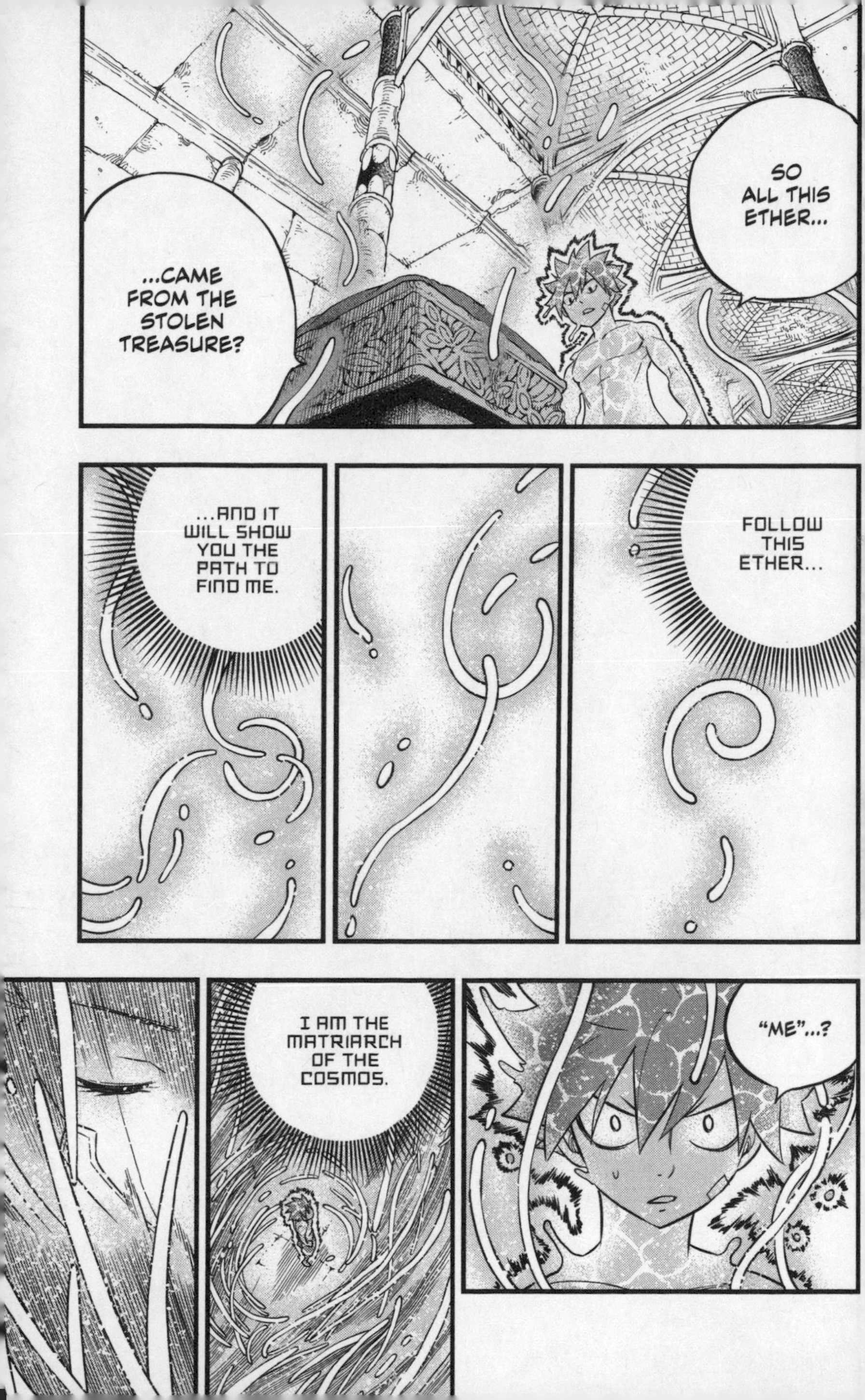
SO ALL THIS ETHER...
...CAME FROM THE STOLEN TREASURE?
FOLLOW THIS ETHER...
...AND IT WILL SHOW YOU THE PATH TO FIND ME.
“ME”...?
I AM THE MATRIARCH OF THE COSMOS.

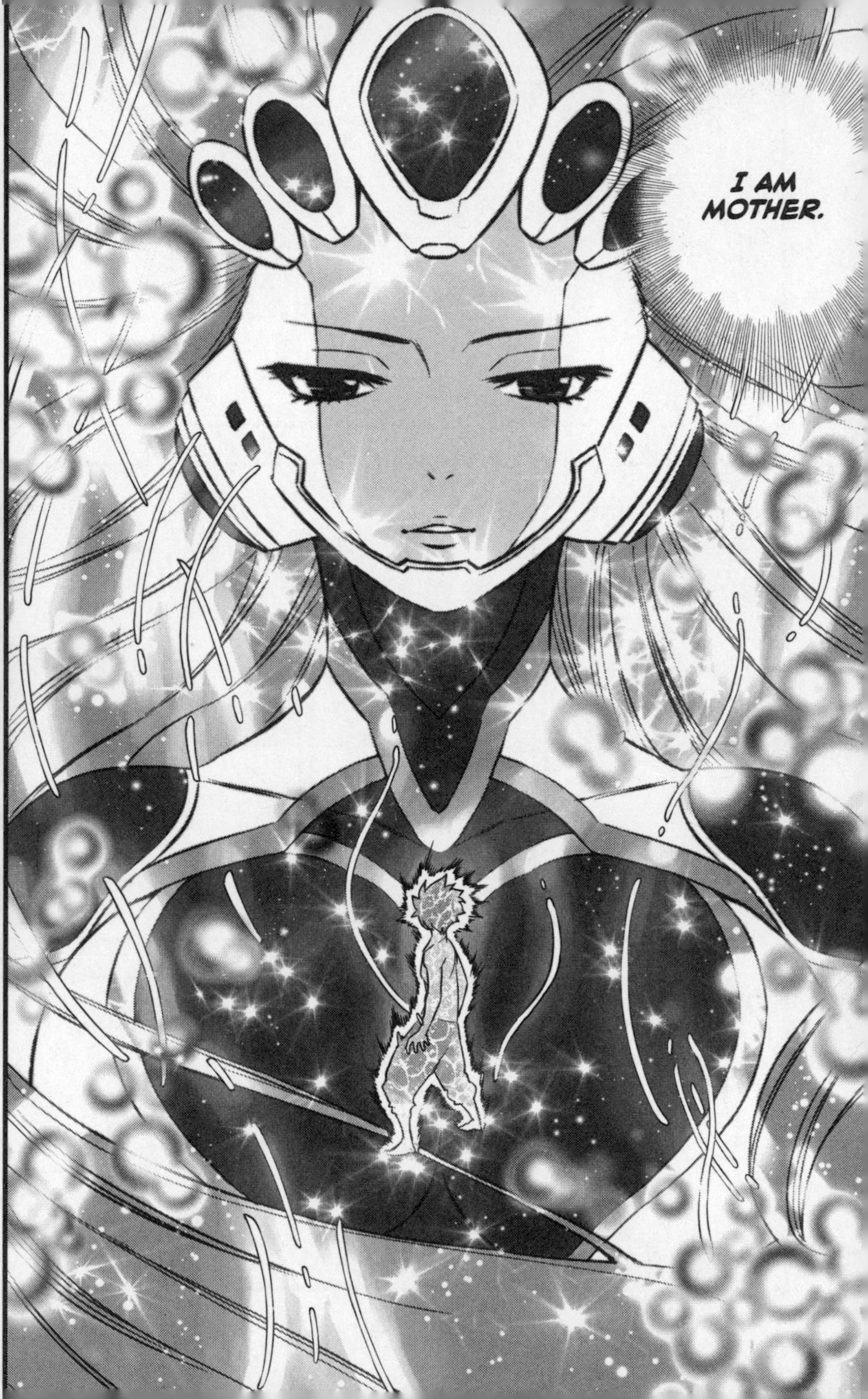
I AM MOTHER.

EDENS ZERO

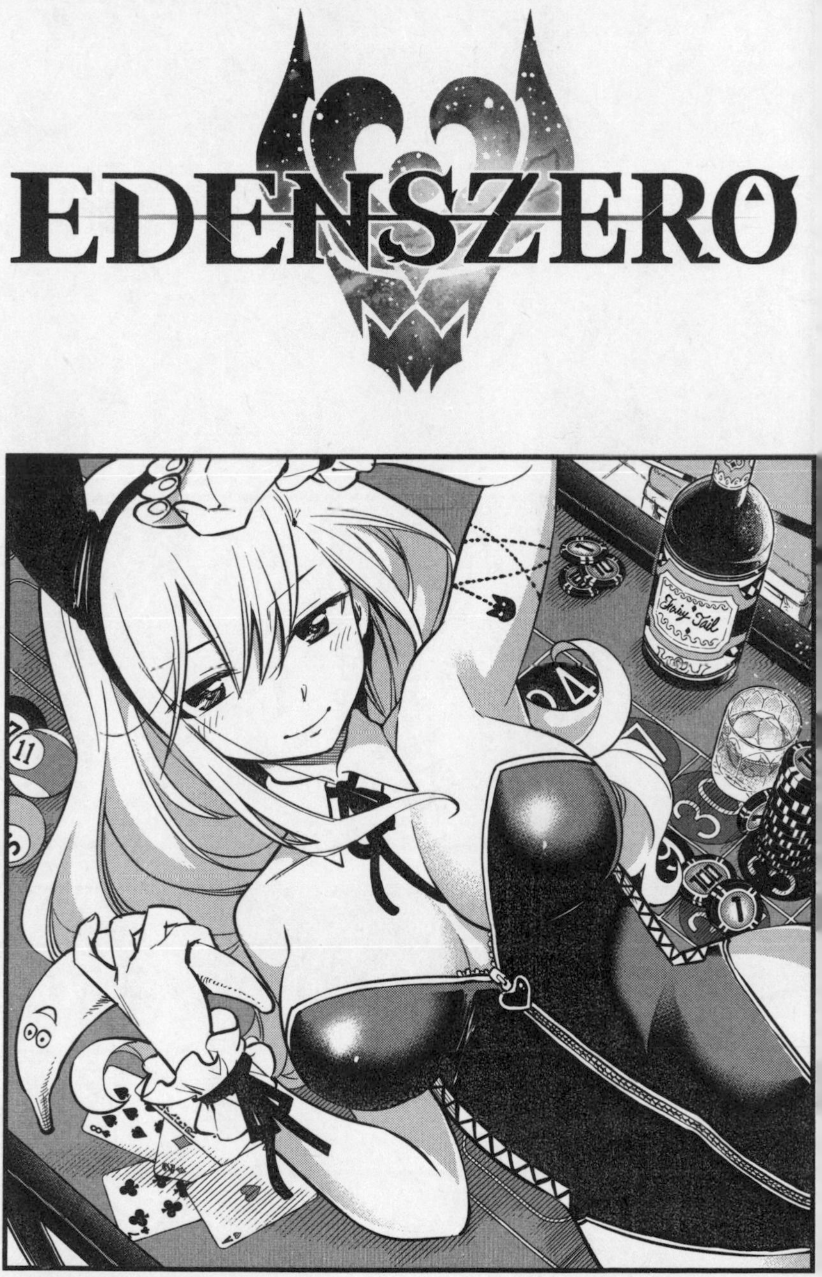
Fairy Tail

CHAPTER 111: THE SKY OF DAYS LONG PAST

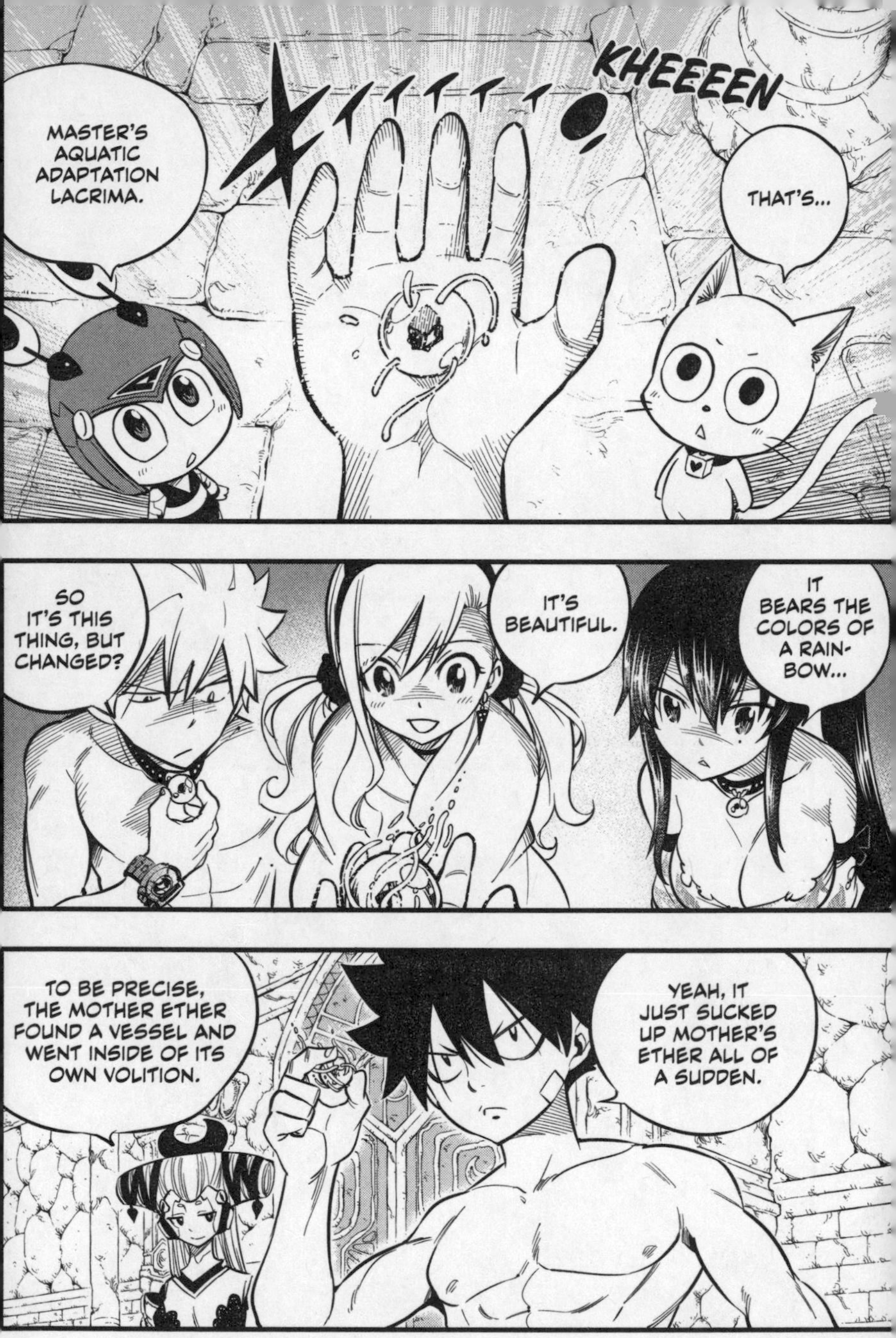
KHEEEEN
THAT'S...
MASTER'S AQUATIC ADAPTATION LACRIMA.
IT BEARS THE COLORS OF A RAIN-BOW...
IT'S BEAUTIFUL.
SO IT'S THIS THING, BUT CHANGED?
YEAH, IT JUST SUCKED UP MOTHER'S ETHER ALL OF A SUDDEN.
TO BE PRECISE, THE MOTHER ETHER FOUND A VESSEL AND WENT INSIDE OF ITS OWN VOLITION.

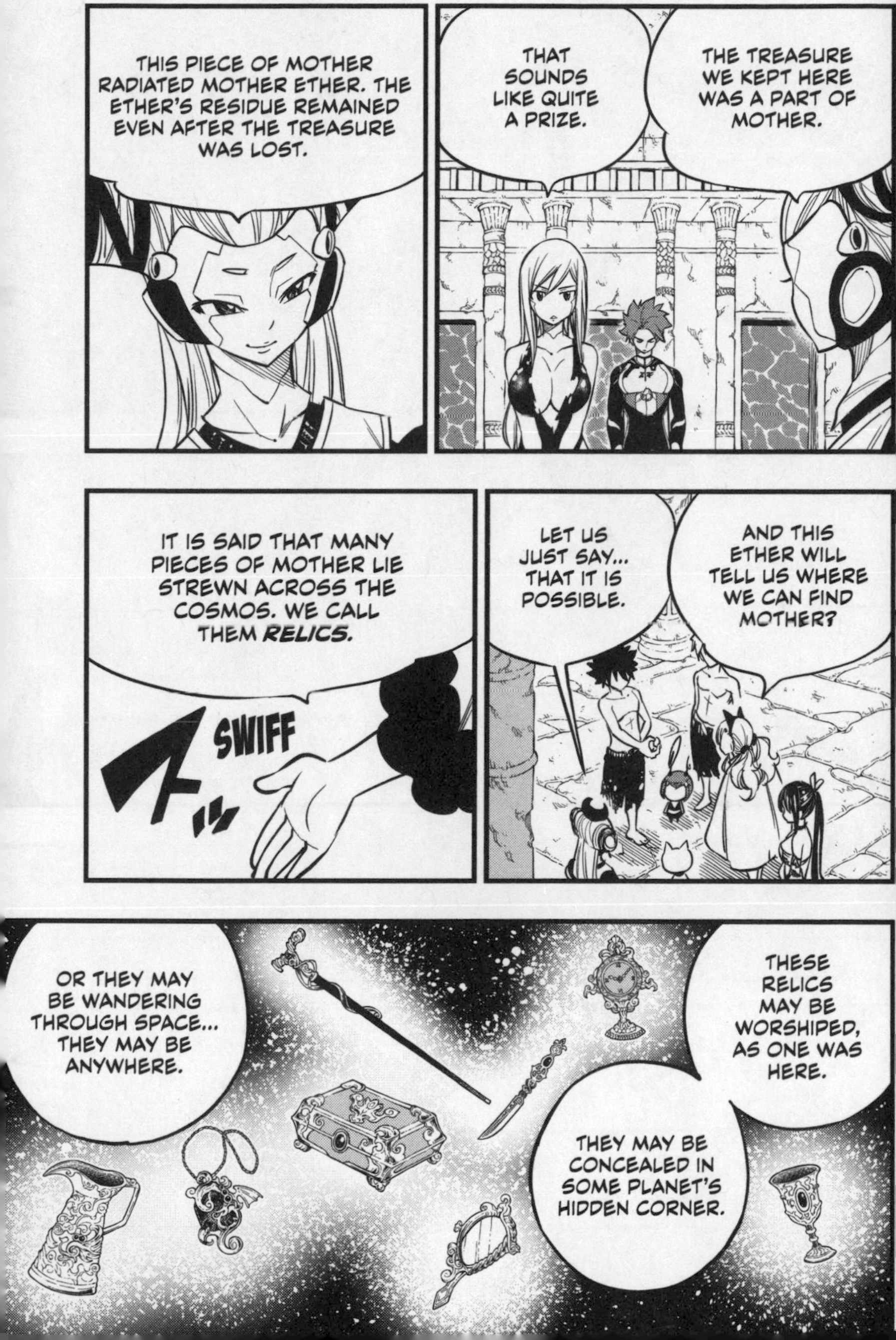
THE TREASURE WE KEPT HERE WAS A PART OF MOTHER.
THAT SOUNDS LIKE QUITE A PRIZE.
THIS PIECE OF MOTHER RADIATED MOTHER ETHER. THE ETHER'S RESIDUE REMAINED EVEN AFTER THE TREASURE WAS LOST.
AND THIS ETHER WILL TELL US WHERE WE CAN FIND MOTHER?
LET US JUST SAY... THAT IT IS POSSIBLE.
IT IS SAID THAT MANY PIECES OF MOTHER LIE STREWN ACROSS THE COSMOS. WE CALL THEM *RELICS.*
SWIFF
THESE RELICS MAY BE WORSHIPED, AS ONE WAS HERE.
THEY MAY BE CONCEALED IN SOME PLANET'S HIDDEN CORNER.
OR THEY MAY BE WANDERING THROUGH SPACE... THEY MAY BE ANYWHERE.

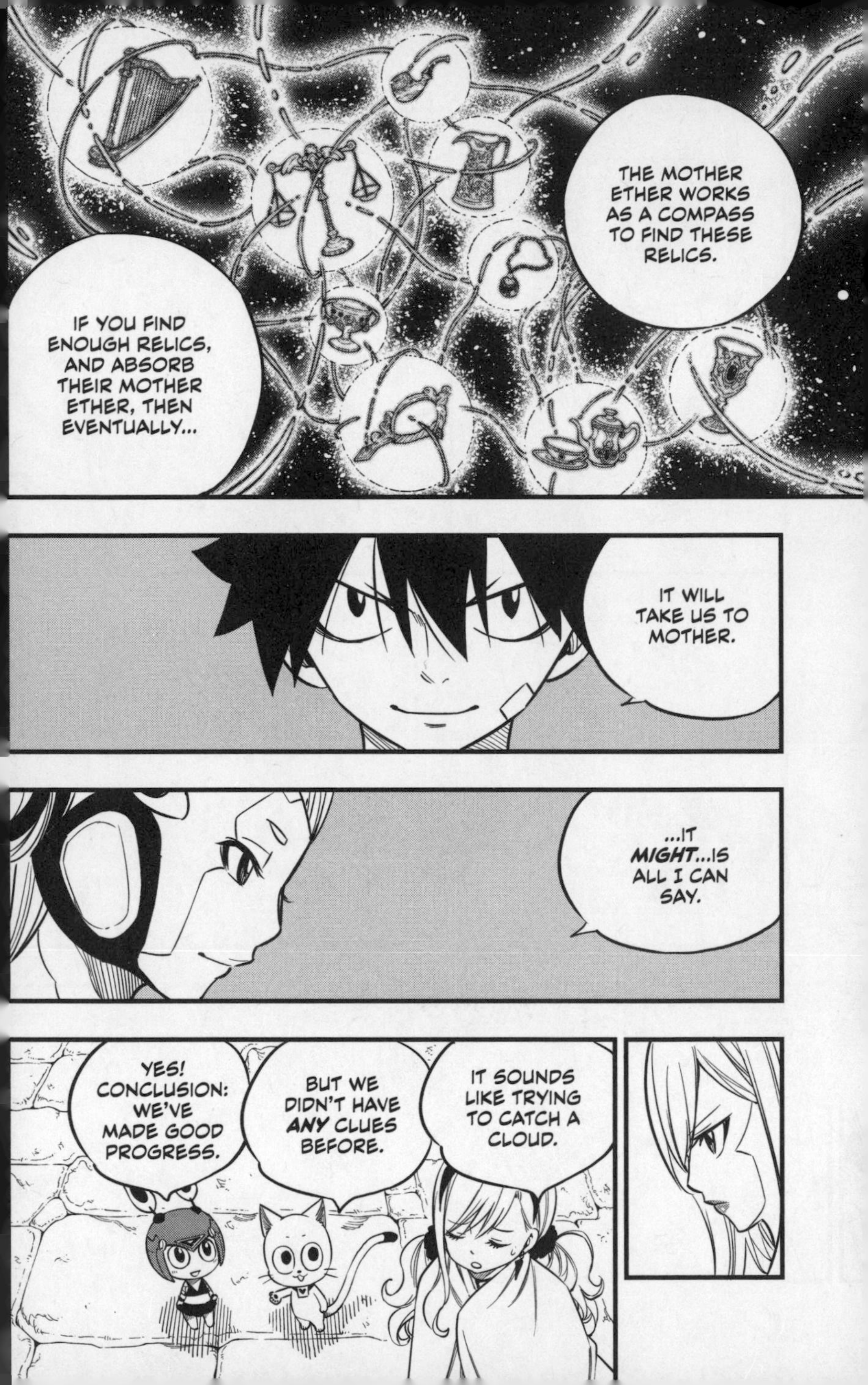
THE MOTHER ETHER WORKS AS A COMPASS TO FIND THESE RELICS.
IF YOU FIND ENOUGH RELICS, AND ABSORB THEIR MOTHER ETHER, THEN EVENTUALLY...
IT WILL TAKE US TO MOTHER.
...IT *MIGHT*...IS ALL I CAN SAY.
IT SOUNDS LIKE TRYING TO CATCH A CLOUD.
BUT WE DIDN'T HAVE *ANY* CLUES BEFORE.
YES! CONCLUSION: WE'VE MADE GOOD PROGRESS.

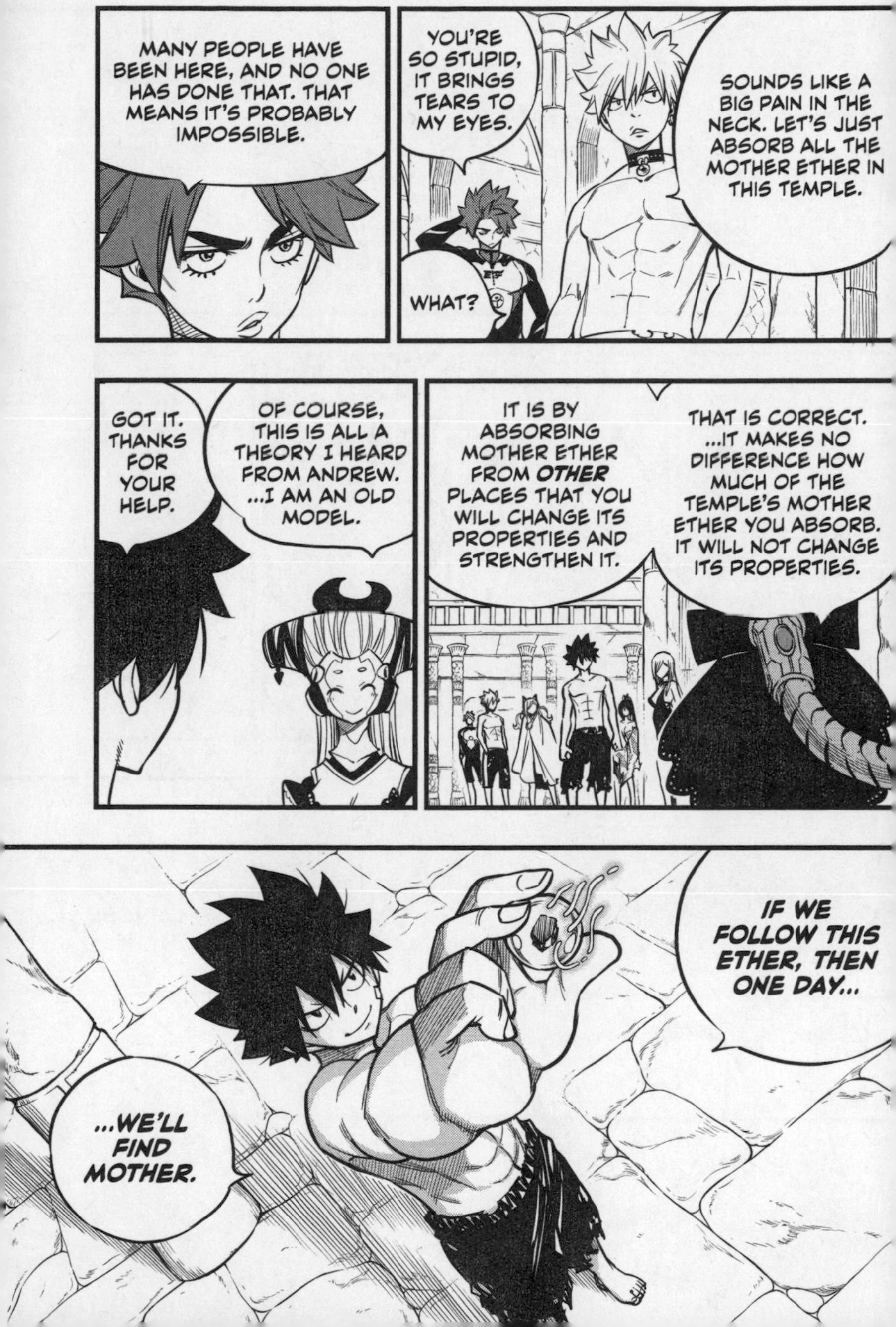
SOUNDS LIKE A BIG PAIN IN THE NECK. LET'S JUST ABSORB ALL THE MOTHER ETHER IN THIS TEMPLE.
YOU'RE SO STUPID, IT BRINGS TEARS TO MY EYES.
WHAT?
MANY PEOPLE HAVE BEEN HERE, AND NO ONE HAS DONE THAT. THAT MEANS IT'S PROBABLY IMPOSSIBLE.
THAT IS CORRECT. ...IT MAKES NO DIFFERENCE HOW MUCH OF THE TEMPLE'S MOTHER ETHER YOU ABSORB. IT WILL NOT CHANGE ITS PROPERTIES.
IT IS BY ABSORBING MOTHER ETHER FROM *OTHER* PLACES THAT YOU WILL CHANGE ITS PROPERTIES AND STRENGTHEN IT.
OF COURSE, THIS IS ALL A THEORY I HEARD FROM ANDREW. ...I AM AN OLD MODEL.
GOT IT. THANKS FOR YOUR HELP.
IF WE FOLLOW THIS ETHER, THEN ONE DAY...
...WE'LL FIND MOTHER.

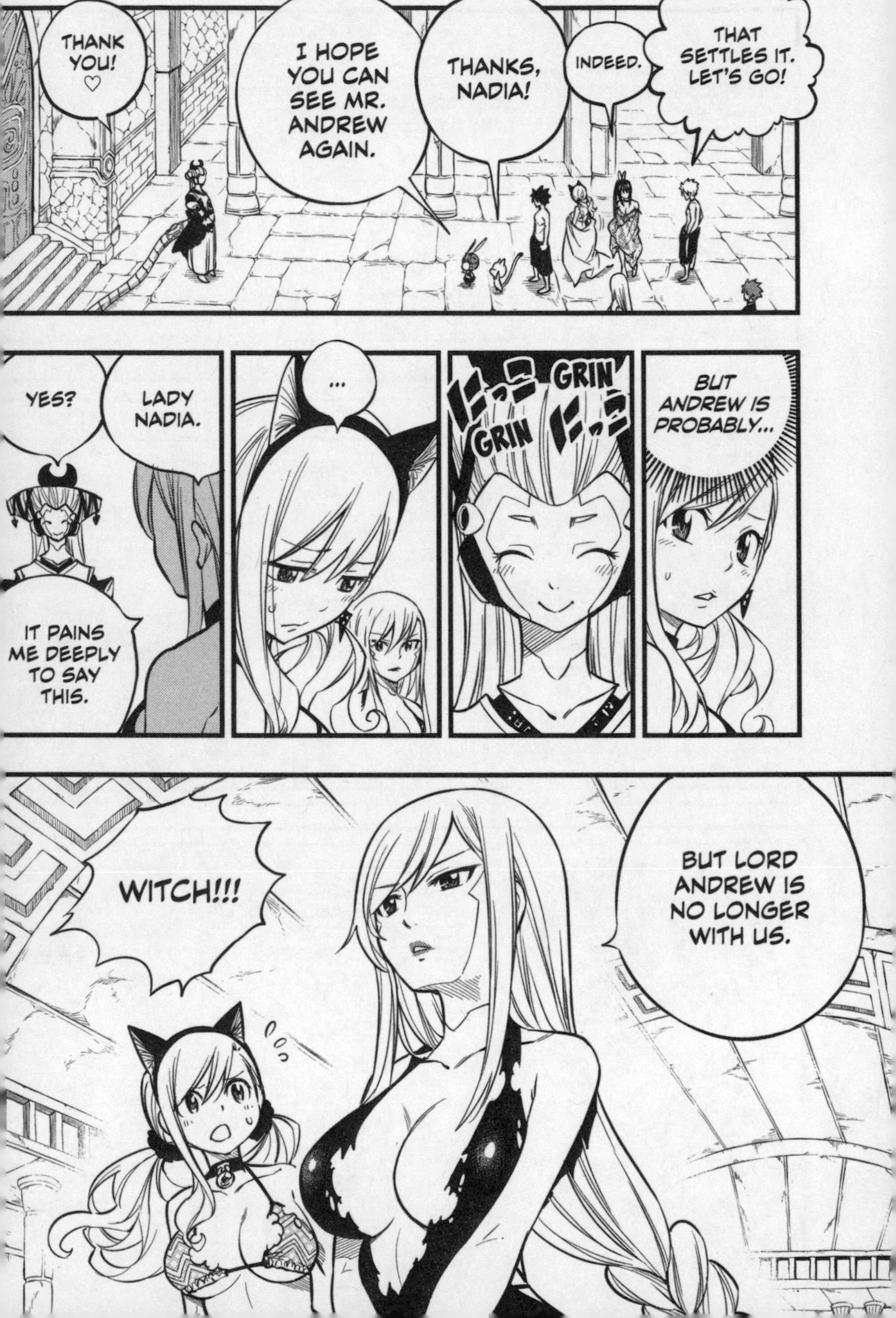
THAT SETTLES IT. LET'S GO!
INDEED.
THANKS, NADIA!
I HOPE YOU CAN SEE MR. ANDREW AGAIN.
THANK YOU! ♡
BUT ANDREW IS PROBABLY...
GRIN
GRIN
...
LADY NADIA.
YES?
IT PAINS ME DEEPLY TO SAY THIS.
BUT LORD ANDREW IS NO LONGER WITH US.
WITCH!!!

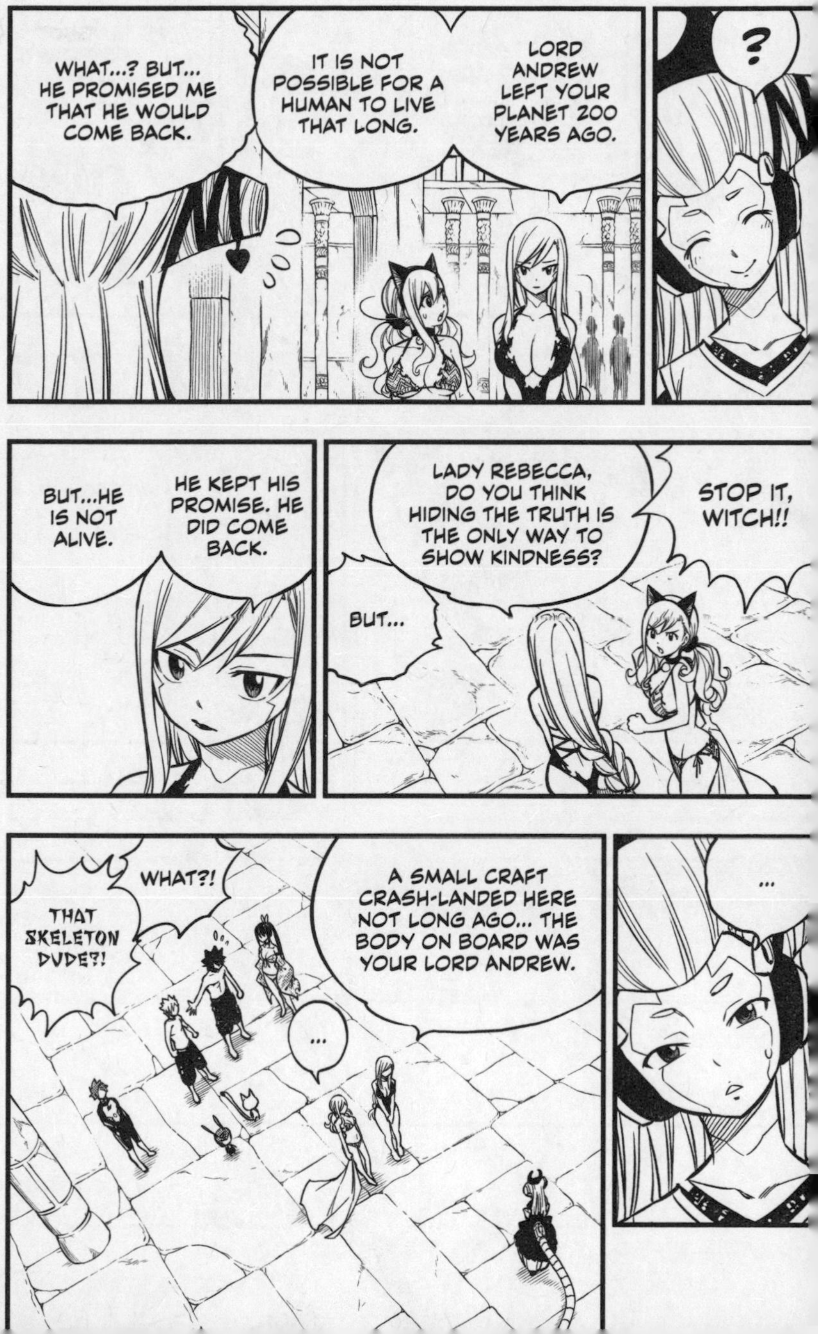
?
LORD ANDREW LEFT YOUR PLANET 200 YEARS AGO.
IT IS NOT POSSIBLE FOR A HUMAN TO LIVE THAT LONG.
WHAT...? BUT... HE PROMISED ME THAT HE WOULD COME BACK.
STOP IT, WITCH!!
LADY REBECCA, DO YOU THINK HIDING THE TRUTH IS THE ONLY WAY TO SHOW KINDNESS?
BUT...
HE KEPT HIS PROMISE. HE DID COME BACK.
BUT...HE IS NOT ALIVE.
...
A SMALL CRAFT CRASH-LANDED HERE NOT LONG AGO... THE BODY ON BOARD WAS YOUR LORD ANDREW.
WHAT?!
THAT SKELETON DUDE?!
...

THE ANSWERS ARE IN THIS MEMORY CHIP.

ギラ゛GLINT

BUT...BUT HOW CAN A CORPSE PILOT A...

!

FSH

ハラ。 VVN

LOADING

CLICK

P-PLEASE, YOU MUST LET ME SEE IT!!

I FOUND IT ON HIS SHIP.

DAY 6, MONTH 7, X290... HEY, NADIA, HOW ARE YOU DOING?

THIS SHOULD PUT EVERYBODY ON RED CAVE BACK TO NORMAL, AND YOU WON'T NEED THAT CABLE ANYMORE.

I GOT THE RELIC BACK. WE'RE LUCKY THE THIEF WAS JUST A SMALL-TIME CROOK, AND THAT I HAVE A FRIEND IN THE GOVERNMENT.

ANDREW...

IT TOOK A WHOLE YEAR. I'M SORRY. I CAN'T WAIT TO SEE YOU AGAIN.

I'VE MISSED THE SKY WE ALWAYS WATCHED TOGETHER.

I'M PRETTY CLOSE TO RED CAVE NOW.

I LOVE YOU.

CRASH

GAH!

!

BEEP
BEEP
BEEP

...UH-OH...
THAT'S NOT
GOOD...

ANDREW.

...

ANDREW!!!

KZHHH

ANDREW!!!

ANDREW

RED CAVE

METEOROID

IT WAS A
METEOROID...
FROM OUR
CALCULATIONS, I'D
SAY IT RENDERED
HIM UNCONSCIOUS
AND UNABLE TO
STEER...

THE COLLISION
KNOCKED HIS SHIP
OFF COURSE, AND
AFTER 200 YEARS,
HE CRASH-LANDED
ON THE PLANET.

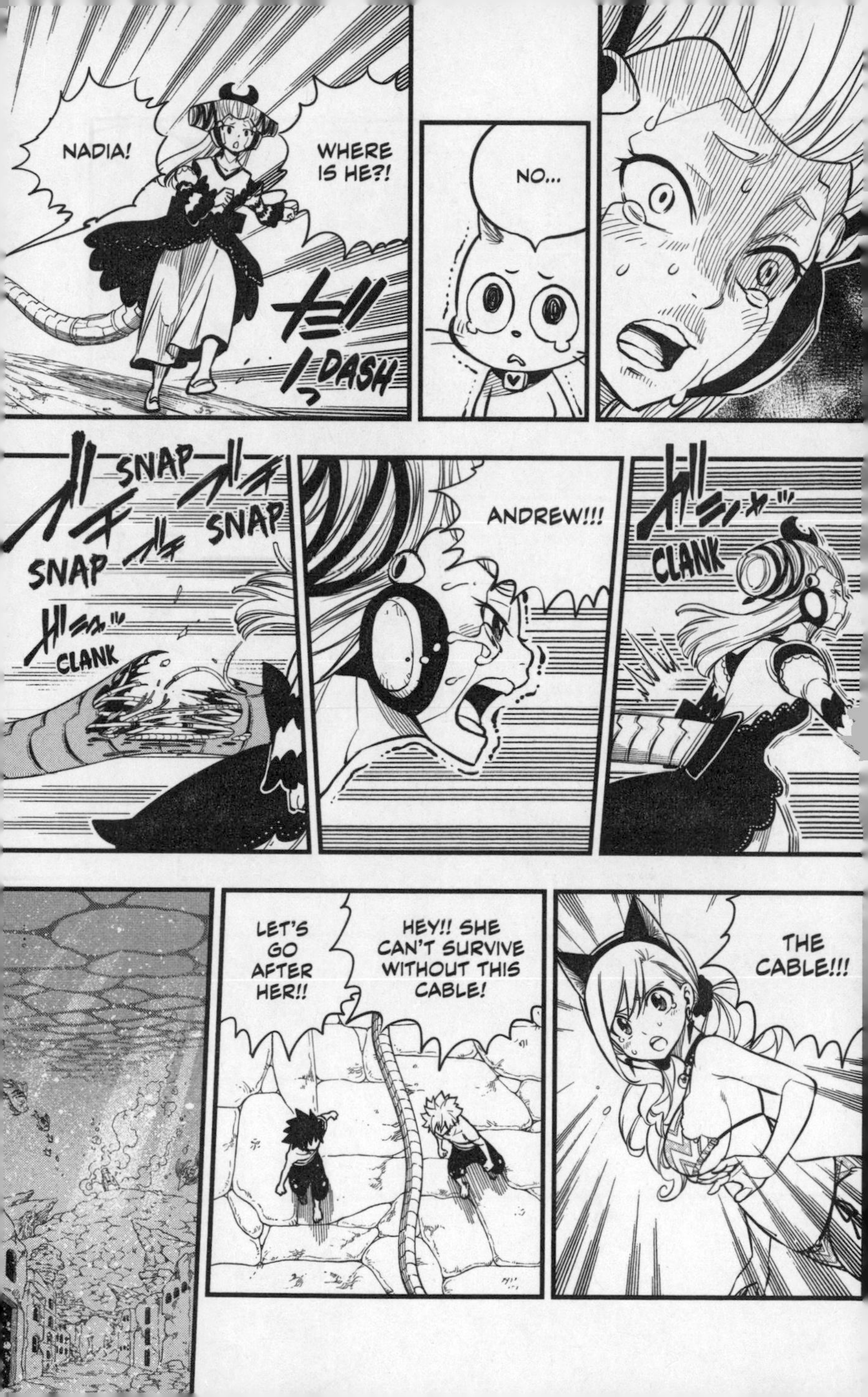
NO...
WHERE IS HE?!
NADIA!
DASH
CLANK
ANDREW!!!
SNAP
SNAP
SNAP
CLANK
THE CABLE!!!
HEY!! SHE CAN'T SURVIVE WITHOUT THIS CABLE!
LET'S GO AFTER HER!!

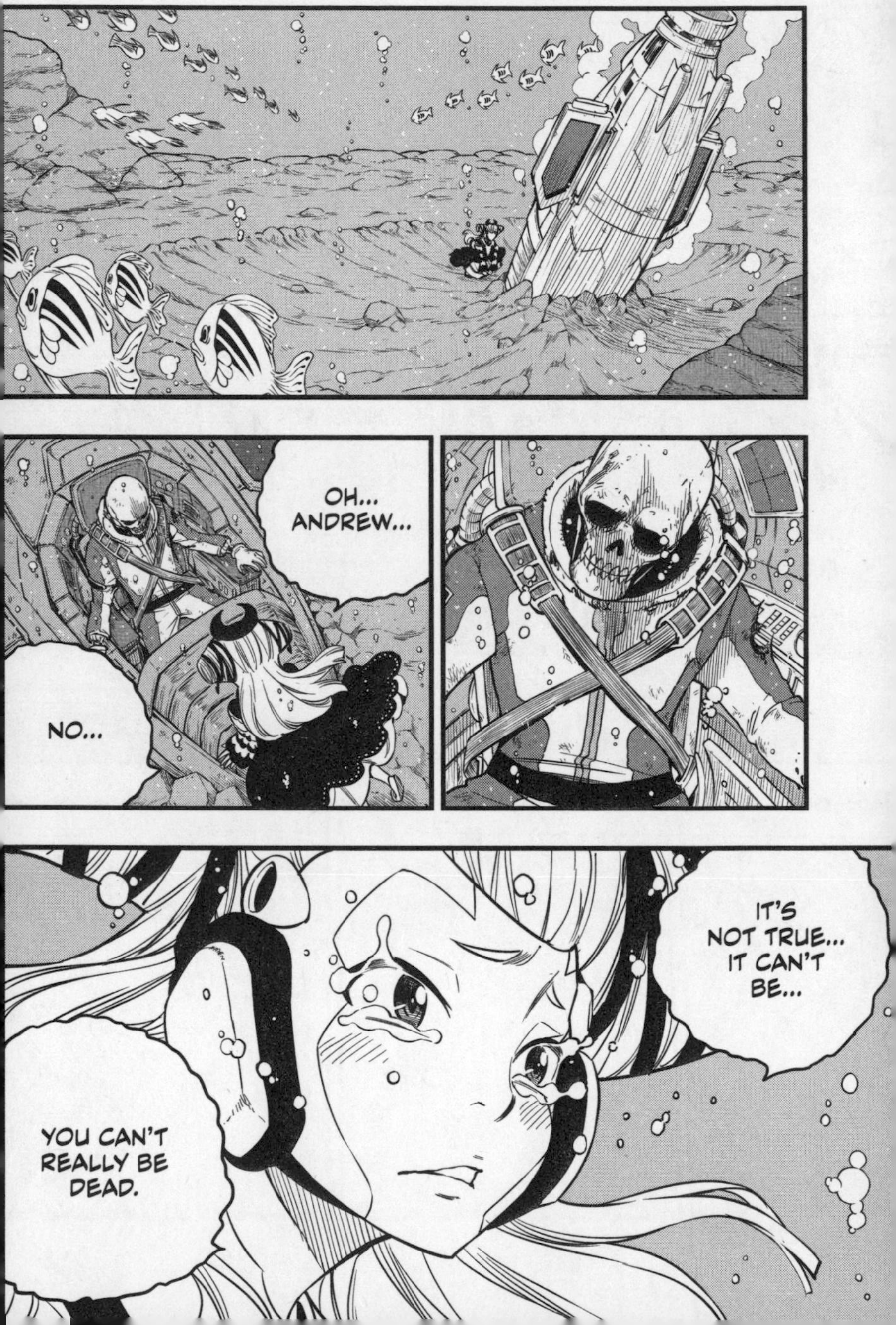
OH... ANDREW...
NO...
IT'S NOT TRUE... IT CAN'T BE...
YOU CAN'T REALLY BE DEAD.

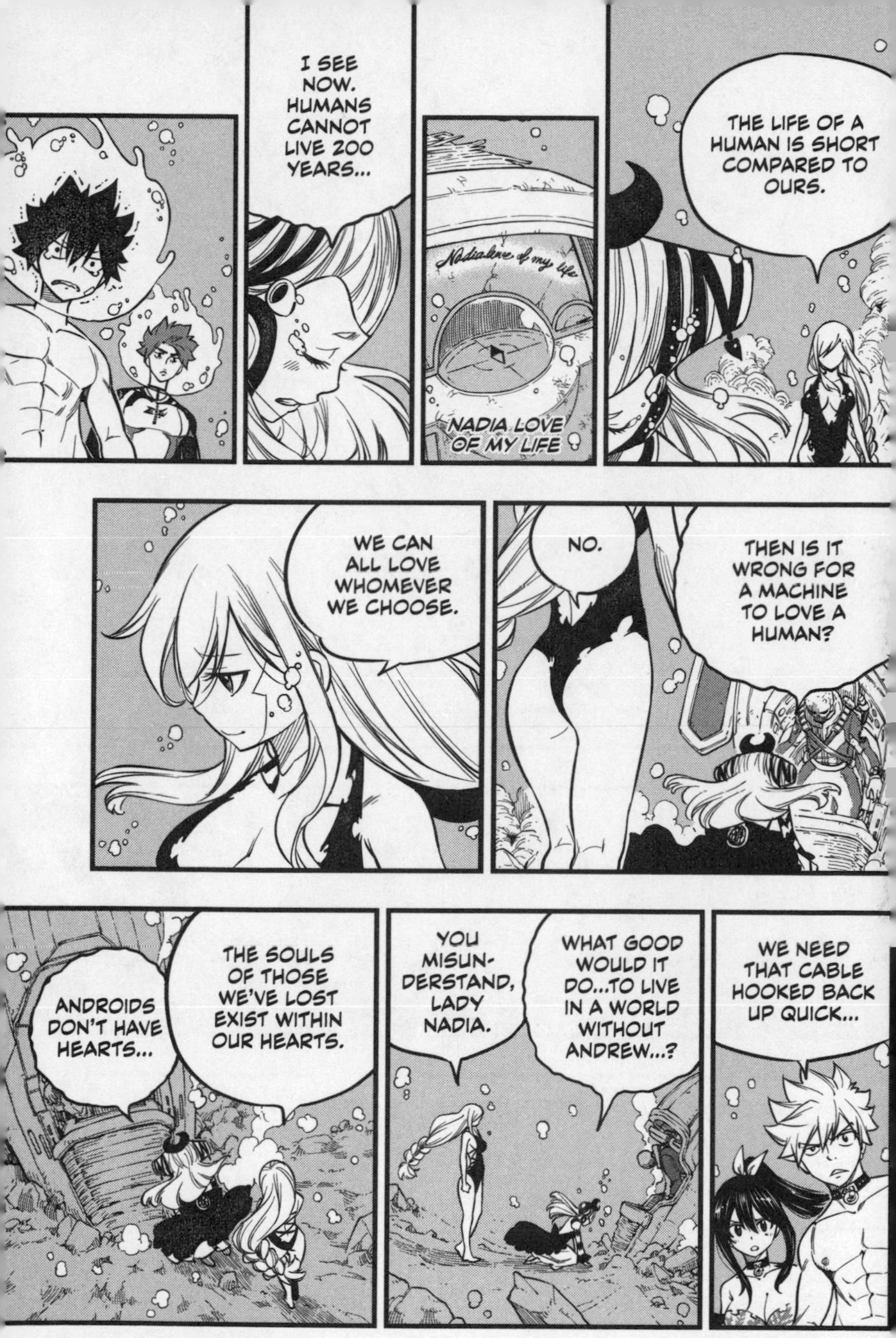
THE LIFE OF A HUMAN IS SHORT COMPARED TO OURS.
Nadia love of my life
NADIA LOVE OF MY LIFE
I SEE NOW. HUMANS CANNOT LIVE 200 YEARS...
THEN IS IT WRONG FOR A MACHINE TO LOVE A HUMAN?
NO.
WE CAN ALL LOVE WHOMEVER WE CHOOSE.
WE NEED THAT CABLE HOOKED BACK UP QUICK...
WHAT GOOD WOULD IT DO...TO LIVE IN A WORLD WITHOUT ANDREW...?
YOU MISUN-DERSTAND, LADY NADIA.
THE SOULS OF THOSE WE'VE LOST EXIST WITHIN OUR HEARTS.
ANDROIDS DON'T HAVE HEARTS...

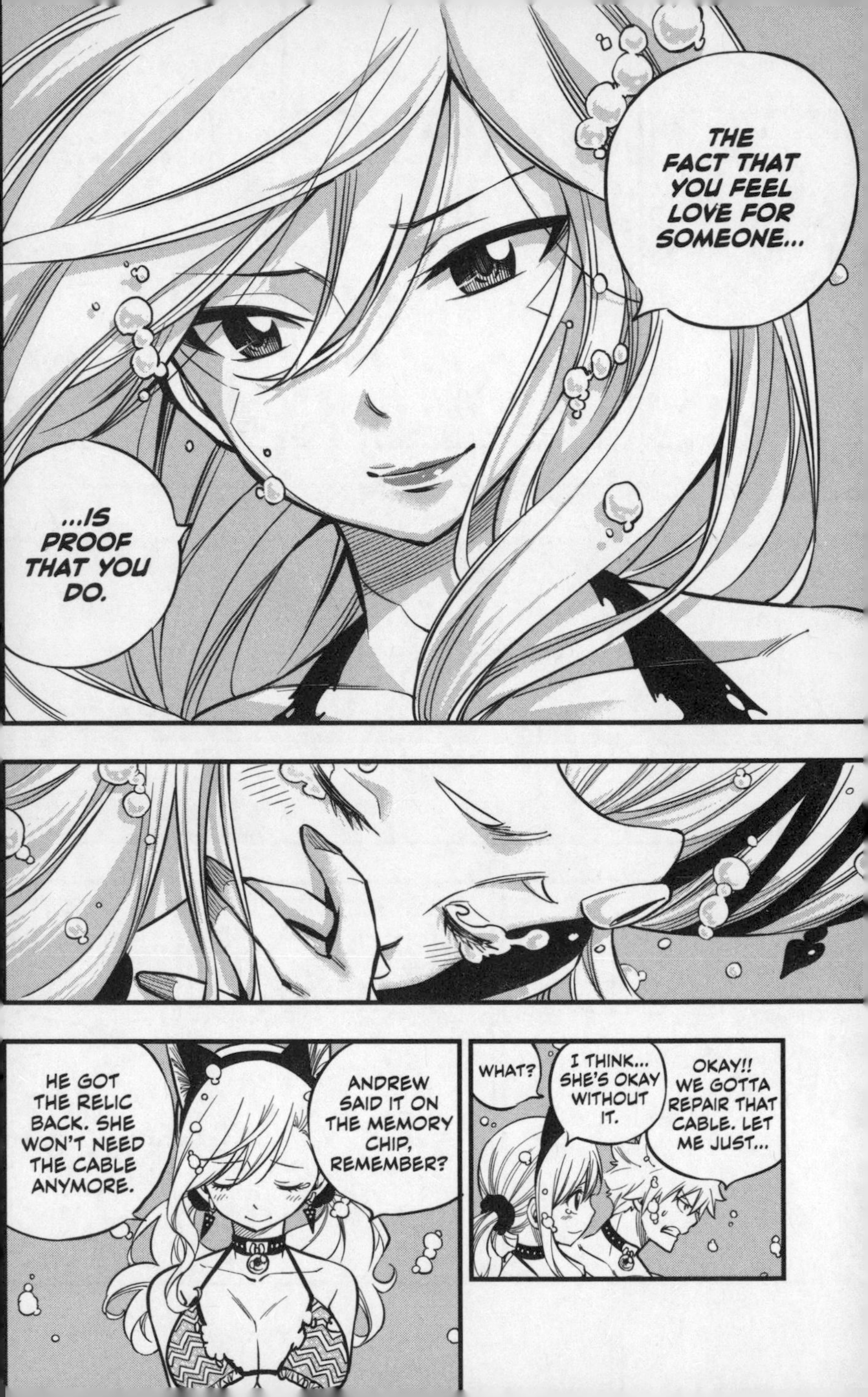
THE FACT THAT YOU FEEL LOVE FOR SOMEONE...
...IS PROOF THAT YOU DO.
OKAY!! WE GOTTA REPAIR THAT CABLE. LET ME JUST...
I THINK... SHE'S OKAY WITHOUT IT.
WHAT?
ANDREW SAID IT ON THE MEMORY CHIP, REMEMBER?
HE GOT THE RELIC BACK. SHE WON'T NEED THE CABLE ANYMORE.

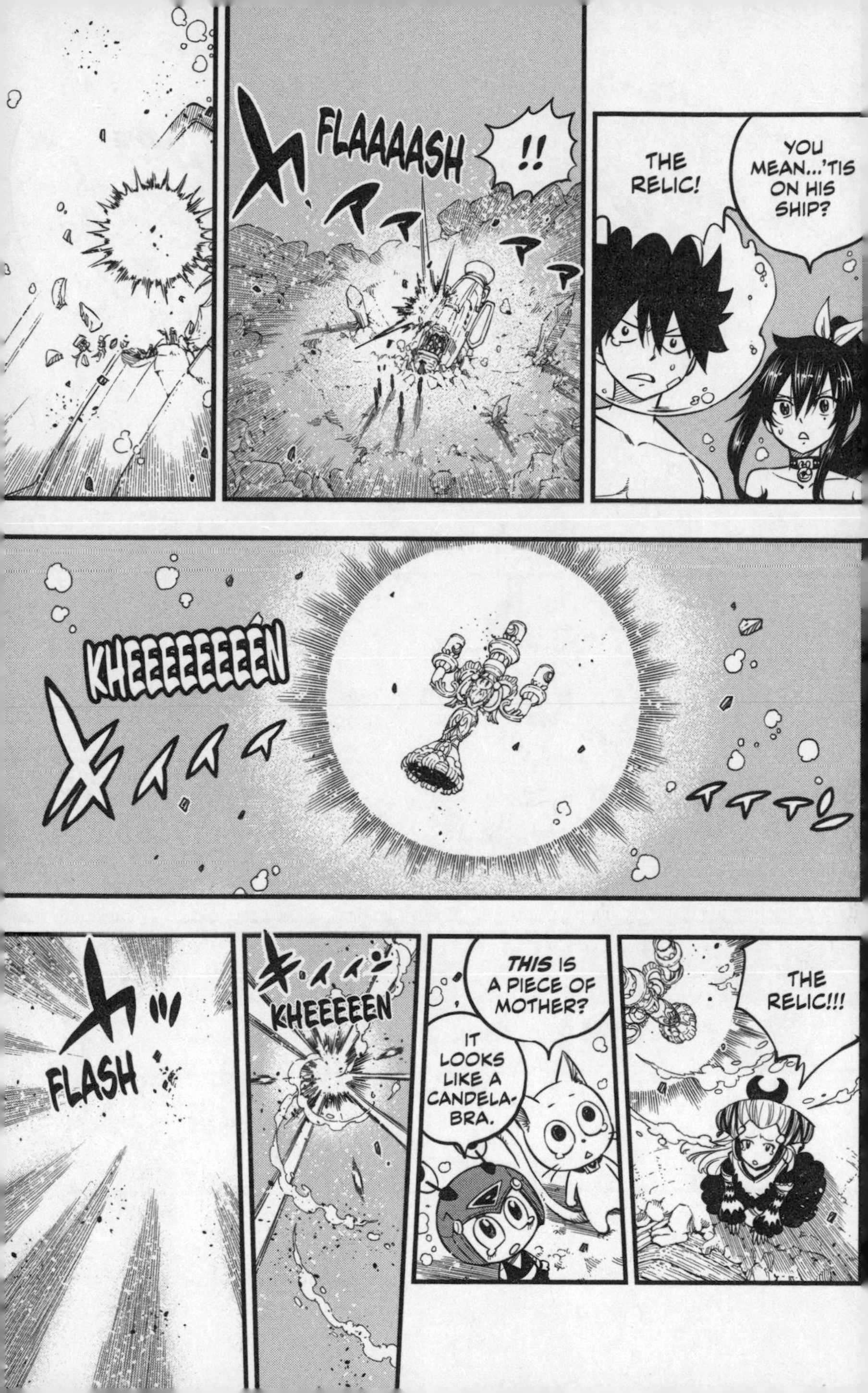
YOU MEAN...'TIS ON HIS SHIP?
THE RELIC!
!!
FLAAAASH
KHEEEEEEEEEN
THE RELIC!!!
THIS is A PIECE OF MOTHER?
IT LOOKS LIKE A CANDELA-BRA.
KHEEEEEN
FLASH

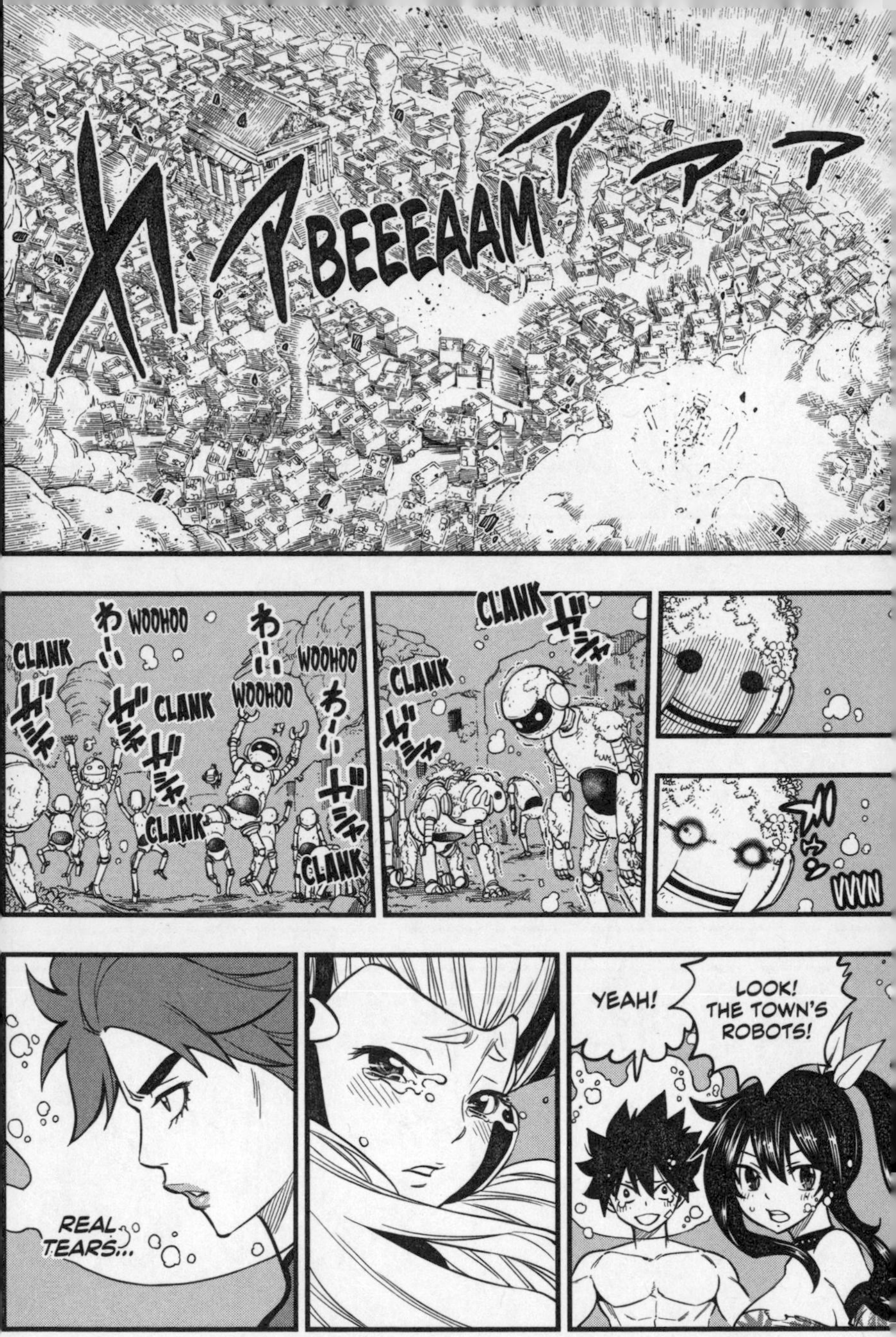
BEEEAAM
VVVN
CLANK
CLANK
WOOHOO
WOOHOO
WOOHOO
CLANK
CLANK
CLANK
CLANK
LOOK! THE TOWN'S ROBOTS!
YEAH!
REAL TEARS...

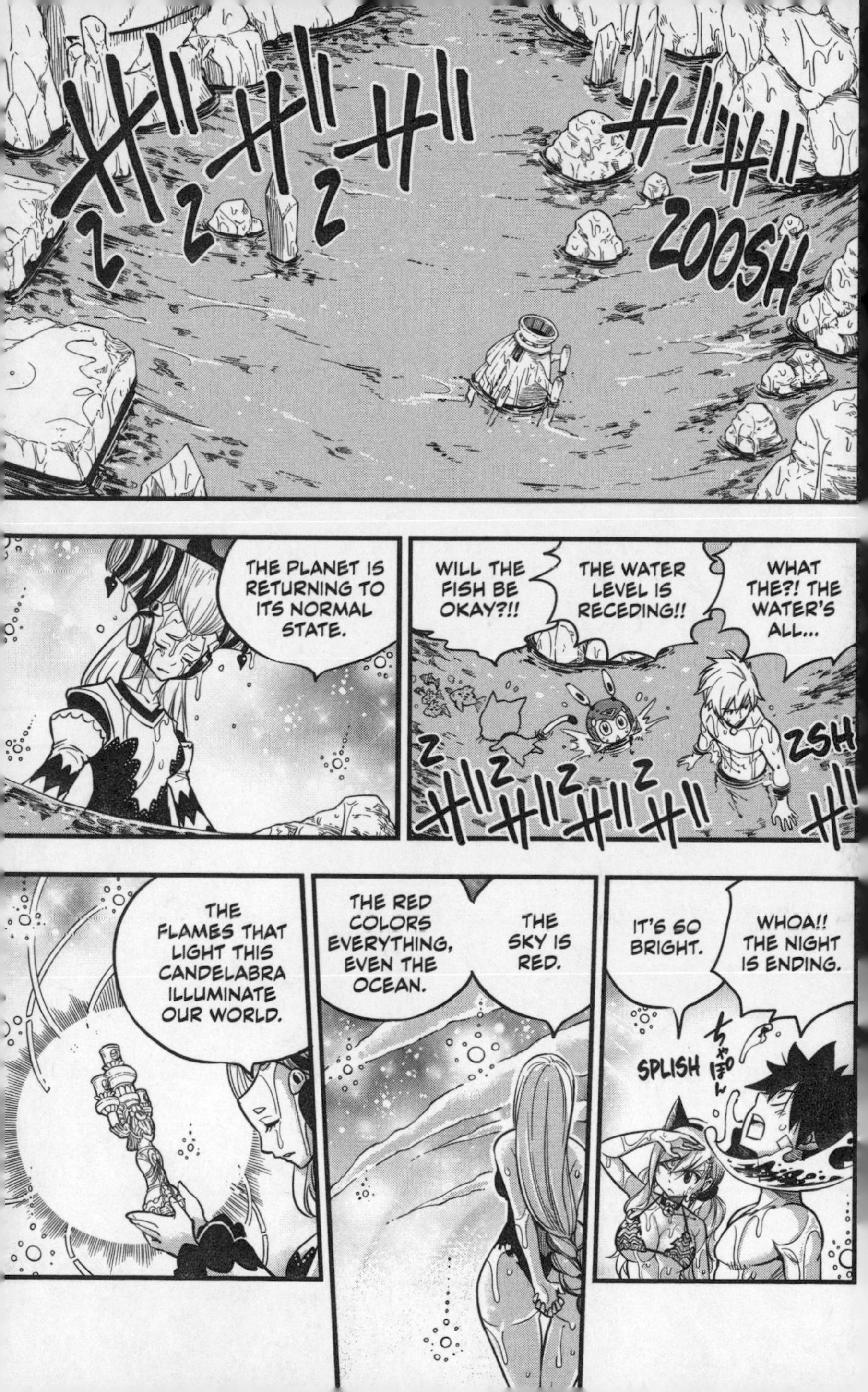
ZOOSH
WHAT THE?! THE WATER'S ALL...
THE WATER LEVEL IS RECEDING!!
WILL THE FISH BE OKAY?!!
ZSH
THE PLANET IS RETURNING TO ITS NORMAL STATE.
WHOA!! THE NIGHT IS ENDING.
IT'S SO BRIGHT.
SPLISH
ちゃぽん
THE SKY IS RED.
THE RED COLORS EVERYTHING, EVEN THE OCEAN.
THE FLAMES THAT LIGHT THIS CANDELABRA ILLUMINATE OUR WORLD.

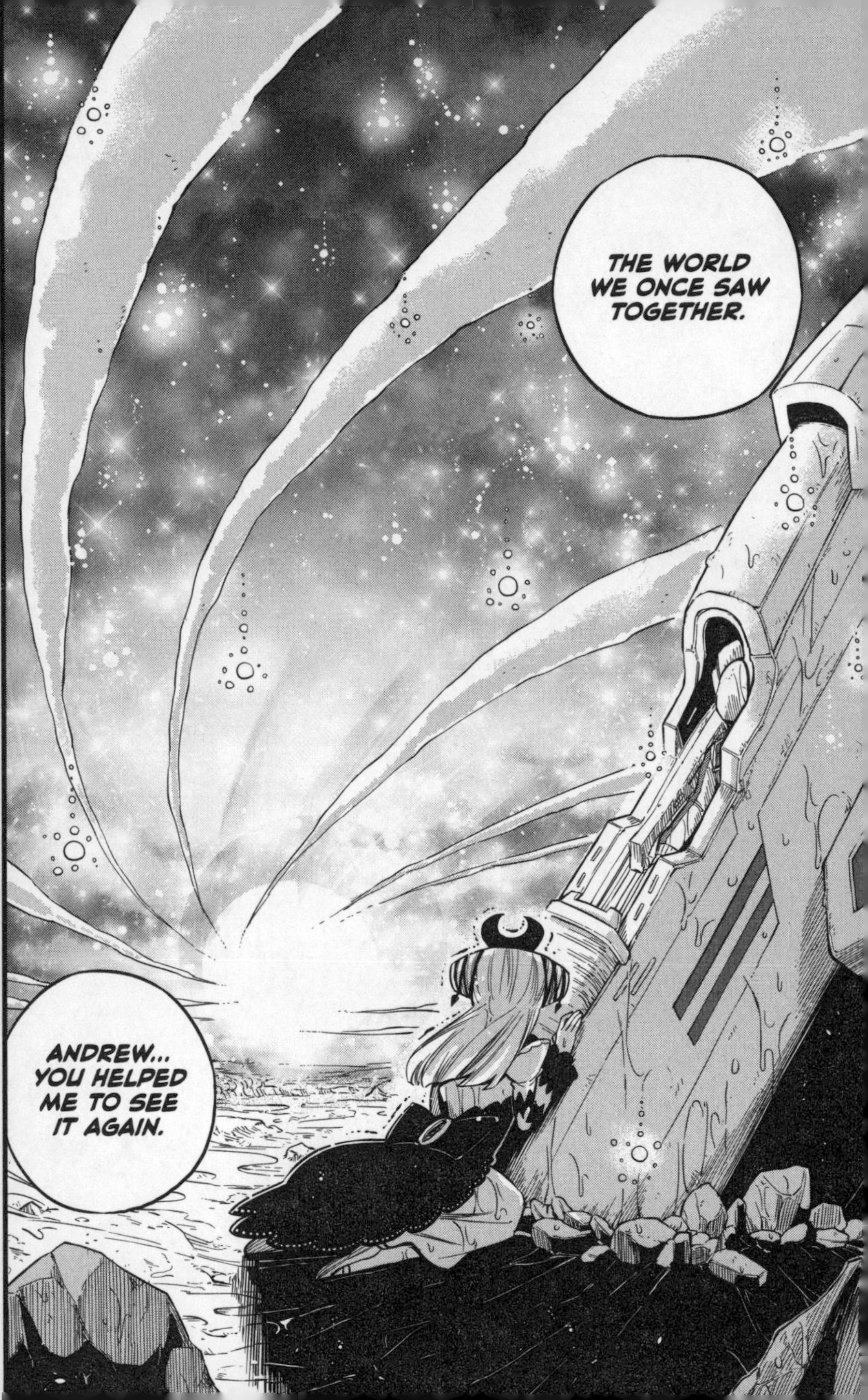
THE WORLD WE ONCE SAW TOGETHER.
ANDREW... YOU HELPED ME TO SEE IT AGAIN.

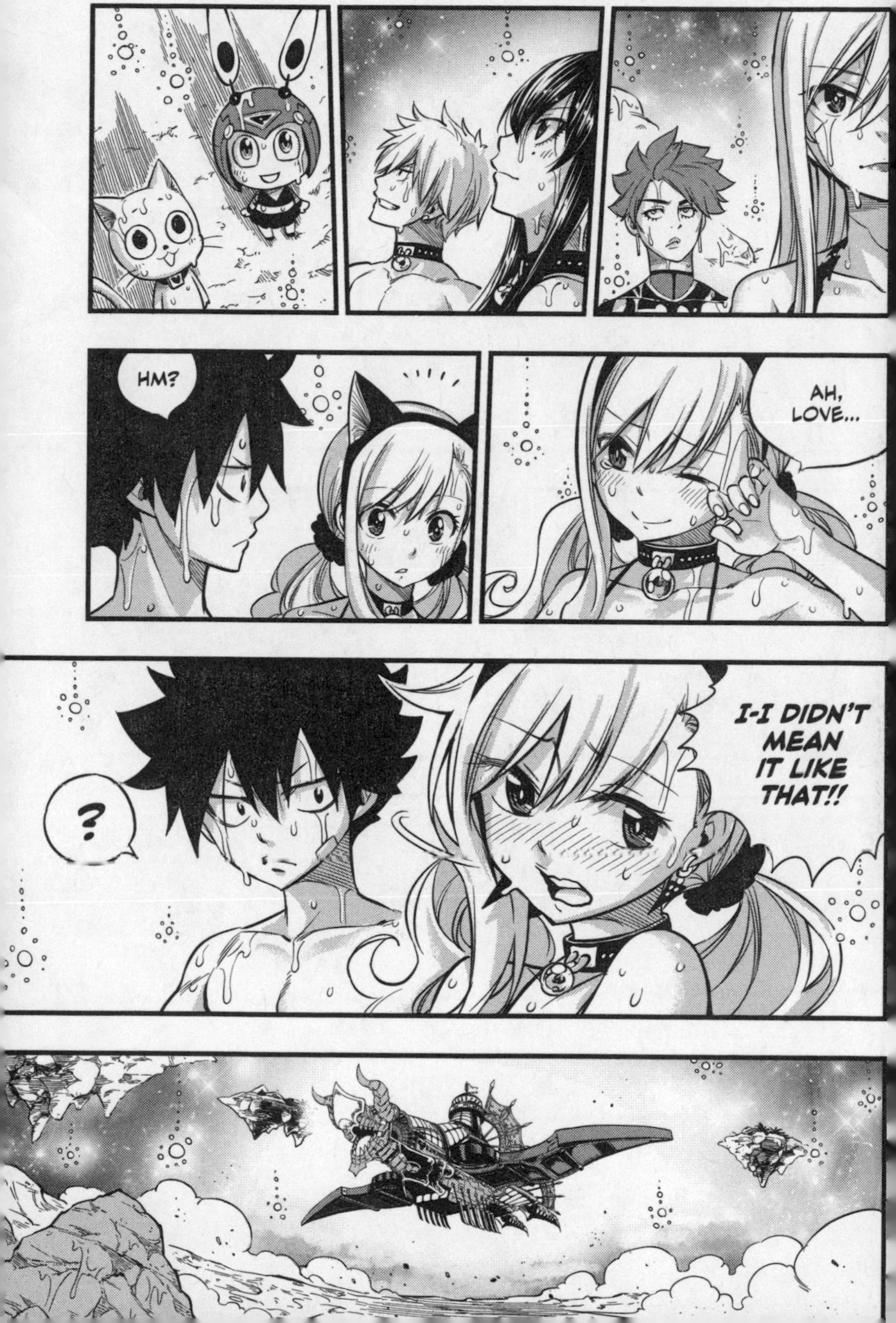
AH, LOVE...
HM?
I-I DIDN'T MEAN IT LIKE THAT!!
?

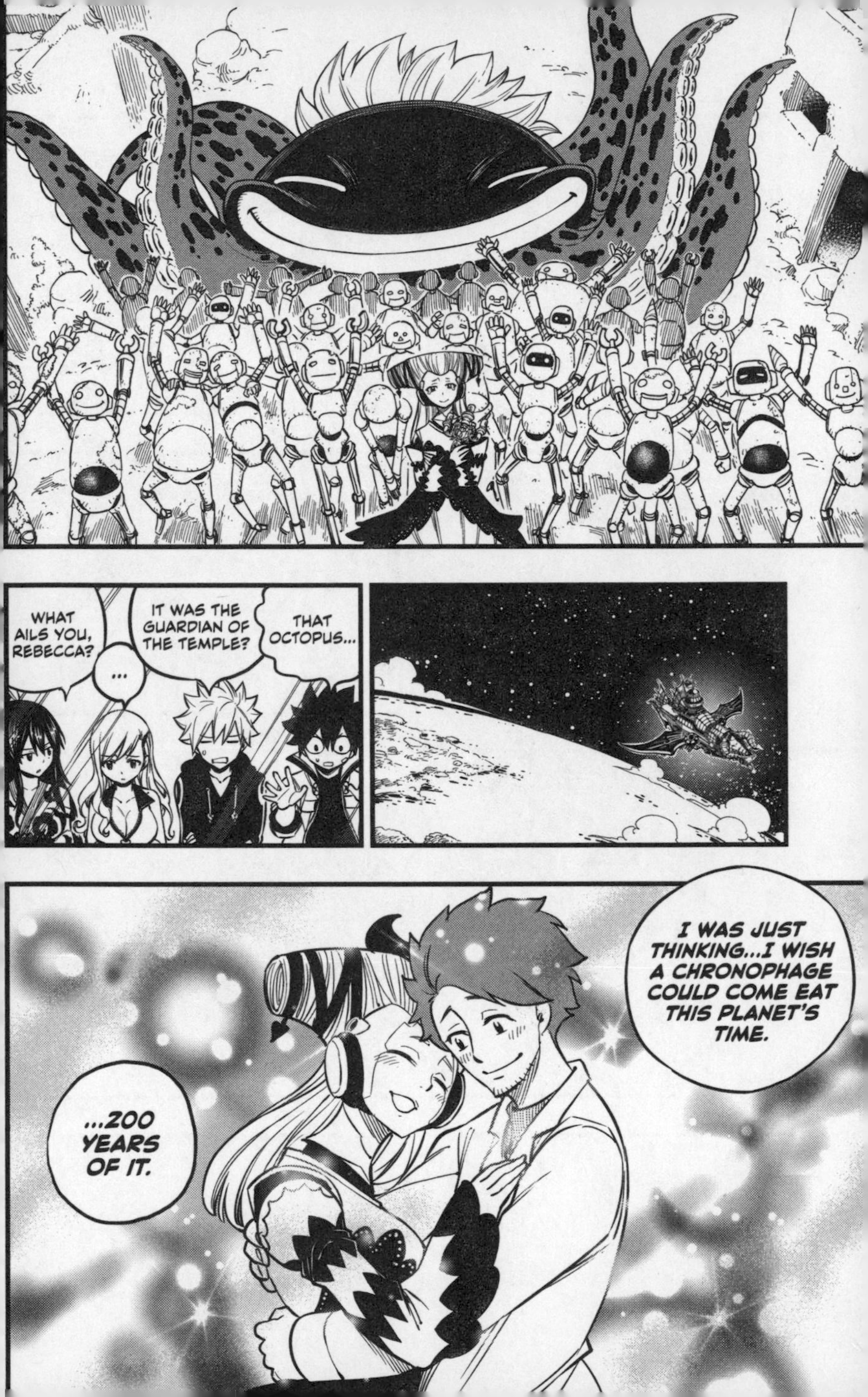
THAT OCTOPUS...
IT WAS THE GUARDIAN OF THE TEMPLE?
...
WHAT AILS YOU, REBECCA?
I WAS JUST THINKING...I WISH A CHRONOPHAGE COULD COME EAT THIS PLANET'S TIME.
...200 YEARS OF IT.

EDENS ZERO

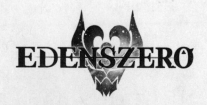

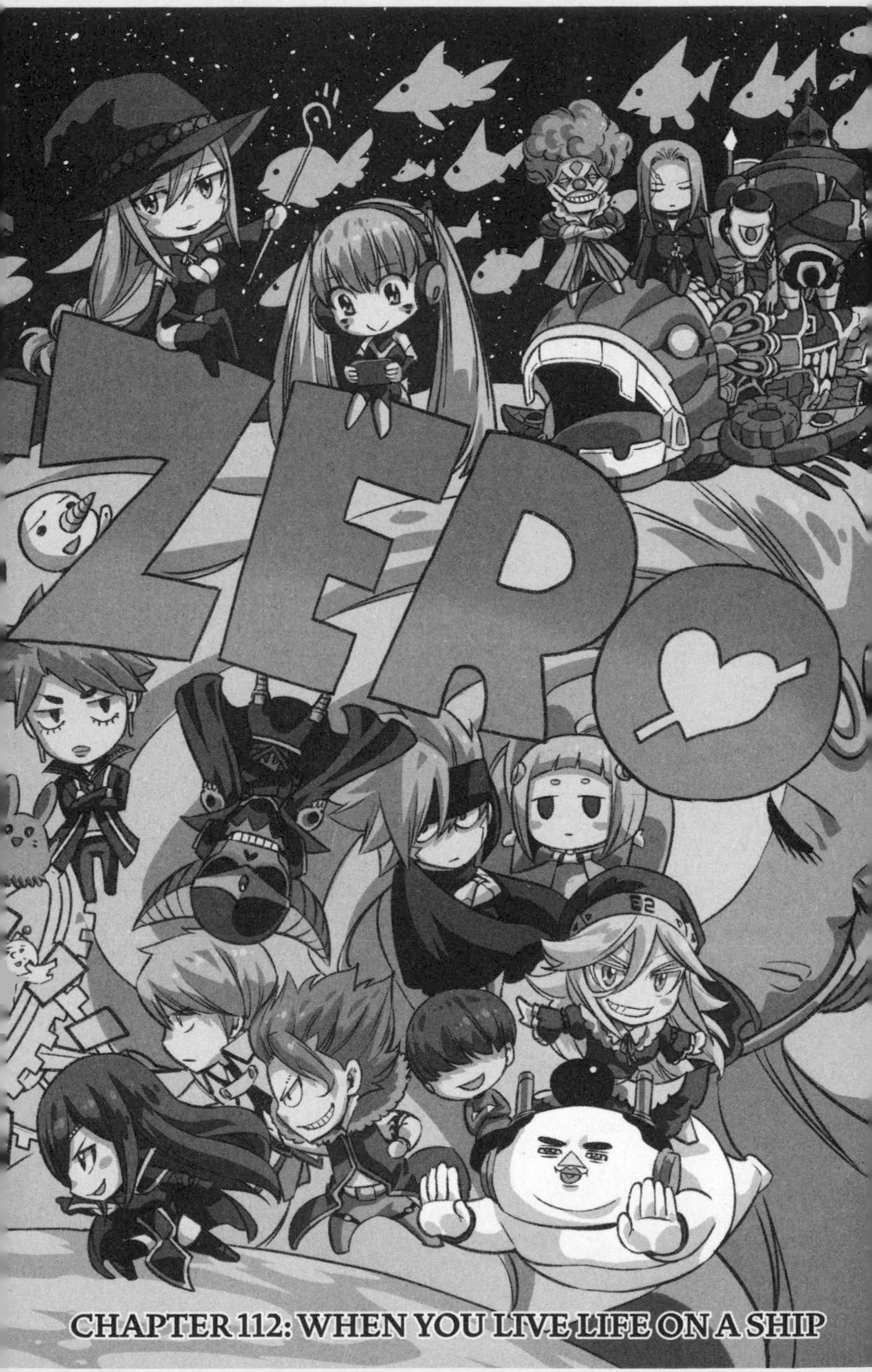
ZERO
62

CHAPTER 112: WHEN YOU LIVE LIFE ON A SHIP

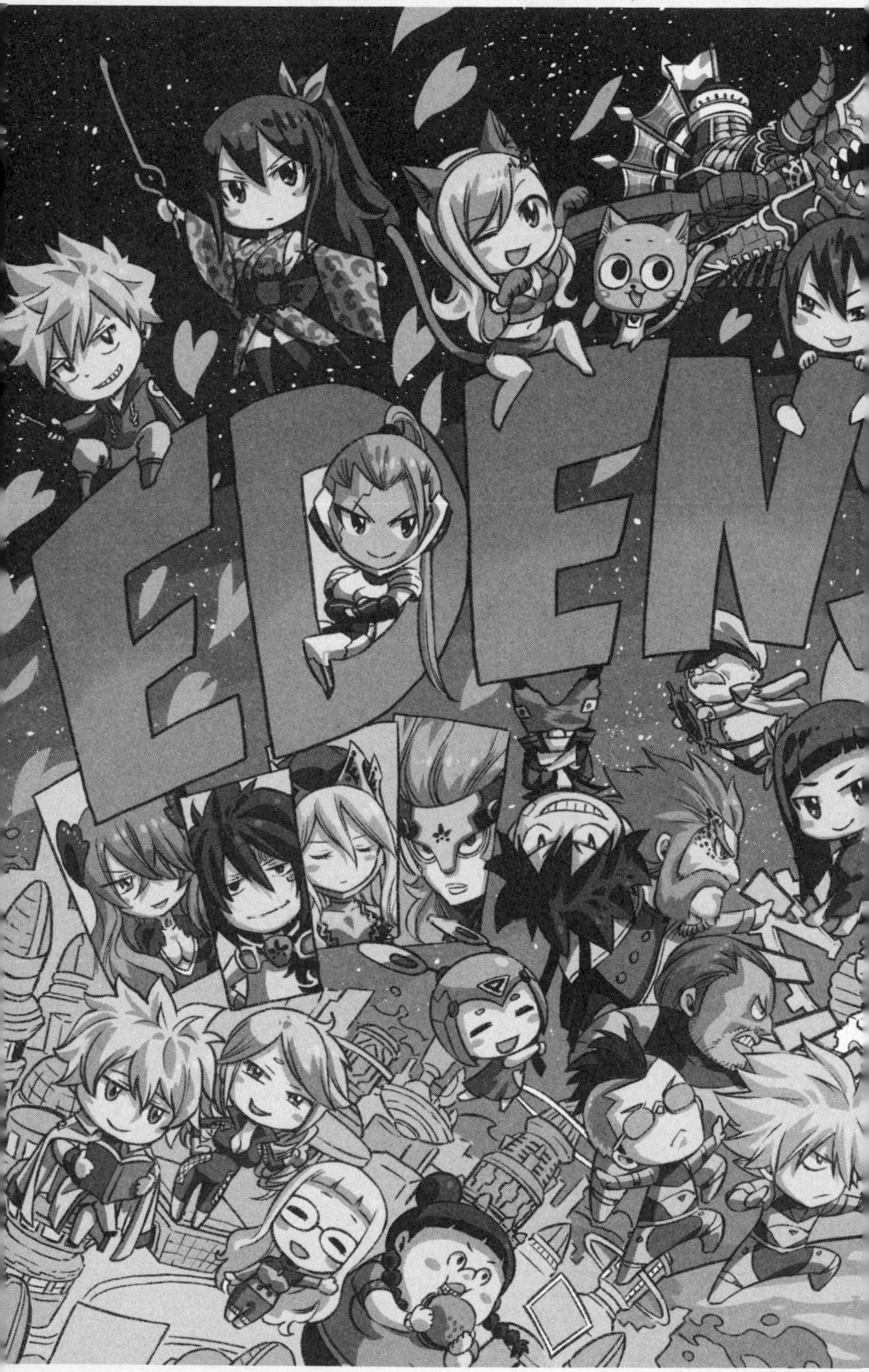

EDENSZERO

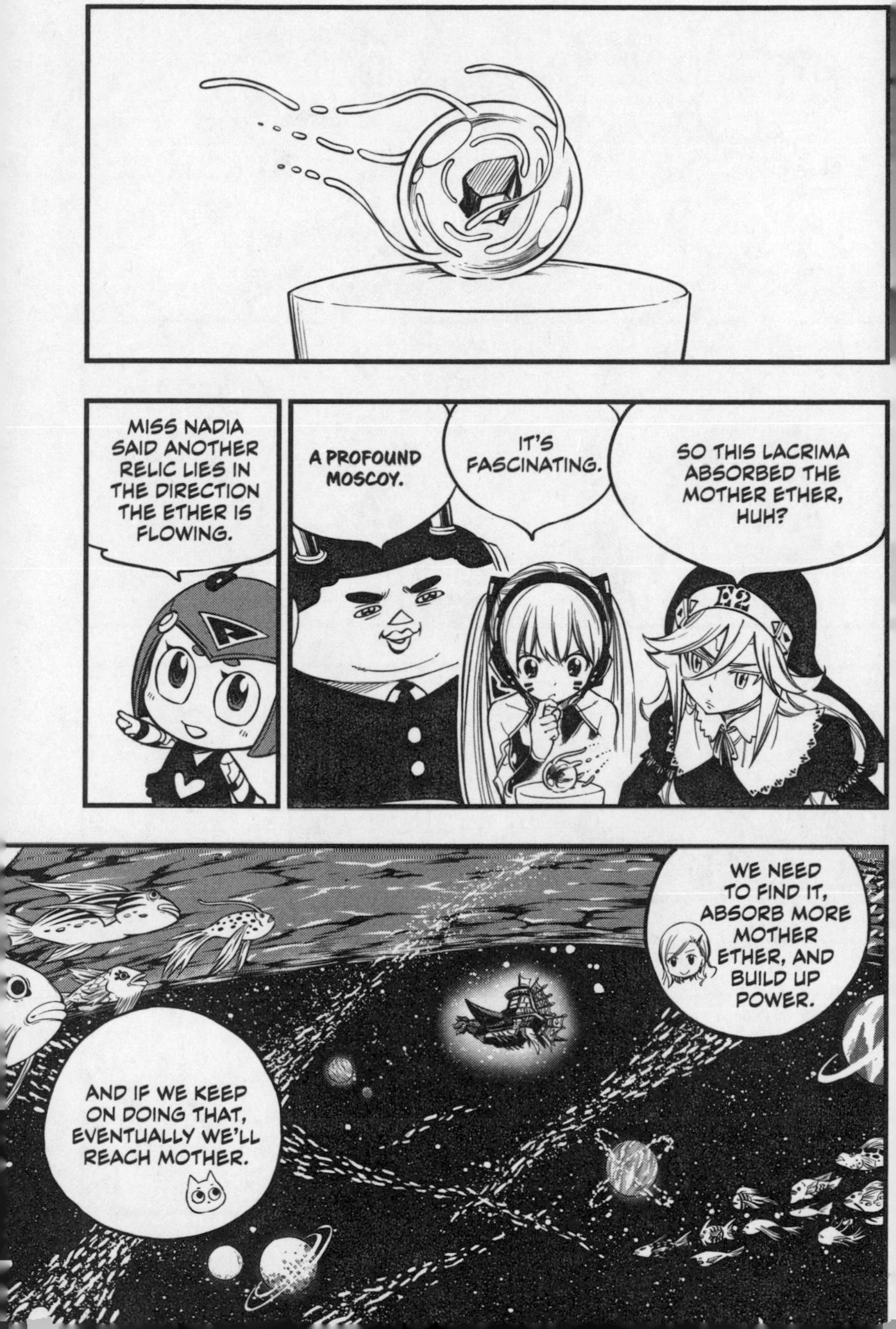
SO THIS LACRIMA ABSORBED THE MOTHER ETHER, HUH?
IT'S FASCINATING.
A PROFOUND MOSCOY.
MISS NADIA SAID ANOTHER RELIC LIES IN THE DIRECTION THE ETHER IS FLOWING.
WE NEED TO FIND IT, ABSORB MORE MOTHER ETHER, AND BUILD UP POWER.
AND IF WE KEEP ON DOING THAT, EVENTUALLY WE'LL REACH MOTHER.

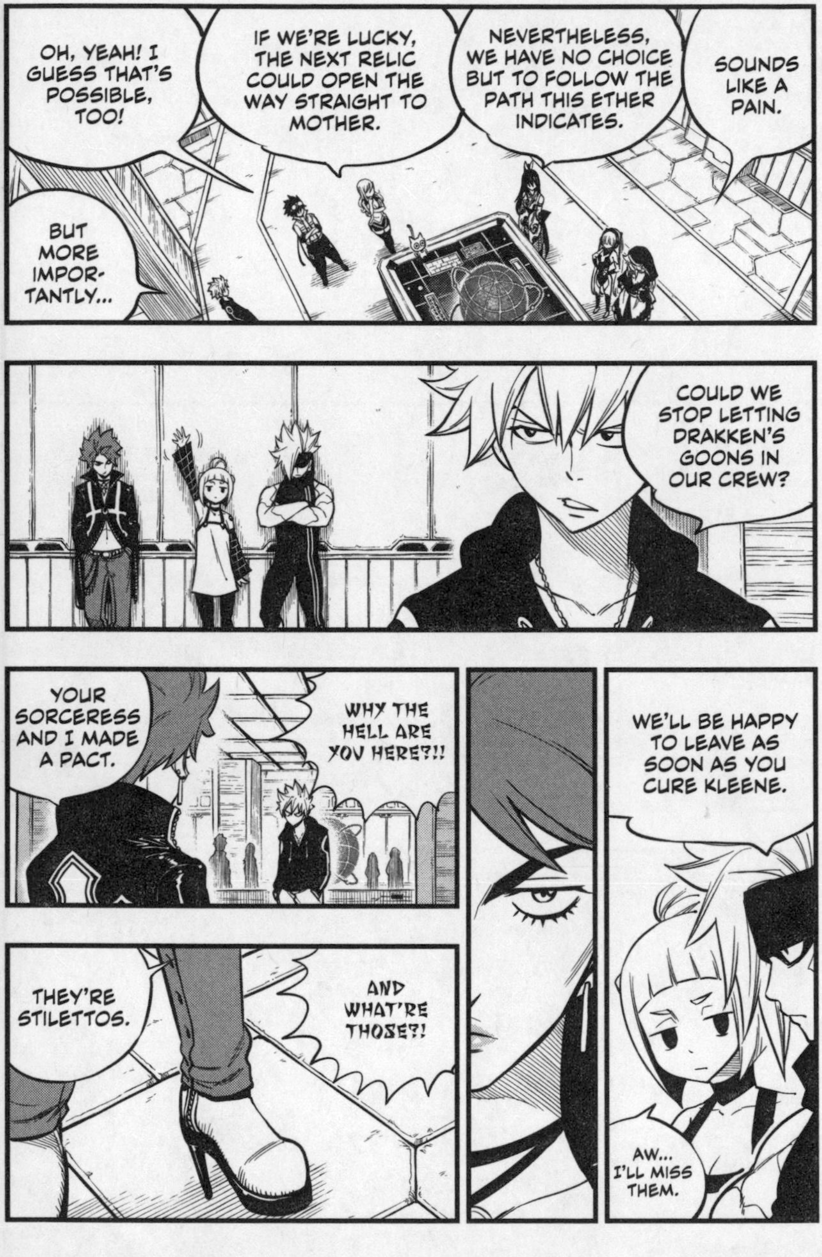
SOUNDS LIKE A PAIN.
NEVERTHELESS, WE HAVE NO CHOICE BUT TO FOLLOW THE PATH THIS ETHER INDICATES.
IF WE'RE LUCKY, THE NEXT RELIC COULD OPEN THE WAY STRAIGHT TO MOTHER.
OH, YEAH! I GUESS THAT'S POSSIBLE, TOO!
BUT MORE IMPORTANTLY...
COULD WE STOP LETTING DRAKKEN'S GOONS IN OUR CREW?
WE'LL BE HAPPY TO LEAVE AS SOON AS YOU CURE KLEENE.
AW... I'LL MISS THEM.
WHY THE HELL ARE YOU HERE?!!
YOUR SORCERESS AND I MADE A PACT.
AND WHAT'RE THOSE?!
THEY'RE STILETTOS.

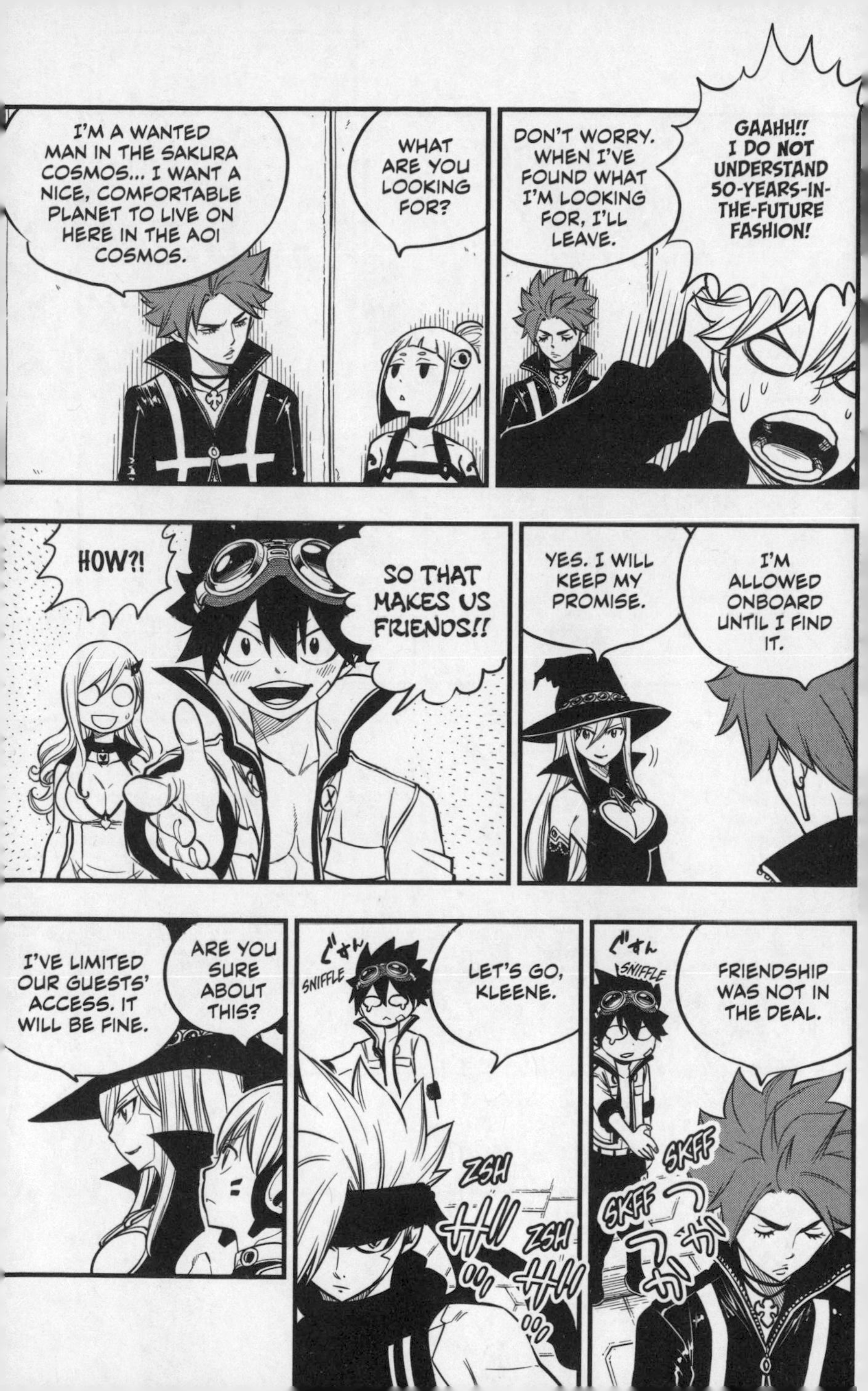
GAAHH!! I DO NOT UNDERSTAND 50-YEARS-IN-THE-FUTURE FASHION!
DON'T WORRY. WHEN I'VE FOUND WHAT I'M LOOKING FOR, I'LL LEAVE.
WHAT ARE YOU LOOKING FOR?
I'M A WANTED MAN IN THE SAKURA COSMOS... I WANT A NICE, COMFORTABLE PLANET TO LIVE ON HERE IN THE AOI COSMOS.
I'M ALLOWED ONBOARD UNTIL I FIND IT.
YES. I WILL KEEP MY PROMISE.
SO THAT MAKES US FRIENDS!!
HOW?!
FRIENDSHIP WAS NOT IN THE DEAL.
SNIFFLE
SKFF
SKFF
LET'S GO, KLEENE.
SNIFFLE
ZSH
ZSH
ARE YOU SURE ABOUT THIS?
I'VE LIMITED OUR GUESTS' ACCESS. IT WILL BE FINE.

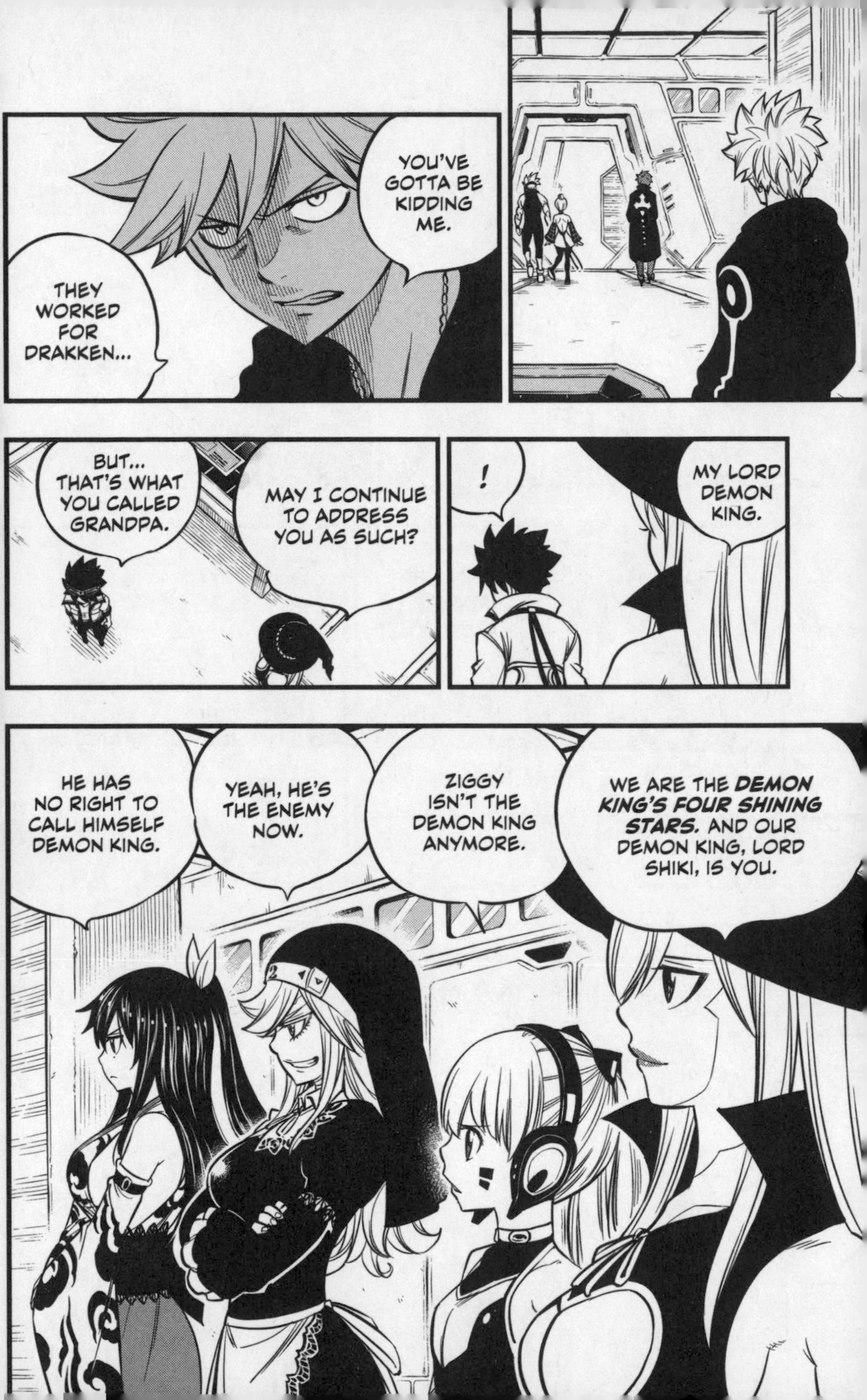
YOU'VE GOTTA BE KIDDING ME.
THEY WORKED FOR DRAKKEN...
MY LORD DEMON KING.
!
MAY I CONTINUE TO ADDRESS YOU AS SUCH?
BUT... THAT'S WHAT YOU CALLED GRANDPA.
WE ARE THE *DEMON KING'S FOUR SHINING STARS.* AND OUR DEMON KING, LORD SHIKI, IS YOU.
ZIGGY ISN'T THE DEMON KING ANYMORE.
YEAH, HE'S THE ENEMY NOW.
HE HAS NO RIGHT TO CALL HIMSELF DEMON KING.

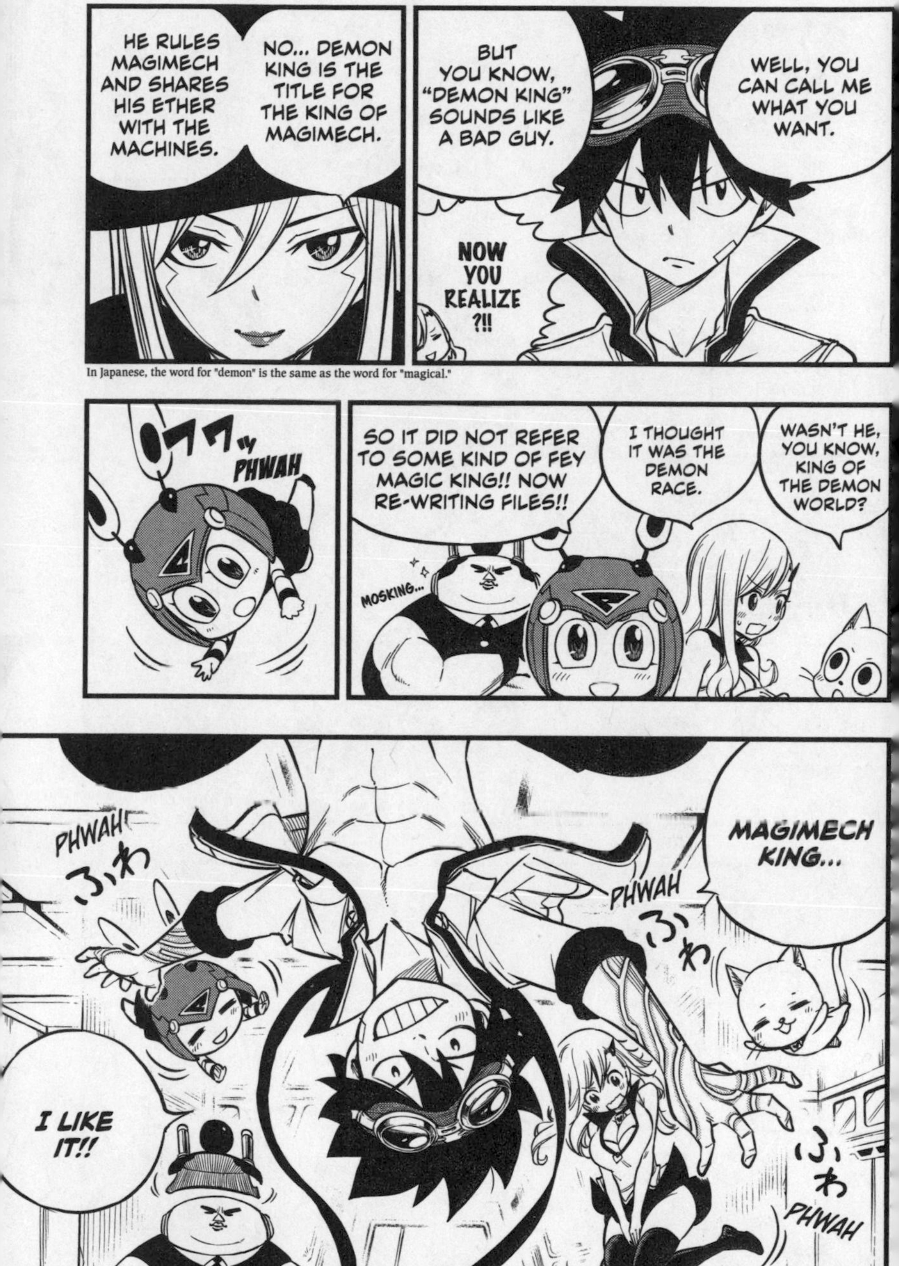
WELL, YOU CAN CALL ME WHAT YOU WANT.
BUT YOU KNOW, "DEMON KING" SOUNDS LIKE A BAD GUY.
NOW YOU REALIZE ?!!
NO... DEMON KING IS THE TITLE FOR THE KING OF MAGIMECH.
HE RULES MAGIMECH AND SHARES HIS ETHER WITH THE MACHINES.
WASN'T HE, YOU KNOW, KING OF THE DEMON WORLD?
I THOUGHT IT WAS THE DEMON RACE.
SO IT DID NOT REFER TO SOME KIND OF FEY MAGIC KING!! NOW RE-WRITING FILES!!
MOSKING...
PHWAH
MAGIMECH KING...
PHWAH
ふわ
PHWAH
ふわ
I LIKE IT!!
ふわ
PHWAH

In Japanese, the word for "demon" is the same as the word for "magical."

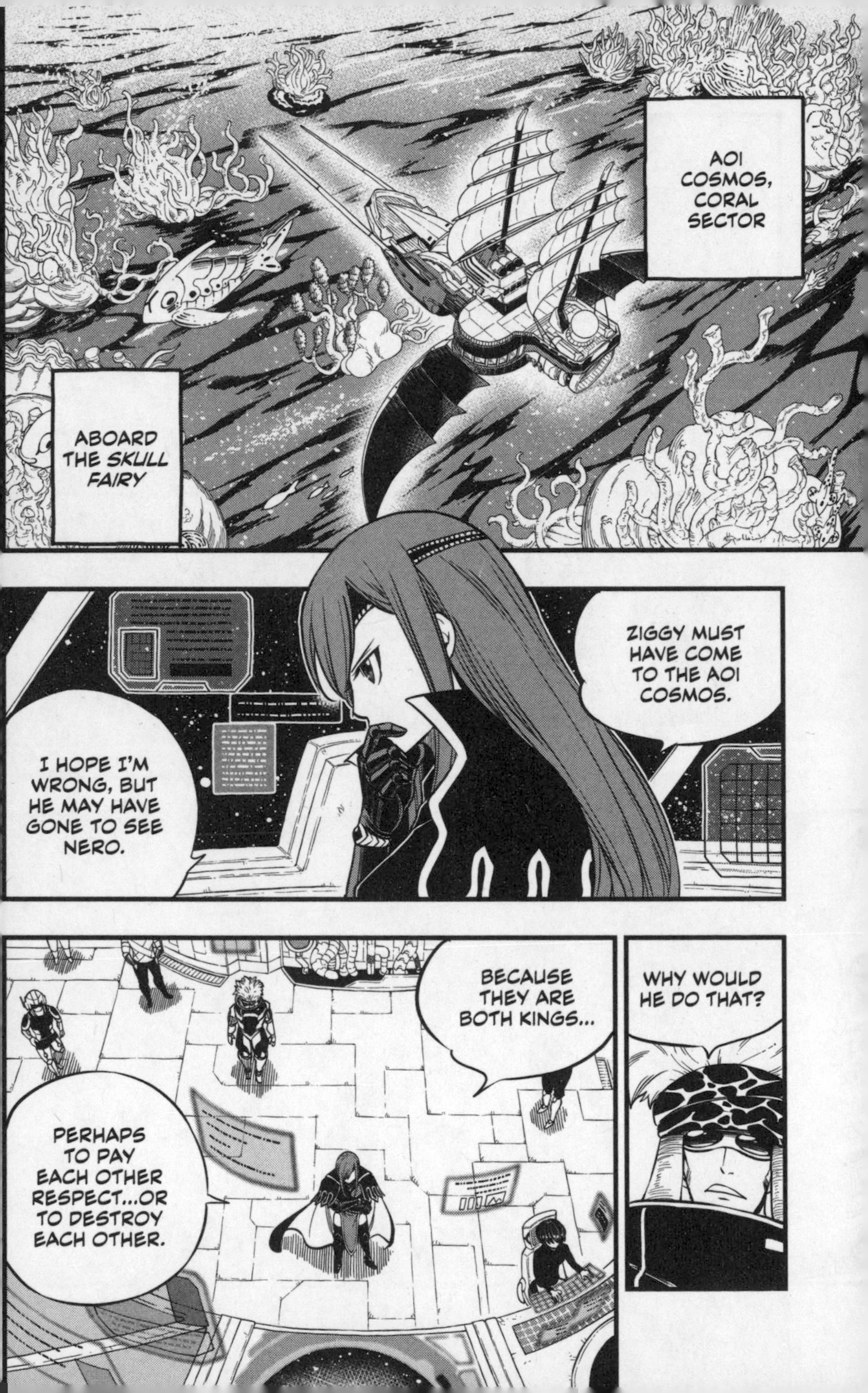
AOI COSMOS, CORAL SECTOR
ABOARD THE SKULL FAIRY
ZIGGY MUST HAVE COME TO THE AOI COSMOS.
I HOPE I'M WRONG, BUT HE MAY HAVE GONE TO SEE NERO.
WHY WOULD HE DO THAT?
BECAUSE THEY ARE BOTH KINGS...
PERHAPS TO PAY EACH OTHER RESPECT...OR TO DESTROY EACH OTHER.

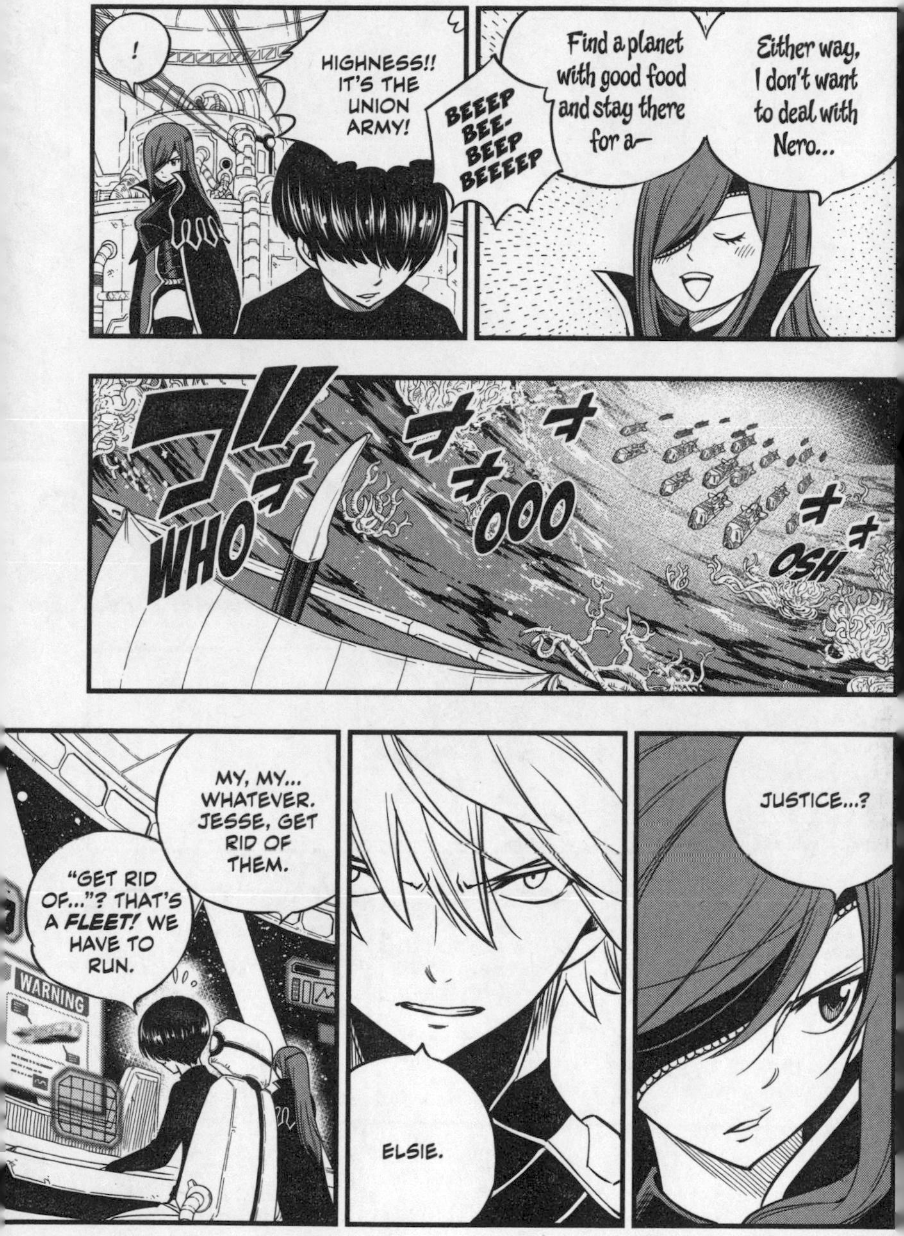
Either way, I don't want to deal with Nero...
Find a planet with good food and stay there for a—
BEEEP BEE-BEEP BEEEEP
HIGHNESS!! IT'S THE UNION ARMY!
!
WHOOOOSH
JUSTICE...?
ELSIE.
MY, MY... WHATEVER. JESSE, GET RID OF THEM.
"GET RID OF..."? THAT'S A *FLEET!* WE HAVE TO RUN.
WARNING

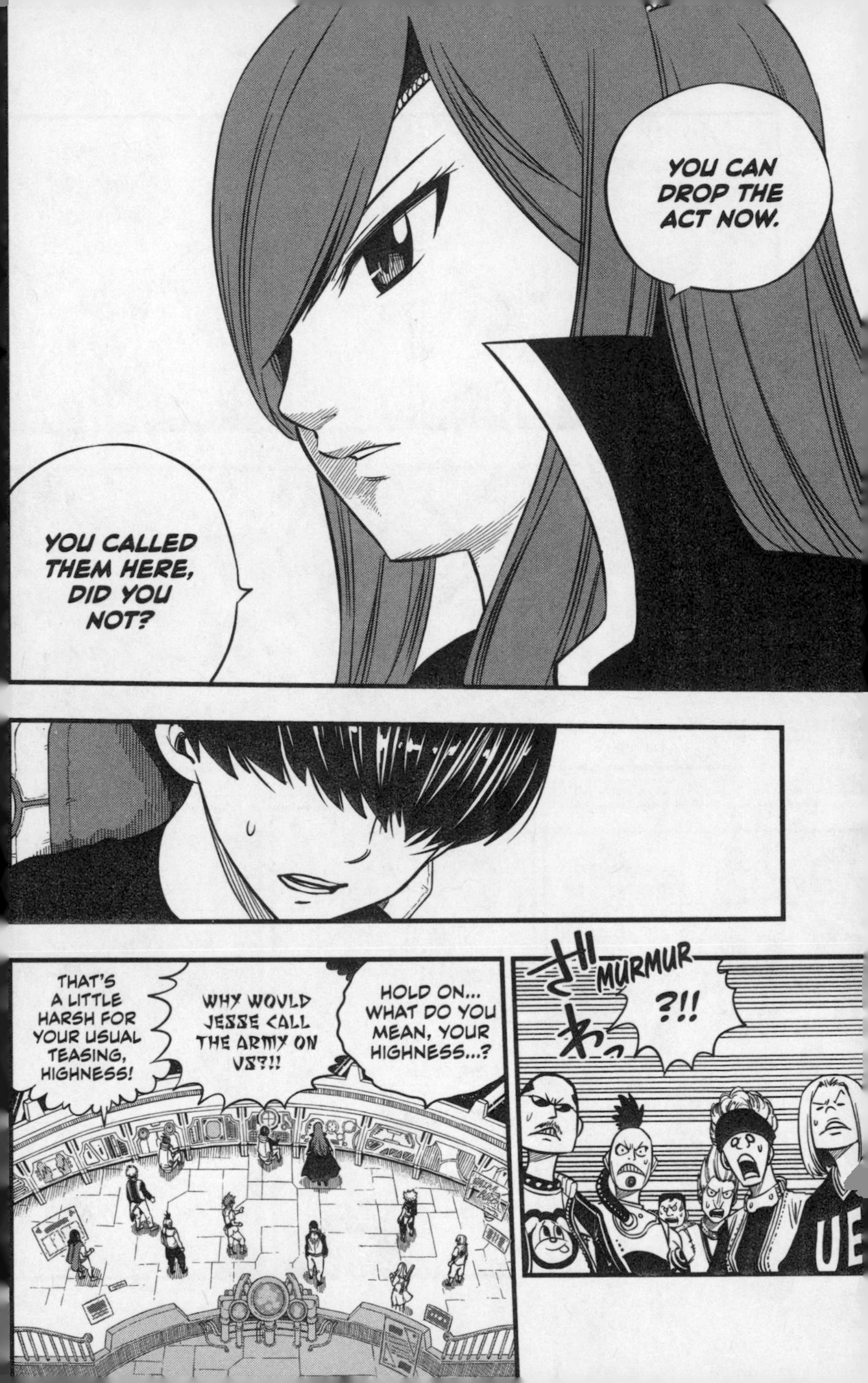
YOU CAN DROP THE ACT NOW.
YOU CALLED THEM HERE, DID YOU NOT?
ざわっ
MURMUR
?!!
HOLD ON... WHAT DO YOU MEAN, YOUR HIGHNESS...?
WHY WOULD JESSE CALL THE ARMY ON US?!!
THAT'S A LITTLE HARSH FOR YOUR USUAL TEASING, HIGHNESS!

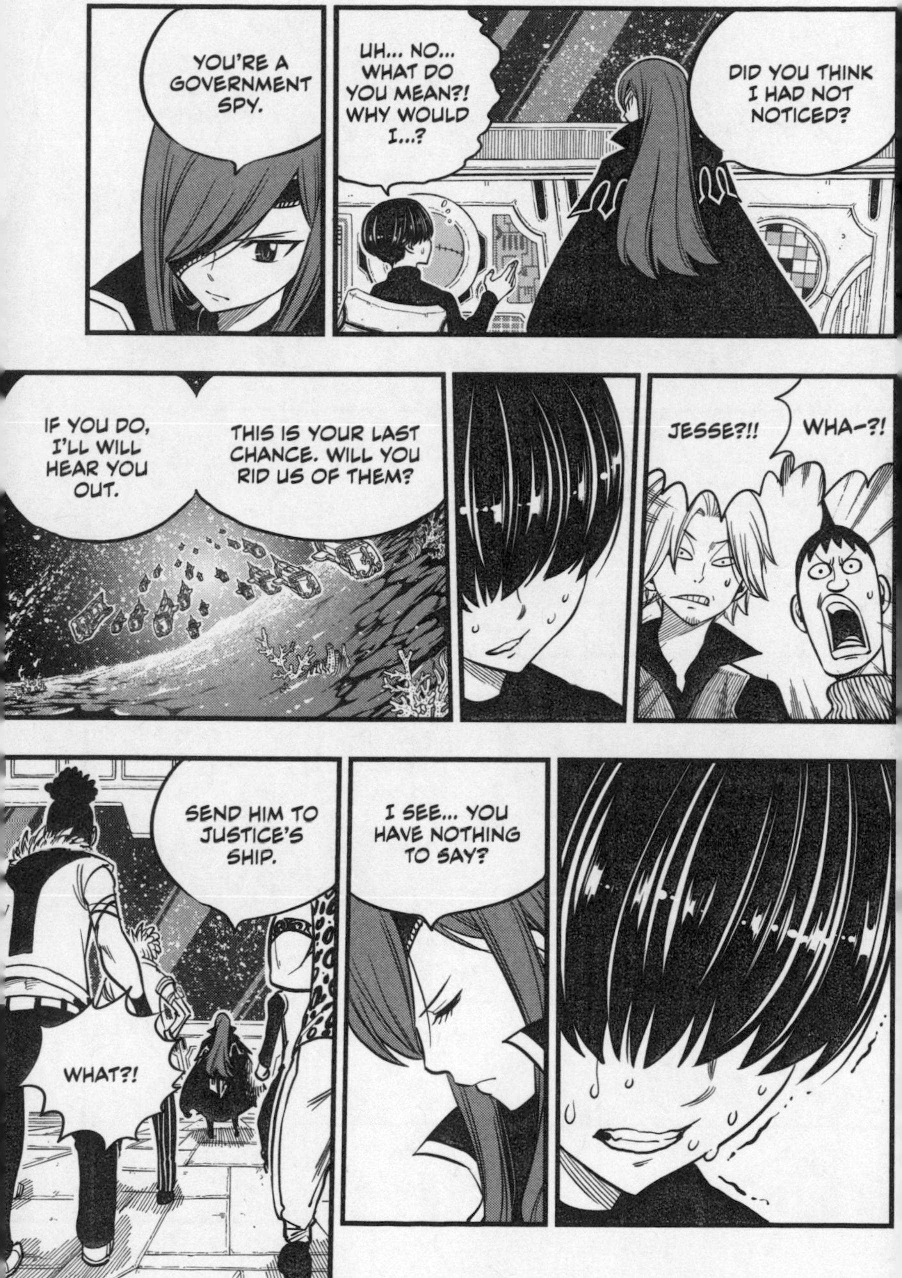
DID YOU THINK I HAD NOT NOTICED?
UH... NO... WHAT DO YOU MEAN?! WHY WOULD I...?
YOU'RE A GOVERNMENT SPY.
WHA-?!
JESSE?!!
THIS IS YOUR LAST CHANCE. WILL YOU RID US OF THEM?
IF YOU DO, I'LL WILL HEAR YOU OUT.
I SEE... YOU HAVE NOTHING TO SAY?
SEND HIM TO JUSTICE'S SHIP.
WHAT?!

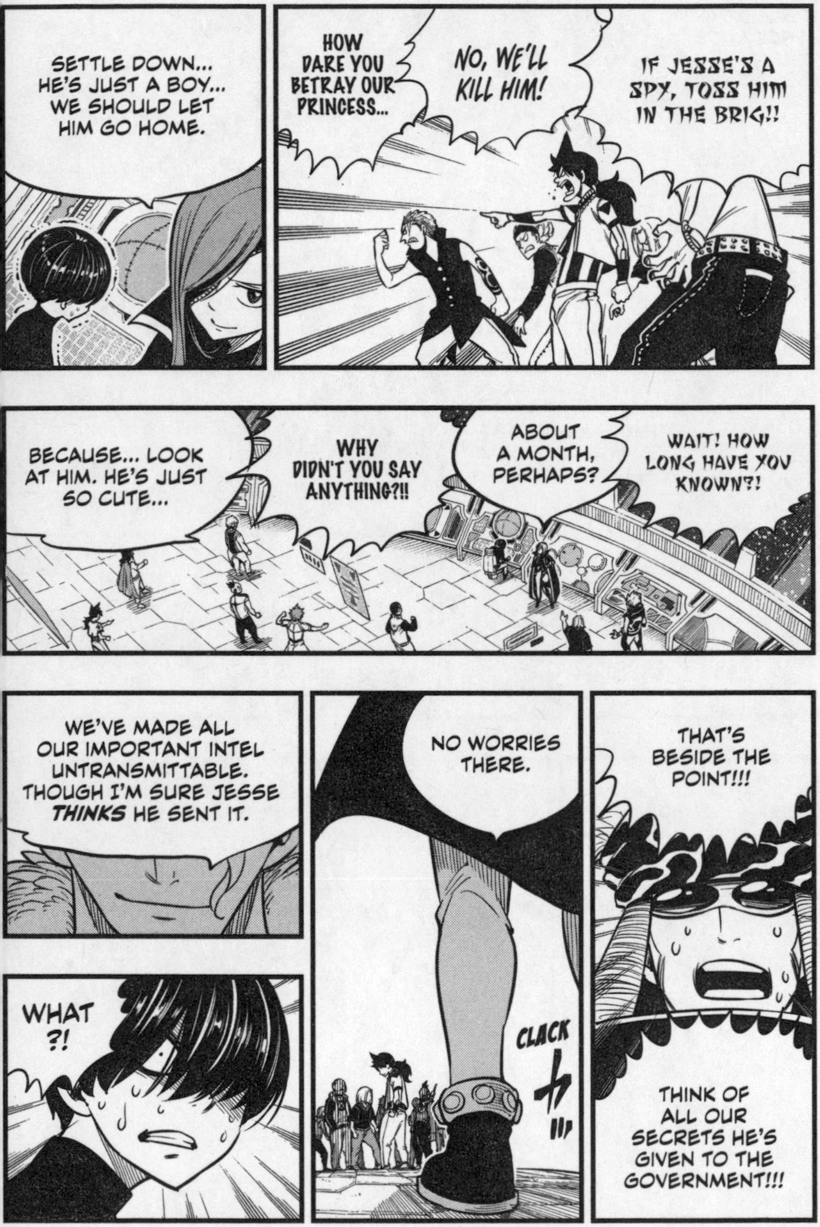
IF JESSE'S A SPY, TOSS HIM IN THE BRIG!!
NO, WE'LL KILL HIM!
HOW DARE YOU BETRAY OUR PRINCESS...
SETTLE DOWN... HE'S JUST A BOY... WE SHOULD LET HIM GO HOME.
WAIT! HOW LONG HAVE YOU KNOWN?!
ABOUT A MONTH, PERHAPS?
WHY DIDN'T YOU SAY ANYTHING?!!
BECAUSE... LOOK AT HIM. HE'S JUST SO CUTE...
THAT'S BESIDE THE POINT!!!
THINK OF ALL OUR SECRETS HE'S GIVEN TO THE GOVERNMENT!!!
NO WORRIES THERE.
CLACK
WE'VE MADE ALL OUR IMPORTANT INTEL UNTRANSMITTABLE. THOUGH I'M SURE JESSE *THINKS* HE SENT IT.
WHAT?!

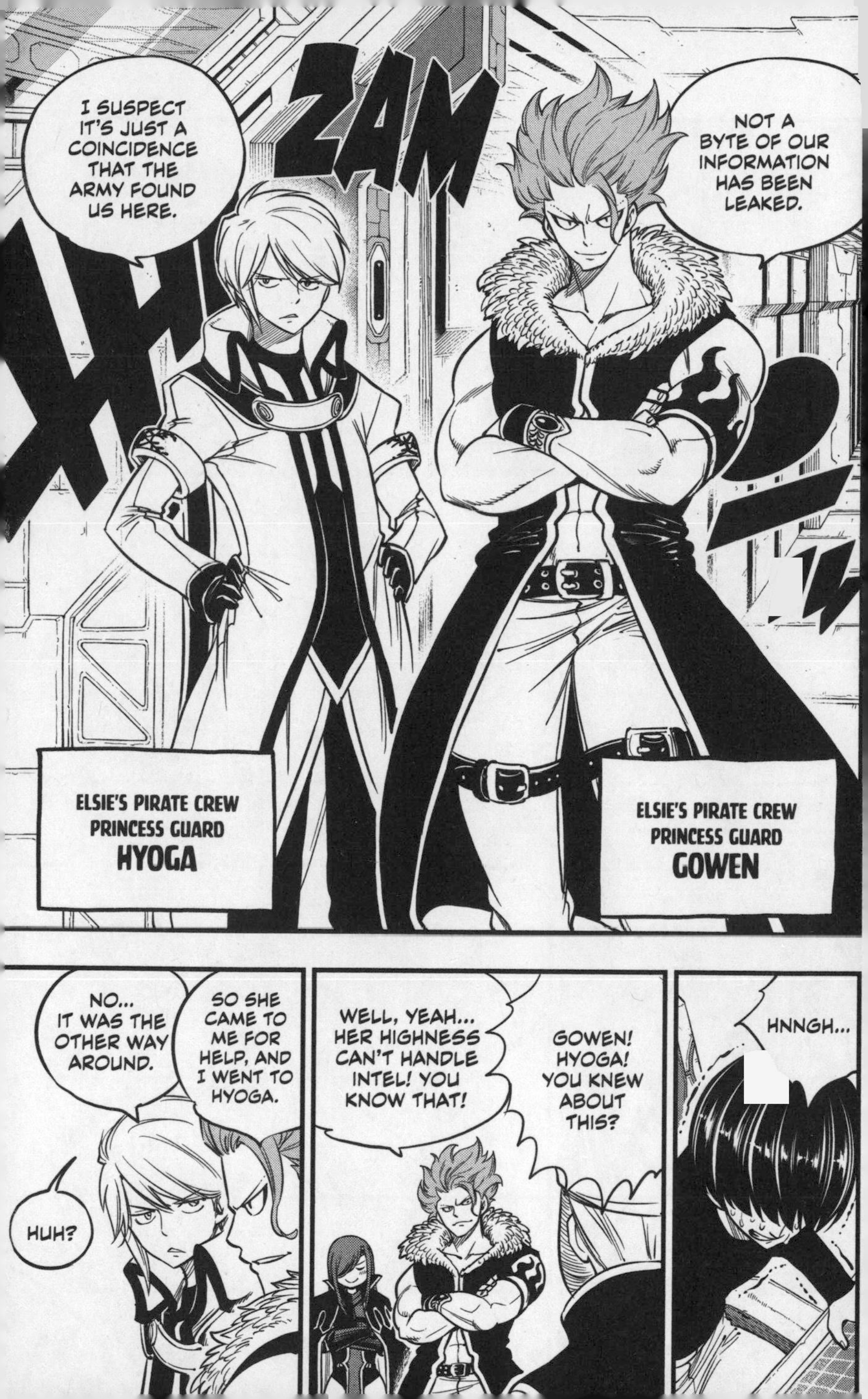
NOT A BYTE OF OUR INFORMATION HAS BEEN LEAKED.
ZAM
I SUSPECT IT'S JUST A COINCIDENCE THAT THE ARMY FOUND US HERE.
ELSIE'S PIRATE CREW PRINCESS GUARD GOWEN
ELSIE'S PIRATE CREW PRINCESS GUARD HYOGA
HNNGH...
GOWEN! HYOGA! YOU KNEW ABOUT THIS?
WELL, YEAH... HER HIGHNESS CAN'T HANDLE INTEL! YOU KNOW THAT!
SO SHE CAME TO ME FOR HELP, AND I WENT TO HYOGA.
NO... IT WAS THE OTHER WAY AROUND.
HUH?

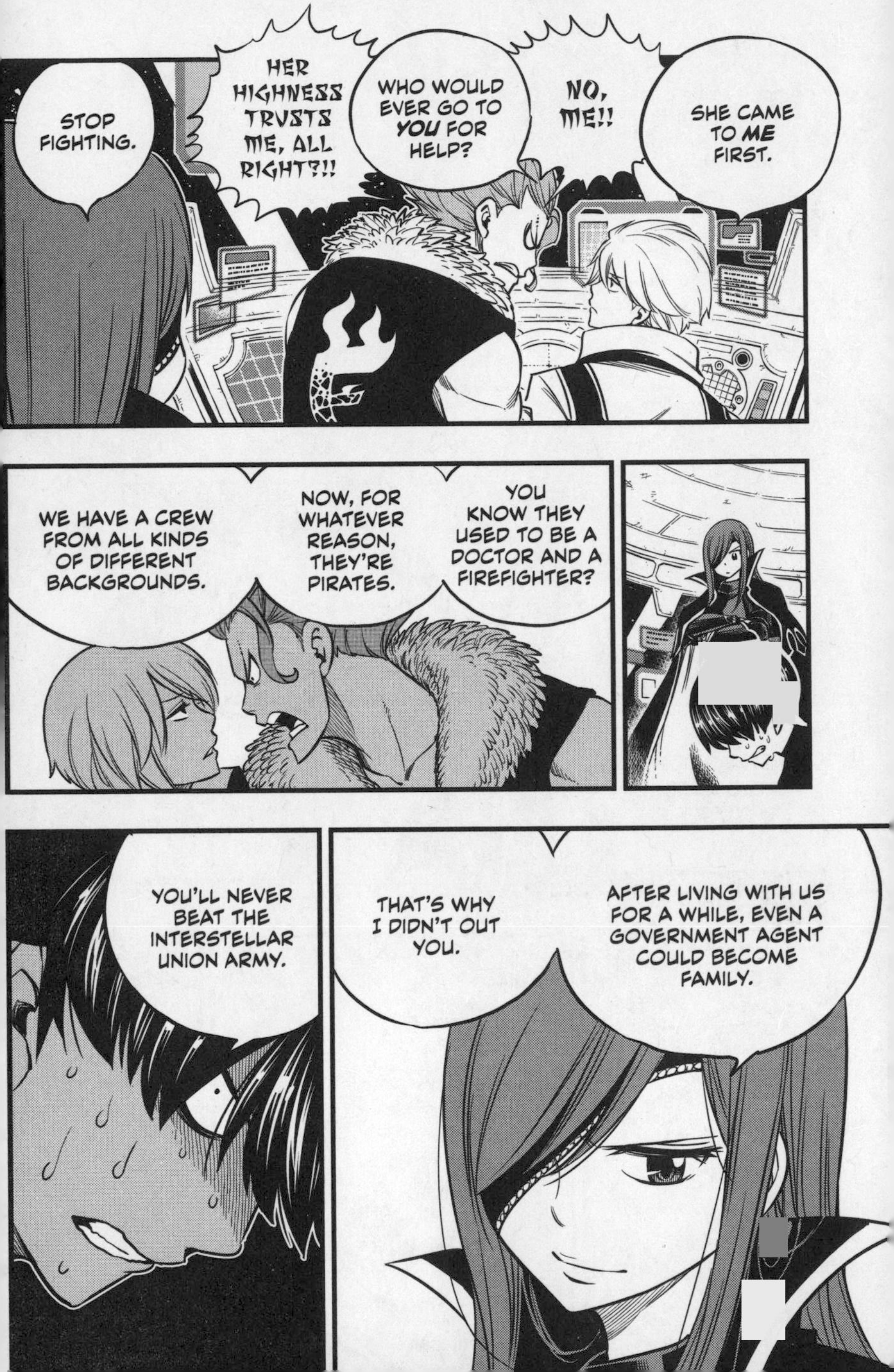
SHE CAME TO ME FIRST.
NO, ME!!
WHO WOULD EVER GO TO YOU FOR HELP?
HER HIGHNESS TRUSTS ME, ALL RIGHT?!!
STOP FIGHTING.
YOU KNOW THEY USED TO BE A DOCTOR AND A FIREFIGHTER?
NOW, FOR WHATEVER REASON, THEY'RE PIRATES.
WE HAVE A CREW FROM ALL KINDS OF DIFFERENT BACKGROUNDS.
AFTER LIVING WITH US FOR A WHILE, EVEN A GOVERNMENT AGENT COULD BECOME FAMILY.
THAT'S WHY I DIDN'T OUT YOU.
YOU'LL NEVER BEAT THE INTERSTELLAR UNION ARMY.

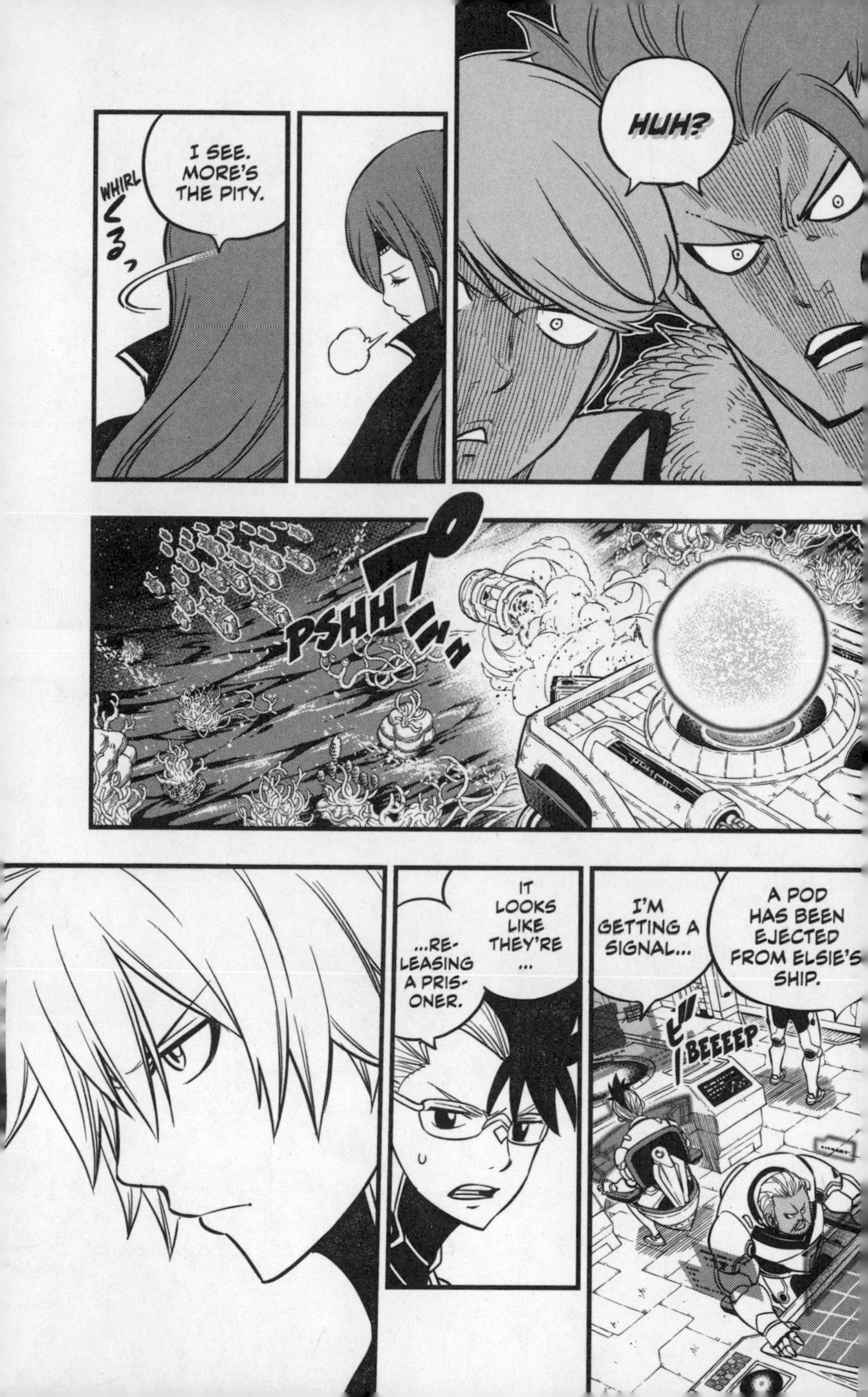
HUH?
I SEE. MORE'S THE PITY.
WHIRL
PSHH
A POD HAS BEEN EJECTED FROM ELSIE'S SHIP.
I'M GETTING A SIGNAL...
BEEEEP
IT LOOKS LIKE THEY'RE ...
...RE-LEASING A PRIS-ONER.

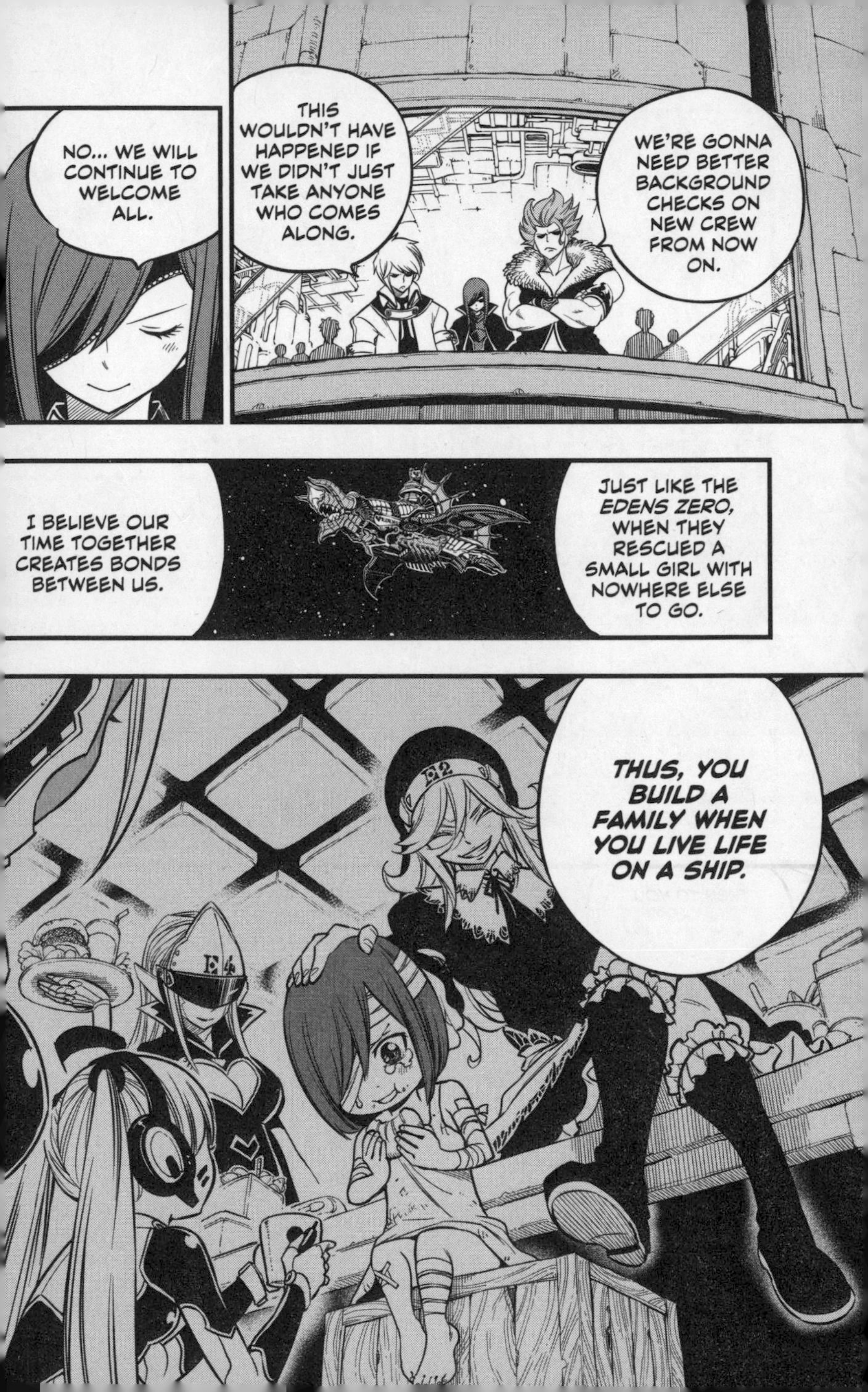
WE'RE GONNA NEED BETTER BACKGROUND CHECKS ON NEW CREW FROM NOW ON.
THIS WOULDN'T HAVE HAPPENED IF WE DIDN'T JUST TAKE ANYONE WHO COMES ALONG.
NO... WE WILL CONTINUE TO WELCOME ALL.
JUST LIKE THE *EDENS ZERO*, WHEN THEY RESCUED A SMALL GIRL WITH NOWHERE ELSE TO GO.
I BELIEVE OUR TIME TOGETHER CREATES BONDS BETWEEN US.
THUS, YOU BUILD A FAMILY WHEN YOU LIVE LIFE ON A SHIP.

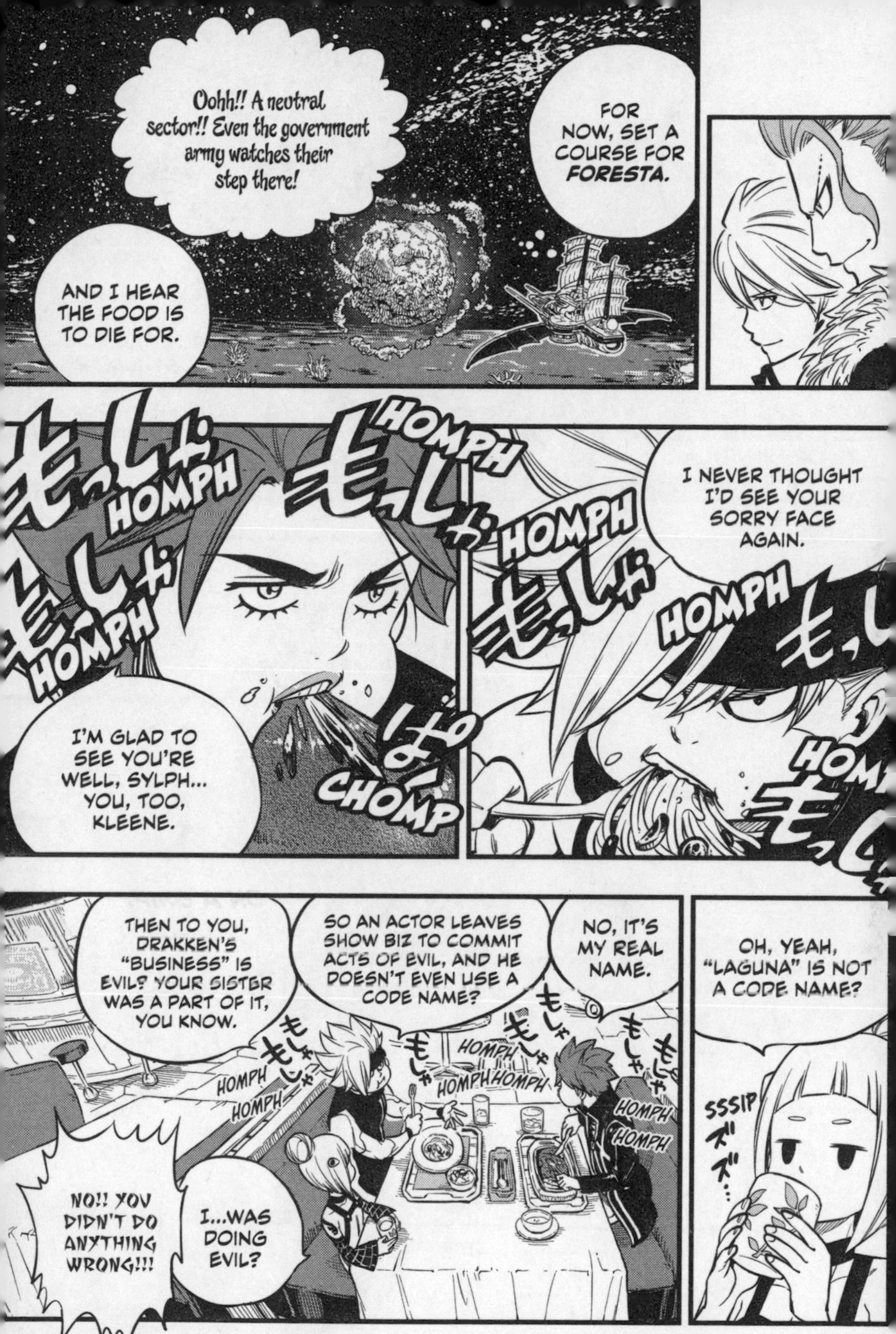
FOR NOW, SET A COURSE FOR FORESTA.
Oohh!! A neutral sector!! Even the government army watches their step there!
AND I HEAR THE FOOD IS TO DIE FOR.
I NEVER THOUGHT I'D SEE YOUR SORRY FACE AGAIN.
HOMPH
HOMPH
HOMPH
HOMPH
HOMPH
I'M GLAD TO SEE YOU'RE WELL, SYLPH... YOU, TOO, KLEENE.
CHOMP
OH, YEAH, "LAGUNA" IS NOT A CODE NAME?
SSSIP
NO, IT'S MY REAL NAME.
SO AN ACTOR LEAVES SHOW BIZ TO COMMIT ACTS OF EVIL, AND HE DOESN'T EVEN USE A CODE NAME?
THEN TO YOU, DRAKKEN'S "BUSINESS" IS EVIL? YOUR SISTER WAS A PART OF IT, YOU KNOW.
HOMPH HOMPH
HOMPH HOMPH
HOMPH HOMPH
I...WAS DOING EVIL?
NO!! YOU DIDN'T DO ANYTHING WRONG!!!

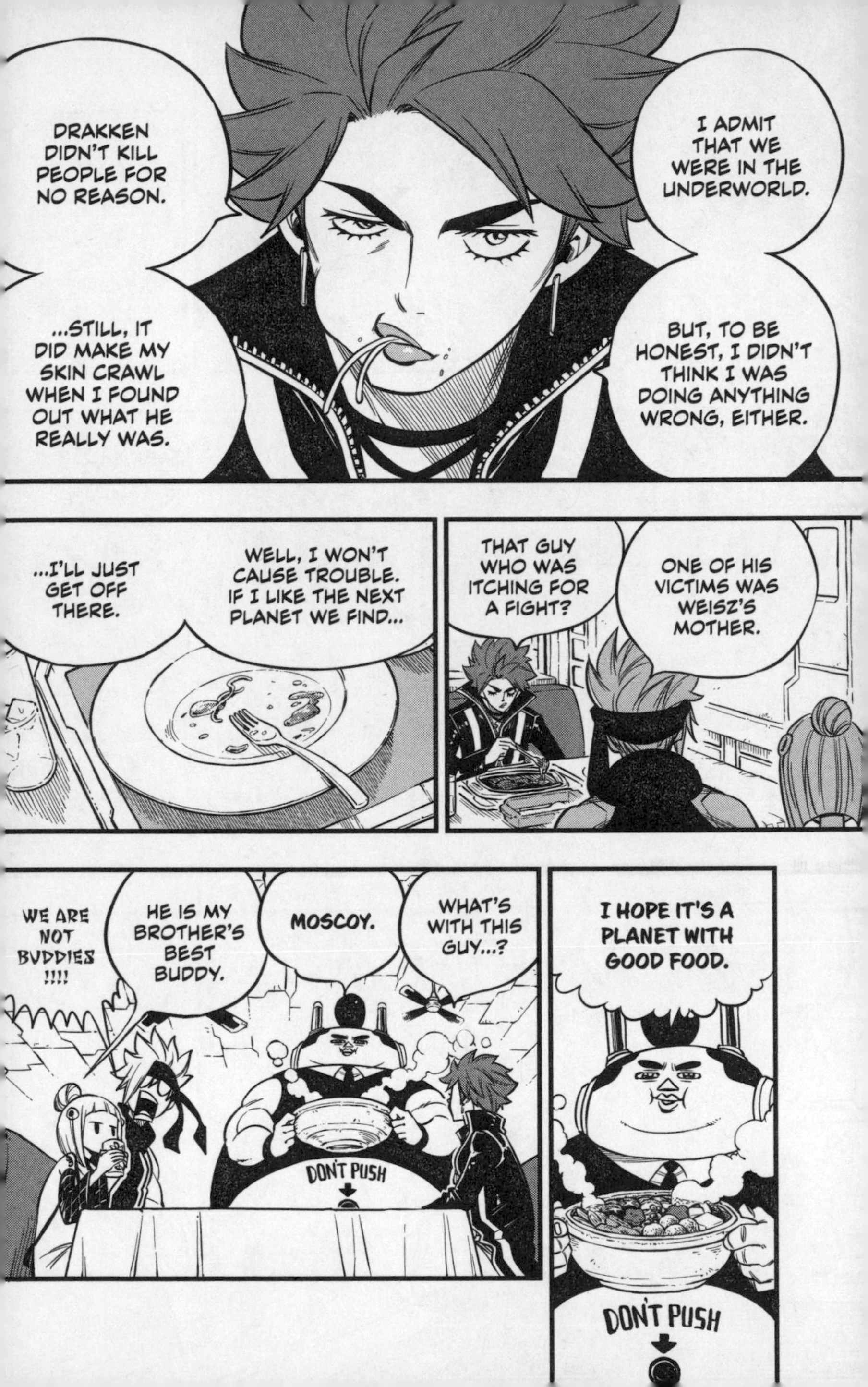
I ADMIT THAT WE WERE IN THE UNDERWORLD.
BUT, TO BE HONEST, I DIDN'T THINK I WAS DOING ANYTHING WRONG, EITHER.
DRAKKEN DIDN'T KILL PEOPLE FOR NO REASON.
...STILL, IT DID MAKE MY SKIN CRAWL WHEN I FOUND OUT WHAT HE REALLY WAS.
ONE OF HIS VICTIMS WAS WEISZ'S MOTHER.
THAT GUY WHO WAS ITCHING FOR A FIGHT?
WELL, I WON'T CAUSE TROUBLE. IF I LIKE THE NEXT PLANET WE FIND...
...I'LL JUST GET OFF THERE.
I HOPE IT'S A PLANET WITH GOOD FOOD.
DON'T PUSH
WHAT'S WITH THIS GUY...?
MOSCOY.
HE IS MY BROTHER'S BEST BUDDY.
WE ARE NOT BUDDIES!!!!
DON'T PUSH

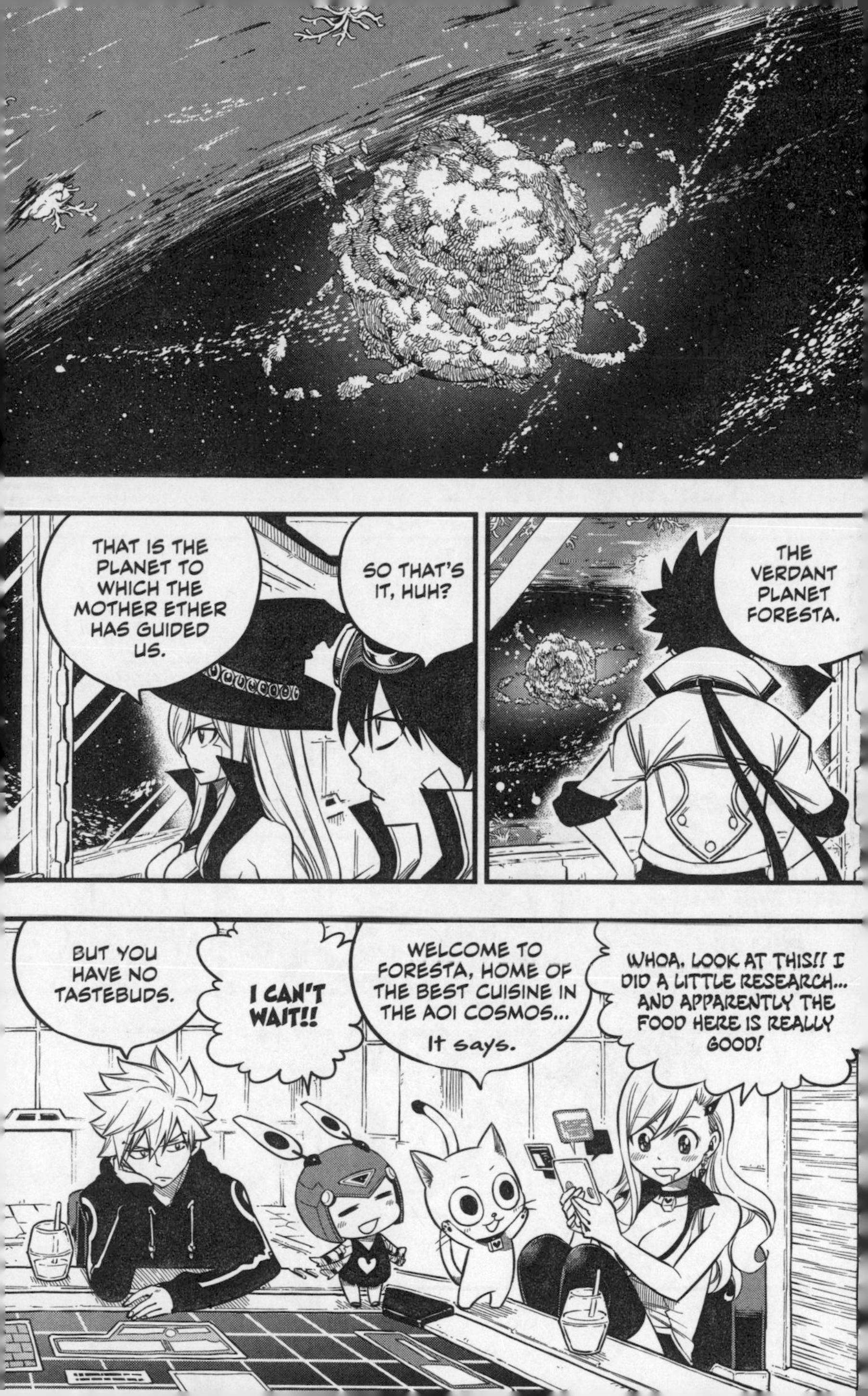
THE VERDANT PLANET FORESTA.
THAT IS THE PLANET TO WHICH THE MOTHER ETHER HAS GUIDED US.
SO THAT'S IT, HUH?
WHOA, LOOK AT THIS!! I DID A LITTLE RESEARCH... AND APPARENTLY THE FOOD HERE IS REALLY GOOD!
WELCOME TO FORESTA, HOME OF THE BEST CUISINE IN THE AOI COSMOS...
It says.
I CAN'T WAIT!!
BUT YOU HAVE NO TASTEBUDS.

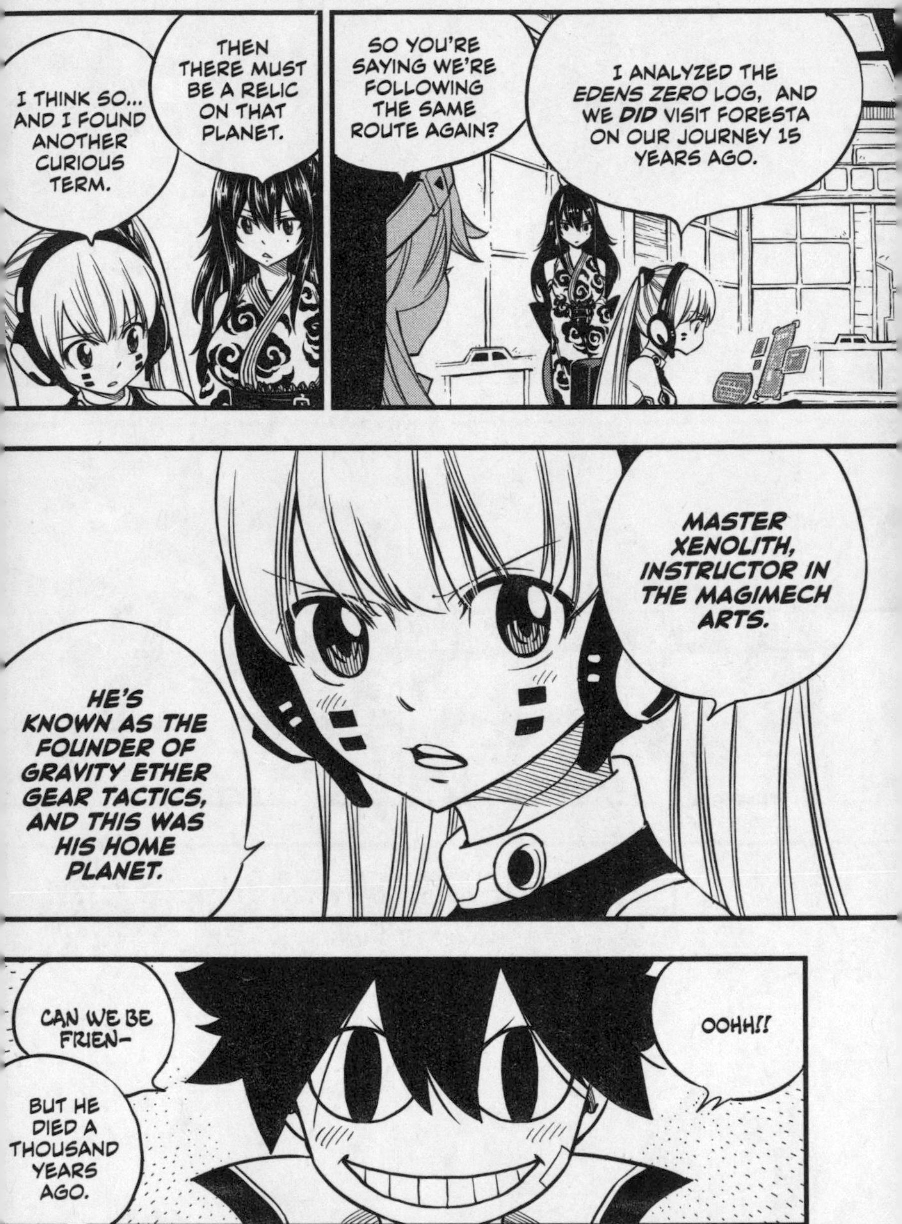
I ANALYZED THE EDENS ZERO LOG, AND WE DID VISIT FORESTA ON OUR JOURNEY 15 YEARS AGO.
SO YOU'RE SAYING WE'RE FOLLOWING THE SAME ROUTE AGAIN?
THEN THERE MUST BE A RELIC ON THAT PLANET.
I THINK SO... AND I FOUND ANOTHER CURIOUS TERM.
MASTER XENOLITH, INSTRUCTOR IN THE MAGIMECH ARTS.
HE'S KNOWN AS THE FOUNDER OF GRAVITY ETHER GEAR TACTICS, AND THIS WAS HIS HOME PLANET.
OOHH!!
CAN WE BE FRIEN-
BUT HE DIED A THOUSAND YEARS AGO.

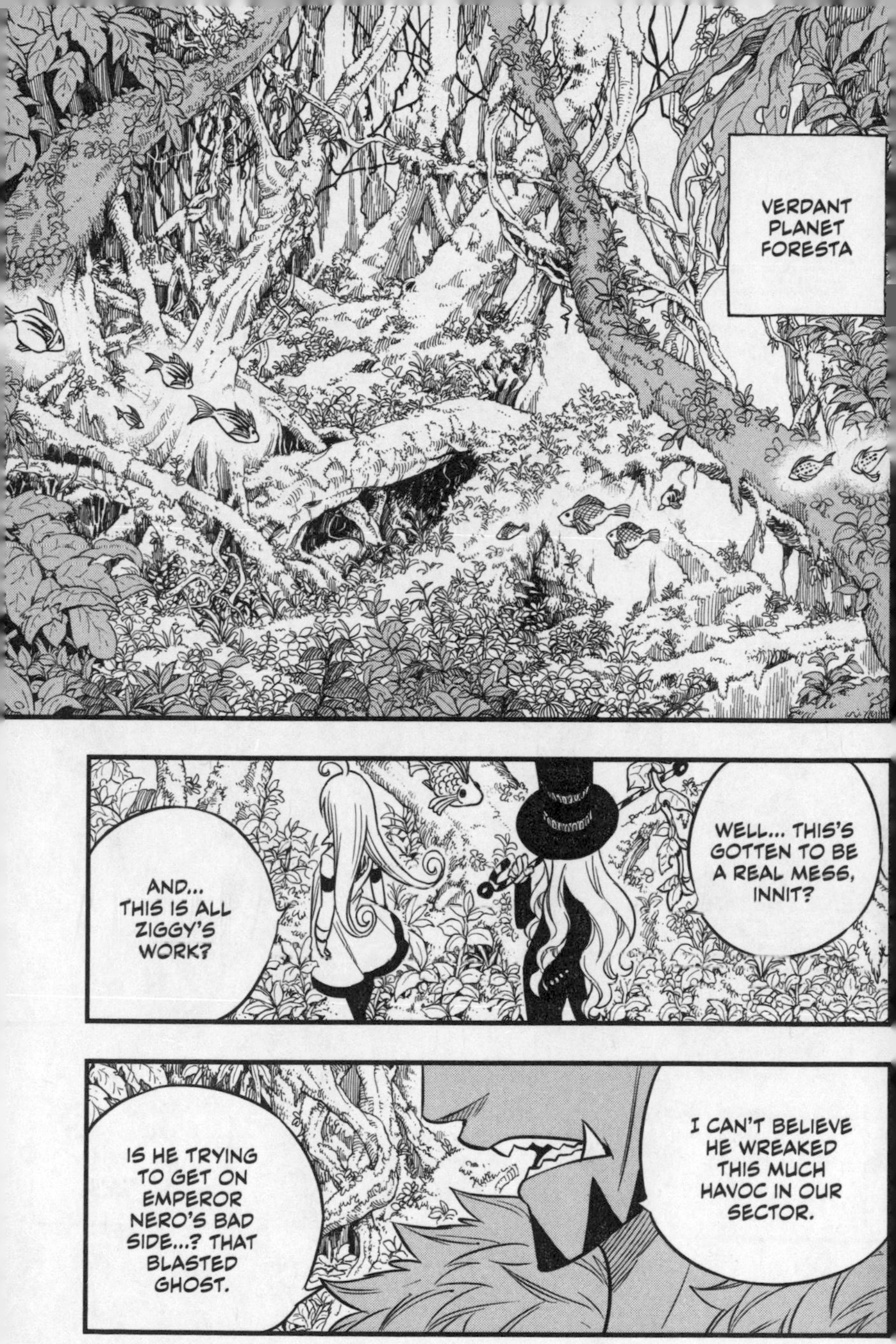
VERDANT PLANET FORESTA
WELL... THIS'S GOTTEN TO BE A REAL MESS, INNIT?
AND... THIS IS ALL ZIGGY'S WORK?
I CAN'T BELIEVE HE WREAKED THIS MUCH HAVOC IN OUR SECTOR.
IS HE TRYING TO GET ON EMPEROR NERO'S BAD SIDE...? THAT BLASTED GHOST.

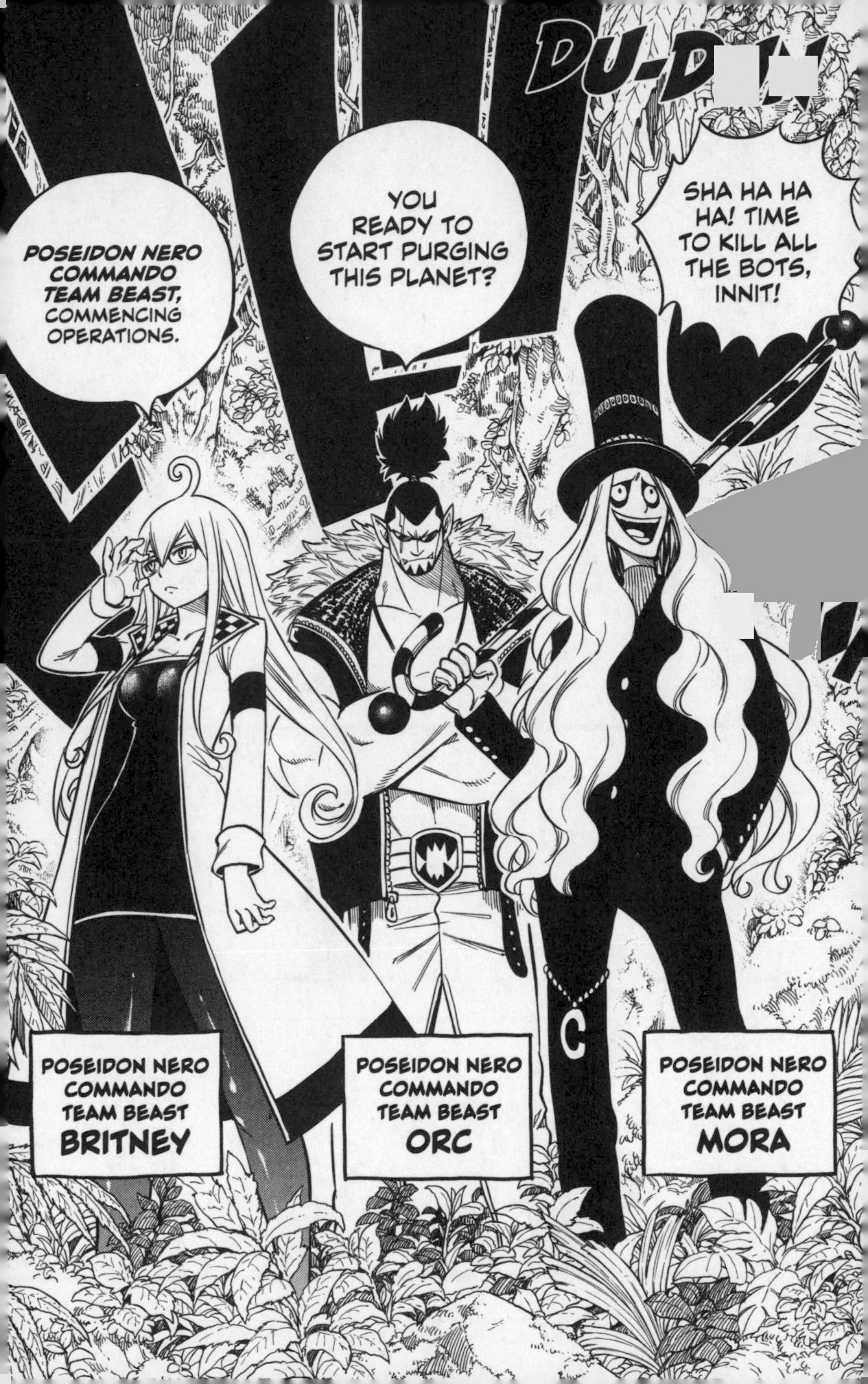
SHA HA HA! TIME TO KILL ALL THE BOTS, INNIT!
YOU READY TO START PURGING THIS PLANET?
POSEIDON NERO COMMANDO TEAM BEAST, COMMENCING OPERATIONS.
POSEIDON NERO COMMANDO TEAM BEAST MORA
POSEIDON NERO COMMANDO TEAM BEAST ORC
POSEIDON NERO COMMANDO TEAM BEAST BRITNEY

EDENS ZERO

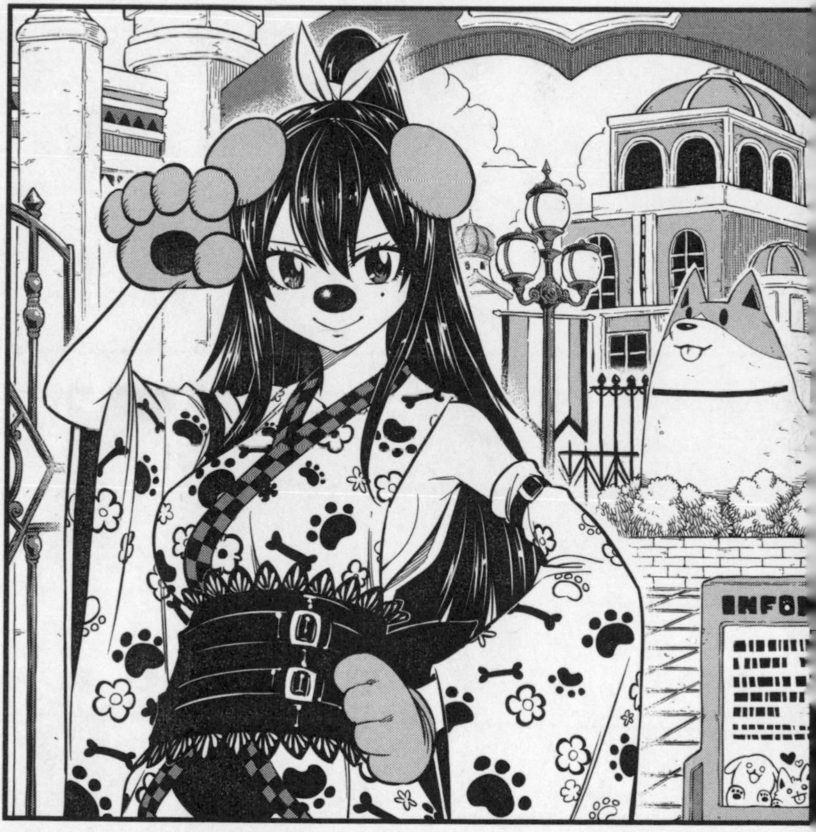

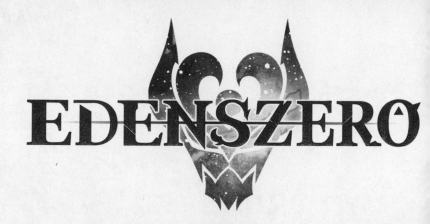

CHAPTER 113: IN THE DOGHOUSE

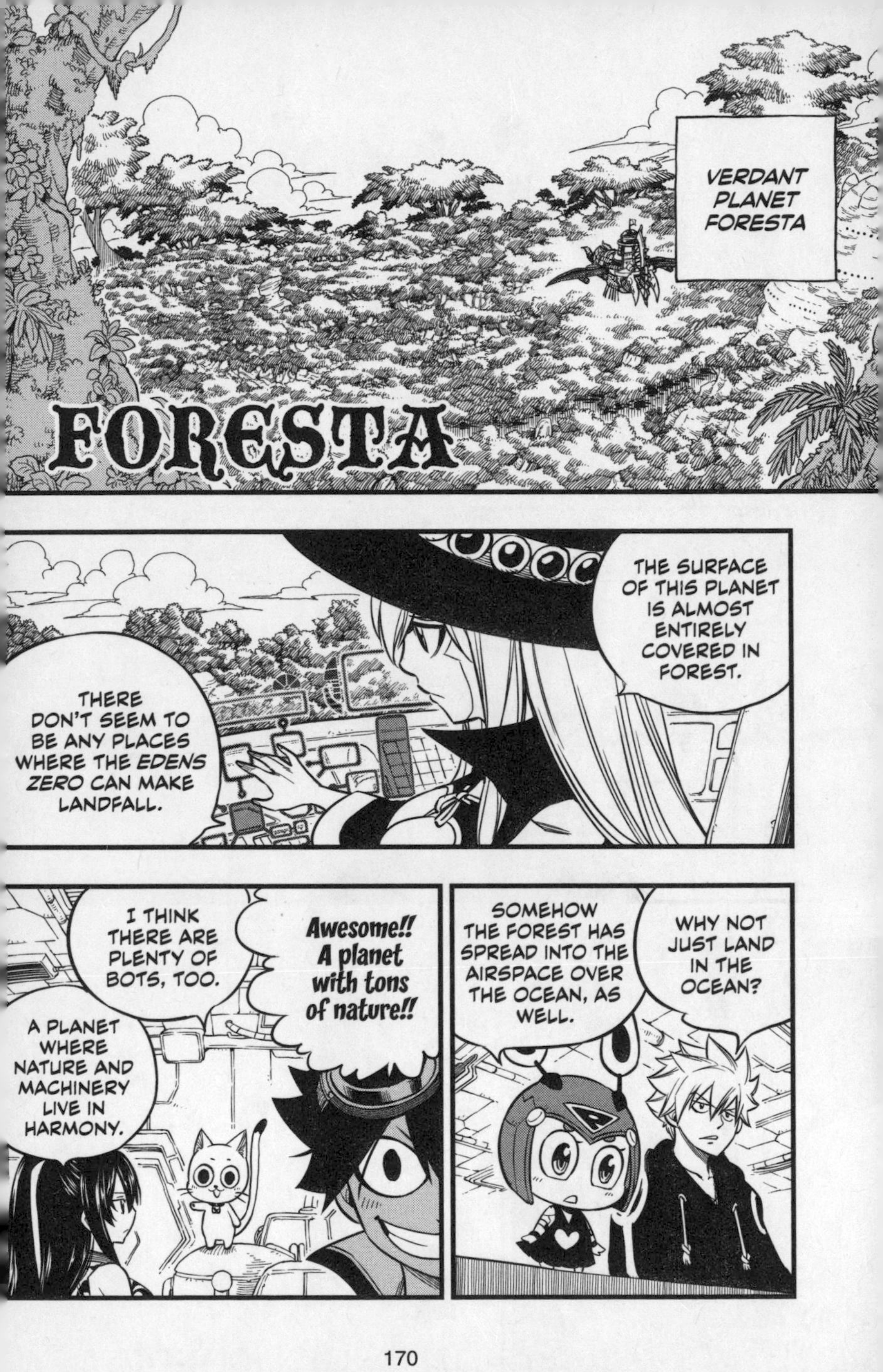
VERDANT PLANET FORESTA
FORESTA
THE SURFACE OF THIS PLANET IS ALMOST ENTIRELY COVERED IN FOREST.
THERE DON'T SEEM TO BE ANY PLACES WHERE THE *EDENS ZERO* CAN MAKE LANDFALL.
WHY NOT JUST LAND IN THE OCEAN?
SOMEHOW THE FOREST HAS SPREAD INTO THE AIRSPACE OVER THE OCEAN, AS WELL.
Awesome!! A planet with tons of nature!!
I THINK THERE ARE PLENTY OF BOTS, TOO.
A PLANET WHERE NATURE AND MACHINERY LIVE IN HARMONY.

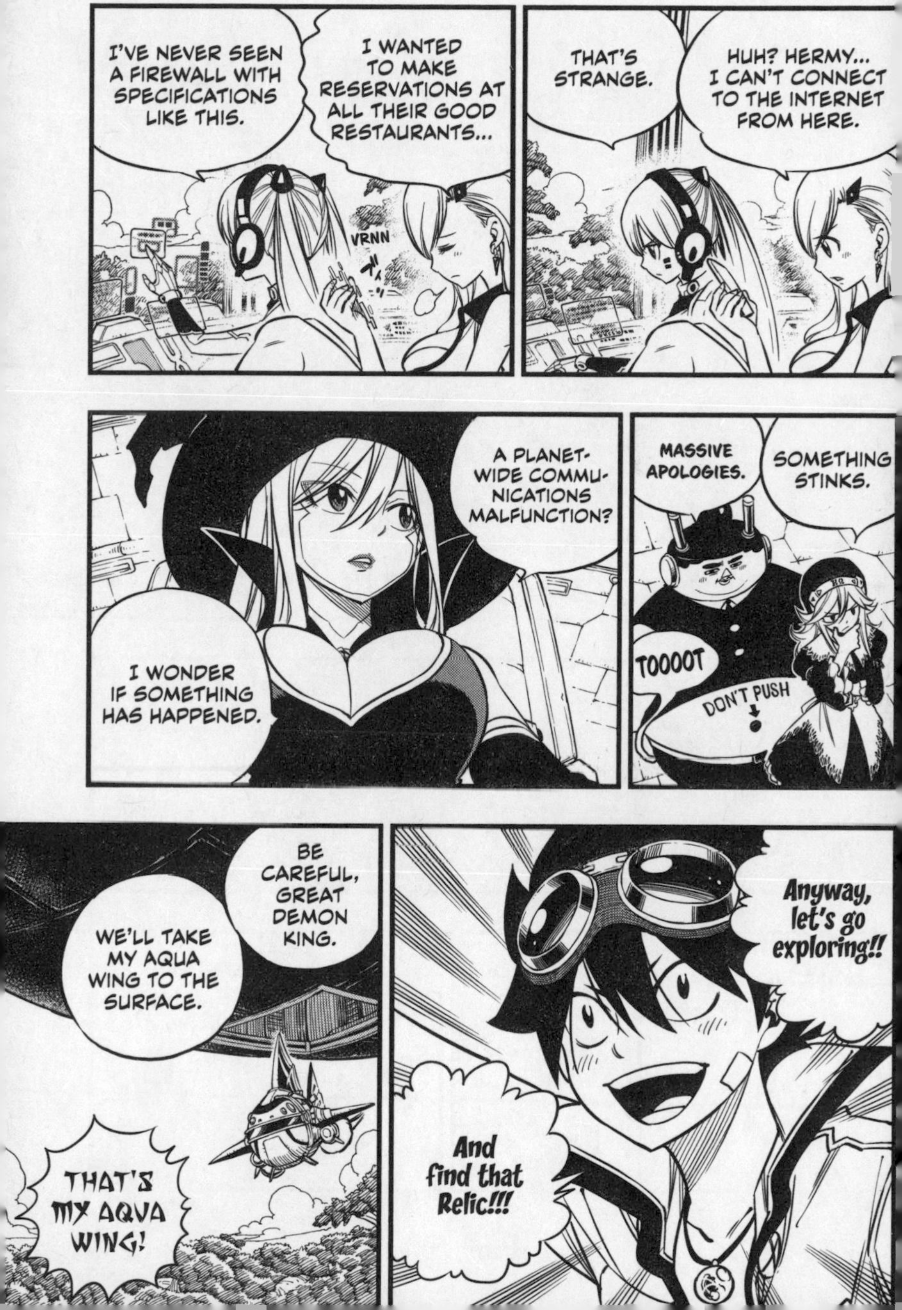
HUH? HERMY... I CAN'T CONNECT TO THE INTERNET FROM HERE.
THAT'S STRANGE.
I WANTED TO MAKE RESERVATIONS AT ALL THEIR GOOD RESTAURANTS...
VRNN
I'VE NEVER SEEN A FIREWALL WITH SPECIFICATIONS LIKE THIS.
SOMETHING STINKS.
MASSIVE APOLOGIES.
TOOOOT
DON'T PUSH
A PLANET-WIDE COMMUNICATIONS MALFUNCTION?
I WONDER IF SOMETHING HAS HAPPENED.
Anyway, let's go exploring!!
And find that Relic!!!
BE CAREFUL, GREAT DEMON KING.
WE'LL TAKE MY AQUA WING TO THE SURFACE.
THAT'S MY AQUA WING!

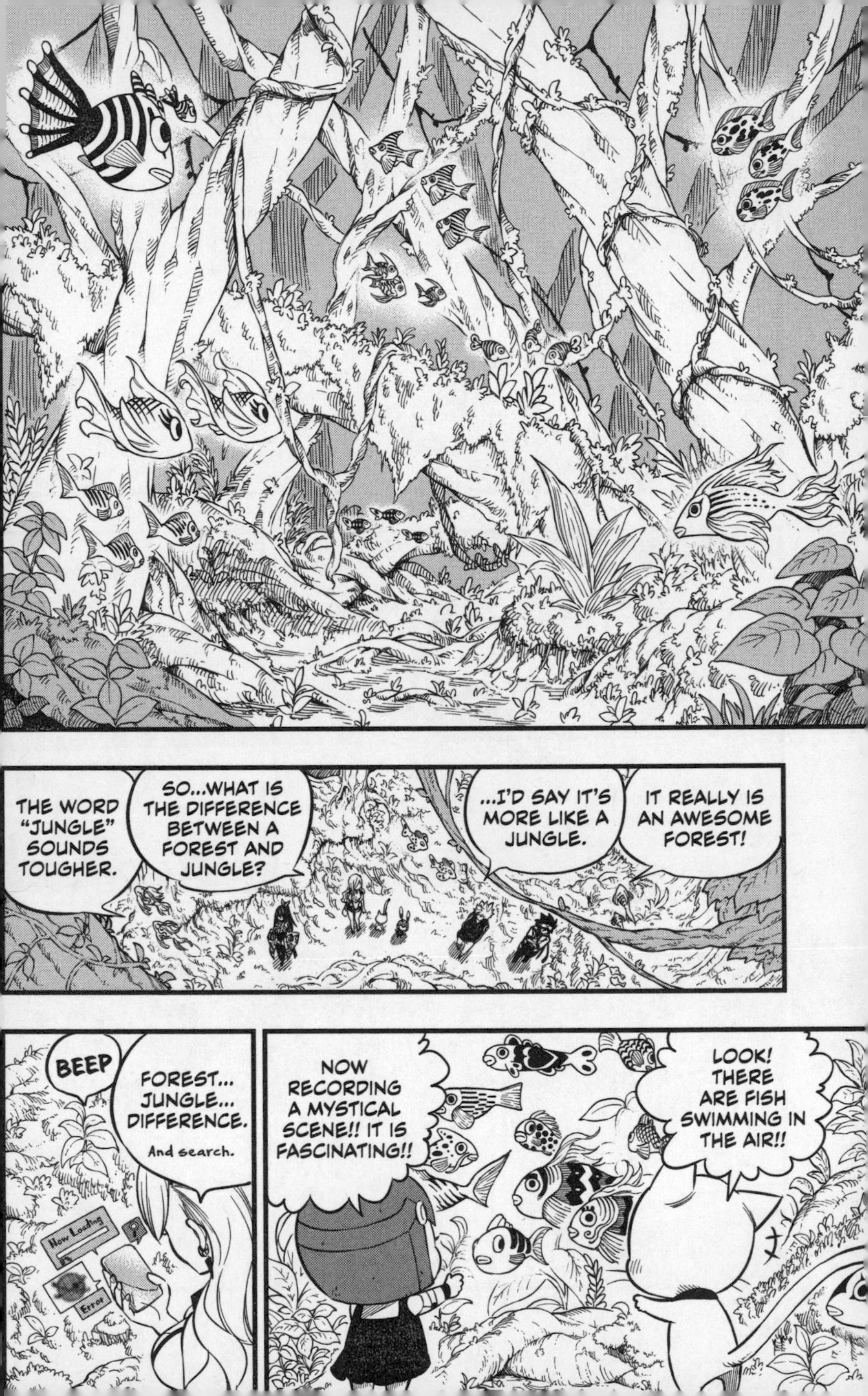
IT REALLY IS AN AWESOME FOREST!
...I'D SAY IT'S MORE LIKE A JUNGLE.
SO...WHAT IS THE DIFFERENCE BETWEEN A FOREST AND JUNGLE?
THE WORD "JUNGLE" SOUNDS TOUGHER.
LOOK! THERE ARE FISH SWIMMING IN THE AIR!!
NOW RECORDING A MYSTICAL SCENE!! IT IS FASCINATING!!
BEEP
FOREST... JUNGLE... DIFFERENCE.
And search.
Now Loading
Error

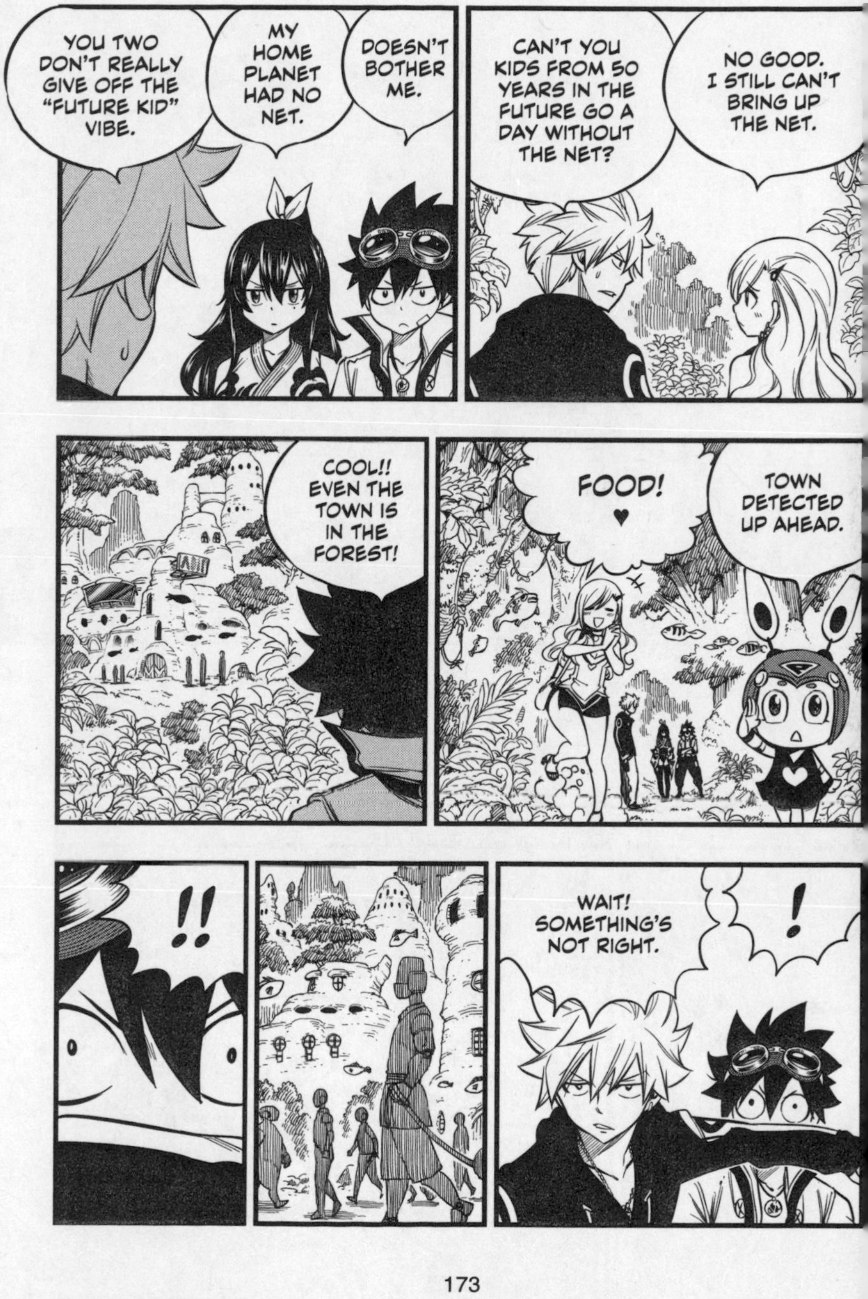
NO GOOD. I STILL CAN'T BRING UP THE NET.
CAN'T YOU KIDS FROM 50 YEARS IN THE FUTURE GO A DAY WITHOUT THE NET?
DOESN'T BOTHER ME.
MY HOME PLANET HAD NO NET.
YOU TWO DON'T REALLY GIVE OFF THE "FUTURE KID" VIBE.
TOWN DETECTED UP AHEAD.
FOOD! ♥
COOL!! EVEN THE TOWN IS IN THE FOREST!
!
WAIT! SOMETHING'S NOT RIGHT.
!!

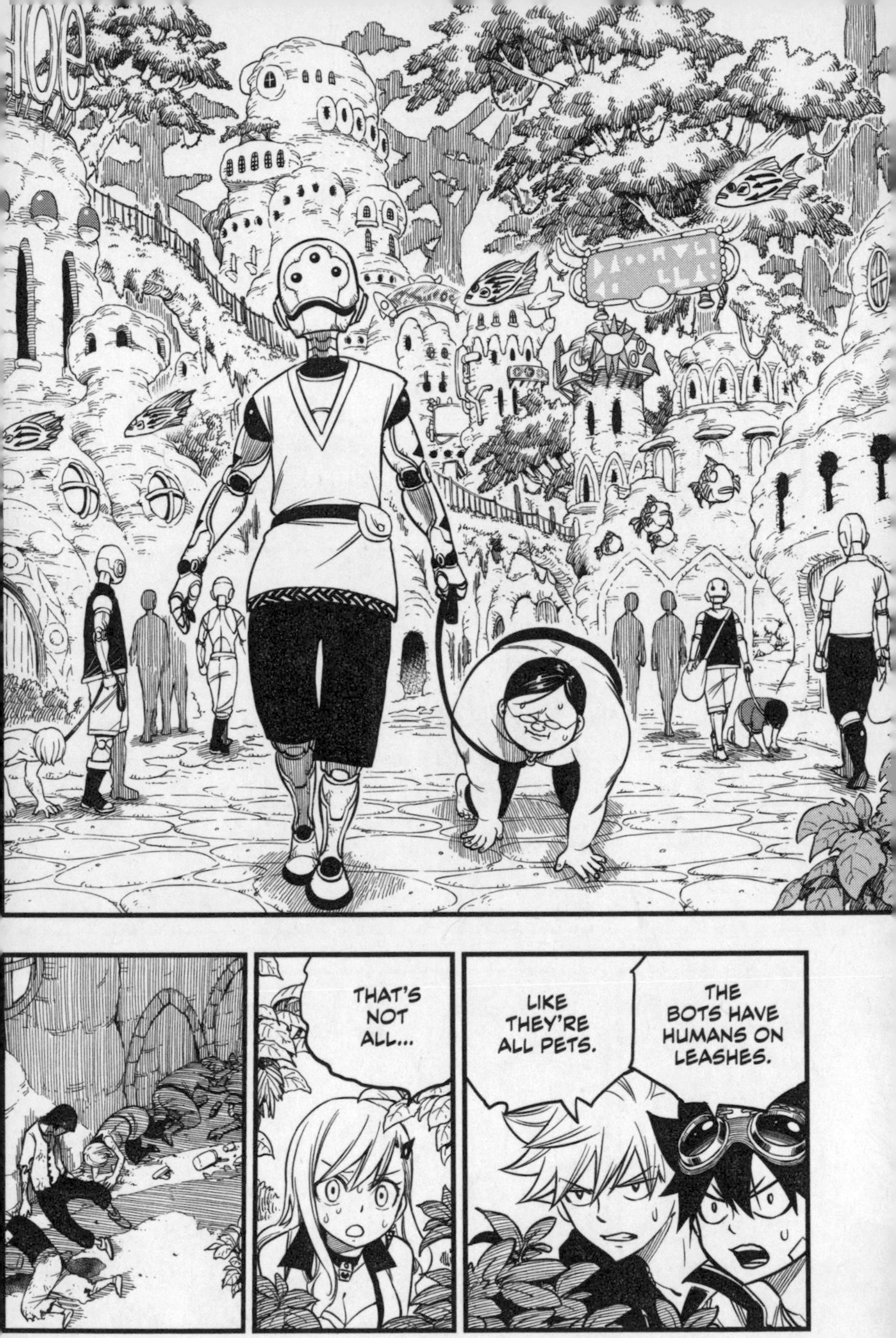
THE BOTS HAVE HUMANS ON LEASHES.
LIKE THEY'RE ALL PETS.
THAT'S NOT ALL...

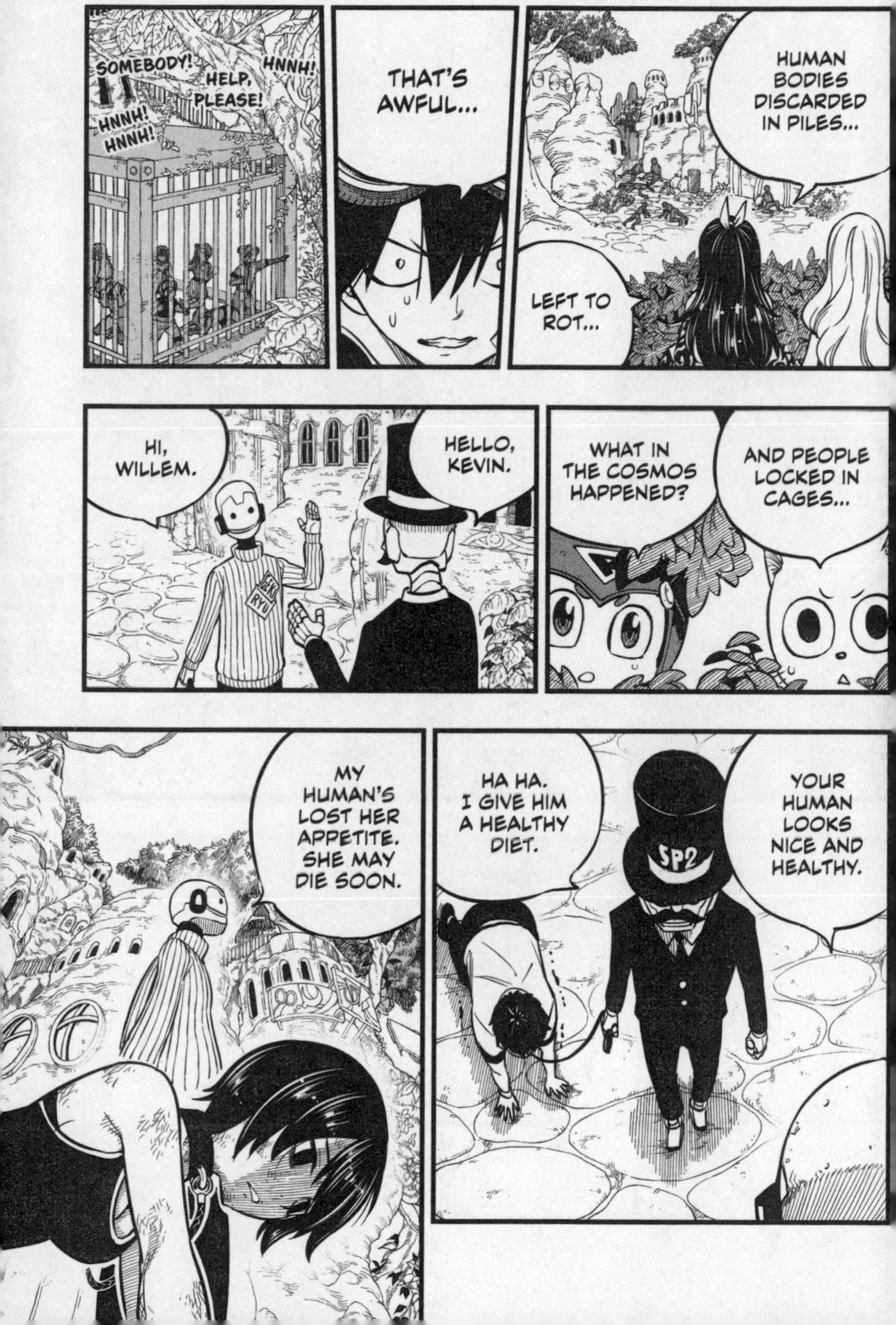
HUMAN BODIES DISCARDED IN PILES...
LEFT TO ROT...
THAT'S AWFUL...
HNNH!
HELP, PLEASE!
SOMEBODY!
HNNH! HNNH!
AND PEOPLE LOCKED IN CAGES...
WHAT IN THE COSMOS HAPPENED?
HELLO, KEVIN.
HI, WILLEM.
YOUR HUMAN LOOKS NICE AND HEALTHY.
HA HA. I GIVE HIM A HEALTHY DIET.
MY HUMAN'S LOST HER APPETITE. SHE MAY DIE SOON.

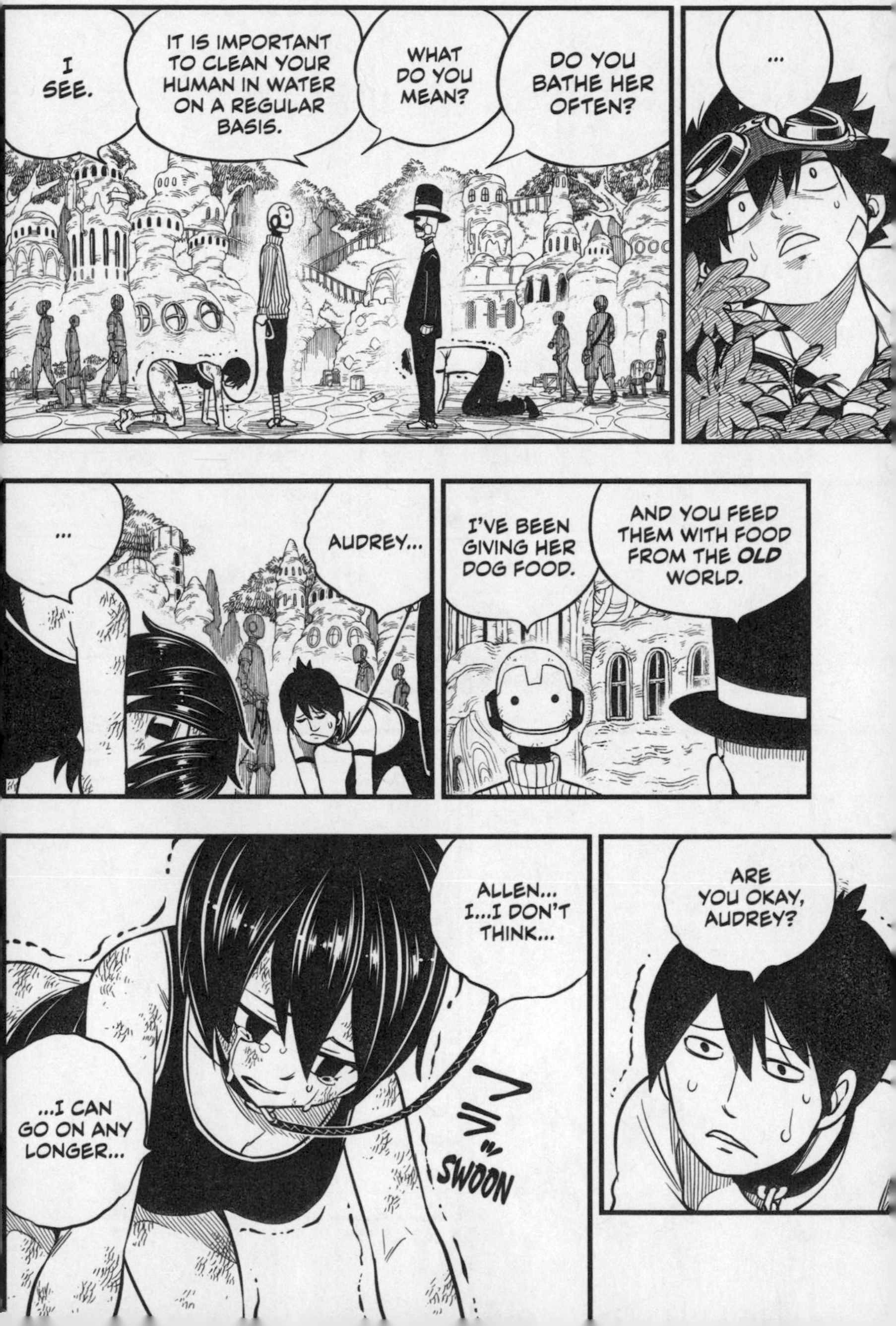
...
DO YOU BATHE HER OFTEN?
WHAT DO YOU MEAN?
IT IS IMPORTANT TO CLEAN YOUR HUMAN IN WATER ON A REGULAR BASIS.
I SEE.
AND YOU FEED THEM WITH FOOD FROM THE **OLD** WORLD.
I'VE BEEN GIVING HER DOG FOOD.
AUDREY...
...
ARE YOU OKAY, AUDREY?
ALLEN... I...I DON'T THINK...
SWOON
...I CAN GO ON ANY LONGER...

STOP! PLEASE! AUDREY WAS MY FIANCÉE!!

TAKE THAT!! AND THAT!!

AH!

OW!

WHAM

AAHH!

I'M SORRY!!

I TOLD YOU NOT TO SPEAK, YOU DUMB HUMAN!!

!

IN THE **OLD** WORLD, HUMANS WOULDN'T THINK TWICE ABOUT BREAKING US.

YOU MUSTN'T ABUSE HER.

...

AUDREY...

WAIT, SHIKI!!

THOSE EVIL–!!!!

GRK

I CANNOT AGREE.

HUMANS ARE MUCH MORE DIFFICULT TO REPAIR. YOU MUST TAKE CARE NOT TO BREAK THEM.

THE OLD WORLD?

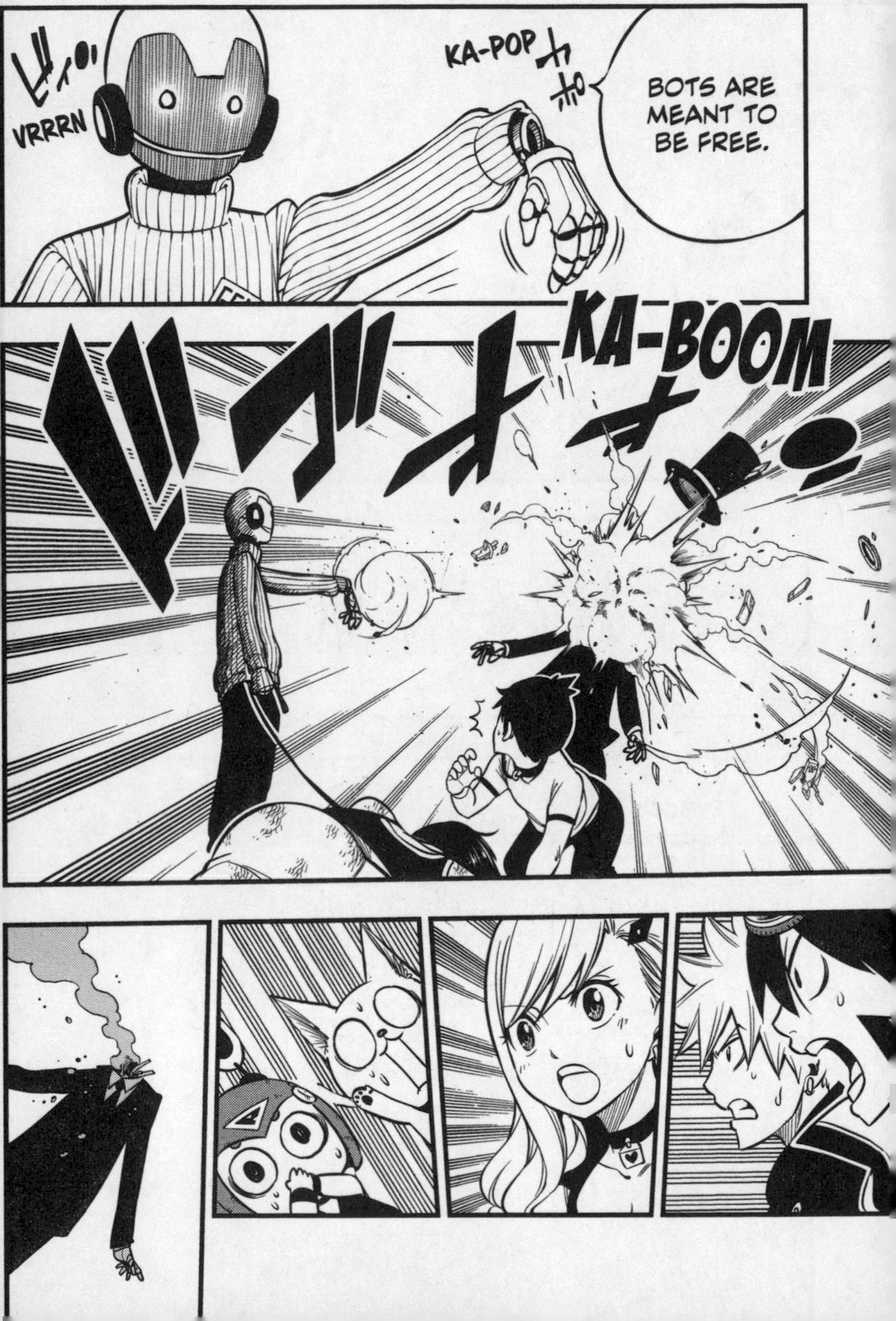
BOTS ARE MEANT TO BE FREE.
KA-POP
VRRRN
KA-BOOM

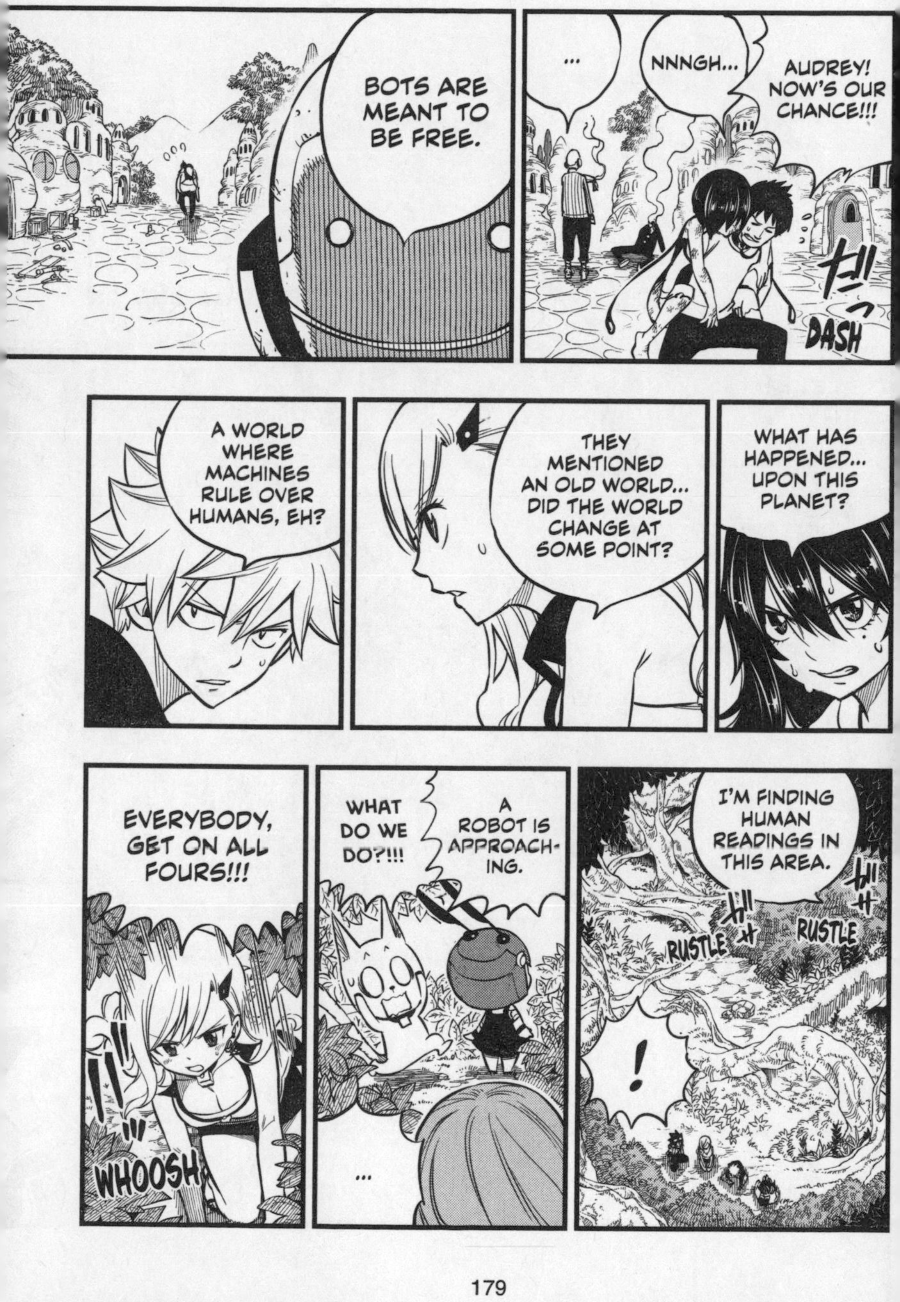
AUDREY! NOW'S OUR CHANCE!!!
NNNGH...
...
DASH
BOTS ARE MEANT TO BE FREE.
WHAT HAS HAPPENED... UPON THIS PLANET?
THEY MENTIONED AN OLD WORLD... DID THE WORLD CHANGE AT SOME POINT?
A WORLD WHERE MACHINES RULE OVER HUMANS, EH?
I'M FINDING HUMAN READINGS IN THIS AREA.
RUSTLE
RUSTLE
!
A ROBOT IS APPROACH-ING.
WHAT DO WE DO?!!!
...
EVERYBODY, GET ON ALL FOURS!!!
WHOOSH

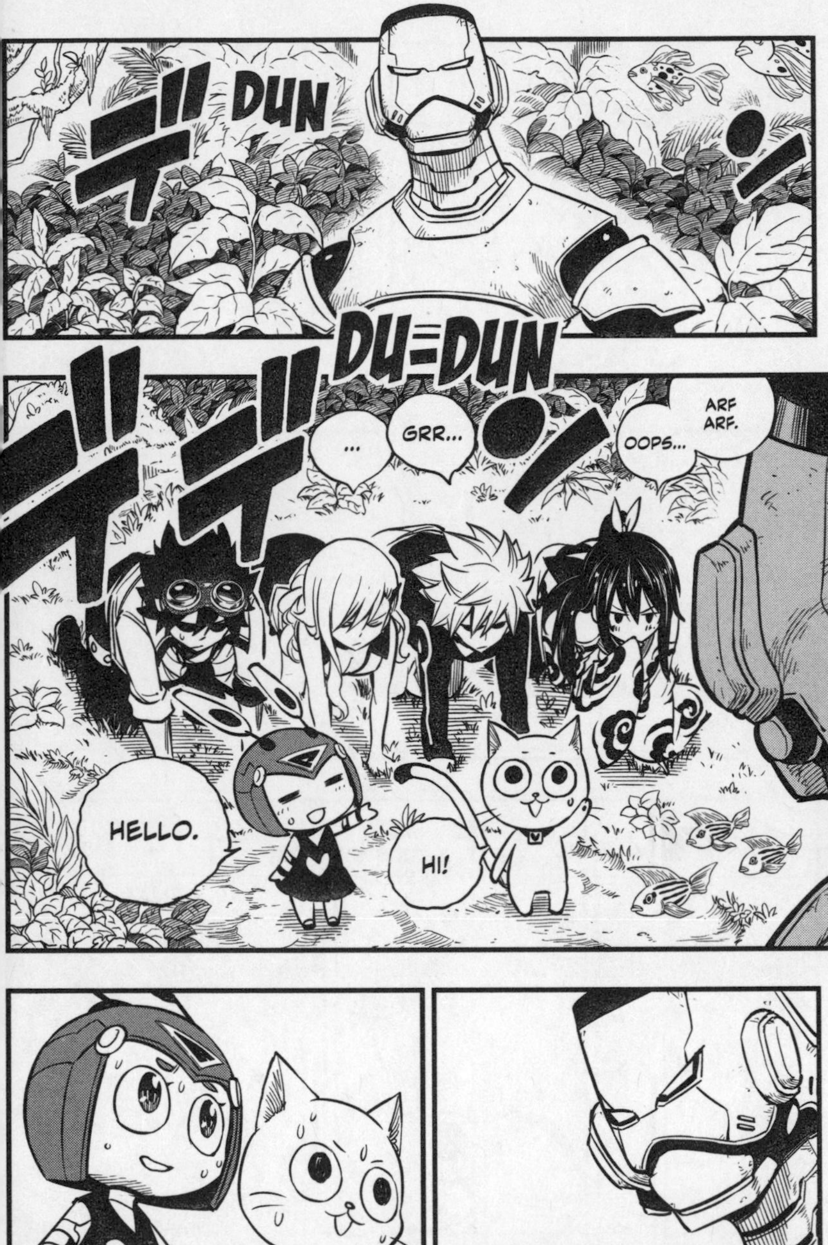
DUN
ARF ARF.
OOPS...
DU=DUN
GRR...
...
HI!
HELLO.

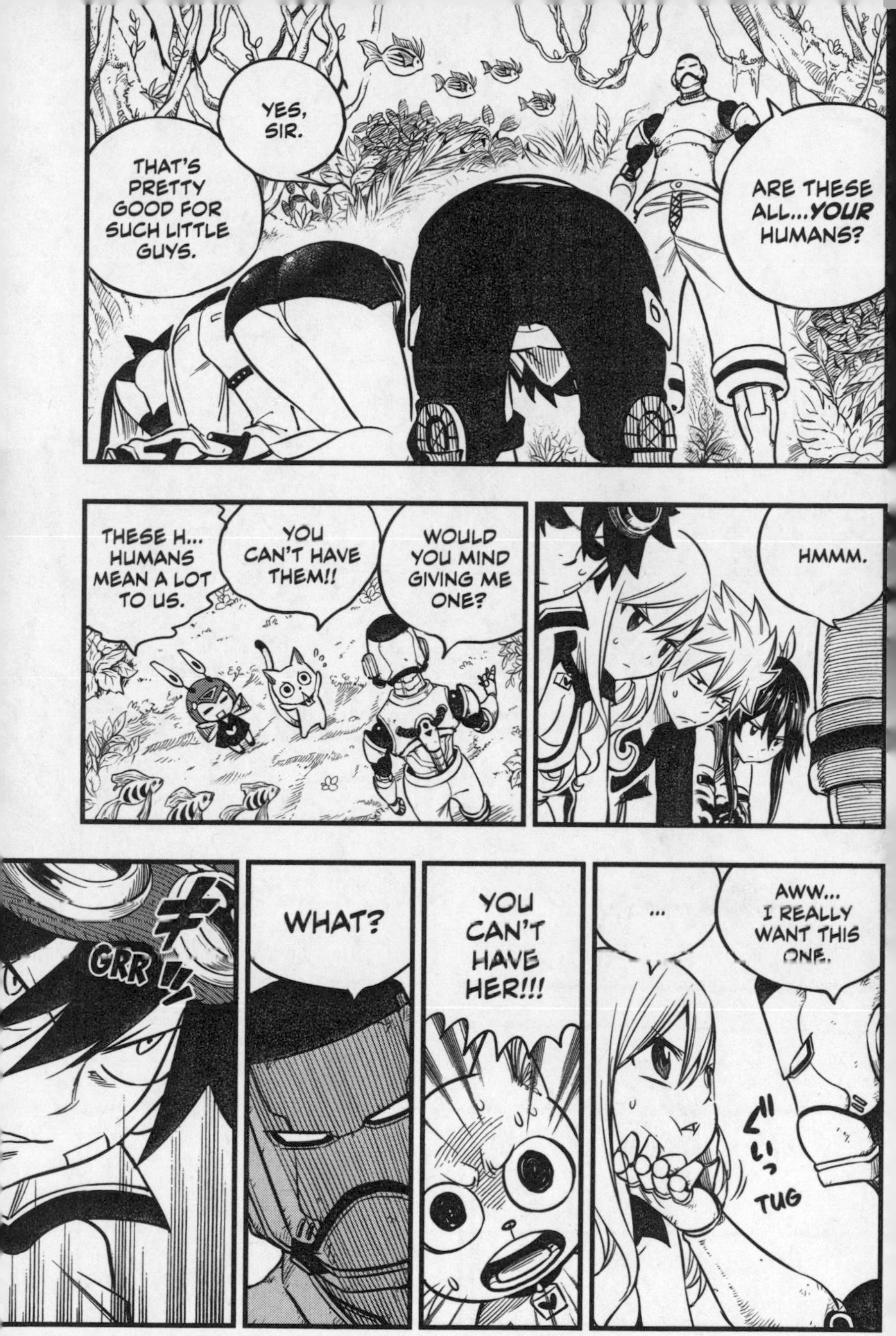
ARE THESE ALL...YOUR HUMANS?
YES, SIR.
THAT'S PRETTY GOOD FOR SUCH LITTLE GUYS.
HMMM.
WOULD YOU MIND GIVING ME ONE?
YOU CAN'T HAVE THEM!!
THESE H... HUMANS MEAN A LOT TO US.
AWW... I REALLY WANT THIS ONE.
TUG
...
YOU CAN'T HAVE HER!!!
WHAT?
GRR

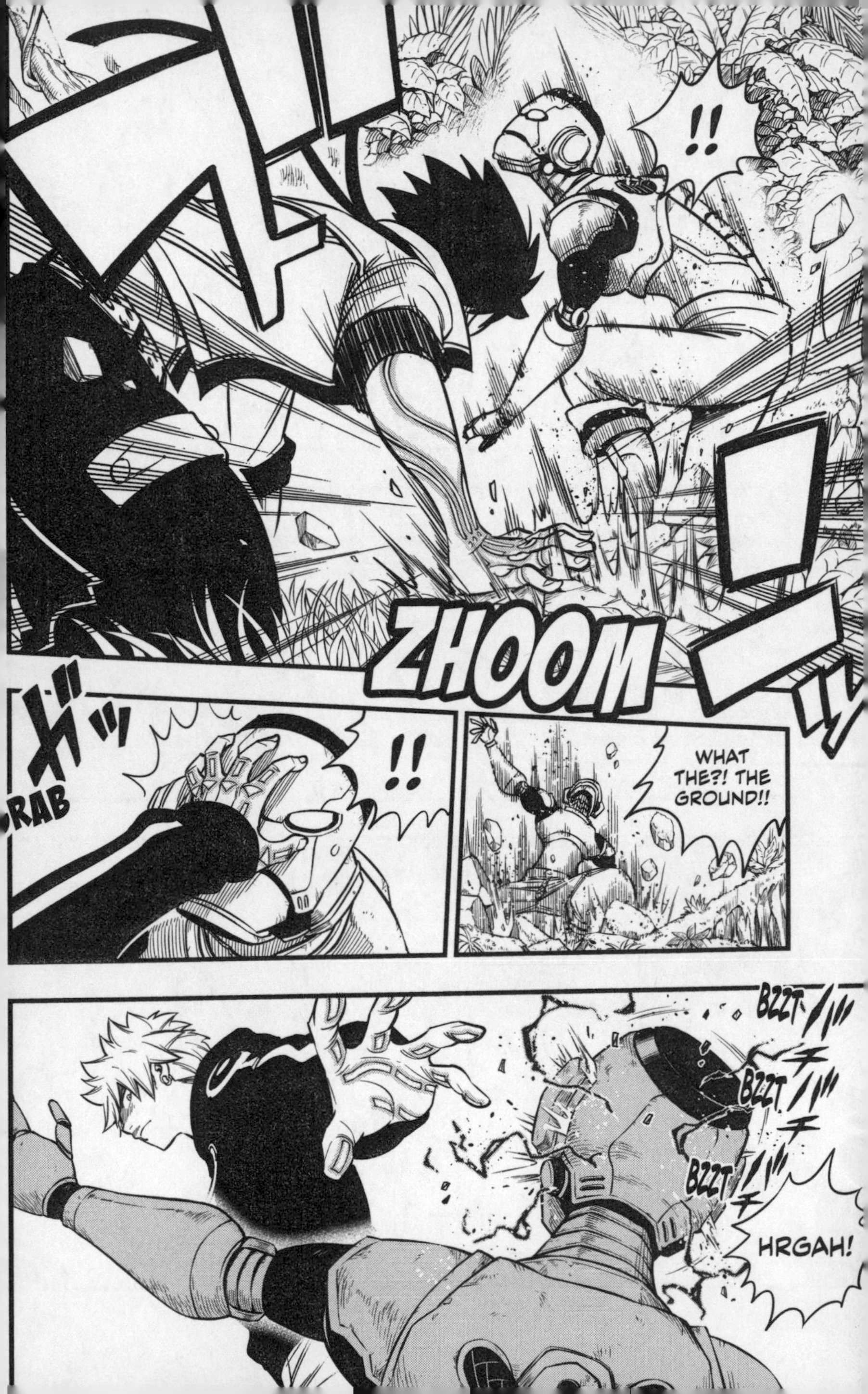
!!
ZHOOM
WHAT THE?! THE GROUND!!
!!
RAB
BZZT
BZZT
BZZT
HRGAH!

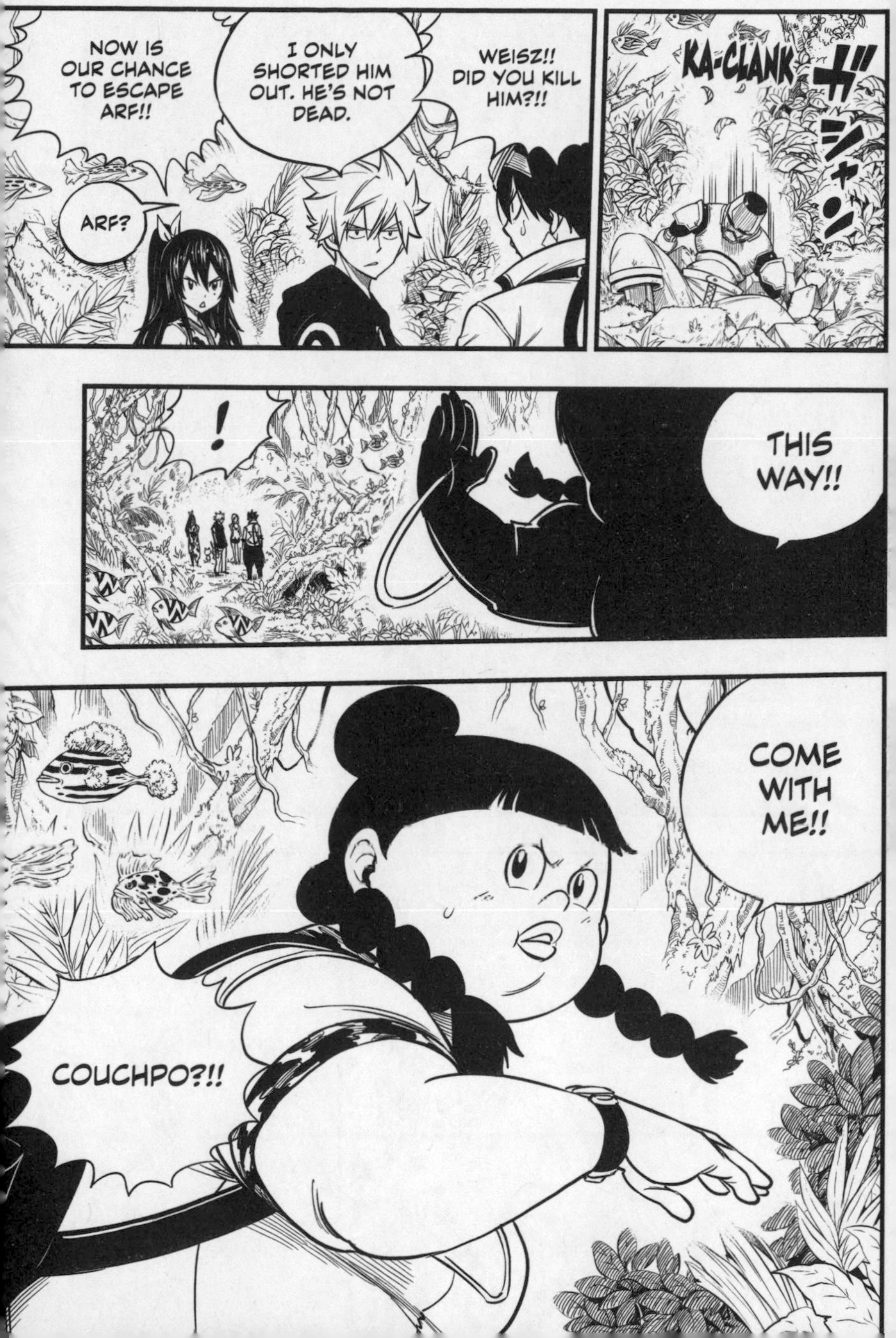
KA-CLANK
ガシャン
WEISZ!! DID YOU KILL HIM?!!
I ONLY SHORTED HIM OUT. HE'S NOT DEAD.
NOW IS OUR CHANCE TO ESCAPE ARF!!
ARF?
THIS WAY!!
!
COME WITH ME!!
COUCHPO?!!

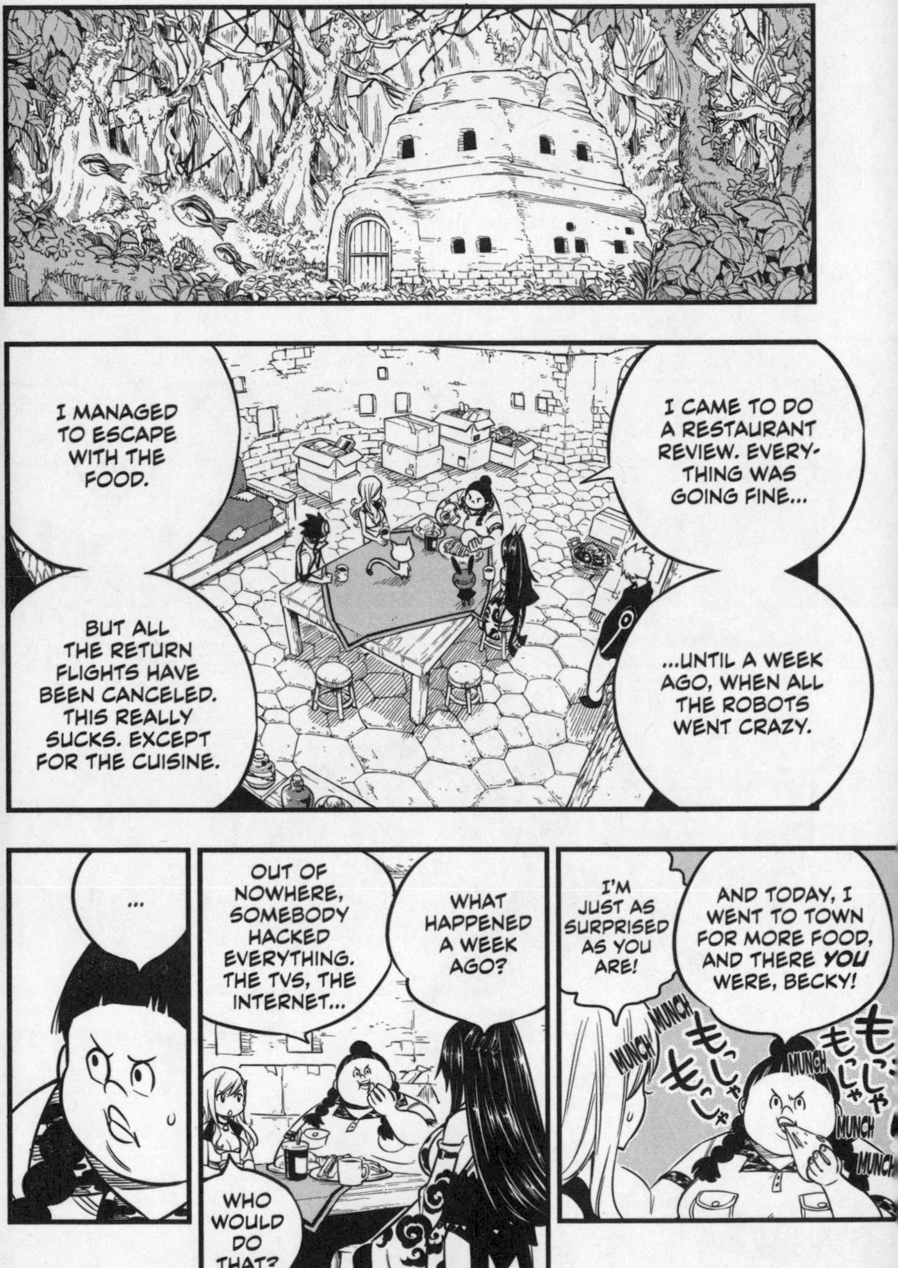
I CAME TO DO A RESTAURANT REVIEW. EVERY-THING WAS GOING FINE...
...UNTIL A WEEK AGO, WHEN ALL THE ROBOTS WENT CRAZY.
I MANAGED TO ESCAPE WITH THE FOOD.
BUT ALL THE RETURN FLIGHTS HAVE BEEN CANCELED. THIS REALLY SUCKS. EXCEPT FOR THE CUISINE.
AND TODAY, I WENT TO TOWN FOR MORE FOOD, AND THERE *YOU* WERE, BECKY!
I'M JUST AS SURPRISED AS YOU ARE!
MUNCH MUNCH
MUNCH MUNCH
MUNCH
WHAT HAPPENED A WEEK AGO?
OUT OF NOWHERE, SOMEBODY HACKED EVERYTHING. THE TVS, THE INTERNET...
WHO WOULD DO THAT?
...

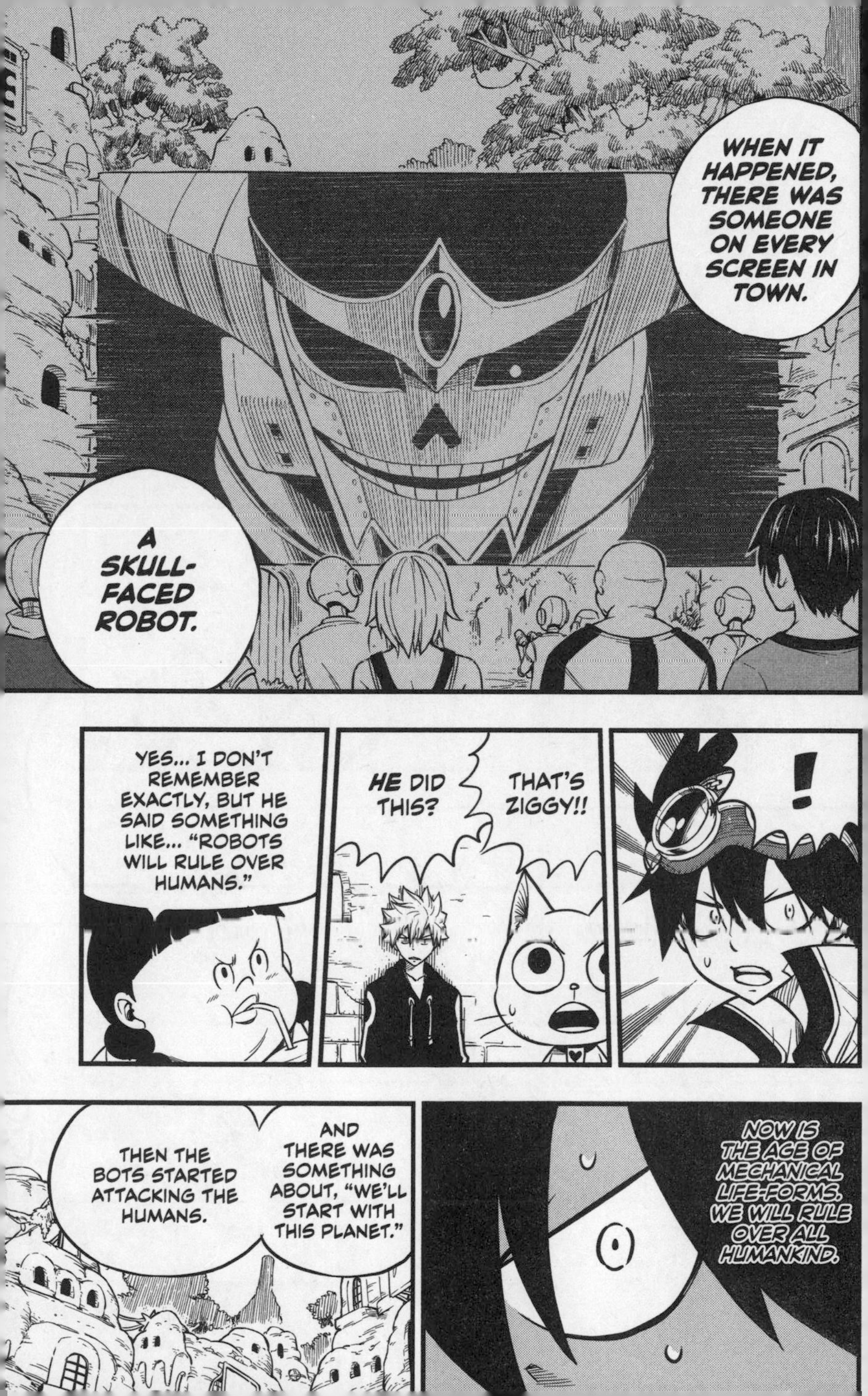
WHEN IT HAPPENED, THERE WAS SOMEONE ON EVERY SCREEN IN TOWN.
A SKULL-FACED ROBOT.
!
THAT'S ZIGGY!!
HE DID THIS?
YES... I DON'T REMEMBER EXACTLY, BUT HE SAID SOMETHING LIKE... "ROBOTS WILL RULE OVER HUMANS."
NOW IS THE AGE OF MECHANICAL LIFE-FORMS. WE WILL RULE OVER ALL HUMANKIND.
AND THERE WAS SOMETHING ABOUT, "WE'LL START WITH THIS PLANET."
THEN THE BOTS STARTED ATTACKING THE HUMANS.

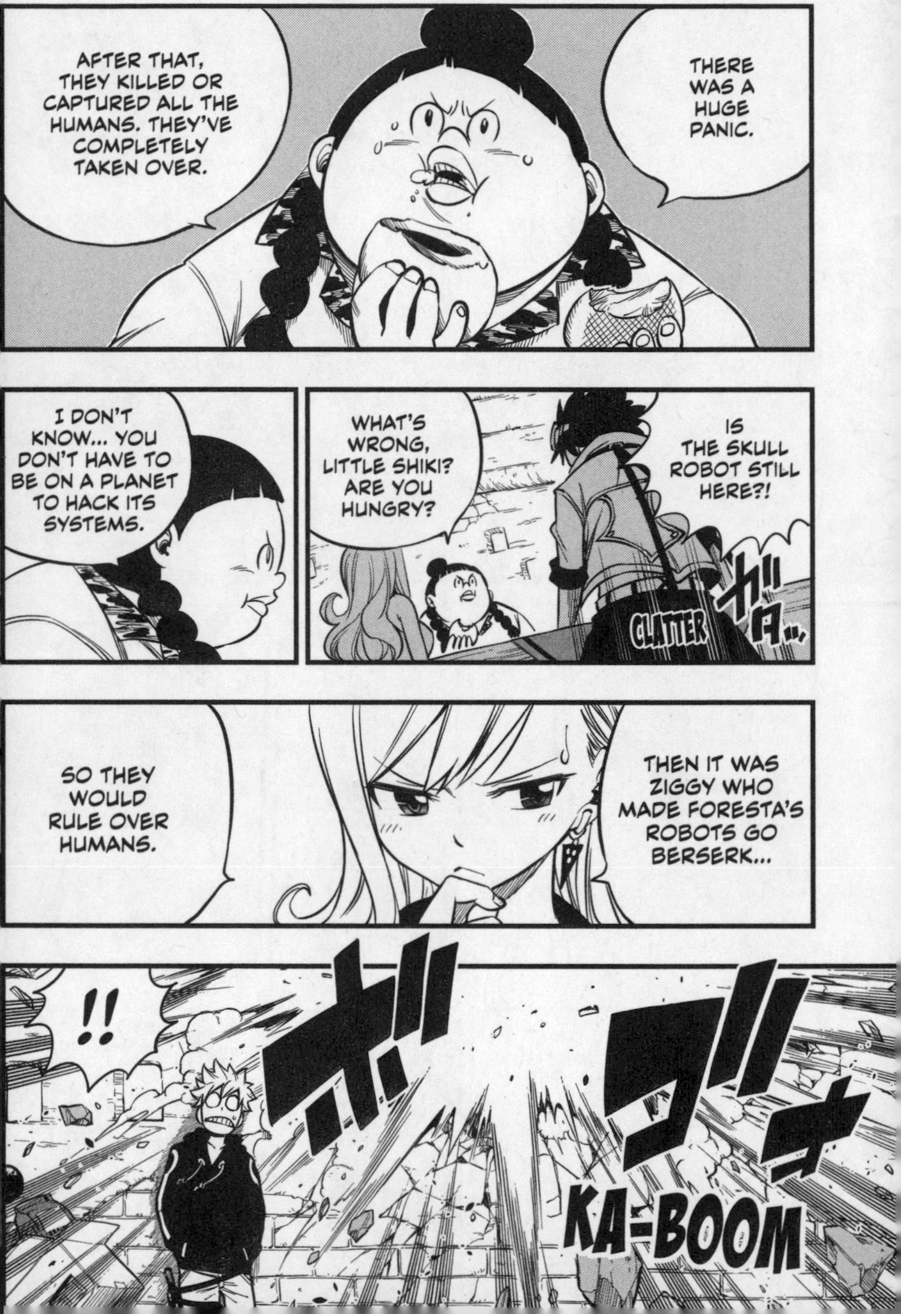
THERE WAS A HUGE PANIC.
AFTER THAT, THEY KILLED OR CAPTURED ALL THE HUMANS. THEY'VE COMPLETELY TAKEN OVER.
IS THE SKULL ROBOT STILL HERE?!
WHAT'S WRONG, LITTLE SHIKI? ARE YOU HUNGRY?
CLATTER
I DON'T KNOW... YOU DON'T HAVE TO BE ON A PLANET TO HACK ITS SYSTEMS.
THEN IT WAS ZIGGY WHO MADE FORESTA'S ROBOTS GO BERSERK...
SO THEY WOULD RULE OVER HUMANS.
KA-BOOM
!!

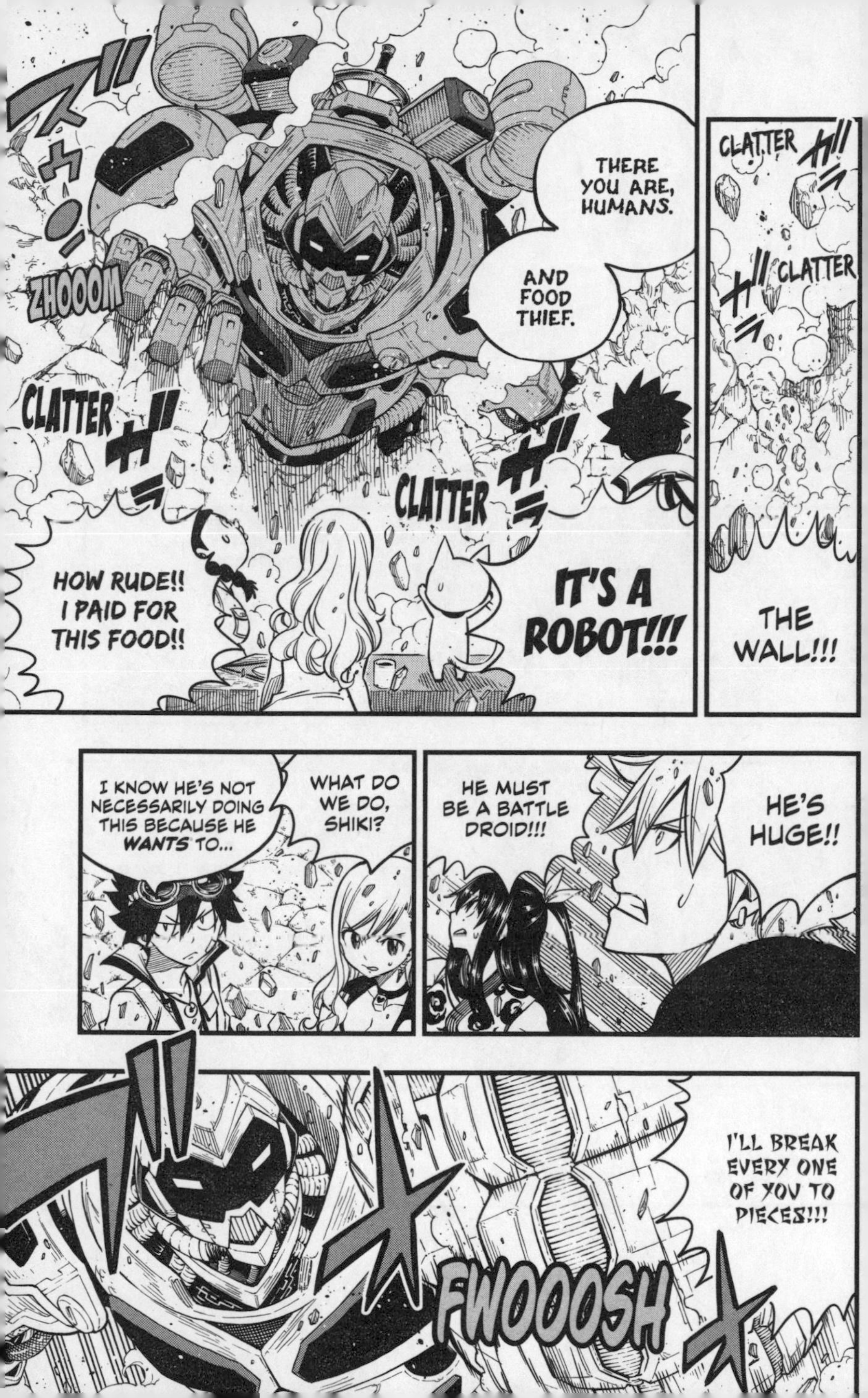
CLATTER
CLATTER
THE WALL!!!
THERE YOU ARE, HUMANS.
AND FOOD THIEF.
ZHOOOM
CLATTER
IT'S A ROBOT!!!
CLATTER
HOW RUDE!! I PAID FOR THIS FOOD!!
HE'S HUGE!!
HE MUST BE A BATTLE DROID!!!
WHAT DO WE DO, SHIKI?
I KNOW HE'S NOT NECESSARILY DOING THIS BECAUSE HE *WANTS* TO...
I'LL BREAK EVERY ONE OF YOU TO PIECES!!!
FWOOOSH

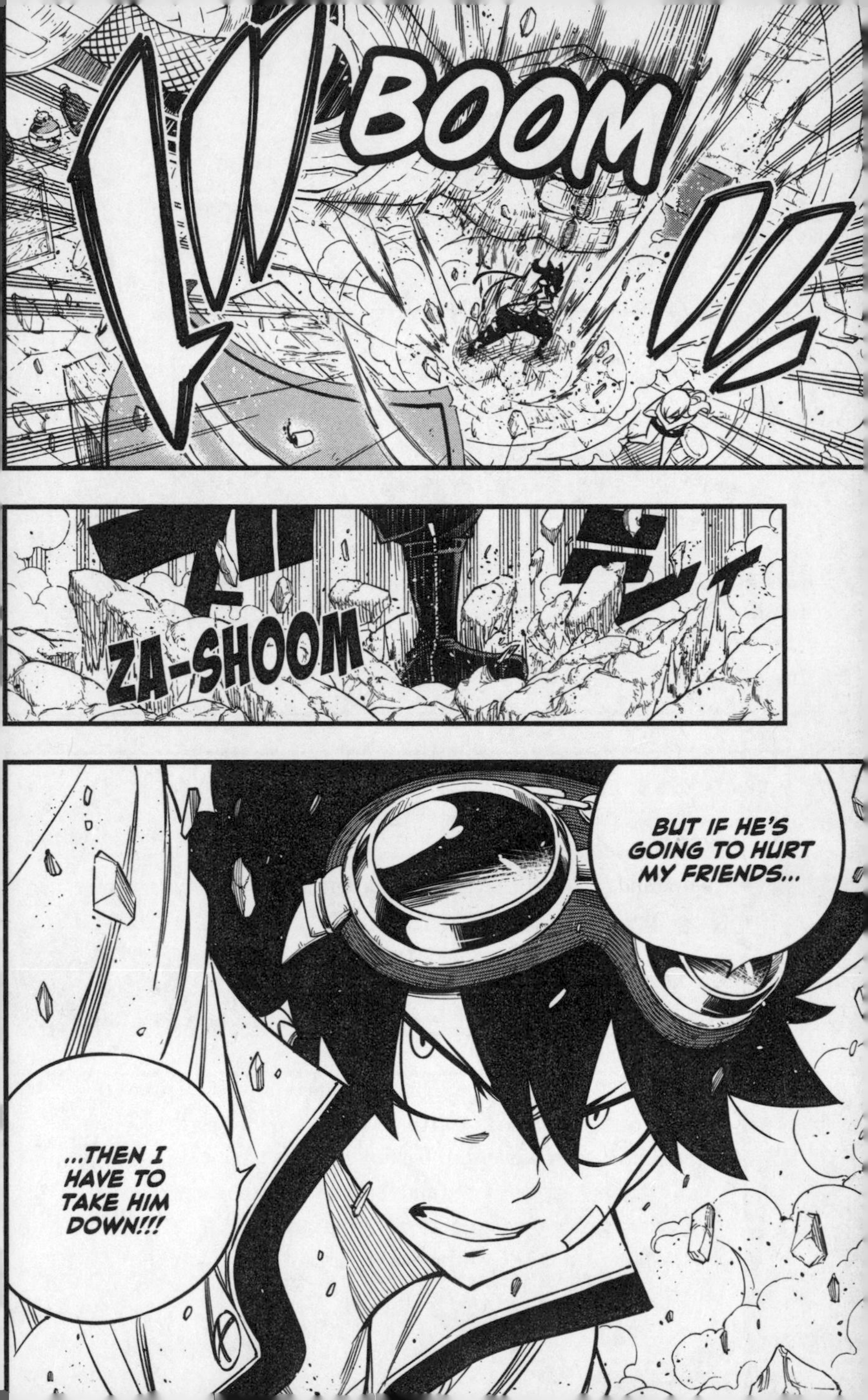
BOOM
ZA-SHOOM
BUT IF HE'S GOING TO HURT MY FRIENDS...
...THEN I HAVE TO TAKE HIM DOWN!!!

AFTERWORD

Mashima: I did it! I messed up! Oh, I'm so embarrassed! In the character profile for Hermit that was published in Weekly Magazine and volume 11 (first printing), I wrote her name as Milon. I already used that name! Aaaaahh! One of the B-Cubers that was captured with Rebecca was Milon from the Tokkô Channel. I can't believe I only just realized it....

Mashima: This does happen, but really very rarely. I'm really, really sorry. In fact, there are characters in my previous series *Fairy Tail* who have the same name. Their name is Yuri, and just like this time, one of them is an important character and the other is a bit character. Even more recently, there's a manga I do the story for called *100 Years Quest*, and I used the name of a character from my previous previous series, *Rave Master*, and I didn't realize it until the artist for the series said, "They have the same name—is that okay?" (This one was revised before publication.)

Mashima: Realistically, there are lots of people in the same world who have the same name, but that sort of realism is the kind of thing that's not good to carry over into stories. It's best when characters don't share the same name.

Mashima: So, it's a little late, but I've decided to change Hermit's name and make the new one official. Hermit Milon is now Hermit Mio. Mio is her official name.

Mashima: "Mio" comes from the Japanese word, *miotsukushi*, meaning "channel marker," something that marks the navigable path in a waterway. It's my understanding that this word was used in old Japanese poetry as a pivot word to mean both "channel marker" and "give one's all (*mi wo tsukushi*)." I thought of Hermit, and how she gives her all to help her friends, and that's how I came up with this name.

Mashima: Most readers probably didn't notice, but as the author, I am extremely embarrassed and I am very sorry about this error. I will focus harder and try not to make the same mistake in the future.

Mashima: But I really am pretty haphazard about naming characters.

Young characters and steampunk setting, like *Howl's Moving Castle* and *Battle Angel Alita*

Beyond the Clouds © 2018 Nicke / Ki-oon

A boy with a talent for machines and a mysterious girl whose wings he's fixed will take you beyond the clouds! In the tradition of the high-flying, resonant adventure stories of Studio Ghibli comes a gorgeous tale about the longing of young hearts for adventure and friendship!

The boys are back, in 400-page hardcovers that are as pretty and badass as they are!

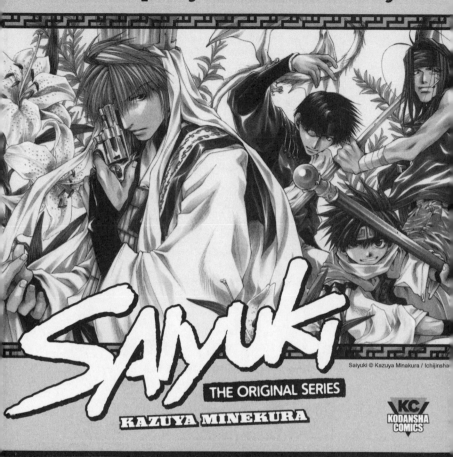

Saiyuki © Kazuya Minakura / Ichijinsha

SAIYUKI
THE ORIGINAL SERIES
KAZUYA MINEKURA

KC KODANSHA COMICS

"AN EDGY COMIC LOOK AT AN ANCIENT CHINESE TALE." —YALSA

Genjo Sanzo is a Buddhist priest in the city of Togenkyo, which is being ravaged by yokai spirits that have fallen out of balance with the natural order. His superiors send him on a journey far to the west to discover why this is happening and how to stop it. His companions are three yokai with human souls. But this is no day trip — the four will encounter many discoveries and horrors on the way.

FEATURES NEW TRANSLATION, COLOR PAGES, AND BEAUTIFUL WRAPAROUND COVER ART!

A Kodansha Comics Trade Paperback Original
EDENS ZERO 13 copyright © 2021 Hiro Mashima
English translation copyright © 2021 Hiro Mashima

Published in the United States by Kodansha Comics, an imprint of Kodansha USA Publishing, LLC, New York.

Publication rights for this English edition arranged through Kodansha Ltd., Tokyo.

First published in Japan in 2021 by Kodansha Ltd., Tokyo.

ISBN 978-1-64651-223-2

Original cover design by Narumi Miura (G x complex).

Printed in the United States of America.

www.kodansha.us

1st Printing
Translation: Alethea Nibley & Athena Nibley
Lettering: AndWorld Design
Editing: David Yoo
Kodansha Comics edition cover design by Phil Balsman

Publisher: Kiichiro Sugawara

Director of publishing services: Ben Applegate
Associate director of operations: Stephen Pakula
Publishing services managing editors: Madison Salters, Alanna Ruse
Production managers: Emi Lotto, Angela Zurlo